S0-BNI-310

The Lord's First Night

THE MYTH OF THE DROIT DE CUISSAGE

Alain Boureau

Translated by Lydia G. Cochrane

THE UNIVERSITY OF CHICAGO PRESS

CHICAGO AND LONDON

Alain Boureau is directeur d'études at the École des Hautes Études en Sciences Sociales, Paris.

The University of Chicago Press, Chicago 60637
The University of Chicago Press, Ltd., London
© 1998 by The University of Chicago
All rights reserved. Published 1998
Printed in the United States of America
07 06 05 04 03 02 01 00 99 98   1 2 3 4 5

ISBN: 0-226-06742-4 (cloth)
ISBN: 0-226-06743-2 (paper)

Originally published as *Le droit de cuissage: La fabrication d'un mythe (XIIIᵉ–XXᵉ siècle)*, © Éditions Albin Michel S.A., 1995.

Library of Congress Cataloging-in-Publication Data

Boureau, Alain.
    [Droit de cuissage. English]
    The lord's first night : the myth of the droit de cuissage / Alain Boureau ; translated by Lydia G. Cochrane.
        p.   cm.
    Includes bibliographical references and index.
    ISBN 0-226-06742-4 (alk. paper). — ISBN 0-226-06743-2 (pbk. : alk. paper)
    1. Jus primae noctis. 2. Feudalism. 3. Sexual harassment—History. I. Title.
JC116.S5B6813   1998
392'.5'0940902—dc21   97-36598
                                                         CIP

♾ The paper used in this publication meets the minimum requirements of the American National Standard for Information Sciences—Permanence of Paper for Printed Library Materials, ANSI Z39.48-1992.

392.5
377

July - 01
379755570

FOR JACQUES LE GOFF

CONTENTS

ACKNOWLEDGMENTS

T his study was first sketched out in two seminars, one in Paris at the École des Hautes Études en Sciences Sociales during the winter of 1990–91, the other at the University of California at Berkeley in the autumn of 1991. My thanks to the participants in these seminars for their suggestions, notably to R. Howard Bloch, Véronique Campion-Vincent, Daniel Duchêne, Geoffrey Koziol, Maria Matesanz, and Jacques Merceron. My thanks to Alain Guerreau, one of a small number of experts on the question of *cuissage* and the author of a stimulating study, *Le féodalisme: Un horizon théorique* (Paris: Le Sycomore, 1980), for fruitful discussions about feudal society and the *droit de cuissage*. Many friends and colleagues have offered suggestions and information, among them Marie-Madeleine Charlier, Colette Collomb-Boureau, Sophie Houdard, and Christian Jouhaud. Philippe Buc, Bernard Lepetit, and Jacques Revel read the manuscript attentively and subjected it to friendly but vigilant criticism. Amaia knows how much I owe to her. Finally, my gratitude to Jacques Le Goff, who urged me some years ago to take on this project, which fascinated me. This book is dedicated to that great discoverer, man of science, and friend.

I n 1991 and 1992 the French National Assembly deliberated a total refashioning of the Penal Code, producing a new code that became law on 7 July 1992. Among the new problems it dealt with were some monstrous crimes against humanity and some banal offenses like *le taggage* (spray-painted graffiti) and *le squat* (illegal occupation of buildings), but one problem, both new and old, presented the legislators with a lexical difficulty: how to describe practices, ranging from the violent to the trivial, that employ professional power for sexual ends without borrowing the American term *sexual harassment* (in French, *le harcèlement sexuel*). Even though the previous version of the code used the verb *harceler, harcèlement sexuel* was inappropriate because the expression refers metaphorically to a system of assault and warfare and is better suited to the American version of English common law.

Instantaneously, however, the French press found a native equivalent: the new law repressed *le droit de cuissage*. Curiously, the French language preserved the memory of a custom that, although never common, was long ago alleged to have existed in the Middle Ages, a time even further in the past. The transmission of the expression appeared to have ceased: For decades schoolbooks had made no mention of it. Romantic fiction, where once it had abounded, rarely touches on it anymore. Admittedly, Beaumarchais's play, *Le mariage de Figaro* (1784), and Mozart's more familiar operatic version gave a boost to the idea of the droit du seigneur. Still, the absence of the word *cuissage* in either the play or the opera, and the distance created by the language (Lorenzo Da Ponte's Italian libretto) and fairy-tale atmosphere of the opera, prevent us from crediting to this work the easy availability of the term *droit de cuissage*.

Because we have no sure guideposts for exploring the memory of the

French language, let us take the institutional route and consult a dictionary. The *Petit Robert de la langue française* tells us: "Cuissage. *n.m.* (XVIe; de *cuisse*). *Féod.* Droit du seigneur de passer la première nuit de noces avec la nouvelle mariée (dans l'*express.* droit de cuissage)" (*Cuissage.* masculine noun [16th c.; from *cuisse* (thigh)]. Feudal. Right of the lord to spend the first night of the wedding with the bride [in the expression "droit de cuissage"]).[1]

This definition takes us to the heart of a medieval barbarism, which gave the lord the power to crush his subjects right down to the elementary and irreducible autonomy of their own bodies and their matrimonial choices. This simple bit of common knowledge, shared unexamined by a good many university professors and journalists today, nonetheless presents more difficulties than it seems to.

If we examine the dictionary definition word for word, we detect several filters between the reality we are seeking and what the definition says. First, there is an immediate and striking chronological anomaly: The existence of the word is attested from the sixteenth century on, whereas we are told the abbreviation "*Féod.*" indicates "a special term concerning feudalism used by historians, jurists, etc." We are referred to the Middle Ages even though the term *feudal* appears only in the sixteenth century[2] and even though (the *Petit Robert* to the contrary) historians and jurists make much less use of the expression *droit de cuissage* than do the "etc." it speaks of (that is, polemicists and novelists). The dating of the expression to the sixteenth century, repeated in all contemporary dictionaries, goes back to Littré, who cites Du Verdier's *Diverses leçons* (1557) by way of the *Dictionnaire historique* of Lacurne de Sainte-Palaye.[3] Littré himself published the first volume of the *Dictionnaire historique*, left in manuscript in the eighteenth century. Littré did not check the primary source, Du Verdier's *Diverses leçons;* it does not contain the word *cuissage,* and only vaguely alludes to the custom of placing a leg across the bed of newly married couples. The expression *droit de cuissage* is in fact more recent: It is not to be found in Richelet's dictionary, in Furetière's dictionary, in the *Dictionnaire de Trévoux,* or in the 1762 edition of the *Dictionnaire de l'Académie.* The first authors to use the phrase seem to have been Boucher d'Argis (in volume 5 of Diderot's *Encyclopédie*)[4] and Voltaire (in his *Essai sur Les mœurs*). Lexicographers and encyclopedists noted the custom, but under other designations: *marquette* (Furetière), *prélibation* (*Dictionnaire de Trévoux*), *culage* (in a subsection entitled "Droits abusifs" in Boucher d'Argis's entry, "Droit," in the *Encyclopédie*).

Robert notes that *droit de cuissage* is an "expression": it does indeed seem to be a linguistic creation. In the nineteenth century a latinizing false modesty gave it yet another linguistic mask as "the right of the first night"—the *jus primae noctis.*

These euphemisms conceal a profound uncertainty concerning the reality of this "right." Robert uses "*Féod.*" and "*express.*" as protection and as a means to avoid a definite assertion. We should not blame him for his prudence: In our own century, when polemical passions over the droit du seigneur have subsided, even the most experienced medievalists are not sure about *cuissage.* A minority of scholars—Robert Boutruche among them[5]—postulate its existence. Some take the *droit de cuissage* for granted: One historian of lordship in the late Middle Ages, in a fine study of the Vannes region, remarks (with neither approval nor disapproval) about a fugitive mention of *culléage* in a document, "The droit du seigneur still existed in the fifteenth century."[6] Even more recently, the Galician historian Carlos Barros has attempted to prove the existence of the *derecho de pernada*, the Spanish equivalent of the *droit de cuissage.*[7]

In general, however, historians are less sure. Medievalists avoid the question. Marc Bloch seems to risk a hesitant reference to it (a hesitation caused more by historiographical scruples than by moral compunctions) in *La société féodale* (*Feudal Society,* 1939–40) when he speaks of feudal pressures on the marriage of dependents. He states that toward vassals (and sometimes toward serfs, also personal dependents) what would be considered an abuse of power with subordinates of a different social level was almost universally considered as legitimate. Contemporary historians appear to be coming to the conclusion that such a right never existed and that mentions of it come from confusing it with seigniorial dues connected with the marriage of dependents, such as *maritagium* or *formariage.* Nonetheless, lexical confusion seems too slight a hypothesis to explain an old and widespread quarrel.

The need to answer a simple question—did the *droit de cuissage* really exist?—would by itself be enough to justify the present work. The pertinent vocabulary may at times be frivolous or suggestive, but important things are at stake, notably, measuring the true daily dimensions of the historiographic monster of feudalism. By testing the reality of the *droit de cuissage* and constructing a historical map of claims for it and objections to it, we can measure, by a simple standard, the gradations of a power that is still obscure. Using the *droit de cuissage* as a rudimentary gauge of personal liberty (freedom to dispose of one's own body) will help us trace the real and ideological vicissitudes of the immense question of personal dependence in societies of the Ancien Régime.

There is a second reason for inquiry: real or imaginary, the *droit de cuissage* has been brandished as a proof of the social ignominy of feudalism. We are all aware of the role of the *Marriage of Figaro* in prerevolutionary France; beginning in the thirteenth century many other references to the same "right," under a variety of names, added it to the arsenal of weapons with which to combat lordship. Thus it becomes important to measure degrees of belief or ruse in its utilization and to evaluate its effectiveness. Let me state from the outset that the question is difficult. Now in the twentieth century memory of this "right" seems both ubiquitous and elusive. It failed to crystallize where one might expect to find it, among satirists (authors of fabliaux, for example) or among well-known enemies of the Middle Ages like Rabelais. Memory of it seems localized in certain specific circumvolutions of the human mind grappling with action and history. Native French earthiness, or *gauloiserie,* may be able to teach us something about the invention of collective memory.

Finally, the persistence of this expression in the French language poses a third question: What constructs the idea of the "Middle Ages," both in common understanding and in historiography? The *droit de cuissage,* like such massive entities as Thomism, hierarchy, and the corporation, presupposes an automatic cohesion of the medieval past. This means we need to investigate the status of certain "medieval" traits that nonspecialists (and even some medievalists) take as an integral part of the Middle Ages.

What are those traits? One can hardly speak of an "image." References are shifting, incapable of producing an overall picture. Nor are we dealing with "myths," strictly speaking, because no one attaches any profound belief to them. What we have is a sort of vocabulary without syntax; a vague tradition, understood as pure transmission. How can such poorly defined entities persist? And how can they still evoke a certain essence of the Middle Ages?

The sexual content of the *droit de cuissage* has obviously done much to keep it in memory. The custom fascinates for its total otherness; it feeds the fantasy of an institutional, even a juridical, consent to violence. The very formality of the "right" enchants by its radical inversion of our values. Its paired terms combine the gravity of the law with a whiff of bawdiness in the word *cuisse,* evoking an entire folklore of sexuality.

The emblem has another side to it, however, that may explain its durability. The *droit de cuissage* has been firmly installed as typically "medieval" and barbarous. The word *medieval* has a poor reputation these days, as more than one medievalist has lamented. The *droit de cuissage* is a concentrate of that barbarity. For example, when Soviet troops invaded Afghanistan, the general secretary of the French Communist Party, Georges Marchais, justified Soviet intervention in the name of the Enlightenment, claiming that the "feudal" Afghans practiced the *droit de cuissage*. Articles on some of the less developed regions of our planet report the same sorry privilege. The powerful break represented by the French Revolution of 1789 has naturalized the idea of an earlier savagery, straight out of the Middle Ages. George Orwell gives a good illustration of this notion, enhanced by fiction, in his *Nineteen Eighty-Four*:

> The thing you invariably came back to was the impossibility of knowing what life before the Revolution had really been like. [Winston] took out of the drawer a copy of a children's history textbook . . . and began copying a passage into the diary: "In the old days (it ran), before the glorious Revolution, London was not the beautiful city that we know today. It was a dark, dirty, miserable place where hardly anybody had enough to eat. . . . The capitalists owned everything in the world, and everyone else was their slave. . . . The chief of all the capitalists was called the King, and—" But he knew the rest of the catalogue. There would be mention of the bishops in their lawn sleeves, the judges in their ermine robes, the pillory, the stocks, the treadmill, the cat-o'-nine-tails, the Lord Mayor's Banquet, and the practice of kissing the Pope's toe. There was also something called the *jus primae noctis*, which would probably not be mentioned in a textbook for children. It was the law by which every capitalist had the right to sleep with any woman working in one of his factories. . . . It might very well be that literally every word in the history books, even the things that one accepted without question, was pure fantasy. For all he knew there might never have been any such law as the *jus primae noctis*, or any such creature as a capitalist, or any such garment as a top hat. Everything had faded into mist.[8]

As a way to emerge from that mist, I propose to construct a genealogy of the constitution of the diffuse knowledge that gave the medieval emblem its forms and colors. We will have to work backward because no evidence is disinterested or unprejudiced. We grasp sources only to have them shy off, disappear, and reemerge elsewhere.

This means I shall begin, almost experimentally, with the current perception of the *droit de cuissage*. Before we impute a particular belief to past agents, it is a good idea to define our cognitive frameworks for lending meaning to the *droit de cuissage*, whether the context is protest, interpretation, or projection (chapter 1). Next we will return to the nineteenth century, because most of the texts and proofs brandished today were established during an extremely lively controversy, beginning in 1854, centered on Louis Veuillot, a champion of a pure and pious Middle Ages. Veuillot, as a propagandist for the Christian cause, was supported by a cohort of paleographers and professors at the École des Chartes; the opposing camp mobilized scholars of a local history that was just beginning to be institutionalized (chapters 2 and 3). Next we will need to sift through the documents collected in that controversy, completed by other sources, and evaluate proofs and refutations—an operation that will take us back to the scene of the crime, the heart of the Middle Ages (chapter 4). The first mention of our "right" comes from the thirteenth century, which is no guarantee of its reality. At the risk of ruining any suspense, let me state clearly that this "right" is certainly mythical. This means, however, that we need to comprehend the meaning of so powerful a myth. We shall try to do so within two contexts, relations of personal dependence in rural societies of the Ancien Régime (chapter 5), and Christian doctrines and customs of medieval marriage (chapter 6). With that as a base we can attempt to trace the historical continuity of references to the *droit de cuissage* up to the French Revolution in two worlds, that of village confrontations among peasants, lords, and the Church, and that of the royal jurists of the Ancien Régime. Beginning in the sixteenth century mention of the *droit de cuissage* (under a variety of names) entered juridical discussions at the crucial moment of the definition of the status of the various systems of law in France (chapter 7).

This return trip into the past and back will, I hope, allow the construction of a total history of the *droit de cuissage*, with the one restriction that, aside from an occasional comparison, I shall consider only the French sphere. It would be nearly impossible to achieve a fully explicated history of the myth and a precisely contextualized analysis of its occurrences for more than a limited geographical area; moreover, the historical object of the *droit de cuissage*, systematically considered, is essentially French. It is important to try to understand why this was so. Traces of analogous customs remain in many other regions; I shall try to explain, beginning in chapter 1, why they do not fit into the sort of interpretation I propose, founded on a contextual analysis of historical remnants.

Remnants and Persistences

I n France today the notion of *droit de cuissage* enjoys a virtual existence: latent in the language and common knowledge, it is activated under certain circumstances without passing through the construction of a precise definition or recalling a historical referent. I shall start from this odd remnant, this after-image of something glimpsed long ago. I have no intention of compiling a historiographic dossier or a list of follies; what I hope to do is identify some ongoing lines of meaning that have kept alive the memory of a medieval "place." That brief phenomenology of ordinary discourse may cast some light on the modes of existence of this notion through history: From the thirteenth century to the nineteenth, the *droit de cuissage* seems already to have become a virtual object, coming back into existence now and then after long periods of latency.

To that effect I shall consider three crystallizations of meaning and three types of interpretive use of the image of the *droit de cuissage* today: a militant use where the *droit de cuissage* is an explicit figure for sexual oppression; an anthropological interpretation that discerns a powerful and primitive taboo beneath the medieval custom; and a sociocultural theme that proves the continuity of a genuine dialectic of the master and the female servant.

DROIT DE CUISSAGE AND SEXUAL HARASSMENT

In March 1989 *Le nouvel observateur* printed a front-page announcement of a series of feature articles under the heading "Sexual Blackmail: Women Accuse; The *Droit de Cuissage* Returns to the Workplace."[1] This metaphorical use of the expression was evidently aimed at finding a concise, lively way to evoke the widespread but not easily labeled problem of male use of social power for sexual ends. In France memories of a violent and "male" Middle Ages (as Georges Duby would say), rekindled by a long polemical and literary tradition, furnished a convenient term. The lexical difficulties involved were clearly shown in the title of one of the first books devoted to the question in France: *De l'abus de pouvoir sexuel: Le harcèlement sexuel au travail* (On the abuse of sexual power: Sexual harassment in the workplace). A note explained the author's choice of terms: "Sexual harassment, translated from the English, has the advantage of being concise and clear. *Droit de cuissage* has a wide resonance in mentalities."[2]

This lexical mediation is less innocent than it seems, and it prompts us to ask why the term *droit de cuissage* has remained stubbornly French in both its designation and its references. Anglo-Saxon historiography uses another French term, *droit du seigneur*. A feature in the Italian magazine *L'Espresso* in the spring of 1992, similar to the one published in *Le nouvel observateur*, makes no mention of any medieval droit du seigneur.[3]

In the French sphere sexual harassment seems to derive from an age-old question of domination. The word *droit* evokes the infamous "bizarre, feudal, abusive" rights of the Ancien Régime. Male behavior in a business setting today is referred back to an ancient domination perpetuated in other forms. In France in the late nineteenth century, when the trade union movement touched on women's demands, it evoked the *droit de cuissage* to denounce their exploitation.[4] A strict polarity between dominators and the dominated made the medieval right plausible and metaphorical use of it legitimate.

During the discussions in June 1991 preparatory to the revision of the French Penal Code, no new term was coined in the article adopted relating to the problem. The code condemns "the act of soliciting by order, constraint, or pressure favors of a sexual nature committed by any means by a person abusing the authority conferred by [his] functions on the occasion of or in the exercise of the victim's professional activity."[5] We must admire in passing the article's exquisite choice of words in *favors*, a term redolent of libertine flirtation. In the final draft of the code (book 2: *Sur les atteintes aux personnes*), the verb *harceler*, despite its American connotations, replaces the verb *solliciter*—another term deriving (paradoxically, given that it refers to strong pressures and moral blackmail) from a deep-rooted French tradition of gallantry and libertinage. More important, however, the innovation, which came much later in France than in other European systems of law or in the United States, caused a political split even though the article had little to do with politics. The right (RPR and

UDF) voted against it; the left (Socialists and Communists) voted for it. The press displayed another and more purely cultural split when referring to this article of the new code: the popular press talked of *droit de cuissage*, while the "bourgeois" press called it *harcèlement sexuel*. One rightist deputy opposed to the article condemned it precisely because he thought it a trendy notion imported from America: Pascal Clément (UDF, Loire) called it "a fashionable amendment."[6] I might note that in the new text the gender of neither the oppressor nor the victim is specified (*lui, la personne, la victime*). Unlike law systems founded in common law, French law, which derives from the Roman, proceeds by specifying precise instances within an overall framework: The general principles of law consider only individuals in the abstract, who are supposed equal under the law. A system based in common law is more empirical in its approach and permits more precisely defined particulars. In French law any change needs to be fitted into a free slot in the overall framework, which is why questions of sexual harassment were for many years assimilated to crimes already listed on the books that fell under civil law, labor law (the *Code du travail*), or *jurisprudence prud'homale*, cases of employer-employee disputes tried before special judges.

The recent reemergence of the term thus becomes more understandable: The rigidity of French law long made it difficult to add "sexual harassment" to the list of offenses, and even now the old expression continues to prevent the creation of a new, more lexically appropriate term. Moreover, the new metaphorical life of the term *droit de cuissage* arises at the juncture of a juridical construction from the United States and a French tradition—always referred to the Ancien Régime—of a simple, strongly polarized opposition between dominators and the dominated. Feminist or political militancy aside, the French determination of this offense operates in a context of classes or castes where the more powerful person applies the principle of "might makes right" and takes the law in his own hands. Sexual violence is but one of the guises of this eternal predatory attitude; the Middle Ages, seen within the feudal myth, supplies its perfect prototype.

Americans construct "sexual harassment" with no such seigniorial genealogy for the excellent reason that the United States has no medieval past. As American history is taught and transmitted, the only prelude to today is "colonial history"—that is, the history of the peopling of the North American continent before the colonies won their independence from Great Britain. For Americans the medieval history of Europe is just one island in the archipelago of Elsewhere, and when American women rise in protest, they do not construct their image of the male predator on the model of the feudal lord.

Furthermore, sexual harassment has won a place in American law thanks to the gradual elaboration of individual rights: Although these were originally founded on an absolute affirmation of the autonomy of the citizen, as time passed they have been extended to take into account groups left out in the free play of individual wills. Slavery, a festering sore from the earliest days of a society defined by the coexistence of liberties, required slow treatment or brutal extirpation. The law, ceaselessly redefined by the law courts and the decisions of the Supreme Court, is in tension between maintaining constitutional principles exalting the abstract individual and protecting the collective rights of "minorities" and righting an initial injustice (as the Supreme Court stated, "to compensate for historical discrimination"). Beginning in the 1960s the women's movement worked to define women as a minority group of persons long denied full individuality by gender.

Sexual harassment in fact first entered U.S. law in connection with minority rights. In the majority opinion on *Meritor Savings Bank v. Vinson* (1986), the Supreme Court declared the sexual harassment of a female employee by her superior contrary to federal law. The term itself came from a book, *Sexual Harassment of Working Women*, written by Catharine MacKinnon, a professor of law and the founder of a feminist theory of law.[7] The Supreme Court may have wanted to compensate for the failure of the Equal Rights Amendment in 1982, a measure that attempted to bring minorities under the direct protection of the Constitution. Still, the 1986 decision derives its juridical meaning from a longstanding tradition, repeatedly revised and constitutional in origin: the ten first amendments to the Constitution (the Bill of Rights), which solemnly affirm the rights of the individual. In 1868 the Fourteenth Amendment established the application of those rights to all citizens in all the states of the Union. That amendment, passed soon after the Civil War, does not explicitly mention races or minorities, but nonetheless it was aimed at making all discriminatory practices illegal: All that was needed was to encompass the legislative liberty of the various states within the framework of the federal Bill of Rights. Discrimination persisted, however, and a century later the Civil Rights Act of 1964 was passed. Title Seven, section 201.(a) of that act guaranteed "full and equal enjoyment" of public places "without discrimination or segregation on the ground of race, color, religion, or national origin." The same act (sections 703.a and 201.a) prohibits discrimination in the workplace on the basis of sex. By referring to the Civil Rights Act, the 1986 legislation continued the process of defining the collective rights of minorities. Women, a gender-defined group, were accorded particular specificity within the idea of discrimination because sexual harassment could not be confined to the moment of recruitment but needed to include day-to-day aspects of dominating behavior. The close connection between sexual harassment and the defense of minorities seems to be confirmed by the introduction of the term *racial harassment* in a 1989 decision of the Supreme Court *(Patterson v. McLean Credit Union).*[8]

Thus metaphorical references to this offense were increasing, in very different contexts, on either side of the Atlantic. In Europe references to seigniorial domination persisted, dramatized by the act of sexual abuse; in the United States sexual harassment was one of a series of vexations in the wars between human groups, and harassment, a lesser version of assault (which was in turn considered an aggravating circumstance in murder cases in English common law from the Middle Ages on) retained a military connotation of guerrilla tactics.

This is why the offense seems so different in these two worlds, as strikingly illustrated in October 1991 by the Clarence Thomas affair. Thomas, nominated to the Supreme Court by President George Bush, was undergoing hearings for Senate confirmation when a former subordinate accused him of sexual harassment. He was not charged with having made any overt attempts at sexual extortion but rather with having made a series of off-color remarks and heavy-handed sexual allusions. In this case harassment consisted in unduly marking a neutral or individual terrain with signs of the culture of the hegemonic group—here, males. The text of a resolution voted by the members of the Conférence Nationale des Intervenants en Harcèlement Sexuel in Canada commented explicitly on this concept, defining sexual harassment as "the intrusion of men into the feelings, the thoughts, the ways of being, the space, the time, the energy, and the body of women without their wanting or desiring it."[9]

The determining agent is thus the "patriarchal" instance, defined as the group of males insofar as it inherits, takes over, and applies an ancestral technique of domination over the female group. Historical reference, anchored in both the ancient tribal world and the authoritarian family universe of the Ancien Régime, skips right over the Middle Ages, perfectly useless to the metaphor.

A recent novel by the Canadian author Margaret Atwood, *The Handmaid's Tale,* is an excellent illustration of this orientation.[10] This work is a narrative of political anticipation in the tradition of George Orwell's *Nineteen Eighty-Four.* At the end of the twentieth century, after a series of ecological and demographic catastrophes and political crises, an extremist organization takes power in the Northeast of the United States and creates the Republic of Gilead, a state founded on caste tyranny and the absolute domination of women by men. A minority of men (the Commanders) enjoy a position of power. They have legitimate wives (who dress in blue) but also have available servant women (dressed in red) for the task of propagation of the species: Once a month the Commander copulates with the servant lying under the body of his wife. Sterile and older women (who dress in green) do the domestic chores. Atwood uses fiction to present patriarchal domination in a pure state based on servitude and reproduction, reinforced by a narrow, constraining ethic, and confirmed by a monopoly of culture, decision-making power, and money. The novelist's feminist point of view does not prevent her from introducing a subtle criticism of the anti-Gileadean feminist movement, which had evolved the matriarchal idea of a separate women's world necessarily defined by reproductive capacity, women's most pertinent differentiating trait. What we need to note is that there is nothing medieval about this neo-archaic republic, except perhaps that the childbearing servants wear a robe and a coif resembling a nun's habit (though as religious dress it is more post-Tridentine than medieval). Gilead is both a "barbarous" universe outside time and a society imbued with the punctiliousness of the Puritan family of the early modern age. The reference to Chaucer in the book's title in no way implies any comparison between the women servants and the female subjects of a feudal lord.

Still, when Atwood's fable situates "patriarchal rights" within a long rivalry between the sexes, it escapes the confines of the ideological landscape of the New World. Her novel might be taken as an illustration in contemporary terms of the theses of the great Swiss thinker Johann Jakob Bachofen (1815–87), best known for his construction of the *Mutterrecht* (the law of the mother), or matriarchy. Basing his hermeneutics on that of Greek myths, Bachofen sought to discover a general law of division between the sexes governing the evolution of all societies. He viewed humanity as passing through three stages. The first was an original "hetaerism" based on the elementary model of the biological reproduction of plants, where sexual promiscuity was uniquely directed toward reproduction and all notion of marriage and family was absent. An annual rite dedicated women of reproductive age to their sacred task (one thinks of Atwood's notion of sacrificial monthly couplings). In those early times humanity followed a purely natural law. The reproducing females gradually reacted, moving to protect their rights by introducing a system of marriage regulated by matrons according to the "principle of Demeter," the goddess of agriculture and family life. A third and final stage of human evolution allowed man to use his superior physical strength to turn to his own profit the familial and hereditary structure matriarchy had devised. History was then governed by war between the sexes based, in the last analysis, on irreducible differences in reproductive capacity.

Although Bachofen does not mention medieval *cuissage,* an equivalent to the droit du seigneur occurs in the transition period between hetaerism and matriarchy: "The sacrifice that was at first made once a year is now performed only once; originally practiced by the matrons, hetaerism is now limited to young women. It is now practiced only before marriage, and even under those conditions is no longer promiscuous but reserved to certain chosen persons."[11]

Bachofen's thesis was echoed in an entire literature of ethnosexology, to which we shall return. For the moment let me simply note a recent example in Georges Bataille's work, *L'érotisme* (1957). Bataille gives no scholarly sources in this study, but his theory of marriage as transgression has an astonishing kinship to Bachofen's thesis of primitive promiscuity. Where Bachofen speaks of the vegetative part of man's nature urging him to disordered growth, Bataille invokes the model of the cell: eroticism is inhabited by a nostalgia for a time of continuity before people were separated into distinct individuals. Marriage, which separates individuals from the milieu of their origin, was acceptable only as a "sanctioned violation" of natural order:

> Recourse to a power of transgression not given to the first person to come along seems to have been commonly held as favorable when it applied to a serious act such as the violation operated on a woman *for the first time* [and] to the vague prohibition [placing] copulation under the sign of shame. Often the operation was entrusted to those who generally had what the fiancé himself lacked—the power to transgress a prohibition. Such people had to be in some way sovereign, enabling them to escape the prohibitions generally affecting the human species. In principle, priesthood designated those chosen to possess the fiancée for the first time, but in the Christian world it became unthinkable to turn to God's ministers for this, and the custom of asking the lord to practice defloration came to be established.

Bataille adds this note: "In any event, the *droit de cuissage,* which justified the feudal lord's performance of this service because he was the sovereign of his domain, was not, as was thought, the exorbitant privilege of a tyrant no one dared resist. Its origin at least was different."[12]

Georges Bataille succeeds in incorporating the European history of *cuissage* into his vast scheme, but at the cost of emptying it of all social resonance. What predominates in Bataille as in Bachofen is a reconstruction of the history of humanity in terms of sexual reproduction and a fundamental division between men and women. A politicized version of that same history structures American feminism.

As Margaret Atwood portrays the contemporary era, it is characterized by a weakened patriarchy and by women's militant aspiration to matriarchy. Her political fiction uses a context of overall crisis in social ties to portray a reaction combining a return to patriarchy with the practice of hetaerism modernized by a recourse to demographics—a question that bears great ideological weight in our societies.

Thus women's militant protest against masculine oppression borrows from two models for its history. The first, predominant in Europe, is founded on the schema of the lord's territorial and corporal domination; its framework is primarily class conflict, and it is only secondarily based in gender. The second, predominant in the United States, privileges the historical figure of the patriarch within a gender-based war that is only secondarily political. Emphasis on the "patriarchal" model perhaps explains why the prolific corporation of American medievalists shows a nearly complete lack of interest in the *droit de cuissage*, despite a high degree of sensitivity to divisive questions of gender. Patriarchal violence is too immemorial and too permanent to be contained within the limits of any particular historical institution. In a recent work on the image of rape in medieval literature, Kathryn Gravdal writes, "The modern notion of the droit du seigneur—a lord's right to deflower the bride of his peasant on their wedding night—typifies this myth of the acceptability of rape in medieval society."[13] More than the mistaken (and widespread) notion that the droit du seigneur is "modern," what is noteworthy here is that Gravdal equates such a right with rape and suggests that the medieval alibi for violent domination by men is a recent construction.

Going beyond ideological constructions and national differences in the reconstruction of the past, however, legal institution of sexual harassment as a criminal offense gives us an essential starting point to which we need not return: Whatever its degree of historical reality, the *droit de cuissage* is one possible occurrence when social power and gender division coincide. Moreover, that coincidence has an objective and universal reality. We need to be careful not to eliminate the concrete possibility that in specific circumstances a male individual endowed with exorbitant powers may have used them for sexual ends. Scattered mentions of a *droit de cuissage* are not necessarily the product of a traveler's imagination or an indication of a longstanding continuity in tradition but may be due to the use of superior force. This is why we need to look critically at another interpretation of the *droit de cuissage* based on a fascination for the archaic and the primordial.

THE IDOL OF ORIGINS: ETHNOGRAPHIC INTERPRETATIONS OF THE *DROIT DE CUISSAGE*

The great nineteenth-century debates over the grandeur or the infamy of feudal societies no longer bear much meaning for us, especially since, as François Furet declared, "the French Revolution is over." Except for the metaphorical use that we have just examined, the medieval antecedents of seigniorial domination have lost their relevance; the droit du seigneur is no longer a valid accusation in law. It has nonetheless gained a new pertinence in common discourse by recalling something primordial: The medieval custom, whether it ever existed or not, transcribes extremely ancient nuptial rites related in varying degree to the "taboo of virginity" or "fertility rites" (a vast category into which almost any phenomenon can be fitted). The medieval custom is simply a partial and poorly understood residue of such rites. This interpretation spread beyond academic circles: In 1929 the American dramatist Leslie Stevens wrote a play set in the twelfth century, *The Lovers* (adapted to the cinema in 1965 by Franklin Schaffer as *The Warlord*),[14] showing the droit du seigneur as a fertility rite.

Interpretations of the *droit de cuissage* taking it back to archaic times are not new. Chateaubriand, in a short commissioned work, *L'analyse raisonnée de l'histoire de France*,[15] wrote of the droit du seigneur: "It is to Greek and Roman servitude that these abuses must be traced." We should not be astonished to see the author of *Le génie du christianisme* sloughing off onto classical antiquity a heavy weight of suspicion that burdened the Christian societies of the Middle Ages, but the origin of the *droit de cuissage* was usually shifted to the Celtic and Germanic tribal borderlands of the classical world.

In general, the myth of a survival from barbarian times remains strong among medievalists. Survivals of the sort enable them to shift a variety of difficult problems—questions of royal power, beliefs, law, and more—out of the field of analysis. Moreover, since little is known about the ancient Germanic and Celtic peoples, they can make such assertions without fear of contradiction. Robert Boutruche, a highly reputable historian of feudalism, used survivals to explain medieval mentions of the *droit de cuissage* (which he at least had the courage to mention, unlike other specialists in feudalism afraid of seeming ridiculous or naive). He defines these as "local resurgences of probably ancient practices, resulting, in my opinion, from a climate maintained either by clan or tribal life or by slavery and returned to honor thanks to the spread of the 'seigniorial ban.'"[16]

The historiographical benefit of simple reference to something anterior or exterior is insufficient to explain turning the droit du seigneur into an archaic rite. Sexual and matrimonial behaviors are probably among the easiest and the most fascinating approaches to otherness—something that becomes evident in the age of the great discoveries. The Middle Ages were not free of a similar curiosity, but it was channeled through scandalized acknowledgment of an ethical anomaly. In the late eleventh century Lanfranc, archbishop of Canterbury and the master and predecessor of St. Anselm, was concerned about sexual mores in the Celtic borderlands of the Christian world. In 1073–74 he wrote two letters, one to Guthric, king of Dublin, and the other to Toirrdelbach Ua Briain, the king of Munster, expressing his indignation at behaviors reported to him: "There are said to be men in your kingdom who take wives from either their own kindred or that of their deceased wives; others who by their own will and authority abandon the wives who are legally married to them; some who give their own wives to others and by an abominable exchange receive the wives of other men instead."[17] Nothing in these practices resembles a *droit de cuissage*, but this text, which is far from extraordinary in ecclesiastical literature, helps us understand why the first statement about the existence of the *droit de cuissage* in lay lordship should come from a thirteenth-century monastic text. The immense effort launched by the eleventh-century Gregorian reforms for christianizing sexual mores led to a sharpened observation of practice where legitimate suspicions mingle with polemic invention.

The scandalized reaction of Lanfranc, an Italian who went first to Normandy before taking on his duties in England, a country where Celtic customs remained alive, was not an isolated case. Ireland, Wales, and Scotland resisted the Anglo-Norman and Roman clergy both with a paganism only recently and superficially suppressed and with an autochthonous tradition of Irish and Scottish monasticism notably different from Roman norms. More than a century after Lanfranc, Giraud de Barri gave a striking image of Celtic irredentism in his famous account of his travels in Ireland and Wales.[18]

The first mention of the *droit de cuissage* in Celtic lands should probably be understood within this politico-religious and medieval context, even if that mention occurs in an early sixteenth-century text. In 1526 the Scottish scholar Hector Boece (or Boethius) published in Paris a *History of Scotland* written in Latin. Among the good measures instituted by King Malcolm III Canmore (1058–93) in his zeal for reform, Boece mentions the elimination of a custom created by a pagan king of Scotland whom he supposes to have reigned toward the end of the first century B.C. Boece states:

> Ane othir law [King Ewin] maid, that wiffis of the commonis sal be fre to the nobillis; and the lord of the ground sall have the madinheid of all virginis dwelling on the same. And thocht the first two lawis wes revokit eftir be counsall, yit this last law wes sa plesand to the young nobillis, that it couth nevir be abrogat, quhill the time of King Malcolme Cammore, and his blist quene Sanct Margaret; quhilkis thocht the samin sa injurius baith to God and man, that thay solistit the nobillis to revoik the said law, takand thairfore ane goldin penny, callit the marchetis: quhilk is yit payit to the lord of the ground, quhen virginis are to be maryit, in redemption of thair honour and chaistite.[19]

This affirmation, which Boece repeats later in his *History,*[20] had a remarkably successful career.

Boece's *History* was the beginning of a Scottish national historiography, until then limited to one or two manuscript chronicles of limited circulation. The renewal of Scottish nationhood in the sixteenth century and the development of printing brought new life to the genre, and Boece's successors, Bishop John Leslie in 1578 and George Buchanan in 1582,[21] repeated the episode about King Evenus (or Ewin). From the seventeenth to the nineteenth century many authors on the Continent, especially in France, reiterated Boece's passage on the droit du seigneur, and dictionary entries on the *droit de cuissage* cited this Celtic precedent. The anecdote was all the more successful for explaining the etymology of a marriage due, the *merchet* or *marquette,* clearly attested in the British Isles from the twelfth century on (and discussed below in connection with analogous dues in French lands). In 1597 Sir John Skene compiled a lexicon of terms from ancient Scots law that he published in an appendix to a collection of laws, repeating the story of King Evenus under "marcheta." Skene archaizes Boece's simple etymology: the mark, a silver coin, became a word for horse—also *mark* in old French, old Irish, and old Germanic—thus coming to designate the act of defloration in a virile, animal metaphor (the rude barbarians again!).[22]

Boece very probably invented the episode of Evenus. No earlier text mentions any such king, and in general almost nothing is known about the various populations of Scotland (Picts, Angles, Bretons, Scots) before the end of the first millennium. Hector Boece (c. 1465–1536), was born in Dundee of an old Scots family. He studied in Paris at the Collège de Montaigu and became its regent during the last decade of the fifteenth century. Later, with Bishop William Elphinstone (and with the backing of King James IV of Scotland), he helped to found the University of Aberdeen. The bull obtained by the bishop from Pope Alexander VI in support of the creation of the university speaks of the need to bring light to the still savage populations of the northernmost regions of Scotland. The episode of Evenus may echo that intent.

Boece's historiographic activities were shaped by national and local preoccupations: After Scotland's terrible defeat by the English at Flodden in 1513, the Scots felt the need to invent a glorious and complete past for their nation. To that purpose Boece first wrote a life of the bishops of Aberdeen (1522) before turning to his *History of Scotland* in 1526. He is not parsimonious with glorifying episodes: The chronicle gives one Scotia or Scota, the daughter of the pharaoh of Egypt, as the founder of the nation, along with her consort Gathelus, "ane richt illuster and vailyeant knight, discending be lang progressioun and linage of the blud riall of Greece"— a pair indisputably of greater antiquity than the founders of the Irish, Welsh, and English nations. Boece did his utmost, but his national history takes on consistency only with Malcolm III, who easily figures as the new founder of the nation: He united the Scots clans, resisted William the Conqueror, and, with his wife Margaret, reformed Scotland's religious customs, until that date subject to Irish influence. It is probably the happy conjunction of Scots "nationalism" and the Romanization of the region that inspired Boece to include an episode proclaiming that barbarian mores had been left behind with conversion to Christianity. He needed a bad ancestor, and Evenus, carefully placed in the epoch immediately preceding christianization, filled the bill. Evenus was certainly an invention: John Major, a fellow student of Boece's at the Collège de Montaigu and a man who shared his culture, wrote a history of Scotland in 1521, five years before Boece, using many of the same references as Boece, but he says not a word about King Evenus.[23]

The episode of Evenus, which played an important role in the dossier of the *droit de cuissage* and led to a long series of citations and borrowings, had no polemic pertinence in Boece, who was operating as a mythologist. Boece probably believed in Evenus no more than he did in Scotia: Both were simply roles in a rhetoric of foundation common in medieval historiography. The episode does not seem inspired by the theme of the droit du seigneur: The tyrant's exorbitant sexual appetite evokes the voracity of the Minotaur, annihilated in the end by the civilizing hero, the Scottish Theseus, Malcolm III. What gives this story a function in the history of the *droit de cuissage* is instead the etymological pains Boece takes to tie Malcolm's action to the payment of merchet. The misunderstanding over Evenus should be treated as a linguistic event situated at the meeting-point of three historical contexts. The first of these, a notion woven into the fabric of the ecclesiastical Middle Ages, might be expressed: "The savages of the borderlands fornicate like beasts so long as they remain untouched by the grace of conversion." The second context, narrower in scope since it operated at the moment of the constitution of nation-states in the late Middle Ages, might be: "A civilizing king has constructed the nation by seizing its savage forces and redirecting them." It is easy to see the connection between these two propositions and to grasp the ambivalence of a barbarian past that both horrifies and fascinates. The second context modified the first. The third context, of a different order, was established throughout Europe at the difficult moment of the compilation of local customs and practices within the framework of monarchical laws, a topic to which we shall return. Here the proposition was: "There are payments that serve as compensation for an ancient custom of barbarian fornication." The combination of these three contextual propositions produced the episode of Evenus; a later decontextualization removed the story's fabulousness and transformed it into a remembrance of an institutional reality.

The Celtic borderlands furnished other ancient "proofs" of the *droit de cuissage*. We need not linger over them, as they repeat the same mechanisms: In Ireland, for example, clan legends furnish several episodes involving unmarried Minotaur-like kings avid for virgin flesh. In these cases the institutionalized expedient of merchet is missing, but in Wales a Gaelic word, *amobyr* (often deformed as *amachyr*), probably designating a marital fee, is attested in the laws of King Hywel (tenth century) and was seized on by champions of the existence of the *droit de cuissage* as early as the seventeenth century as an equivalent to the Scottish merchet. The simple act of extracting the term from its Welsh context lent it the mystery required to serve the myth of *cuissage*.[24]

The long centuries of ecclesiastical culture in the Middle Ages offer another example of this mechanism for projecting ethical censure toward the ethnic borderlands. In the Netherlands at the end of the seventeenth century, Fathers Henschen and Papebroch, continuing the immense hagiographic work of the Jesuit Jean de Bolland, repeated the story of

Evenus in the collection of documents concerning St. Margaret of Scotland they published in 1688, where they attribute Malcolm's reform to her and cite the inevitable Boece.[25] These two scholars did not have to read Scottish history to discover the *droit de cuissage,* however: Thirteen years earlier, in 1675, as they were preparing to publish the acts of the obscure St. Forannan, they encountered a document from the twelfth century in which a noble made a donation dispensing his dependents from payment of the *bathinodium (bathinodii questu).* The context does not explain this due, and anyone accustomed to reading medieval charters knows they include an infinite variety of fiscal designations, presenting a problem of terminology further complicated by transcription of local expressions into Latin. The Jesuits nonetheless took this unusual word as a mask for *cuissage,* stating in a somewhat surprising note:

> *Bathinodium:* I understand by this what we might call "bed-nood" in a more supple dialect, signifying the necessity for payment in compensation for the common couch or bed. This operated between the *serfs de la glèbe,* as they were called (peasants in Belgium were at one time of this kind and many still are found in Frisia and in Germany) and their lords. . . . Vestiges of this right lasted until our own day in country areas, where it is said that the peasants purchase back from the lord of the domain [a dominio fundi], by payment of a due, the right of the first night [jus primae noctis].[26]

Dutch and German erudition of the eighteenth and nineteenth centuries did indeed see Frisia as the frontier of barbarity because conversion had proven extremely difficult in that territory.[27] The *Acta sanctorum* gave the Bollandists' commentary a broad circulation, and *droit de cuissage* benefited from the learned Jesuits' backing. Later polemics made wide use of this "proof."

Thanks to exegesis, an obsession with origins and a mixture of attraction and repulsion concerning barbarian sources of institutions was easily transmitted from the clergy to the clerisy—from churchmen to historians. As Marc Bloch noted in a famous denunciation of the "idol of origins": "Now, this preoccupation with origins, justifiable in a certain type of religious analysis, has spread in a doubtlessly inevitable contagion into other fields of research where its legitimacy is far more debatable. Moreover, history oriented towards origins was put to the service of value judgments."[28] Between the seventeenth century and the eighteenth, differences of opinion between the partisans and the adversaries of the existence of *cuissage* masked their profound agreement that fiscal exactions or odd rites must be explained by primitive origins—clerical for one school, pagan for the other.

Beginning in the sixteenth century, however, accounts of bizarre sexual customs among remote peoples took on a totally different resonance. The many travel narratives that were published (often padded with materials from the classical or medieval tradition) created a taste for a sexual exoticism offering both the pleasure of sin by procuration and an affirmation of the relativity of mores and doctrines. The appeal of that relativization is particularly clear at the end of the sixteenth century, when the shock of the Wars of Religion led to widespread doubt about the universality of truth. The external zones of the domain of certitude (rites, behaviors, even dogmas) tended to shrink, taking refuge in the internal space of individual faith.[29]

Montaigne's two allusions to a *droit de cuissage* in far-off lands in the chapter in his *Essais*, "De la coustume et de ne changer aisément une Loy receüe" (Of Custom, and That We Should Not Easily Change a Law Received), probably written in 1572, should be read in this context. These two passages appear as part of a long list of varied and apparently aberrant practices demonstrating the preeminence of custom in the conduct of human affairs. Montaigne loosely connects the deliberate disorder of this mosaic with "there are countries where . . . where . . . where." First he speaks of lands where premarital chastity is not required of women, then he adds: "And in another place, if it is a merchant who marries, all the merchants invited to the wedding go to bed with the bride before him; and the greater their number, the greater is her honour and her reputation for strength and capacity; and if an officer marry, it is the same; the same if it is a nobleman, and so of all others except labourers or men of mean condition, for then it is the lord's privilege; and yet a severe loyalty during marriage is strictly enjoined."[30] The last detail, which appears in the additions to the *Essais* in the 1588 edition, comes from the French translation of the *History of the Spanish Conquest of Mexico* by Francisco López de Gómara, *Histoire générale des Indes occidentales et terres neuves qui jusquà présent ont esté découvertes*, the fifth edition of which was published in 1584.

Still, López de Gómara was not the only spur to Montaigne's interest in this type of nuptial "rite," since the first version of the chapter, begun in 1572 and published in 1580, includes a similar passage about a land "where the women wear copper greaves upon both legs, and if a louse bite them they are bound in self-respect to bite back, and dare not marry till they have made their king a tender of their virginity, if he please to accept it."[31]

Here Montaigne borrowed from Pierre Saliat's French translation of Herodotus, published in 1575.[32] The passage occurs in Herodotus' narration of the Persian expeditions in Libya and is part of a brief description of the Adyrmachidae, the first Libyans that the Persian invaders encountered after the Egyptians. We need not linger over this fragment as it simply repeats the Minotaur theme.

Their placement within an immense catalogue of ethnological oddities makes these observations only relatively important for the medieval *droit de cuissage,* never mentioned in Montaigne's *Essais,* a work that nonetheless reflects their author's curiosity and free-ranging mind. The social rites associated with marriage that Montaigne lists show a strong sense of hierarchy founded on an exceptional being (the "king" in the second passage) or based on an organization of society into distinct castes (the merchants, officers, nobles, and laborers in the first passage). Marriage norms are no different from Western usages in that only the moment of the nuptials calls for collective participation of the caste in one member's change in state; the rite seems to recall an ancient clan-based sexual promiscuity. The mention of "laborers" does evoke medieval *cuissage,* however, because Montaigne's observation moves us from a separation between castes to an interaction between classes in which "labourers or men of mean condition" have to submit their wife to a dominant personage and because there is also a lord (here, the peasant's lord, not a generic nobleman). It is hard to know whether or not Montaigne is alluding to medieval *cuissage* here, because the contorted composition of his list of customs puts among its ethnological oddities some perfectly "normal" Western customs that take on a coloration of the strange and the arbitrary thanks to the context. If we consult Martin Fumée's translation of López de Gómara we see, however, that Montaigne subtly distorted his source.

Francisco López de Gómara (1511–59) was a cleric in the service of Charles V's ambassador to Rome. During the siege of Algiers in 1541, he met Hernán Cortés, whose chaplain he became. Making use of Cortés's memoirs, he published his *General History of the Indies* in 1552, a work that followed the career of that famous conquistador. The book was an immense and immediate success, but it also prompted criticism: Under pressure from the famous champion of the "Indians," Bartolomé de Las Casas, the imperial court prohibited republication of the book, which nonetheless was reprinted in Antwerp, even before translation into all European languages further broadened its circulation. Thus what Cortés states, through López de Gómara, is not totally above suspicion.

The fragment that Montaigne picks up is part of a short chapter on the island of Cuba, which Cortés visited in 1511 in the first stage of his American conquests. Cortés himself tells López de Gómara that his information was secondhand because by the time of his arrival in Cuba, the island had lost all its Indian inhabitants to syphilis and alcohol or deportation to New Spain. Cortés's informants told him that the original Cubans were in all ways like the natives of Hispaniola (Santo Domingo), except that they spoke a different language and went about naked. The only detail of their mores that the voyager noted was precisely this episode of savage nuptials. Fumée's French translation, which closely follows the Spanish original,[33] presents a social and sexual hierarchy quite different from the one Montaigne presents. In Fumée only the tribal chiefs *(caciques)* and merchants practice communal clan sex; "citizens, bourgeois, and workers [citadins, bourgeois et laboureurs]" are excluded. Furthermore, it is "the lord or some priest [le Seigneur, ou quelque prestre]" who deflowers young women. Montaigne westernizes the hierarchy: In López de Gómara the Cuban custom made a special case of castes external to local life (chiefs and merchants); Montaigne separates the three groups from the rest of the population. Defloration by the priest or lord *(un cacique suprême)* orients the custom toward religious practices Gómara had noted in Mexico. Moreover, by specifying that after the nuptial ceremonies matrimonial norms impose monogamic fidelity, Montaigne makes the festive moment of loss of virginity a special and astonishing rite. In López de Gómara, to the contrary, the Cubans' marital behavior confirms the extreme savagery of their mores and in part explains the rapid disappearance of the population: Spouses repudiate one another without formalities, the men are sodomites, and the women indulge in the wildest sort of sexual fantasies. López de Gómara is still in the medieval tradition of the ethnic otherness of the savage: The Cubans' nature is in fact a self-destructiveness counter to nature; humanity's true nature is conferred by grace or by its secular analogue, progress. Representations of sexuality in the New World are in reality more complex, as Pierre Ragon has recently demonstrated. They cluster around three narrative themes: sodomy among the Indians, the existence of Amazons, and the natives' lascivious but phlegmatic character. It seems possible that mention of an Indian *droit de cuissage* on the part of authors whose works did not have the same success as López de Gómara's helped put the predatory sexual acts of the conquerors, at times operating with the complicity of the native chiefs, in a somewhat better light.[34]

When Montaigne borrowed and altered this episode, he included it in his encyclopedia of relativism: Human nature hardly exists; behaviors are artifacts. Beyond its cascading examples the essay on custom has an ideological coherence. Montaigne begins with a mournful description of the power of habit, "a forcible and treacherous schoolmistress" who relies on the tyranny of the body to dominate the reason. Then little by little, by enlarging his domain of action and presenting a mixture of Western practices and barbarian mores, he moves beyond the antagonism between reason and custom. Reason is illusory: "The laws of conscience, which we say are derived from nature, are born of custom." Hence reason can only be exercised within the individual human conscience: "Private reason has but a private jurisdiction." In the world's forum conformity to established customs must dominate reason: "The Christian religion has all the marks of the utmost justice and utility, but none more manifest than the precise injunction of obedience to the civil magistrate and the maintenance of governments." As he works through his arguments, Montaigne clearly raises a question fundamental to *cuissage:* the status of local (or "feudal") usages. As we shall see, it was the royal jurists who most violently denounced the droit du seigneur. Montaigne energetically defends local law against Roman law: "What can be more strange than to see a people obliged to obey laws they never understood, bound in all their domestic affairs, such as marriages, donations, wills, sales, and purchases, to rules they cannot possibly know, since they are neither written nor published in their own language, and of which they must of necessity purchase both the interpretation and the practice?"[35]

In Montaigne, the Indian mask for the *droit de cuissage* contributes to a defense of a basically conservative moral and epistemological relativism. Until the beginning of the twentieth century an entire tradition I prefer to call ethnographic (to distinguish it from anthropology, more respectful of local contexts) has dipped into the endless variety of exotic customs for an acceptance of its own practices or for the vague satisfaction of vicarious enjoyment. It would be going too far, however, to reduce all expressions of marvel at sexual exoticism to deliberate, scornful indifference. In the eighteenth century European history moved on to another phase in the discovery of the savage. There are Diderot's reveries, for example, in his *Supplément au voyage de Bougainville,* reveries echoed in our own times by the ethnological semi-fictions of Margaret Mead,[36] where sexual mores foreign to our own are connected to a happy, natural sexuality composed of gentleness, tolerance, and a fondness for pleasure. It is thus hardly surprising to find no episodes in the Minotaur mode in these narrations or reflections, whereas from the early eighteenth century on, as we shall see, the droit du seigneur provided subject matter for an entire theatrical genre. In this ethnology of the good savage, different sexual practices serve universalist rather than relativist ends: The humanity observed designates a nature.

This search for authenticity and for a common source of humanity has given our age an "explanation" essential to the ongoing reception of the myth of the *droit de cuissage*. As the argument runs, the truth of *cuissage* has no need of historical proof because it designates a universal tendency in human nature only traces of which, masked by institutions, can be observed as fleeting and imperfect expressions of a transhistorical fact. This truth in turn refers back to something unexpressed and perhaps unconscious: the taboo of virginity and first sexual contact. I shall limit myself to considering two examples, but this model of explanation has a much broader scope: The idea of a primitive ritual significance in the *droit de cuissage* developed diffusely outside these two coherent theories.

The Finnish ethnologist Edward Westermarck (1862–1939) provides the first of these examples. His monumental and well-known *History of Marriage*, begun in 1891, has been translated into many languages and was introduced to the French public in translation by the great folklorist Arnold van Gennep (1934–43). Westermarck's grand obsession was to prove that marriage and the exogamic nuclear family provide structure to all the societies of our planet. He postulates humanity's primitive innocence, thus opposing theorists of a primitive sexual promiscuity, notably Bachofen, whose work had been continued in Germany by an entire school of ethnologists who also drew support from Darwinism. Westermarck's *History of Marriage* is an ethnological compilation much in the taste of the age (only a few years later Sir James Frazer was to publish his enormous catalogue of cults, myths, and rites, *The Golden Bough*), completed by direct observations made in Morocco. The first volume of Westermarck's *History* is in fact aimed at refuting the notion of sexual promiscuity. Chapter 5—which is preceded by a chapter on sexual incontinence before marriage and followed by one on exchange practices within the institution of marriage—is dedicated to the *jus primae noctis,* for Westermarck merely a residual, dubious, and limited form of sexual life. He rejects the reality of a medieval *droit de cuissage,* accepting only a limited amount of evidence in rapidly listed instances from Brazil, the Caribbean, Senegal, Herodotus' Libya, Morocco, Kurdistan, Cambodia, and Malabar. When he speaks of Europe, he repeats the anecdote of King Evenus, mentions Bonifacio Vannozzi in the seventeenth century, and adds a few notes regarding the Celtic and Albanian frontier lands. His choice not only displays the persistence of an uncritical use of unverified sources on the part of a modern ethnologist, but also reveals a specific orientation: In all the cases Westermarck mentions, the nuptial deflowering is relegated to a sanctified figure, a king or a priest, rather than simply to a dominant person. Thus the *jus primae noctis* is a manifestation of a horror or fear of virginal blood and of defloration in primitive societies. Moreover, the custom or rite is only locally associated with a sovereign personage and is often replaced by an artifice (a stick or some sort of artifact), by a man foreign to the community, or by a "professional" deflowerer with no special religious or social privilege. Westermarck's ethnological explanation deserves our attention because it repeats, in "scientific" terms, anecdotes that circulated as early as the Middle Ages and were mentioned by Vincent de Beauvais and John Mandeville in the thirteenth and fourteenth centuries. In the sixteenth century López de Gómara gave a similar explanation of the *droit de cuissage* among the inhabitants of the Americas: "Many submitted [new brides] to the chiefs to be deflowered, either for honor or to save themselves doubts and anxiety."[37]

Sigmund Freud offered a solution analogous to Westermarck's but began from different premises. Freud (1856–1939), an exact contemporary of Westermarck (whose work he knew), treats the question of the *jus primae noctis* in a brief article, "The Taboo of Virginity," written in 1918.[38] Following Krafft-Ebing, Freud investigates the reasons for woman's sexual dependence *(geschlechtliche Hörigkeit)* on man, something that makes loss of virginity both valued and feared. Contemporary sexual morality, far from emancipating the woman from subjection, stressed resisting seduction. Ethnological observation reveals the dangers inherent in the moment of defloration. But, Freud points out, the ethnologists fail to distinguish the physiological aspect of loss of maidenhood from the particular investment in a woman's first sex act. In both the contemporary subjection and the primitive fear Freud saw the same ambivalence and the same mix of attraction and repulsion that creates taboos. Indeed, according to his analysis in *Totem and Taboo* (1913), children, primitives, and neurotics all clearly display the tensions inherent to the monogamous nuclear family, a site of unexpressed tensions. The past of the human species, still visible in "primitive" societies, dismantles the complex, closed unity of the family by manifesting the possibilities of the species before the family was instituted—just as the child expresses the moment before conflicts are integrated or the neurotic flees institutions in marginal symptomatic behavior.

How are we to understand the combined horror and fascination of the initial female sex act constant in human experience? Freud gives four successive answers. First, according to the ethnologists, those emotions have to do with a religious fear of blood and are paralleled by the primeval prohibition of murder and avoidance of contact with menstruating women. Freud finds this explanation insufficient, however, because ancient rites of circumcision and excision feature a beneficent letting of blood. He points to a second cause in a fear of first-time experience that can be classified with neurotic anxieties. But a classification is not an explanation. A third possibility, borrowed from the ethnologist Alfred Ernest Crawley, suggests a more general female taboo. In this view the first sex act manifests the profound difference between men and women by pointing out the danger of sexuality and of its soporific effects. By isolating defloration from daily sexual life, the future male spouse would be refused (or spared, according to how the ambivalent taboo worked) things inseparable from the first sex act: a special bond, a dependence that offends the "narcissism of little differences," the feeling of masculinity. In this sense defloration rites are comparable to neurotics' phobias. Freud prefers a fourth explanation, however, combining the three preceding ones. Returning to the initial question of female sexual dependence, he suggests consideration of the broader question of women's fundamental hostility toward men, a hostility that also appears in female frigidity. The first sex act is traumatizing for the woman because of the pain associated with it, heightened by the narcissistic wound. Furthermore, by its very nature, accomplishment of the sex act delivers less than expected. Lastly and above all, female libido is fixated on the father or the brother, which explains the existence of a *jus primae noctis* where the lord substitutes for the father.

Freud's conclusion approaches Westermarck's because in both cases the lord in the *jus primae noctis* serves as an institutional interpreter of a universal mode of psychic organization, marked in one case by a horror of virginal blood and in the other by the female's desire for the father and the male's fear of the initial bond. In both analyses the history of humanity necessarily leads to the construction of the monogamous family, and the *droit de cuissage* is an ancient or archaic trace of one stage in the process of its creation, a trace that Westermarck absorbs harmoniously and Freud sees as imbued with neuroticism. Freud's hypothesis seems stronger and resists historical criticism better because it is not confined within a reconstruction of origins. For Freud a psychism remains profoundly immutable, so it can never totally coincide with a stage in the evolution of an institution. The tendencies that produced the *jus primae noctis* are always at work, even if they operate differently within the constraints of the Austrian family in the nineteenth century. The construct of the family no more explicitly expresses the tensions at work within the family than the droit du seigneur requires awareness on the part of its actors. In this domain Freudian psychology, like the other "ethnographic" versions of the *droit de cuissage*, totally eludes verification.

Historians will of course have solid objections to offer to these interpretations: How can one account for a continuity between original states and specific mentions of the droit du seigneur occurring between the thirteenth and the seventeenth centuries in a civilization strongly marked by Christianity? Why should the rite be attributed essentially to minor lords firmly implanted on their lands rather than to sublime beings external to the community? How are we to explain the fact that the anxieties about virginity and first sexual contact reemerged just when St. Thomas Aquinas declared that authentic virginity has no relation to a physically intact hymen and when the penalty imposed by thirteenth-century synodal legislation on the deflowerer was merely an obligation to marry his victim or give her a sum of money as a dowry?[39] Criticism is powerless before the hypothesis of the unconscious and its ruses, or before an evocation of the somber depths of human nature. The ethnographic interpretation thus has an excellent chance of retaining the *droit de cuissage* as part of the bric-à-brac of reveries on the sexuality of the Other.

The Dialectic of the Master and the Serving Maid

Quite differently oriented reveries offer their support to the *droit de cuissage:* The medieval fable adopted the fantasy of a domestic sexuality burdened with secret ancillary loves within the privacy of the home.

This transposition is clear in Beaumarchais's *Marriage of Figaro* (1784), a work whose popularity is vastly increased by Mozart's opera and one that continues to nourish belief in this rite. Beaumarchais's play has often been presented as an important prerevolutionary text. Even before it was written, *The Barber of Seville*, with its famous speeches on personal merit, the arrogance of the high and mighty, and the need for liberty placed Beaumarchais within the constellation of Enlightenment luminaries. The long censorship of the *Marriage of Figaro*, until public opinion forced its production five years before the taking of the Bastille, assured Beaumarchais his title as a fighter for liberty. The play's plot seems to espouse the cause of political and social unrest by showing the last throes of a landed aristocracy stubbornly demanding its privileges and its abusive rights: An aristocrat, Count Almaviva, at one time open to the idea of emancipating his subjects, decides to renew ancient seigniorial exactions by demanding the *droit de cuissage* on the occasion of the marriage of two of his subjects, Figaro and Suzanne. The count, Suzanne explains, intends to "get from me, privately, a certain privilege which formerly was the right of the lord of the manor—you know what a grievous right it was." The "feudal reaction" so often analyzed by historians appears clearly in the dialogue between its two victims here:

> *Figaro:* I know it so well that if the Count had not abolished its shameful exercise when he himself was married, I should never have planned to marry you on his lands.
> *Suzanne:* He abolished it right enough, but he has had second thoughts.[40]

As we all know, things turn out for the best: Merit triumphs, thanks to both cleverness and moral superiority, and the intended victims, in alliance with the count's neglected wife, win the day over the count and his henchmen. The gaiety of the finale crowns the blossoming of talent and liberty:

> By the accident of birth,
> One is shepherd, t'other king.
> Chance made lord and underling,
> Only genius threads the maze:
> Twenty kings are fed on praise
> Who in death are common earth,
> While Voltaire immortal stays.[41]

This ancien régime décor is nonetheless the background for another world; it is also the house of a lustful familial despot. Once the young Almaviva had charmed and married Rosine, he pursued his career as a libertine. In his mature years he seeks pleasure within a harem more bourgeois than classical: "What is going on is that his lordship Count Almaviva is tired of pursuing the beauties of the neighborhood and is heading for home—not to *his* wife, you understand, but to yours."[42] The two targets of the *droit de cuissage* are members of the master's household, not rural dependents: Suzanne is "chief chambermaid to the Countess"; Figaro is "valet to the Count and steward of the castle." The famous scene that opens the play (and the opera) presents the scene of the threatened offense, a bedchamber offered to the newlyweds lying between the count's apartments and the countess's. Far from making a ritual and public demand for a fee in compensation for the *droit de cuissage*, the count maneuvers clandestinely, attempting to use the power of money, secretly "buying back" the old usage by offering Suzanne a dowry.

Beaumarchais's play belongs within an eighteenth-century tradition of comedies of manners that grasped the social pretext of the *droit de cuissage*, brought up to date by juridical polemics, to dramatize scenes where masters make advances to the *soubrettes* of the household. The tradition began in 1699 with Charles Dufresny's *La noce interrompue*.[43] In this work the persecutor is a count who attempts to marry off Nanette, his wife's goddaughter, to a peasant in order to keep her in the household as housekeeper. The *droit de cuissage*—which Dufresny explicitly evokes—figures in the title of an anonymous unpublished play, *Le droit du seigneur* (1732),[44] the first occurrence of the euphemized version of the term *droit de cuissage*. Once again, the feudal custom discovered "in his archives" by Monsieur Poignant, the bourgeois lord of the place, gives a certain removal and externality to the semi-incestuous confinement of his desires: Monsieur Poignant wants to marry his wife's goddaughter to his own godson, the peasant Mathurin, to whom he is willing to pay 100 pistoles to exercise his right. The theme remained in vogue throughout the century, with *Le droit du seigneur ou Le mari retrouvé et la femme fidèle* by Louis de Boissy (1735), Voltaire's *Le droit du seigneur* (performed in 1762 and published in 1763), *Le droit du seigneur* by P.J.B. Nougaret (1763), and *Le droit du seigneur* by Desfontaines (published in 1784). Within this tradition only Voltaire seems to have had any genuinely polemical intent; he is also the only author to give a historical framework to his play (although, curiously, he sets it in the mid-sixteenth century, the age of Henry II, rather than the Middle Ages). Voltaire was also one of the first to use the expression *droit de cuissage* (in his *Essai sur les moeurs*, 1756), and he returned to the notion on several occasions. For the other authors the droit du seigneur remained within the confines of domestic farce.

We cannot reduce the insistence on this theme to a mere theatrical vogue, however, or to attempts to imitate a proven success. When we remove the pseudo-feudal ingredient of comedies on the droit du seigneur, we have early instances of a plot that prospered in the "boulevard theater" of the nineteenth century, one centering on bourgeois adultery committed with the young and pretty lady's maid. This comparison is not purely formal; there is even a degree of chronological concordance between an expanded fictional treatment of adultery with servants and popularization of a belief in the existence of the *droit de cuissage* that developed during the eighteenth century and revived strongly in the years from 1850 to 1880.

Ribald or joking evocations of the domestic amours of the master of the house reflect new tensions in familial structures in Europe in a variety of ways. To hazard a global scheme for a complex and varied evolution, the domestic unit of the nuclear family, focused on the couple and its progeny, gradually gained ground over the extended family or clan. Theories and descriptions have long clashed on this slippery terrain, and recent research has brought new life to old interpretations. Traditionally there were two contrasting theories. The first, which we have already seen in Westermarck, attributes a natural and ethical permanence to the perfect and biblical form of the conjugal nucleus, the husband and wife and their offspring. In this view the extended family, enlarged to include kin, is simply an occasional accident in family history. Conversely, since the nineteenth century historians and anthropologists have noted the strong presence of the extended family in rural Europe and related it to the survival of kinship groups in many so-called primitive societies. In this view, the conjugal nucleus resulted from the Industrial Revolution of the eighteenth and nineteenth centuries, when an exodus of population from rural areas to cities and towns and a shift to salaried labor broke down the solidarities and networks of traditional ways of life.[45]

The painstaking studies of Peter Laslett and the Cambridge Group for the History of Population and Social Structure proposed another chronology and, above all, a more detailed causal structure. In their view, the nuclear family emerged gradually beginning in the late Middle Ages as a specific structure with three solid traits: a later average age at first pregnancy, a relatively small age gap between husband and wife, and a high proportion of domestic servants in the population.[46] Jean-Louis Flandrin proposes a convincing reading of the connection among these characteristics:

> The fact that married children were not usually welcome in their parents' house—proven by the almost non-existence of multiple family households—made marriage more difficult and thus raised the average age at first pregnancy despite the not insignificant rate of illegitimate births. But this also calls into question the Western custom of only marrying a young woman if she had a dowry, the importance of which the Cambridge Group seems to me to underestimate. Moreover and conversely, because of the late age at first pregnancy, it was more likely that young people might marry after their parents' deaths, which inevitably limited the number of extended households. This also points out the relationship between the small age gap between spouses and the advanced age of young women at their first marriage, and therefore at their first pregnancy. Lastly, if parents were unable to provide their daughters with a dowry, they had to earn their dowry by working as servants for many years.[47]

These interactive causes, in turn, may well have emerged from a complex network of social and mental changes. One element that deserves mention is Church pressure, beginning in the twelfth century and culminating in the fifteenth century, in favor of the sanctity of the married couple.[48] Nothing is simple in this area, however, and we shall return to the question of the relationship between *cuissage* and the clerical politics of marriage. I might introduce a bit of leeway into this causality by noting that a recent iconoclastic theory of Robert Jacob's reverses these phenomena for the Middle Ages with the suggestion that in Flanders in the late Middle Ages the extended family replaced the smaller family nucleus of the feudal age.[49] For the moment we can leave aside the vicissitudes of the family in the Middle Ages, simply noting how soon in the early modern period the change occurred and remarking that its connection with an increased number of domestic servants provides a social basis for our "dialectic of the master and the serving maid."

This practical and ideological enclosure of the family had important consequences for sexuality, one of the most spectacular being the fairly sudden end to public bordellos in the late fifteenth century. Nearly everywhere in Europe from the early fourteenth century to the end of the fifteenth century, officially sponsored prostitution was available in houses often created by the municipalities and at times controlled or backed by state or local authorities.[50] One historian of the question, Richard Trexler, has convincingly shown that in Florence during the fifteenth century the sexual initiation of the young bourgeois or aristocratic male no longer took place in the bordello but among servant women originally from the Florentine *contado*.[51] Public houses of prostitution did not disappear completely, but their function became marginal as they primarily served foreigners passing through town.

The history of Florence is also unusual in that there was an intermediate form between venal sex and private use of women servants for the pleasure of their masters. During the fourteenth and fifteenth centuries, as Iris Origo has shown,[52] patrician households in Florence included slave women purchased through Genoese merchants in the trading centers of the Black Sea. Despite their condemnation of slavery in general, the priors of Florence passed a decree in 1363 authorizing the acquisition and possession of slaves on the condition (often ignored) that they did not confess the Christian faith. Cohabitation with a slave woman from the East became part of local mores: In the family chronicles of the Niccolini family, Paolo Niccolini tells us in 1433 that when he married Cosa Guasconi his household included a slave woman, Lucia, who had borne him two children. Despite condemnation by Pope John XXII and Pope Martin V, this practice persisted on a broad scale until the servant population dried up when the slaves fled or were emancipated or when the market disappeared with the Turkish advance into Europe.

This astonishing resurrection of slavery had economic causes in an expanded commerce with Romania (the Latin East) that led to a broadening of trade items just when the ravages of the Black Death of 1348, which struck hard in Tuscany, made local labor a rare commodity. This use of commerce with the East might also be seen as an early sign of the enclosure of the household.

Although the chronology of patrician sexuality in Florence, with its three steps of public bordellos, domestic slavery, and private use of servants, is remarkably conclusive, it remains the exception. This means that we need to return to a more general and more uncertain examination of the social conditions of the practice of sexual relations with servants. Shrinking family size included a reduction in and specialization of household personnel. The family dwelling was a loose federation involving complex status gradations, where certain members of the kinship group—unmarried younger sons, for example—had an ambiguous and mobile status shifting between participation in the direction of family affairs and subordination. At the beginning of the early modern age, however, family concentration made the existing hierarchical division between masters and servants more rigid. Thus beginning in the sixteenth century relations between masters and serving women became patriarchal: In France an edict of 1557 required that a female domestic servant ask her master's permission to marry.[53]

It would be mistaken, however, to draw any direct connection between reinforcement of the master's authority and sexual exploitation of the servant. Among both Protestants and Catholics the nuclear family crystallized in synergy with a promotion of strict matrimonial values. Peter Laslett and Edward Shorter have shown that these values by and large cut across social classes, and that the lowest rates for illegitimate births in Europe occurred in the eighteenth century.[54] The need for a stable community required either premarital chastity or sexual relations almost exclusively confined within the framework of a promise of marriage. One sixteenth-century magistrate, Christophe de Bordeaux, does indeed speak of the *chambrière à tout faire*—a special sense of "maid of all work"[55]—but if we follow the chronology that Shorter bases on precise statistical analyses, we see that the second phase of premarital sexuality, marked by the master's exploitation of the woman servant, is abundantly attested only in the eighteenth century. This generalization is of course open to a thousand nuances: We may need to draw a clearer distinction between a master's premarital sex with a servant woman when she is first hired and subsequent sexual abuse. G. R. Quaife, for example, has established in a detailed study of sexual behavior among the Puritan inhabitants of Somerset villages in 1645–60 that although the majority of illicit sexual relations took place between an unmarried servant woman and a man living under the same roof, in 40 percent of cases the master belonged to the lowest levels of the peasantry. In such a case the servant woman might legitimately hope for marriage with a young, unmarried master of a social status little different from her own. In another 25 percent of cases, however, the seducer was the master's son, hence a man of higher social status than she, making the obstacle to marriage more considerable.[56]

The fact remains that sexual relations between masters and servant women developed throughout Europe in the eighteenth century. It is as if once the ideological ties of family cohesion were broken, the household became an oppressive shell confining the unequal pair of master and servant in a face-to-face confrontation of domination and daily temptations under the resigned, absent, or accommodating gaze of the wife. Studies have shown the high rate of illegitimate births among servant women (36 percent of all births in Nantes in the eighteenth century, 35 percent in Clermont-Ferrand).[57] Masters could not have been responsible for all these illegitimate births, but legislation indicates a fear of the seduction of servants by young masters and disapproval of patriarchal excesses from heads of families. One ordonnance in 1730 equates seduction of a person under twenty-five years of age by a domestic servant with *rapt de séduction* (abduction by seduction), and Fournel quotes in his *Traité de la séduction considérée dans l'ordre judiciaire* (1781) the opinion Le Brun de La Rochette expressed in the early eighteenth century that "the pregnant domestic servant or concubine are to be believed if they accuse the master of fathering the fruit they bear."[58]

The other face of this protection was anxiety: The serving maid who seduced the young master might come to enjoy the wealth of the father of the family—a menace in a world where the theme of the servant-mistress was beginning to emerge, especially in the theater (it reached full development in *La Rabouilleuse* of Balzac). The time for miracles had passed. Divine will spared Abraham from having to make a choice when Sarah, his aged spouse, conceived. But Sarah's predicament was still a threat, and Hagar and her Ishmaelite descendants still caused anxiety.[59] In the eighteenth century fables about the *droit de cuissage,* in the form of both a "feudal" exoticism and the imaginary construction of the wily serving maid, were reflections in different registers of a real tension that was becoming a genuine social problem. At the time domestic servants represented some 10 percent of the urban population, even though 90 percent of them were of rural origin. The Enlightenment added the myth of rural innocence to the mix, producing the popular figure of the country girl corrupted, the *paysanne pervertie.*

Whether corrupted or corrupting, the servant girl was an image of a social alienation—made innocent by the fable of *cuissage*—that was supposed to have disappeared from the social picture, or at least from the stock images of a complaisant literature. Diderot stated in the article "Soubrette" in the *Encyclopédie:* "Soubrette, f[eminine] n[oun]. In former times, a woman attached to the service of another woman. There are no more soubrettes in our households, but they have remained in the theater, where they are usually wicked, talkative, and lacking in decency, feelings, manners, and virtue. There is nothing in society that resembles this personage."[60]

Nothing makes this sexual oppression or sexual menace at the heart of bourgeois family respectability seem more culpable than denying it. In his *Dictionnaire des idées reçues* Flaubert notes, "*Femme de chambre:* always dishonored by the son of the family." Edmond Goncourt echoes Flaubert in his continuation of the journal he kept with his brother Jules: "This canard consecrated by the theater: the dishonor of a daughter of the people by rich bourgeois."[61] Maupassant sought to destroy the social image of the rural innocence of the poor by describing a sorry lot of deflorations of girls in peasant society, and Dr. Louis Martineau, the author of an investigation titled *La prostitution clandestine*, reached similar conclusions through serial analysis of the defloration of female servants. Denying this social shame and relegating it to the depths of the Middle Ages (as was common in the late nineteenth century) fulfilled the same function. The return to the bordello, both real and literary *(La Maison Philibert, La Maison Tellier),*[62] combined with the appearance of other forms of extra-familial sexual sociability to signal the ethical shattering of the nuclear family.

A final witness gives an impressive image of internal contradictions wearing down the rigid model of the family dominant in human societies since the sixteenth century. In his *Journal d'une femme de chambre* (1900) Octave Mirabeau has a servant, Célestine, speak for herself. Throughout her peregrinations from one master to another (twelve places of employment in two years), she paints a sinister picture of the bourgeois ethos of the family as a place where female tyranny compensates for frigidity and frustration and hen-pecked males use their female servants as an outlet for their lustful impulses. Célestine's mobility, her mocking, critical attitude, and her aspirations for the social autonomy she achieves by marrying the bestial Joseph, a clever but animalistic domestic, illustrate the end of the social microcosm of the patriarchal family. The maid, an agent who has mobility in an unbudging world, leaves the bleak landscape of familial sexuality. Célestine's new-found independence parallels that of Germinie Lacerteux, a servant invented by the Goncourt brothers on the basis of a shocking personal experience of their own. In the novel of that name, the faithful Germinie, a submissive and maternal domestic slave, reveals on her deathbed the radical unconventionality of her own sexually, a belated revelation that uproots the aging bachelors from their sheltered enjoyment of the bourgeois home.[63]

This rapid overview of the sociocultural background of the fable of *cuissage* as an occasion for the projection and expulsion of tensions in the eighteenth and nineteenth centuries by no means suffices to establish what I have called the dialectic of the master and the serving maid. Social submission seems to announce and promise an erotic submission that in practice it thrusts aside. This is the theme of Abbé Prévost's *Histoire d'une Grecque moderne* (1740). A European purchases a young Turkish slave in order to emancipate her and restore her dignity. This done, he comes to desire her, but the beautiful freedwoman clings steadfastly to her newfound virtue. Robert Mauzi has correctly noted the import of this tale, "an exemplary case of amorous ambiguity—that is, of the impossible desire to possess a liberty."[64]

Thus we must leave the sure terrain of historical contextuality for the uncertain zone of atemporal structures of domination and desire, briefly interrogating what Sandra Gilbert and Susan Grubar have called "the eroticism of inequality."[65] In this unsure domain I shall limit myself to a philosophical exemplum interesting for its combination of contemporary philosophy and classical antiquity.

We need to imagine Martin Heidegger relaunching his seminar at Freiburg im Breisgau in the autumn of 1935 after a hiatus in his teaching duties to function as the university's first rector of the Nazi period. We need to imagine him back in a small classroom after the failure of his lofty ambitions to use the new state to construct an empire of thought, facing a handful of students and attempting to reconstruct his defeated ideas, beginning with nothing and working on the basis of will alone, posing the question, "What is a thing?"

> When the question "What is a thing?" arises, a doubt immediately announces itself. One may say that it makes sense to use and enjoy things in our reach, to eliminate objectionable things, to provide for necessary ones, but that one can really do nothing with the question "What is a thing?" This is true. One can start to do nothing with it. It would be a great misunderstanding of the question itself if we tried to prove that

one can start to do something with it. No one can start to do anything with it. This assertion about our question is so true that we must even understand it as a determination of its essence. The question "What is a thing?" is one with which nothing can be started. More than this need not be said *about* it.[66]

Immediately, however, the question returns to Greece, its native land. This allows the reader, like a diver out of his depth, to give the swift kick that returns him to the surface where he can swim. Reference to Plato takes us back to "Greece in the seventh century B.C." as Heidegger reads, translates, and comments on a passage from Plato's *Theaetus:* "This story is that Thales, while occupied in studying the heavens above and looking up, fell into a well. A good-looking and whimsical maid from Thrace laughed at him and told him that while he might passionately want to know all things in the universe, the things in front of his very nose and feet were unseen by him."

The anecdote is surprising, but it permits Heidegger a way out of his aporia. On the following page the question, "What is a thing?" sets off a thought process: "First, what are we thinking about when we say, 'a thing'?" Heidegger has not yet said anything about the thing, but the question itself has entered into a classification that distinguishes someone capable of posing it from someone who is only capable of hearing it:

> Therefore the question "What is a thing" must always be rated as one which causes housemaids to laugh. And genuine housemaids must have something to laugh about. Through the attempt to determine the question of the thing we have *unintentionally* [emphasis added] arrived at a suggestion about the characteristic of philosophy which poses that question. Philosophy, then, is that thinking with which one can start nothing and about which housemaids necessarily laugh.[67]

In the desert of thought and confronted with the flat indefiniteness of usage ("making use of things"), Heidegger erects a minimal relief, a minuscule change of level where the philosopher can assert his own eminence by reversing the order of the real, where the housemaid laughs at the philosopher who has fallen into the well, and reaffirming the order of the ideal, where contemplation of the heavens is superior to a horizontal gaze attached to the objects of this world. The question, which starts from nothing, creates a polarity, a tension between two poles of human experience, and engenders a current of thought. It is important that the positive pole (with regard to custom) and the negative (with regard to the act of thinking) should be a maidservant. Plato does not reduce the woman servant *(therapainís)* to a slave *(doúlê):* She is someone who observes, serves, and honors a cult *(therapeuein)*. She is a foreigner (a Thracian) and an inferior, but she is capable of being familiar *(emmelês)* and is vivacious and joking. There is a male equivalent to the Thracian soubrette in Plato in the child slave *(paîs)* of the *Meno* who is charged, precisely, with reading the *Theaetus*. He too offers a version of human nature foreign to the sage or the master but on familiar terms with him. Since the child slave is male, however, he represents the human potential for knowledge, inscribed in his naive and native prescience: He serves to show that reasoning is innate. The Thracian serving maid, to the contrary, manifests by her social distance and physical proximity the laughing and delectable dialectic between the intellect-master and the senses-slaves. Célestine and Heidegger would agree that to think as a master is to be *porté sur la chose*—to be inclined to things or, in the more trivial sense, to sex.

The considerable literary success of Plato's exemplum tells us much about the power of the maidservant image, an "internalization of/alternative to" virile powers of thought and domination. Associating (or confusing) the woman and the slave makes manifest the combined attraction and repulsion in an objectivation of the other, with its constant threat of subverting order. As Pierre Vidal-Naquet has shown, the Greek world was terrorized by the idea of a coalition between women and male slaves.[68]

The dialectic of the master and the serving maid internalizes the limits of a slaveholding or patriarchal domination, bordering on genuine sexual abuses, that is not exclusive to any culture and has often been confused with the exercise of a *droit de cuissage*. Examples include servile sexuality in ancient Rome,[69] unions between servant women and nineteenth-century Russian landowners, the sexual tyranny of ambitious young men in the business world, and the mores of the Nartes of the Caucasus that Georges Dumézil describes in a note in his *Loki:*

> *Kaevdaesard*, lit., "found in feeding troughs." The *kaevdaesard*, who occupied a bastard situation in noble families, were the children of the master of the house and servant girls or women who lay with him on entering into his service (after which they might lie with anyone they wanted to). These children remained under the authority of the head of the family, who was free to bequeath a small share of his estate to them if he so wished. This social situation disappeared after 1861, along with the entire system of serfdom.[70]

It seems fruitless to run through the universal encyclopedia of sexual relations between masters and servant women: It is a sturdy construct that crystallizes in certain particular historical contexts. At its moment of greatest strength in the eighteenth and nineteenth centuries, the myth of *cuissage* expresses a tension between the social imaginary and a reality that served it altogether too explicitly. The feudal framework simply provides a neutral décor. After that period the realities of domination and exotic reveries gave the myth the modest survival we know. In this sense our investigation could end here, if the crystallization of the myth were not attached to an event of considerable importance: the construction of the Western European Middle Ages. That event brought a good deal more than a historiographic novelty: It expressed, in concrete fashion and in historical terms, the modern sentiment of the sacredness of the individual. This is why this investigation of the *droit de cuissage* must begin in France in 1789, the moment when the abolition of seigniorial rights relegated *cuissage* to history.

CHAPTER TWO

The *Droit de Cuissage* in the Corridors of History

(1789–1854)

W here should we begin the history of *cuissage?* The problem is far from simple: As we have seen, myths and images overlap in the dialectic of the master and the serving maid. *Cuissage* never existed in a pure state, so we cannot begin at the "beginning" with a first occurrence. The myth always refers back to more distant origins. Chronological facility suggests we start where we left off and see what happened to *cuissage* after Beaumarchais, *The Marriage of Figaro*, and the French Revolution. It was in fact with Beaumarchais that the theme became truly public and popular; items for its dossier were accumulated during the Ancien Régime (as we shall see), but the question was confined to the works and debates of jurists and magistrates. On the night of 4 August 1789 seigniorial rights ceased to exist; *cuissage*, which the jurists, then the philosophers and playwrights had made an emblem for seigniorial oppression, became a historical object. Thus we might expect its context to be simplified when its impact was neutralized. We know what happened next, however: In the 1850s a widespread quarrel broke out over the reality of the *droit de cuissage*. The debate was in fact so violent, and the participants so energetically combed the archives and the available texts, that the principal medieval documentary sources were brought to light and crystallized. Few sources have appeared since then. Moreover, the controversy helped to construct a new image of the Middle Ages as a time of radical strangeness eliciting proclamations of a dreamy political nostalgia or rational and social rejection. We can grasp that polarization of the Middle Ages only by tracing the slow preparation of the new view under the Restoration and the July Monarchy. This somewhat heteroclite chapter will thus show how new historical and political interpretations of the Middle Ages gradually molded themes into "fact."

THE PURSUIT AND REVIVAL OF A LITERARY TRADITION

Beaumarchais's brilliant use of the theme of the droit du seigneur did not exhaust the topic. It was even enriched when an anonymous burlesque and satirical poem, *Il fodero, o sia Il jus sulle spose degli antichi signori sulla fondazione di Nizza della Paglia, poema di Colombo Giulio* (Fodero, or, the right over brides of the ancient lords [and] on the foundation of Nizza della Paglia) appeared in Paris in 1786. As we shall see, this frivolous work is probably to be attributed to the Jesuit Giulio Cesare Cordara. It soon had two French translations, *Le droit de jambage, ou Le droit des anciens seigneurs sur les nouvelles mariées* (1790),[1] and *Le vasselage ou Droit des anciens seigneurs sur les nouvelles épousées* (1791).[2] In the 1790s Restif de La Bretonne, writing in a Voltairean vein, composed a brief "Sanclaudette soumise au droit de jambage-prélibation."

The Voltairean spirit persists in a document published by an amiable polygraph, Jean Florimond de Saint-Amans (1748–1831), in his *Voyage agricole, botanique et pittoresque dans une partie des Landes de Lot-et-Garonne et de celles de la Gironde* (1812), a work marked by a precociously romantic taste for the savage side of nature and bygone eras. Evoking the Gothic Middle Ages, he cites a dramatic proof of the existence of the *droit de cuissage:* A judiciary document in 1302 recognized that Jean de Durasfort, lord of Blanquefort and grand sénéchal of Guyenne, possessed the "right of defloration." We need not linger over this document, an obvious forgery perpetrated by Saint-Amans or one of his contemporaries. It uses modern Catalan instead of the old language of the region; it is dated Wednesday 13 July 1302, a much later usage, and 13 July was not a Wednesday in 1302. It respects no medieval juridical formulas. Moreover, at that time the seigneurie of Blanquefort belonged not to the Durasfort family but to King Edward I of England. If the episode is at all interesting, it is because the text, cobbled together as it is, was republished in 1818, translated into French in 1820, and used during the great dispute of 1854–57.

Clearly little had changed. Crowned by Beaumarchais and Mozart, *cuissage* obstinately continued to enjoy a modest success. In 1813 the composer François Adrien Boieldieu (1775–1834), who wrote some forty comic operas in the taste of the Ancien Régime, celebrated his return from a long sojourn in Russia as director of music at St. Petersburg (1803–10) with a one-act opera, *Le nouveau seigneur de village,* set to a libretto by Baron Auguste Creuzé de Lesser and Baron Jean-François Roger (or perhaps Edmond Guillaume François de Favières).[3] The old order and its lighthearted pleasures reigned again in Paris. In 1829 Ferdinand Langlé (a pseudonym for Joseph Langlois) and Émile Morice published *L'historial du jongleur, chroniques et légendes françaises,* a pretty little volume printed by Didot in gothic type with colored vignettes. Among the contents was a narrative in dialogue, "Le droit de nopçage," that Langlé used as the libretto for a four-act opera, *La jacquerie* (1839), performed at the Théâtre de la Renaissance. Finally, in July 1854 Delacour (Alfred Lartigue) and Adolphe Jaime produced a *vaudeville* in three acts at the Théâtre des Variétés, *Les noces de Merluchet,*[4] not coincidentally only two months after the start of the great quarrel over *cuissage* in May of the same year.

With the Restoration this happy continuation of the culture of the Ancien Régime, spiced with a nascent taste for the "Gothic," became fraught with new emotions. The liberal opposition, a mix of republicans and Bonapartists, was on the lookout for any sign of a return to seigniorial and clerical tyranny, adopting a Voltairean tone brought to perfection in the light prose style of Paul-Louis Courier. A more prolix and mediocre writer, however, took on the task of popularizing the theme of *cuissage* in defense of the necessary progress of history. Jacques Collin, who called himself Collin de Plancy after the village where he was born in 1794, had more in common with Rastignac than with Courier or Benjamin Constant. Drawn to Paris in 1812 as a very young man, Collin de Plancy was soon busy churning out hastily compiled narratives and legends marked by anticlericalism and a hostility to feudalism. His *Dictionnaire infernal* (1818) was followed by a *Dictionnaire féodal, ou Recherches et anecdotes sur les droits féodaux* in two volumes (1819), republished in 1820 with a "Tableau de l'Ancien Régime, comparé à l'état actuel de la France." The thrust of this work was made clear in the introduction: It would enable its readers "to understand tyrannical institutions, the violences of power, odious distinctions, and the miseries of slaves among all the peoples of the world." The Middle Ages did not yet figure as a specific era: For Collin de Plancy the essential cut-off point was the French Revolution, while the Ancien Régime that preceded it was an undifferentiated age of barbarity.

Collin de Plancy dedicates a slim section of some twenty pages in volume 1 of his *Dictionnaire* to the droit du seigneur.[5] He derives the *droit de cuissage* from the treatment of slaves in the ancient world. He cites no references, simply giving a series of occurrences, all well known since the seventeenth century and later included in the dossier of the 1854–57 quarrel (Auvergne, Piedmont, the Scotland of King Evenus, Somloire, plus a list of instances of an ecclesiastical droit du seigneur involving the bishop of

Amiens, the clergy of Picardy, the canons of Lyons, and the parish priest of Bourges). His mention of the droit du seigneur as a clerical usage is worthy of note: Henceforth and throughout the nineteenth century, this was among the weapons brandished to attack the clergy. In Langlé and Morice's "Droit de nopçage," for example, the lord of Montguiscard and the abbot of Taillefontaine compete to exercise the droit du seigneur in lands where they share sovereignty.

By the Restoration the antiseigniorial movement had dissipated; the new threat was the Catholicism that had returned in the monarchy's baggage trains. Collin de Plancy combines political indignation with a flippant tone and a misogyny typical of the new bourgeois culture. He remarks, for example, that in revolts stemming from the application of the droit du seigneur in Piedmont, "it must be observed that the wives of serfs and vassals never took part in these seditious uprisings and everywhere eagerly sacrificed themselves to the usage, to the lord's wishes, and to the *droit de cuissage.*"[6]

Thus there was nothing really new in a compilation inherited from the jurists of the Ancien Régime and the Voltaireans of the preceding century, although publication gave it broad circulation. Despite his weakness as an authority, Collin de Plancy appears regularly in the arguments of the great quarrel. The same industrious author exploited the theme in a rapid succession of works in other keys (burlesque, naughty, or sentimental): a one-act play, *Les regrets féodaux* (1820); a *poème dialogué,* "Une chanson; les gémissements" (1821); *Abelina, nouvelle historique du XIIIe siècle, suivie des Aventures de M. Lebéjaune, et d'anecdotes et Recherches sur le droit de cuissage* (1823); and a translation (under the pseudonym Eugène Allent) of Cordara's *Il fodero* that Collin reworked from his own earlier translation of the same work (under the pseudonym Jacques Saint-Albin), *Le droit du seigneur, ou La fondation de Nice, dans le Haut-Monferrat, aventure du XIIIe siècle, traduit librement du Fodero de Jules Colomb, avec l'histoire de M. Bejaune, et un grand nombre d'anecdotes sur le droit de cuissage et sur les variétés de ce privilège* (1820).[7]

Before we leave this curious figure and obsessive littérateur who played a quantitatively important role in the diffusion of the myth of *cuissage* in the nineteenth century, we must follow his later career for a moment. Collin de Plancy founded his own bookstore in 1821; from 1824 to 1830 he moved on to real estate speculation, an activity that brought him wealth but exile to Belgium from 1830 to 1837. On his return to France he proclaimed himself a convert to Catholicism, and until his death in 1881 this former anticlerical polygraph (who had boasted falsely of being kin to

Danton) channeled his energies into a vast enterprise of clerical publishing, the Société de Saint-Victor, organized after the model of the impressive, industrial-scale Catholic publishing ventures of Abbé Jacques-Paul Migne. In a curious irony of history, Migne published a new version of Collin's *Dictionnaire infernal* in his *Encyclopédie de théologie.*[8] In the nineteenth century anticlericalism (which, as we shall see, was the bearer of the myth of *cuissage*) paid well.

Another cultural development that helped establish the *droit de cuissage* in European literature was the rise, beginning in the 1820s, of the historical and social novel. The genre was often adopted by liberals who used narrative evocations of the past—especially the Middle Ages—to highlight popular and national values. Sir Walter Scott scarcely mentions the droit du seigneur, nor does it appear in the many works his novels inspired on the Continent. There is one rapid allusion to the right in Scotland, compensated by payment of a fee, in Scott's *Fair Maid of Perth* (1827).[9] It is only later, with Eugène Sue, that the theme emerges fully in two long narratives, *La coquille du pèlerin, ou Fergan le carrier* (1849) and *Li trépied de fer* (1856). After his great socialist novels, among them the famous *Mystères de Paris* (1842–43), Sue moved on to anticlerical fiction with *Le Juif errant* (1843–44). The first of Sue's "medieval" novels was adapted for the stage by an anonymous playwright as *Les droits du seigneur, ou Un drame à Jersey* (1859).

In 1850 another, less well-known author, Charles Fellens, published a strongly didactic novel, *La féodalité, ou Les droits du seigneur: Événements mystérieux, lugubres, scandaleux, exactions, despotisme, libertinage de la noblesse et du clergé, suivis de la marche et de la décadence de la féodalité depuis le Moyen Âge jusqu'à nos jours.* In spite of his long, bannerlike title, Fellens was no more an ardent ideologue than was Collin de Plancy. He was a secondary-school teacher apparently ambitious for literary fame; before this highly successful work (reprinted in 1851, republished in 1880, and even translated into German) he had written works of a quite different sort for a narrower public: *Bruits de guerre, poésie nationale* (1840); *Les caprices du pensionnat* (1842); *Le calcul de tête* (1846); *Les jours heureux du pensionnat* (1849).

The minor literary works that appeared in the early nineteenth century brought no reaction from the partisans of order and the Church. Until 1854 only one work attempted to refute the commonly accepted opinion that the *droit du cuissage* had indeed existed. This was a brief treatise by Jean Joseph Raepsaet titled *Les droits du seigneur: Recherches sur l'origine et la nature des droits connus anciennement sous les noms de droits des premières*

nuits, de markette, d'afforage, marcheta, maritagium et bumede, published in
Ghent in 1817.[10] This text deserves a closer look: Because it comes from
outside the French political and cultural context, it neutralizes some
specifically French elements (such as the break represented by the French
Revolution), and it offers a rare opportunity to observe a national variant
on a pattern that remained for the most part French.

A FLEMISH AND ZEELAND PARENTHESIS: THE RAEPSAET MOMENT

Jean Joseph Raepsaet (1750–1832) was not a historian by either profession or training. A citizen of Audenarde, he devoted his life to defending
the traditional liberties of Flanders. As the son of a prominent citizen, he
became a barrister for the Council of Flanders at a young age and a clerk
of the castellany of Audenarde; in 1785 he became a municipal official.
His career was far from tranquil, however, because it paralleled a time of
serious political troubles that gave his treatise a special thrust. After the
Treaty of Utrecht in 1713 the southern Netherlands, which had long been
separated from the independent United Provinces, passed from the Spanish crown to the ruling house of Austria. Emperor Joseph II, who was
crowned in 1765 but became sole ruler only at the death of Maria Theresa
in 1780, carried on his mother's ideal of enlightened despotism, though
with stricter controls. Maria Theresa had attempted to centralize and ra-
tionalize the management of the empire, but she had worked step by step,
and reform had hardly begun in the Low Countries. Joseph II proved ven-
turesome on the social plane, moving against the seigniorial classes by
suppressing serfdom and the *corvée* and attempting to institute a single tax
collected by the state. A second political program, known as "josephism,"
promoted secularization by such measures as an edict of toleration, the institution of civil marriage, and the specification of clerical functions. Both
aspects of Austrian policy struck hard in the southern Low Countries,
which had inherited a long tradition of municipal autonomy and had built
up a strong regional identity by opposing an ultramontane Catholicism to
the Calvinism of Holland. Revolt against the reforms of Joseph II broke
out in 1792 in a movement that suffered some defeats and won some vic-
tories before the armies of the French Republic occupied the Netherlands
in 1792 and again in 1794. Raepsaet played an important political role as
a delegate from Flanders in the provincial Estates-General. He even
spent time in prison in 1789, and later he helped draft projects for a constitution and for a union of the Provinces. From 1803 to 1813 he was a
deputy to the National Assembly in Paris; after the fall of the empire he

helped to draw up the fundamental law that was to create a new kingdom with the United Provinces. Throughout his political career Raepsaet remained stubbornly conservative and firmly supportive of ultramontane Catholicism.[11]

Raepsaet's works, written late in life when he had retired from politics, were aimed especially at supporting Flemish and Belgian particularism. This was notably true of his lengthy *Analyse historique et critique de l'origine et des progrès des droits civils, politiques et religieux des Belges et Gaulois.*

It is easy to see why Raepsaet should have been interested in the *droit de cuissage:* He was attempting to refute the notion that traditional customs and practices were tyrannical. Josephism had long since ceased to be a threat, but the "Belgian" rebellion had not united behind an absolute conservation of traditions. In Brabant a division between clerical conservatives (the "statists" of Hendrik Van der Noot) and liberals (followers of Jean-François Vonck) had enabled Austria to put down the rebellion. Invasion by the forces of the French Republic had revived the conflict, which was raging during the fifteen years Raepsaet was writing his text, and various solutions were being tried for defining what later became Belgium. Raepsaet, who was usually very discreet about the relevance of his arguments to current events, nonetheless speaks of the pressure of opinion that may have led him to write his treatise: "Pamphlets of the present times threaten the finer sex with a return to that abominable right should feudalism and seigniory be restored."[12]

The political relevance of the question had a special meaning in the Low Countries because of an erudite discussion a century earlier. Some Dutch scholars, men far removed from the French tradition, had noted the possible existence of a *droit de cuissage* in the outermost provinces. In 1696 the Dutch scholar Matthijs Smallegange noted in a compilation of chronicles of Jakob Eyndius and Johann Reygersberg that the lord of Kortgene in Zeeland "was said [word geseit]" to hold an ancient right over virginity, later satisfied by payment of a fee.[13] That prudent statement (based on no written trace) was picked up by Matheus Gargon twenty years later as positive fact: "the lord of Kortgene held . . . [Had oud tijds]."[14] Ten years later (in 1727) Pieter van der Schelling, a retired Remonstrant pastor turned jurist, asserted that in olden times the right of the first night had existed in Zeeland in the seigniory of Voshol and its dependent villages and towns, Zwammerdam, Langeraar, Koteraar, Reewick, and Middelburg.[15] With the arrival of Christianity the pagan right had either disappeared or been transposed into a money payment reflected in several taxes still being collected. These writers imputed the barbarian and pagan origins of the right to the Frisians, a Germanic people who had resisted conversion by the Carolingians. Van der Schelling probably based his remarks on a text by Adriaan Pars (first published in 1697) that he edited for republication in 1745.[16]

That same year (1745) Gerard van der Loon refuted van der Schelling's assertion, showing that no proof existed of a genuine connection between a supposed barbarian right of the first night and the various seigniorial taxes on marriage.[17] Van der Loon attacked the myth of the Frisians, noting that neither Tacitus's description of Germania nor the writings of St. Boniface, the evangelizer of the Frisians, made any mention of the custom. Furthermore, van der Loon argued, how could anyone imagine that the Carolingian conquerors would have tolerated transforming such an abominable right into a money payment? We need not linger over this minor Dutch controversy: It simply reiterated on a local scale debate on the origins of seigniorial dues related to the marriage of dependents, a question we shall return to in detail.

We do need to note that this discussion was complicated by reference to the Frisian past of the Low Countries, a question we have already encountered in a learned note of the Bollandists Henschen and Papebroch. It is significant that the debated events took place in Zeeland. In the sixteenth and seventeenth centuries that maritime province was the heart of Protestant resistance to Spain and offered a refuge to Flemish, Brabantine, and Walloon Calvinists. Zeeland remained a center of resistance of the most puritanical tendencies of Calvinism against the moderate and Arminian bourgeoisie of the dominant province, Holland. When local scholars attacked the barbarity, first pagan then Christian, of the ancient population of Zeeland, they cast the new Calvinist colonization as a liberation. In other words, they attributed to the Calvinist Reform the function that the French Revolution fulfilled in French liberal thought. Significantly, Adriaan Pars credits the provincial Estates of Zeeland with a collective commutation of marital taxes. The Calvinist view also directly imputed the survival of pagan barbarity to Catholicism, situating the persistence of *cuissage* in Gelderland, the eastern province that formed the southern edge of the northern zone, where old-style Catholicism was concentrated in the seventeenth century. In 1698 the jurist Johann Voet noted in his commentaries on the *Pandects* payment for dispensation from the right to the first night in Gelderland, in particular in Zutphen.[18]

Thus Raepsaet had to take into account the Calvinist offensive against local traditions and their Catholic basis. He was acquainted with van der Schelling and van der Loon's arguments, which he cited in his treatise. He attempted to prove that the *droit de cuissage* had never existed by showing that the various words seeming to designate it really referred to two other customs, neither of which had anything to do with sexual abuse. The words *marcheta, markette,* and *maritagium* evoked the ancient right of the king (later the lord)—a right that Raepsaet considered perfectly justified—to consent to the marriage of the daughter of a subject or dependent. This limitation of the subject's liberty was compensated by a *garde noble* obliging the suzerain to find a husband and a dowry for his vassals' daughters. When some suzerain rights were abolished and replaced with money payments, the sum paid to compensate for abandoning the requirement for the lord's consent was called *rapchat*, paid during a procedure known as *marchié*. The other terms supposedly referring to *cuissage* were connected with particular customs: *cullage* referred to a wedding gift or ritual collation offered by the new groom; *prélibation* had the same meaning but implied a lighter refreshment. *Afforage* was a banal tax on wine and beer. Strange and salacious designations for matrimonial dues can be explained by a sort of lexical revolt against seigniorial power: That was the meaning of the "tradition" invoked by the partisans of the *droit de cuissage*. Paradoxically, Raepsaet, a fervent conservative, analyzed in very modern terms what is known today as "the invention of tradition," a notion constructed to fit the imaginary long timespans of the folklorists and historians of ideas.

A second basis for the right of first nights came from Christian marital discipline. The Church founded its attempt to impose a period of nuptial abstinence on exegesis of the biblical book of Tobias, where the young Tobias and his bride Sara vanquish the demon Asmodeus by practicing chastity for the three days following their marriage. Various prescriptions of councils and synods (one of which appears in Gratian's *Decretum*) bear witness to this notion. From the twelfth century on the faithful could satisfy a good many penitences by payment of a fee, and the various sums paid to waive first nights' chastity reflect these monetary compensations.

Raepsaet's treatise is instructive for other reasons as well. Nascent Belgian nationalism much enhanced the circulation of the work (it had made little stir when first published in 1817), and when it was republished in Raepsaet's *OEuvres complètes* (1838–40) it became available in many French libraries. The protagonists of the great quarrel of 1854–57 made sweeping use of the work. The supposed neutrality of an austere and learned Belgian (Raepsaet's political commitments were unknown in France) increased his authority. His secondhand use of van der Schelling and van der Loon contributed to tactics of scholarly intimidation. Raepsaet also was the first to subject the myth of *cuissage* to systematic investigation. Before him only expressions of doubt referring to specific occurrences of the right had appeared in learned publications. Raepsaet, an amateur historian but a man of some learning in ecclesiastical history, introduced no new sources, but he found an original way to base demonstration and proof on a global reinterpretation of the perennial bits of evidence from juridical tradition.

Although Raepsaet's treatise was little known before 1854, his philological deconstruction was not an isolated event. It brought up to date works from the eighteenth century to his own day preparing the discovery of the Middle Ages and, more particularly, the dossier on *cuissage*. When the nineteenth-century discovery of the Middle Ages mobilized scattered investigations made during the Ancien Régime, it enhanced the stature of the people and the nation, making them actors in history and endowing them with a language and a coherence of their own.

THE PEOPLE'S WORDS: THE DROIT DU SEIGNEUR AS FOLKLORE

As a matter of course the scholars and dilettantes who took up the question of the droit du seigneur, whatever its designation in the medieval texts, regularly consulted the current dictionaries of medieval Latin. Even today medievalists still use Charles Du Cange's solid and monumental medieval Latin dictionary, *Glossarium ad scriptores mediae et infimae latinitatis*, first published in 1678. Before Du Cange there had been few attempts to codify the prodigious verbal creativity of the Latin Middle Ages in theology and administrative practice. In the three centuries since the *Glossarium* first appeared, the lexicography of medieval Latin has made striking progress: The dictionaries of Forcellini, Niermayer, and Blaise, and more recently the *Mittellateinisches Wörterbuch* and the *Nouveau Du Cange* published by the Centre National de Recherche Scientifique have gradually supplanted Du Cange's dictionary, but without replacing it completely because the range of its documentation defies competition.

The protagonists of the great controversy used the edition of Du Cange's *Glossarium* that had recently been edited by G.A.L. Henschel, published in Paris in 1840 by Didot. Moving from volume to volume, thanks to Du Cange's cross-references, they found various words revolving around the notion of the *droit de cuissage: bathinodium, braconagium, cochetus, culagium, marcheta.* The entries were enlivened by an abundance of carefully dated examples copied word for word from archival sources. This time the principle of authority worked in support of the existence of the *droit de cuissage*. How could one accuse the venerable Charles du Fresne, seigneur du Cange (1610–88) of deliberate partiality? The learned Byzantinist painstakingly amassed notes for his Latin *Glossarium* (followed ten years later, in 1688, by an equivalent work for the Greek language), while writing the first scholarly work on the Latin empires of the Crusades. Du Cange belonged to the same generation as the great Benedictines of Saint-Maur, the illustrious Mabillon among them, and it was the Benedictines who published the second edition of the *Glossarium* in 1733.

In reality Du Cange's contribution to the corpus on *cuissage* was modest. Most of the relevant texts come from the third revision of the dictionary by the Benedictine Pierre Carpentier, published in 1766 as a four-volume supplement to the *Glossarium*. The 1840 edition combined the layers of the text into one whole, which means that a hasty reader might attribute to Du Cange what was essentially Carpentier's work. The distinction is important because the two men were operating in quite different cultural contexts. This means that we must restore lexicographical chronology if we hope to comprehend Dom Carpentier's orientation and method.

Under the entry for *braconnage* (Latin *braconagium*) Du Cange gives only a laconic "Vide Brodaeum, Cons. Paris., t. I, p. 198."[19] This refers to Julien Brodeau, a *conseiller* (judge) in the Parlement de Paris, who mentions the story of King Evenus of Scotland (which, as we have seen, circulated widely in the seventeenth century) in a commentary on Parisian custom. He notes that the story "is related to the right of *braconnage*, mention of which appears in some ancient *aveux, dénombrements,* and other like titles and in the accounts of the domain of Chaulny and of the county of Ponthieu. This right is different from that of *chevel* in Normandy, which is a right of aid in three cases: for the knighthood of the eldest son, the marriage of the eldest daughter, and the imprisonment of the lord."[20] In 1766 Carpentier writes:

> To be added, page 273 of the second edition [of Brodeau's *Coustume*] where the word *braconagium* signifies a certain unusual right of the lord regarding girls who marry that consists in deflowering them the first night of their wedding, as it appears in accounts of the domain of Chaulny and the county of Ponthieu. This meaning is also attested in a feudal acknowledgment of Jean, lord of Mareuil, in 1228, who says, "And I, as lord of Mareuil can and must have the right of *braconnage* over women and girls in my said seigniory if they marry; and if I do not, 2 sols are owed the said seigniory." *Braconner* thus consists in making use of that right. Mention is also made of it in the manuscript customal of

Auxy-le-Château, whose men [dependents] were emancipated by Guillaume III, comte de Ponthieu, at the request of his wife Rugua.

Where Du Cange limited himself to referring to Brodeau's daring hypothesis without actually quoting him, Carpentier gives the paragraph in Brodeau and presents a mini-dossier of three cases. These cases will be evaluated later; for the moment we need only note the singular power of the dictionary as a genre and as an apparently neutral, easily consulted authority. The presumed sexual sense of *braconnage* also appears in the early edition of Émile Littré's dictionary.

Two other entries designate *cuissage* in Du Cange's *Glossarium: bathinodium* and *marcheta.* Under *bathinodium* Du Cange refers to the Bollandists' note in the *Acta sanctorum* discussed in chapter 1. The later editions of the *Glossarium* add nothing since further occurrences were lacking. The notice under *marcheta* is more substantive, referring to the Scottish texts about King Evenus and to Skene, Boece, and Buchanan, all of whom we have already met. Carpentier ends the entry by associating the practice to the law *Regiam majestatem* and Welsh laws, as was common at the time. Under the same entry the Benedictine second edition of the *Glossarium* of 1733 added other references, frequent in juridical scholarship of the age, taken from medieval legislation (Bracton, Henry III), from compilers who repeated the fable of King Evenus and passed on anecdotes from barbarian law (Polydore Virgil, Boxhorn), and from such emblematic episodes as the demand for clerical dues in Amiens. Carpentier continued in the same vein with episodes involving the canons of Mâcon and Vienne.

Du Cange came from a family ennobled through governmental and judicial service—part of the *noblesse de robe.* The son of a royal *prévot* in Amiens, he inherited his father's office, then studied law in Orléans. Clearly, he himself gathered the small lot of anecdotes that suggested (and only suggested) the existence of a droit du seigneur in ancient times, indemnified under Christianity by payment of a due. The Benedictines, Carpentier in particular, show a penchant for certitude, multiplying proofs well beyond the needs of lexicological exposition. This is hardly surprising: Eighteenth-century dramatic and pamphlet literature had done its job. The Benedictines of Saint-Maur, many of whom were also men from the magistrate class who displayed a strong interest in the state, showed no indulgence toward seigniorial abuses.

There is more to the story, however: The Benedictines, Carpentier in particular, provided dictionary entries of a quite different sort, based on different sources. One example is the article on *cullagium (cullage)*. The 1733 edition of the *Glossarium* gives the definition "Tribute that must be paid to the lord by subjects who contract marriage." It offers two examples, the first referring to the Picard customs noted by Eusèbe de Laurière, and the second drawn from a polyptych from Fécamp dated 1235: "When a villein marries his daughter outside the village he owes 3 sous for *cullage* [de culagio]." This is thus a new but typical case of a due implying *cuissage* only by the word's connotations. In 1766 Carpentier wrote a long extension to the entry, adding six French (not Latin) texts. The first is dated 1375: "In the town of Jâlons and the surrounding villages it is a longstanding custom that every young man, unless he is a knight or noble, is held when he marries to pay the other companions and unmarried young men his *bejaune*, called in the said town *coullage*."

Cullage takes on a very different meaning here: rather than dependency, the due confirms departure out of the group of the *varlets*, the young unmarried males of a village, who formed an age class consolidated by rites and festivities and at times formalized as a "youth abbey" *(abbaye de jeunesse)*. When the husband-to-be left the group, he deprived it of his participation and took away one marriageable male; thus he owed it a monetary or symbolic tribute comparable to a compensatory due. Here we are not far from the charivari, a ritual protest against marriages that troubled community order, as when the age gap between the couple was too great. Such marriages were "paid for" by the couple being subjected to noisy teasing or having to pay a real or symbolic compensation.[21] The other examples Carpentier gives clarify the definition and function of *cullage*.

Before taking a closer look at the new orientations that Carpentier gave to the *droit de cullage*, I should note that he was using a totally new source that became important to research on the Middle Ages, the letters of remission in the Trésor des Chartes, a collection of charters and related documents now housed in the French National Archives under the famous call number "JJ." From the mid-fourteenth century to the sixteenth century the royal chancery kept copies of letters from condemned criminals requesting royal pardon for a blood crime. Pardons could be granted only if the crime was unpremeditated and free from all personal motives. This means that supplicants often related (through a notary or scribe) details to prove that their deadly act was accidental or unpremeditated and inspired by passion, incidentally giving details about the circumstances of a quarrel or a provocation. This makes these documents an exceptional source of information about the life of village or urban communities of the late Middle Ages and the Renaissance. For once it is the people who speak, even though, as Natalie Zemon Davis has shown, their version of events is filtered through an official narration. (Even more recently Claude Gauvard has made admirable use of these documents.)[22] Carpentier can be credited with discovering this remarkable resource: He frequently cites letters of remission, giving precise references. In returning to them, I shall cite them somewhat more extensively than Carpentier did.[23]

In Curmont (Haute-Marne) in 1391, Michel Bergier was about to marry Oudote. One Chrestiennot de Chatenay participated in the day-long festivities:

> *And in the evening after the supper for the said wedding, at about the second hour of night, when the said Chrestiennot and the said late Regaudot and several other young people and unmarried men were assembled before the hostelry of Michiel Aubert of the said Curmont, where the wedding was held, a certain great debate arose among them to know to whom the right of *coillage* due for the said bride belonged,* for Simon, the supplicant's brother, and Mongin de Torcenay, the son of Jehan Rebillard, claimed it, and the young people and unmarried men of the said Curmont contradicted this, saying that it was theirs and they should have it, not the said Simon and Mongin, because the said Simon had once been married and the said Mongin was not from their town of Curmont.

The due, here called *droit de coillage*, thus seems to have been a serious matter, given the bitter quarrel that ensued. The affair is known because a man died: The group of young men protested the usurpation of their rights by two intruders, a formerly married man and someone not from the village (a sign that the due was local, not social). Regaudot, one of the *varlets*, took a stick to Chrestiennot, who took out a knife and killed him. In the Curmont affair *cullage* benefited only the unmarried men of the village in a principle of local identity confirmed, in a somewhat different form, by another French text Carpentier cites, where the tribute seems occasioned less by a man's leaving the bachelor group than by his taking a bride from outside the community. Folklorists, Arnold van Gennep in particular, have often found this trait in rural France of the nineteenth and twentieth centuries.[24]

This second episode took place at Montier-en-Der (Haute-Marne) in 1396. The young men of the hamlet of La Grève left toward evening

> to go to the said place of Montier-en-Der in the hope of demanding of Jean Thibaut, vintner, his *coillage*, because that day he had wed a girl from the said locality of La Grève and was celebrating his wedding at

the said Montier-en-Der in the hostelry of the said Jean Thibaut; the which wedding festivities all the above-named attended, and they being at the said hostelry at about the given hour, they spoke to the said Thibaut and several times demanded of him his said *coillage* because he had taken a girl from the said La Grève, as has been said; [but] Jean Thibaut refused to give them anything.

Thibaut offered a compromise: "He would willingly give them some of his bread, his wine, and the goods of his hostelry, and he led them to his barn where he had had tables set out for his said wedding and seated them in the said barn at a table and had them brought a tablecloth, bread, wine, and roast meat." At the same time, however, Jean sent for the police. When the bailiff's lieutenant and his sergeants arrived from Montier-en-Der, they found the five young men from La Grève seated at a table. The lieutenant enjoined them to leave Jean in peace: "Gentle sirs, I beg you to do no harm to Jean Thibaut, who is vintner to the lord of Montier-en-Der. Drink his wine courteously and go home to bed." The young men followed Thibaut, however, and set upon him. The question of the right to *cullage* was probably complicated by Thibaut's status as vintner to the lord of Montier-en-Der and by his prompt call for aid from the local constabulary, a move that simply made his attackers more aggressive. The case also shows that village rites were both recognized and tolerated by the local powers, who cared only that things not get out of hand.

When the bailiff's lieutenant noted that the vintner had fulfilled his duties as a groom by offering wine, he was implicitly referring to one of the ritual forms of *cullage*. Compensation might be no more than an offer of the *vin du cullage* mentioned in Carpentier's second extract and repeated in several entries mentioned as cross-references: *calenum* (the Latin form of *chaudel*), *bannum, nuptiaticum,* and *vinum maritagii*. The *vin de cullage* also went under a name *(cochet)* that Carpentier derived from a different etymology. In the entry for *cochetus* in the *Glossarium* Carpentier cites a letter of remission in Latin (because of its early date, 1350): "Toward evening of the day of the celebration of the said marriage the relatives and friends who had come to the wedding came to the dwelling of the couple for the compensation and to fetch the cock or *cochet* [causa solatii et quaerendi gallum seu cochetum]." At the time the gift consisted of a cock or a hen, and thus had connotations of fertility familiar to anthropologists. As Carpentier's other citations show, the etymology of *cochet* was soon forgotten, the word coming to designate wine offered alone or specially prepared (*chaudel,* implying a mixed hot drink, persists in a number of more or less burlesque variants in later folklore).[25] Another term, *deschaussage* or *deschausaille,* appears in two letters of remission dated 1390 and 1595, but receives no entry of its own in Carpentier, instead appearing toward the end of the article on *culagium.* This is perhaps because Latin attestations were lacking. Here the ritual payment was connected with taking off one's shoes, a gesture analogous to catching the bride's garter and symbolic of participation in the wedding night.[26]

Carpentier thus gave his readers some fifteen texts scattered among six new entries in the *Glossarium.* They sketch a picture of matrimonial rites in medieval village communities, but they also provide an outline for a functional, self-sufficient explanation of the *droit de cuissage* that refers to group pressures on matrimonial choices rather than to a somber past of hierarchical oppression. Still, the entry in the *Glossarium* and the retention and development of articles on *marcheta* and *braconagium* left the question unresolved. Each camp in the great quarrel opened the dictionary to a page that supported its own arguments.

Beyond his considerable contribution to documentation, Dom Carpentier's new approach opened up an entire field of research that came to be called folklore in the nineteenth century. It is difficult to follow the evolution of Carpentier's thought because so little is known of his life, dedicated to learning. He seems somewhat atypical of the scholarly Benedictines of the eighteenth century.

Born in 1697, Carpentier entered the Abbey of Saint-Rémi in Reims, a dependency of the Congrégation de Saint-Maur, in 1720. After only a few years his superiors took notice of his studies on Tertullian and sent him to Saint-Germain-des-Prés, the scholarly hub of the Congrégation de Saint-Maur, to work on the crown archives and take part in the major revision of Du Cange's *Glossarium,* publication of which began in 1733. On that occasion he requested and obtained free access to the Trésor des Chartes, where he found the letters of remission. In 1737 he became *prévôt* of Saint-Onésime in Danchery. He entered the Cluniac Order but did not long remain at the Abbey of Saint-Saulve, requesting permission to return to Paris to pursue his labors. In 1747 he published a work on the *notae Tironianae,* a complex ancient Roman system of shorthand, all the while continuing to accumulate notes for his enormous supplement to Du Cange's dictionary. Carpentier's continuous labors were interrupted only briefly by service with the French ambassador to Vienna in 1750. Throughout his career Carpentier quarreled with the Benedictines over questions of literary paternity. In his new individualism as an intellectual laborer, he was impatient with the anonymity of great collective works, and we may owe his strikingly original revision of Du Cange—a felicitous result displaying a foretaste of philology rather than the imprint of traditional lexicography—to his determination to publish under his own name. He was secularized shortly before his death, perhaps because he became tired of lawsuits and interference. Nothing in his career predisposed him to be sensitive to popular mores in olden times; perhaps his discovery of the letters of remission led him in that direction. He hints as much in the introduction to his supplement, where he says that the registers of the Trésor des Chartes

> contain a great quantity of pardon letters, most of which are written in French. These letters relate in very full detail all sorts of events that took place in various provinces. . . . One can find in them domestic customs that would be sought in vain elsewhere. In a word, I think that it is from these pieces that one can gain the surest knowledge of the mores of the thirteenth, fourteenth, and fifteenth centuries. This Treasury is a sacred depository where trickery and ill-intention were never acceptable.

The latter half of the eighteenth century was also a time of a new turn toward simplicity and rusticity as proof of natural human authenticity. Once again, Restif de La Bretonne and his many descriptions of village society (notably in *Mon père*, 1778), spring to mind. Some writers timidly explored the past of the lower classes and attempted to locate adequate sources. The Jesuit Pierre Le Grand d'Aussy, the author of *Histoire de la vie privée des françois* (1782), was the first to publish the fabliaux of the Middle Ages (1779–81). Before the Middle Ages had been identified as a distinct period, those centuries were viewed in confused fashion as an ancient treasury for the study of simple ways of life.

Romanticism's quest for origins and the deep past contributed to this interest in ancient popular cultures. France never developed the fascination for popular traditions that Herder, Brentano, Arnim, and the brothers Grimm brought to Germany with their collecting activities and their research. Nonetheless, various societies and reviews devoted to French popular traditions were founded in the early nineteenth century, drawing on new aspirations and old antiauthoritarian and regionalist loyalties. This is hardly the place to trace the history of this movement, but I might note that one of the new "folklorists" helped to elucidate the question of the *cullage* connected with weddings. In an early issue of the *Revue des Ardennes* one Duvivier published two articles (in 1825 and 1828) demonstrating the persistence of compensatory customs. He writes of folk customs in Monthois in 1825: "When the young men who paid the compliment—to the dessert—judge that the moment in the meal we have spoken of has come, they come to seek the *pâté de culage* and they shoot off guns. Courtesy dictates they be ushered in and offered something to drink. Afterward they are given their pâté and some bottles of wine. The pâté is sometimes only sham, filled with bones, oakum, and the like." In his later article Duvivier says of folk customs in Givet:

> The *culage* (in patois, *culache*) is a custom established by the young people in several communities consisting of a piece of meat and a loaf of bread or a cake that husbands are expected to give on their wedding day. Usually the meat is a haunch of veal with the tail. The young men then parade about the village carrying this meat and the cake stuck on the end of a spit or a sword, singing bacchic songs, and at the end of each couplet they shout with all their might, "*culache! culache!*" They go to an inn to have the haunch cooked. Sometimes (even most of the time) the young men invite the girls to come share their feast, and when the pieces are nicely cut up on a platter, they present it to the girl thought or supposed to be the most amorous of the company. If by chance a pious girl or a bigot is among them she is picked for the honor, and as good manners dictate that you take what is offered, they make sure she is presented with the tail.[27]

This rite had evidently persisted for centuries, though with a notable change: We still find traces of aggressive behavior (shooting off guns), but the institution of a group based on age and status (unmarried *varlets*) has been lost. By then the threat had shifted to the girls who were still unmarried and focused on their greater or lesser sexual propensities.

Duvivier's remarks on folk customs in the Ardennes probably played no precise role in the controversy over *cuissage,* but they do help us understand why Michelet contributed to a resurgence of the question of *cuissage* among historians in 1837. In the early nineteenth century there was so much discussion of the exotic oddity of local customs that people began to perceive a real continuity in the life of the people from olden times to the present. One of Michelet's obsessions was seeing the past as a series of returns—Vico called them *ricorsi*—where the Middle Ages could be read in present-day customs but also perceived as a return to the "divine and heroic age." Under superficial layers of civilization one could grasp continuity in the words of the tribe.

As a young man Michelet was strongly influenced by Vico's works, and in 1827 he translated into French Vico's *Principi di una scienza nuova d'intorno alla comune natura delle nazioni.* Following Vico, Michelet sought the "wisdom of a community" through language, but especially through what he called "the law" *(le droit),* which he defined as the formulaic utterances and gestures that, by ritual usage, transmit an ancient memory and a nation's soul. He was looking for the "obscure and misunderstood law of the people." Michelet's interest was further stimulated by contact with the work of Jakob Grimm, in particular his *Von der Poesie im Recht*. Just when Michelet was establishing a correspondence with Grimm, the latter's *Deutsche Rechts Alterthümer*, a major collection of rites and formulas of the ancient Germans, was published in Germany. The work so impressed Michelet that in 1837 he published a French adaptation of it preceded by a long foreword, *Les origines du droit français cherchées dans les symboles et formules du droit universel.*[28]

Michelet's "juridical biography of humankind," starting with the family (chapter 1) and going through to old age and death, contains a brief section on feudal rights in a chapter on the state (chapter 3) that speaks of the droit du seigneur. For the most part Michelet repeats Grimm's examples: Rather than forming a coherent whole on the *droit de cuissage*, they give scattered instances of ancient practices pertaining to the matrimonial custom of purchasing the fiancée, reputedly a Germanic tradition. More than elsewhere in his adaptation, Michelet here enriches Grimm's list, adding the usual anecdotes from the French juridical tradition and Carpentier's mention of *cullage*. Michelet uses these additions to reinforce his denunciation of feudal abuses; still, he displays more interest in the archaic and imagistic formulation of these customs than in the reality of the droit du seigneur: "Moreover, nothing indicates that this shameful right ever had to be paid in kind."[29] As with Carpentier, Michelet's sensitivity to popular traditions blunted his questioning of the feudal reality of the droit du seigneur, so that we find side by side expressions of doubt and the traditional examples providing a basis for belief in the reality of *cuissage*. The times were not yet ripe for the great dispute, and Frédéric Ozanam, a Catholic, praised Michelet's *Origines du droit français* (without mentioning this particular passage) in an article in *L'Univers*, a journal that played a prominent role fifteen years later in the crusade to deny the reality of the *droit de cuissage* in the Middle Ages.[30] For the first time, however—if we except Raepsaet, who was more in the tradition of nationalistic antiquarian interests than the historical tradition—the droit du seigneur entered into the writing of history.

Despite the neutrality or ambivalence of lexical notations of the droit du seigneur, at the time of the great quarrel the discoveries of this minor philological and folkloristic tradition were used to demonstrate that such a right had never existed.

To anticipate: In 1866 a paleographer named Anatole de Barthélemy flew to the aid of Catholic opponents of the *droit de cuissage* by publishing in the first issue of the *Revue des questions historiques* an article "demolishing the fetish of the Revolution," entitled "Le droit du seigneur."[31] However, where conservative Catholics attempted a total refutation of the "proofs" that such a right had indeed existed, Barthélemy offered a wholly "folkloristic" demonstration establishing that *cuissage* was simply the ritual of *cullage*. His examples came from Carpentier, but he forged them into a system that provided legitimists with support for the notion of an ancient cultural division between aristocrats and the people: Feudal *cullage* was merely a hierarchical variant of communitarian *cullage*. Barthélemy added to his repertory of examples a case recently discovered by Charles de Beaurepaire and published in 1857 in the *Bibliothèque de l'École des Chartes*.[32] In a charter of 1238 conserved in the municipal archives of Neufchâtel-en-Bray (Normandy), Lord Simon de Pierrecourt renounced the right of *cullagium* over the men of his fief.

The interpretation of the *droit de cuissage* as folklore and as a transposition, whether malicious or ingenuous, of authentic popular rites—an interpretation born of the singular curiosity of a Benedictine antiquary of the eighteenth century and used for political purposes in the nineteenth century—prepared the way for historical anthropology. Both the historian Roger Vaultier in his book *Le Folklore pendant la guerre de Cent Ans d'après les lettres de rémission du Trésor des Chartes* (a work published posthumously in 1965 that rekindled historical interest in letters of remission among anthropologists and revived hope that popular culture could be described) and, more recently, the anthropologist Évelyne Sorlin borrowed generously from Dom Carpentier's work on the vocabulary of *cuissage*.[33]

The People's Acts: The Politicization of the Droit du Seigneur

Conservative opponents of the myth of *cuissage* were not the only people interested in the transfer of the past of the popular classes to a folklore increasingly centered in the Middle Ages. Heightened sensitivity to popular traditions led liberals to a greater interest in popular revolts and jacqueries. For Michelet the Revolution of 1789 had enabled the people to reconstitute their personality and rediscover a soul that had survived in secret in the hidden language of customs. For historians unfamiliar with the popular revolts of classical antiquity, the Middle Ages were a privileged moment of just revolt. The *droit de cuissage* played a functional role in the glorification of the jacquerie because folklore, more than simply registering amusing matrimonial customs, commemorated triumphs over seigniorial abuses, the *droit de cuissage* among them. Folklorists of the early nineteenth century observed that a certain number of festivities to celebrate popular rebellion leading to the abolition of the *droit de cuissage* in a medieval community still persisted, notably in the Alps, the hinterland of Nice, and Piedmont.[34] There was of course no way to trace such oral ritual traditions further back in time: The theme was probably introduced after the Middle Ages when cultural pressures of various sorts led to the invention of traditions. A certain number of mythic foundation narratives were available, and the nineteenth century made use of them.

Let us return for a moment to a text mentioned earlier, *Il fodero*, first published in Paris in 1786 as the work of "Colombo Giulio" (or "Veridico Sincer Colombo Giulio"), republished in Paris in 1788 and again in Turin in 1789.[35] This work was translated into French on three occasions (1790, 1791, 1820); it was popularized by Collin de Plancy and cited repeatedly during the great quarrel.

Il fodero relates the founding of the small town of Nizza della Paglia (now Nizza Monferrato) in 1235. The inhabitants of six villages—Lanero, Calamandrana, Garbazuola, Quinzano, Lintilano, and Belmonte—reached the point where they could no longer tolerate the tyranny of their overlord, the conte di Acquasana, who, with the backing of the marchese di Monferrato, imposed heavy seigniorial dues and enforced the indemnification of the *droit de cuissage* by a tax called *fodero*. The villagers formed a conspiracy, and at the sound of a bell rung in Belmonte the inhabitants of each of the six communities seized the local village lords and killed them. They then destroyed the castles, and with the aid of the inhabitants of the nearby city of Alessandria (with which they were in league) they founded the town of Nizza della Paglia at the confluence of the Nizza and the Belbo Rivers, using the river waters for a system of protective moats. The legend is fairly typical of an extremely old genre, the foundation narrative ennobling the creation of a plains town after emigration from the nearby hills and in opposition to a strong regional power. Here the poor peasants are transmuted into conspirators intent on federation, and the little city's domination of its hinterland provides further justification. The scenario, which recalls recent controversy over the "origins" of Switzerland,[36] corresponds to no real event in medieval Piedmont. The existence of the town of Nizza is attested as early as the eleventh century, and no medieval source relates the 1235 rebellion.

Where did the author of *Il fodero* get his story? He himself gives the source: from the *Annali d'Alessandria*, published in 1666 by Girolamo Ghilini, a churchman from an old aristocratic Alessandria family, who gives no source for his own account. Although we have no basis for evaluating the meaning of Ghilini's narrative (his annals might have remained in total obscurity except for the success of *Il fodero*), I might note that under the same date (1235) Ghilini repeats the old anti-Semitic medieval myth of the Jews' crucifixion of the child Julian of Norwich, a tale no one still believed in the seventeenth century. The tradition of the founding of Nizza begins with Ghilini; the early sixteenth-century chronicler Schiavona says nothing about it. Ghilini's version may have been an interpretation of a real event in the history of Nizza: In 1235 the inhabitants of Alessandria, who were at war with the nearby city of Asti and with Bonifaccio, the powerful marchese di Monferrato, burned the six or seven villages mentioned in the legend. The inhabitants fled to Nizza, which may have come to be called Nizza della Paglia (of straw) because in their haste to find shelter the peasants roofed their new houses with straw.[37] We cannot exclude the possibility that the foundation legend circulated in Nizza in the seventeenth century.

But why should this dubious tale have been exhumed at the end of the eighteenth century? This raises a minor problem of literary history, which has some relevance if we are to give the agents of history credit for their contributions to constructing the myth. All chroniclers of *cuissage*, from the great quarrel of the latter nineteenth century to recent times, followed Jules Delpit in his attribution (1857) of the anonymous work *Il fodero* to one Sincere Rastelli, a translator and professor of Italian in Lyons who was guillotined in 1793. Rastelli may have been the anonymous translator of the French version of 1790, but it is equally possible that Delpit was led astray by his given name, also found in one name for the author of the work, "Veridico Sincer Colombo Giulio," obviously a pseudonym. The true author seems to have been the Jesuit Giulio Cesare Cordara. This is at any rate what his fellow Jesuit Aloysius Marin Burchetti claimed in 1804, barely twenty years after *Il fodero* first appeared, in a lengthy introduction to the posthumous edition of Cordara's complete works, which Burchetti edited.[38]

Cordara (1704–85) had a long career in the service of the Society of Jesus, which he entered as a very young man. He moved from one school to another as both a student and a professor, as was the custom among the Jesuits, teaching rhetoric at Viterbo, Fermo, and Ancona, completing his theological studies in Rome at the famous Collegium Romanum, then teaching philosophy and canon law in Macerata and Rome. At age thirty-five he held the prestigious post of professor at the Collegium Romanum, the Jesuits' intellectual center. During this time, he published satirical poems in both Latin and Italian under his own name or neo-Latin pseudonyms. In 1742 the Jesuits set him the task of continuing the official history of the Society of Jesus begun by Joseph de Jouvancy. This brilliant career as a writer and a Jesuit professor had a melancholy end in 1772 when Pope Clement XIV suppressed the Jesuit Order, which had been rejected throughout Europe. Cordara retired to the Piedmontese village of Calamandrana, his place of birth and one of the six communities in the anti-*cuissage* conspiracy. His father had inherited from an uncle (also of modest extraction) the title of conte di Calamandrana and its attendant holdings. According to Burchetti, Cordara composed *Il fodero* in 1773, toward the beginning of his retirement in his home town. We can easily imagine the circumstances: Cordara's talent for satiric verse no longer found an outlet; the aristocrats in his new society were probably scornful of a family of parvenus with a freshly minted title; he probably read local authors. Ghilini's anecdote offered Cordara a way to take revenge and amuse himself. He did not claim to take the denounced abuses seriously: His work includes a burlesque episode involving the intervention of a demon, and Cordara states clearly in his introduction to the poem that in 1235 the droit du seigneur had been reduced to the collection of a tax, adding that the term *fodero*, in its more general sense, referred to a royal levy to provision the sovereign's troops and horses. The medievalist will recognize in this term the *fodrum* of the early Middle Ages, studied in recent years by Carlrichard Brühl.[39]

The fact remains that in the nineteenth century the light tone of Cordara's rhetoric was forgotten, and the heroic tale of the founding of a free town was ceaselessly recalled. Another foundation narrative—that of Montauban—was associated with it, for example, in the notes to Langlé and Morice's "Droit de nopçage" (1829) and in countless defenses of the existence of *cuissage*. Popular encyclopedic publications, in vogue in the 1840s, when publishing was moving into the industrial era, further circulated the notion. The story of the foundation of Montauban appeared in Girault de Saint-Fargeau's *Dictionnaire des communes de France*, published by Didot in 1845, and in Aristide Mathieu-Guilbert's *Histoire des villes de France*, published from 1844 to 1849 in 184 installments sold for 50 centimes apiece.

According to this version of the story, the serfs of the monks of the Abbey of Saint-Théodard of Montauriol were subjected to the *droit de cuissage*, known by the crude term *jus cunni*. The popular saying, "conduire la fiancée au moutier" (lead the bride to the monastery) came from the same community. Weary of this abuse, the serfs revolted and determined to found the free town of Montauban adjacent to Montauriol.

The truth is quite different: Montauban was created in 1144 on the initiative of Alphonse Jourdain, comte de Toulouse. The count's personal interest is clear in the charter of foundation dated 11 October 1144, where he imposes on the inhabitants the task of building a bridge across the Tarn.[40] Contrary to the views of liberal historians, continued into the twentieth century by Charles Petit-Dutaillis,[41] the foundation of new free towns did not occur unilaterally by popular initiative, but rather took place by seigniorial decision. The text of the charters themselves is insufficient proof: Mention of the will of the future townspeople may well be a cover-up and justification for the lord's attempt to reorganize the territory.[42] In the case of Montauban, the powerful comte de Toulouse hoped to acquire a source of income while also nibbling away the church's lands. Many of Montauriol's serfs and dependents undoubtedly went to Montauban: Albert, the abbot of Saint-Théodard, immediately protested to Pope Eugene III that the count's act was inciting the abbey's dependents to revolt and desertion and that the count had usurped alodial lands belonging to the monastery. On 23 June 1145 the pope ordered Archbishop Arnaud de Narbonne and Bishop Raymond de Toulouse to obtain reparations from Comte Alphonse within forty days; failing this, the diocese of Toulouse and the count's dependencies would fall under interdict. Negotiations began, and in 1148 a compromise was found confirming Raymond V, Alphonse's son, as his successor. The counts and the monastery were to hold equally divided sovereignty over Montauban, and Saint-Théodard was to retain the seigniorial dues. The struggle continued, however, and was complicated when the counts of Toulouse fought at the side of the Cathars attacking the monastery. The defeat of the counts led to the Treaty of Meaux and to a local agreement on Montauban signed in Gaillac in 1231. At that point Saint-Théodard held only one-fourth sovereignty over Montauban. The agreement was reiterated several times during the course of the Middle Ages. Montauban, which was governed by *consulats* after 1185, continued to prosper, and in 1317 Pope John XXII made it the seat of a diocese.

No medieval source mentions the legend of the founding of Montauban as a gesture of protest. Even more telling, we possess an old text extolling the city's mythical origins, a chanson de geste titled *Renaud de Montauban* composed in the late twelfth century. According to this version the city was founded by the four sons of Aymon, who endowed it with a palace and walls and installed five hundred burghers in it, adding one hundred tavernkeepers and equal numbers of bakers, butchers, and merchants, and three hundred craftsmen.[43] This curious mix of chivalric fiction and glorification of the urban and commercial vocation of the city omits any evil role played by the monks of Montauriol.

The first trace of the protest legend came later in a work titled *Histoire de la ville de Montauban,* published in 1668 by Henri Le Bret, *prévôt* of the cathedral. After relating the historical founding of Montauban, Le Bret adds:

> Such is the true cause of this displacement, which the Calvinists of Montauban have attributed to the hatred supposedly kindled against the abbot and the monks of Montauriol by the use they allegedly made of a shameful right: [a] gross calumny and one that displays an ignorance all the greater because this right was merely the *jus cunni*—that is, the right to coin money—for nearly all the lords, along with the power of life and death that they held over their subjects from ancient times, had that one as well, each within his jurisdiction. This right was later transformed into the right to levy tallage when the lord returned from the Holy Land, when he married, when he was knighted, or when he was a prisoner of war. As a result the monks, who did not marry, were not knighted, were not likely to be prisoners of war, and did not go off to conquer the Holy Land, probably changed all these rights into a due they extracted from their vassals when they married and which the engaged couples brought to the church, whence the proverb, "lead the bride to the monastery."[44]

Le Bret's history had a paradoxical success: Attempts to exculpate the monks encouraged the spread of the legend. Toward the end of the seventeenth century Antoine de Cathala-Coture, a Montauban magistrate who had read Le Bret, opted for the accuracy of a sexual interpretation of the *jus cunni*, first in a memoir and then in his *Histoire politique, ecclésiastique et littéraire de Querci,* published in 1785, long after the author's death in 1724.[45] His publisher, P. Th. Cazaméa, seemed to have his doubts, stating in his introduction that Cathala-Coture's version of events had been examined in "a historical memoir inserted in 1778 in the *Affiches de Montauban.*" When Abbé Marcellin and Gabriel Ruck republished Le Bret's book in 1841, furnishing it with a rampart of defensive notes,[46] the fable found a secure place in the dossier on *cuissage.*

Le Bret's hypothesis of a Calvinist calumny seems plausible: Montauban was one of the cities conceded to the Protestants by the Edict of Nantes, and antimonastic resentment may have created or crystallized the legend of the city's founding. More accurately, the legend may have arisen when the Protestants took Montauban during the Wars of Religion. In 1562 Protestant forces burned the cathedral of Saint-Martin, formerly in the monastery of Saint-Théodard, which by then had been enveloped by the city's growth. The fable may have been an a posteriori attempt to justify an act of vandalism on a building odious for its connections with both monasticism and the episcopacy.

One document presents the legend in an early, hesitant stage. In 1564, two years after the burning of the cathedral, a Calvinist named Jean Fournier wrote a work titled *Histoire de l'affliction de la ville de Montauban*, evoking the history of the church and its earlier occupants.[47] The Calvinists were thus fully aware of the cathedral's earlier history. The accusations against the monks of Saint-Théodard primarily concerned fiscal exactions, notably a right of *mainmorte* over the goods of a deceased dependent. Later in his history Fournier speaks in vague terms of "most unworthy things" that the monks made the people endure:

> Once the city was most anciently rooted where one can see the remains of the church of St. Michael that [are used to] support vines, and next to it an abbey had been founded with a monastery built and named for Theodat [Théodart], later the episcopal church of St. Martin. In those times the abbey most ignominiously tyrannized the inhabitants; when someone died it demanded by its right and power one-half of all his goods, and it often forced the townspeople to endure most unworthy things from its notorious monks, which led the inhabitants to put themselves into the hands of the comte de Toulouse, their secular lord, leaving land and the power of the monks, and to go to where they presently live.

It seems possible (though not very probable) that the Calvinist author found the legend frighteningly salacious. Protestant propaganda did not often recoil before descriptions of ecclesiastical debauchery. Rather than being invented wholesale in 1564, the discourse justifying violent acts most likely was constructed piecemeal. In the century of struggles and pressures between Fournier's text and Le Bret's, the fate of Montauban was decided by the religious tolerance imposed by the Edict of Nantes and the Catholic reconquest of the territory, and thus the conditions for constructing the legend of the monks of Saint-Théodard all fell into place.

In his argument against the sexually charged interpretation, Le Bret, the worthy *prévôt* of the cathedral, either out of ingenuousness or because the oral legends used the term, introduced the expression *jus cunni* into his written memoir on *cuissage*. The term had great success subsequently. Le

Bret claims it had no other meaning than the right to strike coins (from *coin*, a die or stamp). This argument was thoroughly discredited in 1853 (one year before the great quarrel over *cuissage* erupted) in an article in the conservative *Revue de numismatique* by Baron Chaudruc de Crazannes.[48] He found Le Bret's explanation highly unsatisfactory: The term was not to be found anywhere in the vocabulary of money. The Abbey of Montauriol never enjoyed such a privilege. Furthermore, Le Bret's reconstruction of marital law revealed a profound misunderstanding of feudal levies, conceived not in relation to land but in relation to an abstract, proto-state sovereignty moving, according to circumstances, from coins to the *maritagium* by way of tallage. Le Bret's attempt to reject a clear designation of the female sex organ (made gleefully explicit by Cathala-Coture) was pathetically weak.

It seems probable that the term *jus cunni* circulated within popular culture as a parallel to *cullage*, as suggested in an astonishing document discovered in 1924 by Léonce Cellier.[49] An *aveu* dated 2 January 1342 states: "Item: *congnage*, that is, from every bride, whether she comes from outside Chauny or is passing through Chauny over the royal bridge or whatever, provided she passes over the said bridge, 5 hairs from her cunt or 5 *sols parisis* [Paris sous]." This farcical choice opens new horizons on the relation between a common culture of Gallic bawdiness and seigniorial rights.

During the Ancien Régime *cuissage* was simply one symptom of a social tyranny whose effects continued to be felt even when it became outwardly less crude. There was nothing specifically medieval about it. As we have seen, theatrical productions that featured it were set in a variety of ages and often in contemporary times. Mentions of it in the Middle Ages were not rare, but they fail to form an overall picture. During the first half of the nineteenth century, on the other hand, the contradictory debate over the Middle Ages, although still muted, took place within a global representation of a certain view of the Middle Ages centered on communal liberties, ancient popular culture, and Christian devotions—an ideological construction of the Middle Ages that gained ground during the course of the century. A great quarrel over the *droit de cuissage* played an important role in the formation of that ideology.

The Great Dispute of 1854–82: The *Droit de Cuissage* and the Invention of the Middle Ages

T he themes traced in chapter 2 are insufficient to explain the scope of the quarrel over the *droit de cuissage* that began in 1854. Scattered allusions in isolated cultural genres began to take on a more global meaning, and the droit du seigneur gradually moved from the domain of curiosities from bygone times to become a symptom of political, religious, and social change. Before it could truly take hold, however, that semiological shift needed to be amplified by an ideological vision of the Middle Ages and the discovery of new texts and documents.

TOWARD THE INSTITUTION OF THE MIDDLE AGES: THE DROIT DU SEIGNEUR UNDER THE WEIGHT OF HISTORY

Restoration France had a real craving for history, as we have seen in connection with the historical novel in the romantic era. France differed from other countries, however, in the prominent role that history played in French politics. As Stanley Mellon noted, every party and every review was served by historians who constructed a vision of the world for it and lent it legitimacy.[1] The situation in 1814, when the French Empire was collapsing under the blows of a coalition of European forces, left France in a great void open to all possibilities, beginnings, and returns. In 1789 France had made a violent break with continuity; it had invented an incongruous imperial regime in 1804; now it was about to receive a new form by political and military decision. Russian, Austrian, and English sovereigns and diplomats imagined a wide variety of institutions for France, fetched from the storerooms of history. The return of the Bourbons was simply one possibility among others.[2] The imposed restoration of the monarchy did not put a halt to the need for history: For the legitimists, the very term *Restoration* implied a desire to wipe out twenty-five years of history. If the scenario of a continuous course of monarchic history interrupted by a regrettable accident was to be believable, the idea of a progressive development of enlightenment culminating in the abolition of royalty obviously needed correction. For liberals, remembering the gains of the Revolution and the Napoleonic era made historical narration and publication a civic duty. One of the most brilliant ornaments of liberal history under the Restoration, Augustin Thierry, confessed this political motivation in a memorable phrase: "In 1817, imbued by a burning desire to make my contribution to the triumph of constitutional opinions, I began to seek in the history books proofs and arguments in support of my political beliefs."[3] Both legitimists and liberals felt it necessary and urgent to explain the French Revolution and set it within a long historical process.

This explains the extraordinary vitality of history in France during the decade from 1820 to 1830. Even before scholars had available the new documentation that was to flood the scene after 1830, the ideological and epistemological framework of the new history was in place.

The Middle Ages crystallized the political historians' new expectations. The concept 'Middle Ages' still lacked the strict periodization and the feeling of remoteness that triumphed in the second half of the nineteenth century. Still, it put down tenuous but tenacious roots of an identity within the "total" history developing out of the desire to explain the destiny of a people and a nation whose revolutionary and imperial experience had endowed them with an indelible image going beyond political uses.[4] Edgar Quinet admirably illustrates this viewpoint:

> The collapse of a world was my first education. I became interested in everything in the past that might present some similarity with the immense human turmoil that had first struck my eyes. Thanks to that analogy, history, which I found intolerable, changed from a dead to a living thing. In many respects the past was the present still troubling me. When I read in Sidonius Apollinaris that the barbarians of his time waxed their moustaches with butter, that little detail quickly replaced what I had seen a hundred times, right under my eyes, in our German, Croatian, and Russian garrisons, and I think that if my contemporaries looked back on their own lives, they would agree that the historical sense of great masses of humanity typical of our epoch was awakened and elicited in them in the same way, by the same spectacle of the people overflowing their former streambed. That at least is why I was so quick to associate (in a comparison I could not explain otherwise) my fondness for Gregory of Tours with my passion for Tacitus. . . . With [Gregory] too, invasion was not just a threat avoided but an actual event. On

all sides endless masses of foreigners were camped, just as I had seen them in my father's house. I too had seen the cauldron of nations [la fabrique des nations] giving birth to one people after another to overwhelm us. In 1814 and 1815 I too had heard the hammer of Attila resounding in our countryside. . . . I set to work to write about Gregory of Tours, following the example of my great commentators, and I still possess that sketch. I was following contemporary models. I kept at it for several years, and I stubbornly continued to study the barbarians until suddenly, in 1822 and 1824, I saw that the fine works launching the fame of M. Guizot and Augustin Thierry had beaten me to it. Early in their careers I judged that the place had been taken and well taken; I was forced to seek another road.[5]

Historians sought ancient ideological and political breaking points in the Middle Ages—moments when the process culminating in 1789 had begun. Political adversaries agreed on one point: In 1814 the comte de Montlosier, a committed reactionary, published *De la monarchie française depuis son établissement jusqu'à nos jours,* a work in which he demonstrated that since the twelfth century the monarchy and the third estate had formed an objective coalition against feudalism. In this sense the monarchy itself had prepared the way for the Revolution of 1789. Augustin Thierry praised Montlosier for having pinpointed the fundamental nucleus of the long time span of French history, although liberals judged that break from a diametrically opposed point of view. Carrion-Nisas, for example, who had been an officer in Napoleon's army and was strongly attached to the memory of the Revolution, stood totally opposed to Montlosier, but presented a similar division of time in his *De la liberté et des factions, ou Coup d'oeil sur l'état de la liberté publique aux diverses époques de notre histoire et sur son état présent* (1819), where he contrasts the primitive liberties of the Frankish nations with a feudal despotism backed by the monarchy until the age of the Enlightenment. The work of Collin de Plancy (discussed in chapter 2) belongs within this antifeudal current, although he wrote on a fairly low, popularizing level.

The dominant factions in political and intellectual life under the Restoration—liberalism and constitutional monarchism—shared the view (with shades of difference) that the locus of the founding of personal liberties was the communes of the twelfth century. This agreement neutralized 1789 as a traumatic rupture and made the Revolution seem more like one incident in a straightforward advance. Not by chance, Louis XVIII called the constitutional text he asked Beugnot to draft a "charter." Moreover, the preamble to that Charte of 4 June 1814 offers an astonishing summary of French history:

Although in France all authority resides in the person of the king, his predecessors did not hesitate to modify its exercise according to differences in the times. It was thus that the communes owed their enfranchisement to Louis the Fat and the confirmation and extension of their rights to St. Louis and Philip the Fair; that the judiciary order was established and developed by the laws of Louis XI, Henry II, and Charles IX; and that Louis XIV reorganized almost all sectors of public administration through a number of ordonnances whose wisdom is as yet unsurpassed.[6]

It was also Louis XVIII who founded the École des Chartes in 1822 as an institution for the publication of medieval documents proving the ancient and solid alliance between the kings of France and the people of the cities, allied against feudal tyranny in the establishment of liberties. The former Cabinet des Chartes of the ancien régime monarchy thus took on a mission of pedagogy and dissemination of information. The right and the left might have viewed the nobility and the Church differently, but the Middle Ages guaranteed both sides continuity with the past and promised a possible future.

The peaceful revolution of 1830 only confirmed this vision. Augustin Thierry wrote in 1840, "That revolution made [us] take a step forward in the logical development of our history." Ten years later, in his last work, significantly titled *Essai sur l'histoire de la formation et des progrès du Tiers État,* Thierry saw the events of 1789 and 1830 as "the providential outcome of the work of the centuries that have passed since the twelfth century." Once the excesses of 1793 had been forgotten, political activity permitted France to "retie the thread of tradition" (Michelet) because "our Revolution throws light on medieval revolutions" (Thierry). Beyond their doctrinal or tactical disagreements, liberal historians (Guizot, Barante, Thierry, Michelet) saw in the events of July 1830 the endpoint and completion of both the French Revolution and history itself; the 1830 revolution was to produce a scientific and "political" historiography and a "veritable history." The two earlier versions of French history that had emerged from eighteenth-century debate agreed in seeing the Middle Ages as the matrix of the order of their own century. The "Romanists" grouped in the Académie Française and the École des Chartes (starting in 1829), where they grouped around Pardessus and Guérard, attempted to link the monarchy and the bourgeoisie through the city and medieval Christianity, both products of ancient Rome. The "Germanists," who included partisans of liberal history and liberal aristocrats, emphasized the contribution to the notion of 'liberty' of medieval Germanic invasions.

The trauma of the revolution of 1848 broke that convergence. The violence and radicalism of the Movement, an informal ideological coalition of the revolutionary, democratic, and liberal left, annihilated the myth of an end to history and a gradual completion of a process begun in the twelfth century. To the right, a parallel with 1793 swept away the notion that 1789 had been positive. Michelet, who was writing his *Histoire de la Révolution française* as the events of 1848–52 were unfolding, abandoned the Orléanist compromise and the ambiguities of liberal history. The harshness of the repression reinforced opposition between liberty and order and between the liberal Movement and the Reaction.

At that point despair born of defeat made images of the Ancien Régime and feudal abuses as menacing and odious as they had been in the eighteenth century. Curiously, rejection of France's "feudal" past was even more decisive when Louis Napoléon Bonaparte seized power. When the last shudders of the 1848 revolution had run their course after the legislative elections in the spring of 1849, Louis Napoléon gradually tried to rally the legitimist and Orléanist monarchists by constructing a party of "order" based on what came to be called the "alliance of throne and altar." Even before the proclerical measures promoted by Fortoul and Falloux in 1850–52, Oudinot's expedition against Rome in July 1849, which aimed at reestablishing Pope Pius IX, against the will of the revolution, proclaimed a similar intention to rally traditional Catholicism. The result was a radical recomposition of ideological forces: In spite of the efforts of some great spokesmen for the Reaction and for ultramontane Catholicism (Bonald, Maistre), Gallicanism retained its traditional hold on many monarchists, even the least liberal among them, such as the comte de Montlosier, a sworn enemy of the Jesuits. Gallican thought was central to the compromise of the July Monarchy. Little by little, however, a renewal of Catholicism that did not derive directly from the Reaction was developing with Lamennais and the partisans of a social Christianity, and after 1848, just when the Enlightenment was losing ground on the left to another form of religious thought, utopian socialism, they offered the party of order a new ideological cement.

The old religious orders were restored, and the problem of the Jesuits was gotten around. In 1833 Dom Guéranguer reconstructed the Benedictine Order, and Lacordaire did the same for the Dominican Order in 1839. A new image of the Middle Ages as a time of total and gentle piety was forming. In 1836 Montalembert published a book on St. Elizabeth of Hungary; Ozanam defended his thesis on Dante in 1839. Around 1845 the courses at the Sorbonne on the Christian Middle Ages taught by Charles Lenormant and Frédéric Ozanam aroused the ire of Gallican and free-thinking liberals. The question of "free" schools (or the clericaliza-tion of the schools) aroused passions in 1843–44 before it was settled in 1850 by the Falloux Law. The odd term for confessional schools, *enseigne-ment libre*, dates from that time; the myth of medieval liberties had some-thing to do with it.

The moment had passed, however, for presenting the Middle Ages as a time of liberties and the birth of the third estate. When troubles shook rural France in December 1851, the conservative press referred to them as jacqueries.

The Middle Ages evoked by the party of order was an age of faith and cathedrals, a time when a severe but just Church stepped forward as the great pacifier. The vital center of the Middle Ages shifted from the twelfth century, the century of liberties, to the thirteenth, "the century of St. Louis." The Movement developed a contrary image of a Middle Ages of obscurantism and fanaticism. This is what is meant by the "invention of the Middle Ages" in the nineteenth century: When contrasted with a dechristianized present, medieval times seemed a radically other, foreign epoch, whether its strangeness provided a positive or negative model. The Restoration had seen the Middle Ages as the beginning of something that ended with the defeat of the revolution of 1848. The terms used in French to designate and evaluate the age (*moyennageux* [1865], *médiéval* [1874]) and to refer to those who make it a specific historical discipline (*médiéviste* [1867]) all date from the later nineteenth century. The notion of transi-tion that had been contained in the term *Middle Ages* when it was forming (*medias aetas*, sixteenth century; *medium aevum*, early seventeenth cen-tury) dissipated before a firm substantive: Henceforth "the Middle Ages" (*le Moyen Âge*) existed as an essence.

Quite understandably, the droit du seigneur, even when hidden in the innermost recesses of a text or a proclamation, aroused violent reactions and invited further research. Opinion was hypersensitive to any hint of the ignominies of the Middle Ages, and *cuissage* was the most striking ex-ample. In the first half of the nineteenth century rapidly accumulating documentation produced new "proofs" of *cuissage*.

This vast machinery for historicizing debate and channeling sensibili-ties was accompanied by a vast movement to publish historical texts. In the early years of the Restoration there were the *Collection complète des mé-moires relatifs à l'histoire de France, depuis le règne de Philippe Auguste jusqu'au commencement du XVIIᵉ siècle* (52 volumes, produced under the general editors Petitot and Monmerqué, and published from 1819 to 1826); the *Nouvelle collection des mémoires pour servir à l'histoire de France* *depuis le XIIIe siècle jusqu'à la fin du XVIIIe siècle,* by Michaud and Poujoulat (32 volumes, published from 1836 to 1839); Buchon's *Collection des chroniques nationales, écrites en langue vulgaire, du XIIIe au XVIe siècle* (46 volumes, published from 1826 to 1828); the *Collection des mémoires relatifs à l'histoire de France depuis la fondation de la monarchie jusqu'au XIIIe siècle,* edited by Guizot (31 volumes, published from 1823 to 1835). This frantic activity to produce publications whose relatively modest prices and wide use of translations made them accessible to a broad public stood in strong contrast to the slow and scholarly publication of weighty and costly in-folio volumes by the Benedictines in the Ancien Régime. Historical works become more scholarly beginning in the 1830s, when the École des Chartes was functioning smoothly, Michelet and Mignet became archivists, and Guizot, then minister of public instruction, used his ministry to launch ambitious publishing projects. Two examples (among many others) of such publications are the French charters put out under the direction of Benjamin Guérard (the author of a famous edition of the polyptych of Saint-Irmion) and the *Recueil des monuments inédits de l'histoire du Tiers État* under the editorship of Augustin Thierry.[7]

One aspect of this development of medieval sources is especially important for our purposes: Local erudition, which had earned its letters of nobility (more properly, of bourgeoisie) under the Ancien Régime, gained new luster and won ideological legitimacy. Although it accomplished little in that direction, the Restoration had stood opposed to Napoleon's tyrannical centralization. People of all political loyalties hoped to revitalize local institutions. Here too, the Middle Ages served to convey this interest, and Joseph Fiévée, a prefect under Napoleon who passed into the service of the Bourbons, never failed to evoke the memory of communal liberties in his administrative reports in 1814–15.[8] It was precisely in documents published in the French provinces that fresh evidence of *cuissage* emerged after 1854, bringing a direct authenticity to the somewhat faded dossier on the droit du seigneur.

What set off the 1854 debate, as we shall see, was the publication of a work by Alexandre Bouthors, *Les Coutumes locales du bailliage d'Amiens, rédigées en 1507* (volume 1, 1845; volume 2, 1853), a work that inaugurated the *Mémoires de la Société des Antiquaires de Picardie.* Was Bouthors a scholar of liberal sympathies? Not necessarily. Jean-Louis-Alexandre Bouthors, a barrister, then (in 1831) recording clerk of the court of Amiens, seems to have been fairly typical of the local scholar in the nineteenth century. He founded the Société des Antiquaires de Picardie and served as its president from 1843 to 1854; he also founded the Société d'Archéologie de la Somme and served as its perpetual secretary, and was president of the Académie d'Amiens. His experience in local matters earned him the post of imperial councilor in 1858 and a chance to participate in the drafting of the *Code rural.* He died in 1866. Nothing in his modest scholarly oeuvre shows any sign of doctrinal commitment. The four or five texts the debate seized on were part of a voluminous dossier of archival materials that Bouthors published in entirety and with notes displaying painstaking application rather than any desire to offer mocking commentary.

A second group of documents emerged in Béarn at about the same time. In Pau in 1841 Adolphe Mazure and Jules Hatoulet published *Les Fors de Béarn, législation inédite du XIe au XVe siècle, avec traduction en regard, notes et introduction.* Although they too had founded a learned society in Pau, Mazure and Hatoulet belonged to social circles quite different from Bouthors's. Hatoulet was a dilettante with a special interest in popular culture, which at the time often meant the early language of the region. In 1817 he wrote a slim volume on the local dialect, *L'idiome béarnais* (reprinted in 1852); in 1862 he produced a collection of *Proverbes béarnais.* Adolphe Mazure was a secondary school teacher who produced a steady stream of textbooks and school editions of the classics. His interest in the customs of Béarn was probably restricted to one phase of his academic career.

Lest it be thought that Bouthors, Mazure, and Hatoulet had any hidden agenda, I might add that many more items in the dossier of the 1854 quarrel came from a third source, the massive *Études sur la condition de la classe agricole et l'état de l'agriculture en Normandie au Moyen Âge* by Léopold Delisle, published in 1851.[9] Delisle's allegiance was never in doubt: He was a member of the conservative and Catholic group centered in the École des Chartes that denied the reality of the *droit de cuissage* throughout the 1850s. Although Delisle had a keen interest in Normandy (his dissertation for the École des Chartes in 1849 had discussed public revenues in medieval Normandy), his illustrious career propelled him to the very heart of scholarship on the national scene. He served as director of the École des Chartes for over fifty years (1852–1905), at the same time serving as director of the Bibliothèque Impériale, where he accomplished herculean labors cataloguing and editing manuscripts. His *Études* was a work of synthesis based on an enormous number of charters and other archival documents, transcribed in his notes, systematically treating all aspects of rural life.

Although Delisle's *Études* reached both the publishing market and the ideological market in troubled times, it reflected the earlier epoch of consensus on the Middle Ages. Its title echoes a question used as the topic for a competition (which Delisle mentions in his preface) sponsored by the Académie des Sciences Morales et Politiques: "Rechercher quelle a été, en France, la condition des classes agricoles depuis le XIIIe siècle jusqu'à la Révolution de 1789" (Investigate the condition of the agricultural classes in France from the thirteenth century to the Revolution of 1789). Where the liberals sought continuity emerging from Frankish freedoms and urban communes of the twelfth century, the conservatives of the Académie and the École des Chartes attempted to establish a tradition of rural well-being that began with the affirmation of monarchic power. The end date stipulated in the academy competition (1789) can probably be read as a suggestion that the National Assembly's abolition of the formal apparatus of seigniory on the night of 4 August 1789 had not only broken up the village communities but also changed them permanently and for the worse. It is ironic that Delisle's documents contributed to the denunciation of feudal abuses and the *droit de cuissage*. But the time has come to plunge into the thick of the great debate of 1854 and examine its dossier.

The Great Debate

It all began on 25 March 1854, when André-Marie-Jean-Jacques Dupin reported to his colleagues in the Académie des Sciences Morales et Politiques on Alexandre Bouthors's work, *Les Coutumes locales du bailliage d'Amiens rédigées en 1507*, the second and final volume of which had just been published in 1853.[10] There was nothing unusual about this presentation: it was among the duties of the institution to call to the attention of the intellectual community throughout the nation outstanding works of local scholarship, which it coordinated and encouraged. As we have seen, Bouthors's work inaugurated the labors and the collections of the Société des Antiquaires de Picardie, a society formed in imitation of its venerable elder, the Société des Antiquaires de Normandie. Moreover, several weeks after Dupin's report, the Académie des Inscriptions et Belles-Lettres honored Bouthors's work with a medal. In his report Dupin praised it as a worthy effort in an erudite tradition begun by the Congrégation de Saint-Maur and carried on with new dynamism by Augustin Thierry, Guizot, and the École des Chartes.

Nonetheless this grave and unexceptional session prompted an intense discussion that occupied the learned world and the general public for thirty years and made *cuissage* a touchstone for what the Middle Ages stood for. In his report Dupin picked out half a dozen texts in customals that seemed to attest the existence of a tax levied by a lord when one of his subjects married, which indemnified a right, by then abolished, that had once given his predecessors first enjoyment of the bride's virginity. In his notes Bouthors himself recalls two cases famous in the juridical culture of the Ancien Régime, one regarding a curé in Bourges and the other the bishop of Amiens. Dupin states, "What is scandalous about this is that ecclesiastical lords should claim exercise of that right." In 1854, soon after the formation of the alliance of throne and altar, that statement, along with a critical allusion to the "posthumous friends of feudalism," resounded like a challenge. What is more, Dupin himself was a good deal more than a modest and venerable scholar.

André-Marie-Jean-Jacques Dupin (also known as Dupin the Elder) began his brilliant career as a liberal.[11] As a young lawyer he took part in Ney's defense before the Chambre de Pairs late in 1815. All through the Restoration he specialized in defending Napoleonic dignitaries, earning the nickname "the marshals' lawyer." He defended Moncey when he was stripped of his title for refusing to sit in the Assembly that had executed Ney. He took on the defense of Carnot, Travot, Poret de Morvan, and Cantillon (accused of having plotted to assassinate the duke of Wellington). He negotiated the return of General Allix from exile (1819) and that of the duc de Rovigo (1819). When the monarchy reopened the dossier of the execution of the duc d'Enghien, Dupin defended Generals Caulaincourt and Hulin (1820), and in 1827 he published an article in Le Constitutionnel theorizing on his experiences defending the marshals, "Les Maréchaux de France, défense de leur titre." Dupin consistently fought for freedom of the press: In 1820 he represented the Abbé de Pradt, accused of attacking the king. The famous Béranger was also one of his clients. In 1825 he defended the newspaper Le Constitutionnel. He later became known in a different context, the combat against the Jesuits and ultramontanism. Liberalism's anti-Roman focus was intensified when Charles X ascended the throne, and in 1825, the year Charles was crowned, Dupin thundered: "Our present-day Pharisees are devising our tortures. Feel the slashes of the sword whose hilt is at Rome and whose point strikes in all directions."[12] In 1826 he joined the thoroughly reactionary comte de Montlosier in his bitter fight to further the interdiction of the Society of Jesus. In 1827 Dupin sent a solemn warning of the dangers of clerical domination to Joseph Villèle, minister of finance.

Among these great liberal causes one minor affair seemed to the Catholics of 1854 to indicate Dupin's longstanding interest in *droit de cuissage* and his crafty approach to the question. In January 1820 Dupin took on the defense of César Eugène Gossuin, the editor of *La bibliothèque historique,* a somewhat mediocre publication specializing in compilations, who was brought to trial regarding some imprudent statements on constitutional questions. It was the *Bibliothèque historique* that printed (in 1819) the shocking text on the seigniorial right to defloration first published in Jean Florimond de Saint-Amans's *Voyage agricole* (1812, reprinted 1818). The trial (which ended with Gossuin's acquittal) made no mention of either that dubious cause or a text that left little imprint on Restoration thought.

Dupin's successes at the bar led to his election to the National Assembly as a liberal deputy, serving from 1827 to 1830. He played a role of some prominence during the July Revolution: On 26 July 1830 the editors of the opposition papers met at the house of his brother and law partner, Philippe.[13] His connections with the Orléans family probably won him the function of unofficial negotiator before Louis-Philippe's election as king. Dupin's courage paid off, and under the July Monarchy he was showered with honors: From 1832 to 1837 he was president of the Chamber of Deputies; he was elected to the Académie Française in 1832 and later to the Académie des Sciences Morales et Politiques. He was subsequently named prosecutor-in-chief *(procureur général)* of the Cours de Cassation. A liberal and then a prominent figure under the July Monarchy, Dupin rallied to the cause of the revolution of 1848. Now a moderate, he presided over the National Legislative Assembly until Louis Napoléon's coup d'état; Dupin's first reaction to that event was the hatred of an official whose place had seemed secure until a usurper reshuffled the cards of the patient political game he excelled at.

Dupin, a man who would not have been out of place in the Enlightenment, was known for his ironic eloquence. One famous bon mot regarded Louis Napoléon's confiscation of the wealth of the House of Orléans in January 1852: "C'est le premier vol de l'Aigle" (It is the Eagle's first flight/theft). The emperor forgave him this witticism, and Dupin eventually rallied to his cause. Before his death in 1865 Dupin was made a senator (1857) and was given the *grand cordon* of the Legion of Honor. I might add, to give Dupin his due for coherence, that his latter-day support of Louis Napoléon came only after the dissolution of the alliance of throne and altar. Dupin retained the obstinate anticlericalism of his liberal past that had inspired his joyous appreciation of Bouthors's discoveries. When ultramontane Catholicism returned, first in 1815 and then in 1845, it prompted the crystallization of a reaction that not only inherited the anticlerical sentiment of the Enlightenment but also mitigated doctrinal differences among liberals, democrats, and partisans of the Movement. The time-honored image of the lustful, greedy priest or monk so familiar in the late Middle Ages and the Reformation returned in force. We cannot comprehend the nineteenth-century image of "feudalism" without including its association with the Catholic Church.

Still, Dupin (who wrote works of piety) remained a moderate and a Gallican liberal. Unlike the new generation of democrats who rushed into the breach his report had opened, he remained as attached to the Middle Ages as the liberal historians had been. Barely a page of his communication to the Académie des Sciences Morales et Politiques was devoted to the *droit de cuissage*. As a whole his speech was essentially a posthumous homage to the grand tradition of liberal historiography. Bouthors's work—which Dupin presented as a step forward in the task of publishing medieval documents launched by Guizot, Thierry, and Guérard—confirmed the impression that "the Middle Ages have once again become fashionable." Echoing Augustin Thierry, Dupin speaks of the "long, bumpy, and twisting road our ancestors followed to reach freedom."[14] Dupin's allusion to the *droit de cuissage*, emphasizing the cases Bouthors had discovered and recalling the traditional proofs of its existence given by ancien régime jurists, simply contrasts the "barbarian elements" in the Middle Ages to the constant advance of liberty.[15]

There is nothing new in Dupin's somewhat antiquated discourse. He adds little to what Michelet had to say, and his prose lacks the vivacity of the fictions of Collin de Plancy and Langlé, let alone the thunder of Saint-Amans's falsities. Still, as we have seen, the situation in 1854 created a political hypersensitivity to any challenge to the Middle Ages or the medieval Church. Dupin stresses the scandal of clerics' use of the droit du seigneur. The person and the place are important: It was not Dupin the jurist, the dilettante antiquarian, or the coauthor of a new edition of Antoine Loisel's *Institutes coustumières* who was perceived as presenting this report, but rather the eminent political figure and the Orléanist who had rallied to the cause of conservative republicanism. The session of the academy illustrates the institutional limits of the vast movement to reorganize Christianity and subject it to order—a movement that the academy and its Orléanist figures resisted, even though the members were far from united on the question. Although the Académie des Inscriptions et Belles-Lettres had awarded a medal to Bouthors's work, that institution had by no means given any seal of approval to "proofs" of the existence of the *droit de cuissage*. In the session of 18 August 1854 Berger de Xivrey declared, speaking for the Commission des Antiquaires de France,[16] that the taxes mentioned in the Picard documents did not refer to *cuissage:* "That right, which has occupied modern people much more than those who paid it and those who received it, was thus a tax and no more." The only Picard text "in which the right in question had a more serious import than a tax and declaration of vassalship" was thus simply "an inconsequential exception."[17]

The March 1854 session of the Académie des Sciences Morales et Politiques did not go unremarked, however: It was mentioned in the *Journal des débats* in its issue of 2 May 1854 in a notice written by Louis Alloury. This was not by chance. Alloury (1805–84), a jurist by training, came from the department of the Nièvre (as did Dupin) and had worked for Dupin. After joining the *Journal des débats* in 1841, he firmly defended Orléanist and Gallican liberalism.[18] He was a moderate who strove in vain to have a political career, losing to a legitimist and republican in the elections of 1846. His 1854 article moved the *cuissage* question into the political arena. At a time when glorification of the age of St. Louis was rampant, Alloury bitterly criticized "that century that some dare to oppose to our own."

The question of *cuissage* emerged from the narrow circles where it had been confined. The threat of wider acceptance of the belief that the Church had encouraged and clergy had practiced that barbarian right became increasingly acute. In 1855 Henri Martin mentioned *cuissage* in the fourth edition of his popular *Histoire de France:* "The existence of the droit du seigneur was thus what one might call [a matter] of public notoriety; it lacked direct proofs; visibly, those proofs were no longer lacking."[19] Somewhat later Louis Laferrière, a man who wrote a measured and hence persuasive prose, opened the doors of higher education to the droit du seigneur in his textbook, *Histoire du droit français.*[20]

God's Party in the Great Combat

The Catholic partisans of order swiftly mounted a response to Dupin, energetically spearheaded by Louis Veuillot, a prominent representative of "God's party." Veuillot's response was printed in *L'Univers,* a review he edited, in a long series of articles appearing on 17, 20, 24, and 29 May 1854. The articles served Veuillot as the basis for a book, which he wrote at top speed: The manuscript was ready by 16 July of the same year and was printed by 23 July. The book was an immediate success, and as early as October of that year the five thousand copies of the first press run of this hefty 490-page volume had already sold out.

Veuillot is the perfect incarnation of the triumphant return of Catholicism in the nineteenth century.[21] Born in 1813 in the Gâtinais, he was the son of a man who worked for a barrelmaker. At age twelve little Louis was already employed as an errand-boy in a government office. He went to Paris as a very young man, where he joined the crowd of ambitious young men (described to perfection by Balzac) bitten by romanticism and avid for a social recognition best achieved in the nascent field of journalism.[22] At age eighteen Veuillot started to write for *L'écho de la Seine Inférieure*, later moving on to *Le mémorial de la Dordogne*, a periodical launched by Bugeaud as a means for consolidating his electoral fief in Périgueux. Veuillot had no hesitations when it came to choosing his camp: "I defended order, which was also my God."[23] With Guizot at the head of the government, Veuillot moved closer to power, working for *La Charte de 1830*, a journal founded by Guizot, then for *La Paix* and *Le moniteur Parisien*. In the spring of 1838, during a trip to Rome with his friend Gustave Olivier, Veuillot converted to Catholicism. The following year he published his first article in *L'univers religieux, politique, philosophique, scientifique et littéraire* (shortened to *L'Univers* in 1843), a journal created in 1833 by Abbé Migne. Migne later produced pious and theological publications on a near industrial scale under the general direction of Dom Guéranguer, who reinstituted the Benedictine Order in 1833 and was the soul of the construction of a new, decidedly Roman, and reactionary Catholicism. Veuillot soon became editor-in-chief of *L'Univers,* and the review gave battle to the liberal and social Catholicism of Lacordaire and Montalembert as expressed in the rival review *Le Correspondant.* While the newly converted Veuillot continued to pursue his political and administrative career (he was *sous-chef de bureau* in the Ministry of the Interior from 1839 to 1840, then attaché to the Guizot cabinet from 1840 to 1842), he was soon remarked for his virulence, particularly in the push to encourage religious schools in the years from 1843 to 1845. When the worker question arose as a distant threat, Veuillot clearly understood that an energetic Catholicism could be the glue that would hold together a new party of order: "Everything falls apart when we are no longer there."

His harsh attacks compromised him in the eyes of the Church and of Rome. In 1845 a committee was formed at the instigation of the hierarchy and Dupanloup to persuade *L'Univers* to soften its violence. Veuillot was forced to accept demotion to assistant editor. The triumph of order in 1852 gave him full liberty once more, and he appealed to his readers to vote for Louis Napoléon, the savior of Pius IX.

Although he was only a journalist, Veuillot played a considerable role in the neo-Catholicism of the 1840s and 1850s. How new was this Catholicism? In a slowly dechristianized world, where the Concordat of 1801 may have done more to marginalize Christian influence than either the triumphs of the Enlightenment or the authoritarian antireligious policies of the Revolution, the Church party worked to establish a new Catholic society founded on the network of parish priests. This gigantic enterprise functioned at all levels of French society. Dom Guéranguer and his circle reintroduced traditional liturgy, while Abbé Migne founded an industry of piety, putting millions of books on the market (the four hundred volumes of his famous *Patrologia* represent only a small part of these). Liturgical objects and ecclesiastical ornaments were widely produced and distributed, and the services of priests were made available to abandoned parishes. Migne's enterprise was aimed at fulfilling the combined functions of the *Encyclopédie,* the academies, and the Masonic lodges in the impious age of the Enlightenment. History was to be given a new start by obliterating the cursed century of unbelief.[24] Veuillot operated on a third level, below Guéranguer and Migne; his self-appointed mission was to the masses, and while the clergy directed the battle and thundered, he spoke for humble folk and for popular Catholicism, playing skillfully on his own simple origins: "We little people, who need leaders, must respect acquired rank, position, and authority," he wrote toward the beginning of *Le droit du seigneur.* He wrote with an easy style and filled thousands of pages with exhortations, denunciations, and edifying tales.

Veuillot's work *Le droit du seigneur,* written with verve and conviction, stands out in an oeuvre that is often tedious. Léon Bloy remarks in his *Propos d'un entrepreneur de démolitions* that Veuillot's *L'esclave Vindex* and his *Droit du seigneur* are "the only two books that will remain from this entire oeuvre."[25]

Le droit du seigneur approaches the question of *cuissage* with some objectivity. Veuillot begins by praising the century of St. Louis (part 1: "Le Moyen Âge," 1–136); next, returning to Raepsaet's demonstration, he establishes the two reasons for misunderstanding the droit du seigneur. Alleged mentions of an ecclesiastical droit du seigneur are in reality an invitation to observe three days of initial conjugal chastity (part 2: "Le droit de Dieu," 137–258); mentions of a secular right simply refer to an innocent tax on subjects' marriages (part 3: "Le *maritagium*," 259–324). In a final section (part 4: "Les faits," 325–490) Veuillot focuses on proofs of the existence of *cuissage*.

The books starts off like a populist Christian manifesto. The honor of the Church, "our" ancestors, and order itself are at stake. Veuillot immediately points out the political implications of a question it would be wrong to dismiss as just ribald trickery: "Although the abuses [Dupin] speaks of may well have dishonored society and the Church in past ages, it is not up to him to reveal them [or] throw them to the commentaries of the mob in these perilous days when respect is so deplorably weak."[26] A publicity notice for the 1871 edition emphasizes the negative effects of a perverse belief in the immorality of the powerful, as confirmed by current events in the Commune: "The people, who furnish a large contingent to the 100,000 prostitutes in Paris, voted against the poor bourgeois out of hatred for the droit du seigneur, which [the bourgeois] are accused of wanting to reestablish."[27]

The Christian Middle Ages reflected a corrected, purified image of present times. Authority, monopolized in 1854 by a state Veuillot detested as a matter of principle, was invested in the lord: "Put the state in the place of the lord, and you will see several epochs of contemporary history." Without the Church as a counterweight, he argues, the contemporary state has kept and aggravated only the most oppressive aspects of lordship. *Mainmorte* (the lord's feudal right to recover a portion of his subject's inheritance) was a modest prefiguration of state taxation of succession; modern conscription went much further than the feudal military service of the *ost*. The harshness of feudal domination was nothing compared to "industrial feudalism,"[28] because in both essence and practice the earlier domination was defined by a respect for individual possessions acquired by merit or birth (here Veuillot speaks of "the droit du seigneur, that is, of the proprietor").[29] He pursues his parallel in details: The bizarre rights and rituals noted by critics of feudalism arose out of a joyous love of forms that persisted in the nineteenth century, albeit in a less spirited version, in "academies and bands of pierrots."[30] Although Veuillot praises the "paternal royalty of St. Louis," he condemns medieval monarchy in general, accusing it of smoothing the way for the oppressive secular state: After St. Louis, "everything went to the royal power with the support of the bourgeoisie and the parlements."[31]

Thus Veuillot offers a fairly close reiteration of the comte de Montlosier's sociohistorical position, with the notable difference that for Veuillot the Roman extraterritoriality of Christianity and the "immense and preponderant party of God," armed with penitence and confession, had introduced justice into the inevitably rough ways of proprietor-lords.[32] The Church civilized the "savage society" that had imposed the subjection of both serfdom and civil law. It protected subjects from the encroachments of secular powers "under the benign conditions of a patronage nearly free of cost for the people, while at the same time it resisted empires with a centralized authority, though with full respect, loyalty, and independence."[33] Even in its apparent brutality, which was no more than justice and firmness, the Church defended society on its left flank, where anarchy lay in wait: "It crushed the Albigensian heresy, which was the socialism of those days."[34]

Veuillot's systematic comparisons (which at times were hilarious or grotesque) between the thirteenth century and the nineteenth played an undeniable part in constructing the idea of the Middle Ages because, far from dehistoricizing medieval times, he broke with the evolutionist view prevalent in liberal history in favor of a cyclical view, or at least a partially cyclical view: The nineteenth century could only revive the thirteenth with a global, deep-rooted return to Christian society. Systematic anachronism, polemical or experimental, has certain heuristic virtues: It requires taking the past seriously and asking real questions of it, even if we may think them biased. When history is cut off from the present, either out of laziness or scruples, it has every chance of being confined to futile description or a viscous relativism.

During the thirty years of the great controversy over *cuissage,* anachronistic comparisons were rampant on both sides. Examples abound, but I shall give only one savory one from *Le droit du seigneur,* a work by Comte Amédée de Foras published in 1884. It need not keep us for long, as it simply repeats Veuillot's views. Foras (1830–99), a Savoyard aristocrat and the author of a monumental *Armorial de Savoie,*[35] championed the seigniorial Middle Ages, but without Veuillot's panache or his taste for bawdy details. Still, Foras uses an anachronistic but effective transposition to reconstruct the feudal system in only a few astonishing pages. Ironically, his analysis, though totally aberrant as theory, comes close to resembling a view of history that seems diametrically opposed to his—the social history of feudalism sensitive to production relations and mechanisms of exchange, developed after Marc Bloch, that rejects the mythical exoticism of feudalism, long considered of no practical importance. In this anachronistic fiction prefiguring the individualization of the economic approach, Foras states:

Arthur, a wealthy proprietor, was saved one fine morning from a great danger, at the risk of their own lives, by Jacques and his son Pierre, foreigners chased out of their homes by some invasion. These unhappy, homeless, landless men did not even have the precious right to vote in the community; their only right was to die of starvation. Arthur, seeing that they were robust, intelligent, honest men and moved by gratitude for the immense service they had rendered him, gave them a lease [emphytéose] for an immense plot of newly cleared land, which promised great revenues one day, for the insignificant rental fee of 2,000 francs per year. He advanced them at interest and for a limited time [in mutuum, ad tempus] a sizable sum of money and gave them livestock in trust [en commende]. The lease contract was drawn up for thirty years. If Jacques were to die before this term, his son Pierre was to have the right to renew the lease on his own and hold it for another thirty years, in which case Pierre would pay the master a "welcome" [relief] of 500 francs. If Arthur were to die, Jacques or Pierre would pay 500 francs to Arthur's heir in like fashion [droit de mutage: ad mutationem domini et vassalli vel tenementarii]. The tenant farmers [emphyteotes] were held to paying the tallage [taillables] due the state and the commune; they must fulfill two corvées [corvéables] per year to the master, not counting other dues in labor or kind [corvées; prestations en nature] owed the state per head of man or livestock [corvéables à miséricorde]. Jacques and Pierre thus had possession [arrière-fief] of a farm for sixty years, thanks to which they were sure of making their fortunes. This farm is the land [glèbe] to which they are attached [attachés], counting themselves lucky to be so.

In this idyllic scheme of a serenely hierarchical society of landowners and tenant farmers living in mutual respect and attentive to one another's needs, a tax on marriages, odiously disguised as a *droit de cuissage*, seems totally legitimate: "Arthur stipulates that if Pierre has only a daughter and if she marries a fine lad from the village [un brave garçon de la commune] capable of tending the fields and of inspiring confidence in Arthur's descendants [a variety of the *foris-maritagium* or *formariage*], the heirs will be obliged to renew the lease for another thirty years, but the taker [Pierre], given the immense value of the property he has acquired, will pay a double rent plus a 'welcome' of 4,000 francs [droit de relief, de nouvelle investiture, de sufferte]."[36]

To return to 1854 and Veuillot, after Foras's astonishing outline for a "feudal" social contract founded on an original act of charity (rather than on natural equality), the rest of *Le droit du seigneur* holds little interest for us. After Veuillot's pompous remarks on the century of St. Louis, parts 2 and 3 of his work owe their power of persuasion to Raepsaet's arguments (discussed in chapter 2). We shall return to the hypothesis of a dual transposition of *cuissage* into *formariage* and church prescriptions regarding marriage. The last part of Veuillot's work, which refutes "proofs" of the existence of *cuissage,* have a certain technical strength borrowed from French scholars to whom he pays tribute. Veuillot's brother-in-law Charles Arthur Murrier, a young paleographer, helped him by transcribing the text of a decision of the Parlement de Paris in 1409 (to which we shall return). Veuillot salutes in passing the École des Chartes and its major figures, Benjamin Guérard and Léopold Delisle: "It is to that school directed by true scholars and that trains scholars that we owe (finally!) a history of the Middle Ages."

As years passed and a republican defense of the existence of the *droit de cuissage* was organized, traditional paleographers lent their support. In 1857 Charles de Robillard de Beaurepaire (1828–1908), a man whose training included the Faculté de Droit and the École des Chartes (1850), published a brief article in the *Bibliothèque de l'École des Chartes* that contained a new, apparently modest but in fact highly important document. Beaurepaire, who had been named director of the Archives de La Seine-Inférieure after his graduation from the École des Chartes in 1851 and remained there until he retired in 1905, found it in the municipal archives of Neufchâtel-en-Bray, a modest cantonal seat in the department of Seine-Inférieure.

This text was a charter dated 1238, accorded by Simon de Pierrecourt, lord of the homonymous locality (now the commune of Blangy), in the *arrondissement* of Neufchâtel. It states:

> I, Simon de Pierrecourt, knight and lord of this same domain, make known to all present that with the assent of my wife Agnes and my first-born Guillaume, for the care of my soul and that of my ancestors and all my friends, both in what concerns me and in what belongs to my heirs, will, concede, and ordain, confirming it by the present charter, that from this day forward and in perpetuity all my dependents of Pierrecourt shall be entirely free and quit of all tallage that I collected from them each year by just or unjust title. I also dispense these same people from a certain payment called *cullage* [cullagium] that they owe me when they marry their daughters. In order that this decision remain in effect in perpetuity, I have reinforced the present letter with the witness of my seal. Done at Pierrecourt in the presence of Master Robert, abbot of Foucarmont, and the parish priests of Pierrecourt on the day of St. Mary Magdalen.[37]

The meaning of this document is clear: The lord of Pierrecourt was emancipating his dependents *(homines)* from personal subjection—which of course did not abolish their dependence where land or justice was concerned. We need not linger over Simon's personal motives, though the mention of his soul's salvation and his choice of clerics as witnesses must have enchanted Veuillot. This de facto emancipation sprang from a widespread movement, the territorialization of the seigniorial demesne, which had economic and social reasons, to which we shall return in chapter 5. The manor had obviously not been under serfdom for some time. The document's importance for the participants in the great quarrel lay in its clear definition of *cullage* as a marital tax or a tax of *formariage*. That means that *cullage* could be dissociated from the earthy connotations attached to *cul* and could be brought back into the lexical family of *cueillir* or *recueillir* (in the sense "to collect"). In the Middle Ages many specific taxes had generic designations, and several attestations can be found where *cullagium* has no relation to marriage (notably, in a tax on salt).[38]

Another paleographer, Anatole de Barthélemy, flew to the aid of Veuillot with an article in *L'Univers* on 19 April 1856. Barthélemy was a man who participated more in the debate as his administrative career advanced. An older man than Beaurepaire, Barthélemy graduated from the École des Chartes in 1842. In his youth he served as the editor of *La revue de numismatique*. He obtained an administrative post in the Côtes-du-Nord on the accession of Napoleon III and, in 1855, the post of assistant prefect of Belfort. This was a brilliant beginning, but he was compromised in the Keller affair and sent in disgrace to an obscure post—by an odd coincidence—at Neufchâtel-en-Bray.

In 1866 Barthélemy published an article on the droit du seigneur in the first issue of the conservative *Revue des questions historiques* (as we have seen in chapter 2) that offered a new interpretation of *cuissage* based on folklore.

Thus the paleographers (and Raepsaet's intuitions in the previous generation) enabled the Catholic clan to chalk up some fine successes in their campaign. The last combatant to enter the fray, the comte de Foras, stressed the importance of scholarship. Although he praised Louis Veuillot's vigor and applauded the "strong correction" that Veuillot had inflicted on his opponents, Foras announced that the time had come for a truly scientific approach to the Middle Ages: Veuillot's demonstration "was not a complete success." "Despite his immense talent," Veuillot was not "a man familiar with charters"; "one has to be a paleographer and have spent his entire life studying documents to be able to speak about the Middle Ages." The Middle Ages, by then a well-defined period ("It is a conventional epoch of history beginning with the barbarian invasions in the year 395 after Our Lord Jesus Christ and ending in 1453 with the taking of Constantinople") and thoroughly studied, had become a specific scholarly discipline. Thus in the late nineteenth century, just when the paleographer and the philologist belatedly triumphed in France, this distinguished Savoyard aristocrat cast off the role of the dilettante or the antiquary in favor of a new role: "Bent day and night over dusty parchments, I study the things and events of the Middle Ages not from tales [racontages] but from the original sources in search of truth, my only goal and my one aspiration. After an entire life of rude labors and fascinating work, I know just enough to realize how much I still have to learn." From then on the rationality of partisans of the reality of *cuissage*, like their model Flaubert's Homais, lost credit: "A school that does not believe in God becomes of an ineffable credulity when it comes to believing in diabolical yarns and tall tales."[39]

Republican Resistance

The fight continued, however, because the opponents of the party of God and St. Louis, not content with simply popularizing their own ideas, were also intent on contributing to and making use of the "science" of medieval history.

Gustave Bascle de Lagrèze was the first scholar after the great combat between Dupin and Veuillot to defend the existence of *cuissage*. Like Bouthors, he was a provincial antiquary. A grand-nephew of Bernadotte's, Bascle de Lagrèze was a magistrate, serving first as substitute prosecutor and then as king's prosecutor in Lourdes and Pau. He played an essential role in the great debate by contributing two important pieces to the dossier on *cuissage*. In 1840, when a young barrister at Pau, he subscribed to the publication in five installments of Adolphe Mazure and Jules Hatoulet's edition of texts of customs in the county of Béarn gathered together in the late fifteenth and early sixteenth centuries but including much older dispositions. Their collection was indeed of genuine interest, and it deserves the critical attention it has received in recent years.[40] Mazure and Hatoulet, the first a lawyer, the second a schoolteacher, were members of an extremely modest learned society. Their painstaking edition, which they furnished with notes and a French translation, raised little interest. Only four or five of the work's one hundred or so subscribers lived outside the circles of the intellectually curious and the magistrates of Pau. The only institutions to acquire the volume were the municipal library of Pau and the departmental archives.

Bascle was thus among the happy few who might have read Mazure and Hatoulet's long note on the fate of the *questaux* (a local word for serfs) of Béarn, as reported in two documents dated 1538 where local lords boldly demanded their right to *cuissage:* "We have before our eyes a *dénombrement* of the lord of Lobier [Louvie-Soubiron] in which revolting rights many would be tempted to regard as fabulous are stipulated with a most shameful naïveté. Such documents are important for history, and a false delicacy must not oblige us to stifle them."[41] Their boldness did not go so far as translation of the phrases they mention, however. We shall return to these texts in detail.

Bascle may even have had direct access to these documents. In 1845 a question of communal rights brought the village of Louvie-Soubiron before the courts. The lawyers prepared an astonishing dossier for this case, including some extremely old documents deciphered and translated from Béarn dialect by Mazure and Hatoulet. A young lawyer, Marcel Barthe (who later had a fine career as a progressive deputy), collected documents, the 1538 text among them, into a memoir. I have been unable to locate the 1845 edition of this memoir, if it ever existed, but Barthe republished its contents in 1874.[42] It seems probable that Bascle had direct acquaintance with the document in one form or another.

Bascle, a corresponding member of several provincial academies and ministerial committees, had means for circulating the newly discovered documents. Moreover, he had become a genuinely competent archivist whose skills are visible in a work published in 1851, *Le Trésor de Pau: Archives du Château d'Henri IV,* the first detailed guide to the departmental archives of the Basses-Pyrénées. Even before the beginning of the dispute, he spoke in this work of the "revolting occurrences" that Mazure and Hatoulet had discovered.[43] Thus he was able to locate the *dénombrements* presented in Mazure and Hatoulet without specific references. But it was certainly the Dupin-Veuillot affair and the broader scope it gave to these documents that most excited Bascle's paleographic zeal. Bascle published the texts and his conclusions in an article in *Le Droit* on 23 July 1854 and separately in 1855.[44] More and more fascinated by the *cuissage* question, he wrote to Dupin, who responded somewhat noncommittally on 3 April 1855: "I said only what they had said." Bascle then turned to the jurist Laferrière, who proposed a subtler explanation than the one he later put in his textbook: "No law, no usage authorized by the Church, but particular acts and local charters asserting fact raised to a right." Bascle then returned to the ancient dossiers on the droit du seigneur and appealed to the highest authority available to scholarship in that age: "I have engaged a German scholar to search the libraries and the archives of Berlin."[45]

By now Bascle spoke as an eminent specialist in feudalism in the Pyrenees and was recognized as such by the Académie des Sciences Morales et Politiques, where he presented a memoir on the topic in 1864.[46] His patient obsession had finally taken him to the pinnacle of knowledge. In reality, however, despite his growing pile of extracts and books, Bascle did little more than add somewhat more current information to the discoveries of the obscure and modest Mazure and Hatoulet. Unlike the other participants in the debate, he enhanced his position by taking a moderate stance on the question of the *droit de cuissage*. He stated in 1867: "I have tried to demonstrate that these acts of infamous immodesty were never sanctioned by any law but existed as an abuse attempting to bear the appearances of a right. I have victoriously established that the magistrature and the Church, far from having been accomplices in such disorders, have always condemned them as contrary to religion and right conduct."[47] Still, the broad circulation of the Béarn documents made the *droit de cuissage* seem more plausible by adding another region to the places where it had been found, which now stretched from one end of France to the other.

Dupin received another helping hand from the provinces in 1855. Victor Vallein, editor in chief of *L'Indépendant* in Saintes, a liberal newspaper founded in 1848, published a summary of the quarrel in 1854. Veuillot gave Vallein unexpected notoriety by quoting one of his more vehement statements:

> At this moment *L'Univers* is proving that France of the Middle Ages, with no roads, no canals, no commerce and no industry, deep in mud, miserable poverty, and ignorance, constantly decimated by plagues and recurrent famines, prey to all tyrannies, having neither government, laws, nor justice other than might makes right, was better than France of the nineteenth century, than this grand and glorious country marching at the head of the world's civilization today. One cannot discuss such absurdities.[48]

Vallein hastened to capitalize on this publicity by organizing his attacks on the medievalism of the pious reactionaries in a work published at Saintes, *Le Moyen Âge, ou, Aperçu de la condition des populations, principalement dans les XIe, XIIe, et XIIIe siècles.* Under the spur of debate the Middle Ages gradually took firmer shape.

The true assault on Veuillot came somewhat later. In 1857 Jules Delpit, a scholar who affected the rough simplicity of a provincial dilettante in both the title of his work and the tone of his demonstration, took aim at the centralizing, Roman, Parisian, Catholic, and Chartist arrogance of the censors of the *droit de cuissage*. His *Réponse d'un campagnard à un Parisien, ou Réfutation du livre de M. Veuillot sur "Le droit du seigneur"* was published in Paris, with an enlarged version appearing in 1873.[49] This posture of humility, which was just as much a tactic as the arrogance of the Catholic paleographers, by no means reflected Delpit's true career as a liberal historian.

Jules Delpit had earned a degree in law before attending courses at the École des Chartes, where he was a classmate of Louis Quicherat, a noted philologist. He soon worked with Augustin Thierry, who recommended him (in 1842) to François Villemain, minister of public instruction, for a mission to England in search of the royal archives of Philip Augustus. This mission resulted in the publication (beginning in 1847) of an important project, the *Collection générale des documents français qui se trouvent en Angleterre: Inventaire des lettres et documents.* Earlier, with his cousin Martial Delpit, a paleographer who also had worked with Augustin Thierry, Delpit had successfully conducted another scholarly expedition, this one to Wolfenbüttel in view of an edition of the *Recognitiones feodorum,* a close analysis of which appeared in the *Notices et extraits de la Bibliothèque du Roi* in 1843.[50] Delpit delved into local scholarship as well, editing the history of Bordeaux of Father Gaufreteau (early seventeenth century)[51] and a catalogue of manuscripts regarding Bordeaux. He founded the Commission des Archives Municipales (1845) of that city and the Société des Bibliophiles de Guyenne, and was head of the *secrétariat général* of the Académie de Bordeaux.

The challenger facing Veuillot was thus no simple "peasant from the banks of the Dordogne," as Delpit was fond of saying, but a formidable liberal anticlerical scholar with a sure knowledge of the Middle Ages (qualities that did not prevent him from skillfully manipulating texts, a practice he shared with all the Veuillot clan). Until the end of the century Delpit's book remained the textbook for partisans of the existence of the *droit de cuissage.* I shall use it as a collection of dossier items to be explored, and although publications continued to appear and invective was exchanged for some time to come, I shall end my chronicle of the republican battle with it. One later work, Léon de Labessade's *Le droit du seigneur,* published in 1878, added no more novelties to Delpit's work than the comte de Foras had brought to Veuillot's. If I mention it and recall Foras's text here, it is simply to note that reiterated arguments signaled the end of the quarrel.

The years 1878 and 1884 frame the effective beginning of the French Republic after ten years of a moral "order" where the old royalist and Bonapartist solutions still seemed to have some chance of being realized. After the disappearance of claimants to the throne, the national expiation of defeat in the Franco-Prussian War, and the Commune, the time had passed for an ideological reconstruction of the Middle Ages. The Trojan horse of anachronism and historicism was crammed with old parchments rather than fighting men. Henceforth the paleographer could advance unmasked because he no longer had anything to hide, even if somewhat later the Dreyfus affair showed that scholarship regarding writings no longer enjoyed the privilege of impartiality. Between our two framing dates the first nonpolemical work on the *droit de cuissage* appeared (in 1881). It was published in German in Freiburg im Breisgau and was written by Karl Schmidt, a judge in Colmar in occupied Alsace (another form taken by expiation and the liquidation of tensions in the years from 1850 to 1880).[52] Schmidt firmly concludes that the *droit de cuissage* never existed, but he attaches no ideological expectations or corollaries to his judgment. In the book, written in a serene tone of critical consideration of sources, he discusses a long series of references, examining case by case all attestations of the *droit de cuissage* from the dawn of time. This lengthy and meticulous work, whose rather myopic erudition somewhat dates it, still has no worthy successor, even taking into account the compilation closely based on his text recently published in Germany.[53]

In 1881 the Middle Ages, circumscribed by ideological debates, closed its gates and sent packing the passions it had engendered. Henceforth the question of *cuissage* belonged to the domains of cliché or personal opinion, where it was restrained by the fear of seeming ridiculous or naive.

The great debate over *cuissage* that emerged from a sweeping political and religious redistribution of roles early in the Second Empire contributed greatly to the construction of the idea of a Middle Ages essentially different from other epochs and a foil or model for them. Even today popular opinion and some historians are prisoners of this ideological vision. The violence of that debate provided a wealth of sources and arguments. We will take that rich dossier as a point of departure for investigating "proofs" of the existence of the *droit de cuissage*.

CHAPTER FOUR

Seventy-two Proofs

W hy approach the dossier of "proofs" of the existence of *cuissage* through Delpit's polemical work? First, it seems advantageous to seize the question when debate was still lively but was informed by polemical research, before Schmidt imposed his flat erudition on it; and second, Delpit's presentation facilitates examination of the items in the dossier. The longest part of his work is a painstaking review of all the data available in 1857: chapter 2 ("Summary Analysis of the 72 Facts Contradicting the System of M. Veuillot") and chapter 3 ("Proofs and Discussions of Facts Misunderstood or Falsified by M. Veuillot and Which Establish That the Droit du Seigneur Existed") take up nearly one-half the book. In the rest of his book Delpit attacks Veuillot's ignorance (chapter 4) and his aggressive bad faith (chapters 4 and 5), then considers the Middle Ages (chapter 6), Christian marriage (chapter 7), and the fanaticism of the Church (chapter 8). In his ninth and final chapter Delpit asserts the reality of the *droit de cuissage*, presenting it as the clerical and feudal equivalent of an oppressive slavery. May the reader forgive me for not discussing these chapters, often droll and unfailingly imbued with anticlerical republicanism, where Delpit rejects the amiable image of the Middle Ages typical of the liberal historians of the preceding generation. Delpit's frame of mind should already be clear in its dialectical contrast to Veuillot's.

Our basic dossier is thus made up of the seventy-two proofs that Jules Delpit examines and Veuillot repeats in the second edition of *Le droit du seigneur* (1871). Schmidt did not lengthen this list except to add the exotic or ancient cases discussed in chapter 1 above.

Delpit's compilation is a fine illustration of accumulation and amalgamation, time-honored tactics of the partisans of the existence of *cuissage*. The technique was to assemble references and texts of extremely varied status and provenance, a few with a troubling content, in the hope that the whole would be permeated with that trouble or a persuasive sense of certainty. Beginning in the sixteenth century tireless repetition of the same proofs had augmented the list by its own momentum when at each reiteration the secondary or tertiary source added its own authority. Delpit pushed this procedure to an extreme, inserting into the traditional lot thirty-two proofs that had only recently been published (two cases from Mazure and Hatoulet in 1841, six from Bouthors in 1845–53, twenty-three from Delisle in 1851, and one from Beaurepaire in 1857). I shall follow Delpit's full list as we sift through and examine the texts. His total needs to be reduced somewhat from the outset, however, eliminating items 71 (on *formariage*) and 72 (on "tradition"), which refer to groups of cases rather than precise factual proofs. With the classification I propose, I hope to reach the nub of the argument by eliminating purely imaginary and irrelevant sources, which are present in great number in the dossier.

FABLES AND FORGERIES

A first group of cases consists of forgeries or legends of recent origin (from the sixteenth to the nineteenth century) with no medieval attestation, some of them examined in earlier chapters.

Item 64: This is the forged charter of Blanquefort (see chapter 2 above) published in 1812 by Saint-Amans and written by its editor or one of his contemporaries.[1]

Items 39 and 40: The legend of King Evenus (which played such an important role in diffusing the myth of *cuissage*) emerged in 1526 in Hector Boece's history of Scotland (*Scotorum historiae ab illius gentis origine*) discussed in chapter 1. Boece invented Evenus, backing up his narrative with a false mention (uncorroborated by any reference) of *cuissage* near Louvain (item 40): "And that is no different from what occurred in a place not far from Louvain, where a husband paid the lord of the locality an indemnity for the rape threatening his wife."[2]

Items 37 and 38: Several legends concerning merchet among the ancient kings of England and Wales deriving from the famous case of King Evenus, arising in the same circles, and transmitted in parallel fashion should be set aside as well. See chapter 5 for a discussion of Eleanor Searle's explanation of that marital tax.[3]

Item 66: The first written attestation of the narrative of the founding of Montauban (see chapter 2) is in Henri Le Bret's refutation of it (1668); an oral version may have accompanied or followed the destruction of the cathedral of Saint-Martin (formerly part of the monastery of Saint-Théodard) by the Calvinists in 1562.[4]

Item 50: The history of the town of Nizza della Paglia (Nizza Monferrato), which first appears in 1666 in Girolamo Ghilini's *Annali di Alessandria,* goes back at best to a popular tradition in the seventeenth century.[5]

Items 48 and 49: The scheme of city foundation narratives was a productive one. In 1704 Eusèbe de Laurière in his *Glossaire du droit français* (under *cullage*) added to the great classics of *cuissage* the story of the emancipation of the lands of Prelley and Persanni in Piedmont. In fourteenth-century Savoy under Amedeo VII the vassals of the lords of these two fiefs disinfeudated themselves because their lords refused to abolish the right of *cuissage,* here called *cazzagio,* transferring their subjection to Amedeo. The story calls up no echoes: No place in Piedmont corresponds to these place names; Savoyard chronicles say nothing of the episode. We shall return to the clear connection between the propaganda of royal jurists and the propagation of the myth of *cuissage:* The figure of the king emancipating vassals from local servitudes seems all too convenient. This unattested fable owed its prominent place in the corpus on *cuissage* to the new term it offered, *cazzagio* (belief has a penchant for realism, passing easily from a name to a thing), and to the wide circulation of Laurière's dictionary.[6]

Items 43–46: An effect of sheer mass (seventy-two proofs!) is at times obtained by dubious means: Mention of four neighboring seigniories in Zeeland where indemnification for the *droit de cuissage* was alleged to have been practiced in the seventeenth century occupies four spaces on Delpit's list, whereas Dutch sources give the same data globally and without detail (see chapter 2). To recall: The first mention is dated 1696 and occurs in a text by Matthijs Smallegange that relies on oral tradition ("it is said") but fits in too suspiciously well with the circumstances behind the compiling of the chronicle—a campaign supporting the legitimacy of Calvinist colonization in Zeeland—to permit belief in a genuine, deep-rooted tradition.[7]

Item 62: Delpit himself enriches this series of forgeries and fictions by borrowing from the Bordeaux manuscripts an extract from the *Notes et observations sur Bordeaux* written in the eighteenth century by Abbé Bellet, the canon of Cadillac: "*Marquetes des femmes.* The *captal* [captain] of Buch formerly had this right to lie with new brides on the first night of their wedding, or to take whatever gift he ordained. This right contrary to good mores and that could only be waived for slaves was suppressed in 1468 by a decree of the Parlement of Bordeaux, which replaced it with a right in money." Twenty years after the publication of his book Delpit himself located the probable source of Abbé Bellet's comment in a fragment from the *Chronique bordelaise*, a collection of notes and manuscript texts written in the 1630s by Jean de Gaufreteau (1572–1639), a Bordeaux judge who later took religious orders. Delpit published the entire text of the *Chronique* in 1877. Under the year 1468 Gaufreteau remarks: "In that year, the *captau* of Buch had the right to lie, if he wanted to, with brides on the first evening of the wedding or to take a present, as he ordained, in all the lands and parishes of his captalcy. But this right was abolished as contrary to the commandments of God by decree of the Parlement of Bordeaux, and in its place was ordained a certain right of *fouage* [hearth tax] in money over [the captal's] subjects."[8] Neither the judiciary archives of Bordeaux nor chronicles preceding Gaufreteau's contain any mention of this case. Once again, a local microcontext reinforced a fable. A feeble echo of this same tale surfaces in 1812 in the *Voyage agricole* of Saint-Amans, who probably was unaware of Gaufreteau's and Bellet's manuscript texts: Saint-Amans does not mention *cuissage*, but he does speak of the tyranny of the captal of Buch, by then probably a vaguely defined feudal bogey-man in Bordeaux and Guyenne oral tradition. This legend merits a closer look, however, because it gives the fabulation an exceptionally rich context.

This story seems surprisingly disproportionate: The tiny seigniory of Buch, near Arcachon, is an unlikely candidate for stirring up dreams. Nonetheless, it played an important role in Bordeaux life. It was constituted in the thirteenth century by grouping a dozen or so smaller domains. Through the Arcachon basin it furnished Bordeaux with a good part of its fish and facilitated its maritime commerce. The captal enjoyed a right of *clie*, reaffirmed in the seventeenth century by the duc d'Épernon, giving him a monopoly on the sale of fish in Bordeaux. The captal's residence, originally the castle of La Teste (by which the captalcy was known) soon moved to the Château Puy-Paulin in the heart of Bordeaux. This urban command over a rural seigniory—rare in feudal society in its traditional form—may offer a key to the myth of *cuissage* as an urban representation of relations between peasant and lord. The myth gained added impact from this bipolar captalcy—part urban, part maritime and rural—because the western part of the region of Buch was reputed to be a savage place: Gaufreteau calls it "un lieu affreux et sauvage" where priests were illiterate and backward, sorcerers abounded, and a commission of Bordelais magistrates who ventured there was decimated by a mysterious illness.[9] The flat forested Landes of Buch were the final stage in transhumance for the redoubtable shepherds of Béarn.

The families who held lordship over the captalcy of Buch also added to its importance. From the late thirteenth century the domain had been in the hands of the Grailly family. The most famous captal was Jean III de Grailly (1321–76), who succeeded his father Pierre II and his brother Jean II. Jean III was in the service of England and was the Black Prince's lieutenant in Guyenne during the Hundred Years War; in 1356 he was among the victors at Poitiers but was defeated by Du Guesclin in 1364. Was this a first reason for detesting the captal, at least retrospectively, when the idea of national integration began to be constituted in France in the late Middle Ages? Jean III may also have left bitter memories for the role he played at the head of a harsh repression of the peasant uprising at Meaux in 1358. Be this as it may, he was an imposing figure. The next generation of the Grailly family intermarried with the families of the counts of Béarn, the viscounts of Foix, and the Albret family. Later the captalcy passed to the younger branch of this powerful lineage: The captal in 1468, Jean IV de Grailly (presumably the man who lost the suit over *cuissage*) had followed the pro-English career of his predecessor Jean III a century earlier. He lived in England, where he married the daughter of the duke of Suffolk, Marguerite de la Pole, who brought him the county of Candale. During Jean IV's absence from Guyenne, Charles VII confiscated the captalcy and gave it in appanage to his son, the future Louis XI. When Louis became king in 1461, he persuaded Jean IV, now Jean de Foix-Candale, to return to France by offering to restore him to his captalcy. Jean accepted the offer, and Buch regained its captal. In 1488 Jean's son and successor Gaston II de Foix-Candale received the title of grand seneschal of Guyenne. As it happens, Saint-Amans's 1812 forgery mentions both a grand seneschal of Guyenne and the Durasfort family. As we have seen, all the details, including dates and genealogical data, were false in this document. We might well wonder whether tradition had reconstructed events askew, attributing to the Durasforts a legend that had sprung from the detested lineage of the captal of Buch.

The suit in 1468 was no simple case of *cuissage*, referring rather to a charter (known in the local dialect as *baillettes*) of Jean IV according his dependents certain customary rights in exchange for their help to fight fires in the pine forests. How are we to understand the transposition to the version circulating in seventeenth-century oral tradition and collected by Gaufreteau? One possible explanation might be that certain specific rights pertaining to the captalcy were misinterpreted, such as the right to *concage* over one-tenth of the cargos discharged in the domain. The English past of Jean IV, a foreigner who returned as master of a portion of

Bordeaux territory, may have crystallized memory of the other "traitor," Jean III, although Gaufreteau's chronicle suggests that in the seventeenth century the English presence in the area was remembered with some nostalgia. Did the League factions in Guyenne use calumny to take vengeance on the maternal lineage (the Albret family) of the apostate Henri IV, the last count of Foix? This would suppose too global a sense of genealogy in an age when all lineages were split by religious troubles. It seems to me more likely that the fabulation arose out of urban and patrician vengeance against the invasive presence of an overly powerful seigniory.

The power of the Foix-Candale family did in fact give a symbolic eminence to a wild captalcy: Gaufreteau notes that when deaths, marriages, or births occurred in the seigniorial family, delegations of *jurats* (municipal magistrates) came with full solemnity to the castle of Cadillac, the residence of the Foix-Candales.[10] The lineage took a prominent part in the life of the city: Another Jean de Foix-Candale was archbishop of Bordeaux from 1501 to 1529; the penultimate Candale captal, Henri, became mayor of Bordeaux in 1571. His heir, François, bishop of Aire, reinforced the connection between grandeur and oddness that seemed to mark the captalcy: Well-versed in alchemy, he invented an *eau de Candale* and acted as both benefactor and tyrant, protecting and endowing the Collège de Guyenne but also (in 1582) laying claim to the public square facing the Château de Puy-Paulin.[11]

Toward the end of the sixteenth century the captalcy passed, on the marriage of Marguerite de Foix-Candale in 1587, to the famous duc d'Épernon, a prominent figure under Henry III—a king detested by the League, which was quick to point to the duke's humble origins as "a notary's grandson." In Gaufreteau's day the duc d'Épernon was governor of Guyenne and had built a sumptuous château in Cadillac, near Bordeaux (and we might recall that Abbé Bellet was the canon of Cadillac).

In 1633 a much-talked-about incident occurred between the duke and the archbishop of Bordeaux, Henri de Sourdis. The duke publicly attacked the archbishop, who retaliated by excommunicating the governor (with the support of Louis XIII and Richelieu). The people of Bordeaux and some of the bourgeoisie (the Catholic party in any event) backed the archbishop against Épernon, as Gaufreteau himself relates. The phantom of the terrible fourteenth-century captal of Buch may have evoked horror thanks to hatred of his successor.[12] The image of an arrogant captal detested by a city proud of its patrician traditions continued in the next generation: Ten years or so after the death of both Gaufreteau (in 1639) and the duc d'Épernon (in 1642), an anonymous *mazarinade* in verse from Bordeaux (also published by Jules Delpit), *Le prince ridicule*, attacked the duke's younger son, Bernard, who had received the captalcy as part of his legacy from his father. Bernard d'Épernon, who plotted vaguely (but seriously enough to merit a death sentence) against Richelieu, later married the archbishop's niece and obtained his pardon. Bernard seems to have served Mazarin faithfully, which probably explains the hatred the *frondeurs* of Bordeaux felt for him. More important for our purposes, the *mazarinade* confirms the tenacious image of the captal as an uncivilized tyrant whose visible presence at the heart of the city in the Puy-Paulin was an offense to the city's dignity. This "Prince of resin and tar / Monarch of rays and soles / . . . Sovereign of quicksands" claimed to exercise his right of *clie* over the city's fish market while displaying a usurped grandeur: "If your principality makes us laugh / Your tyranny makes us weep."

Item 58: The bitterness and seriousness of the polemics of 1854–57 made the participants unable to see that the "proofs" they quarreled over might be humorous tales on a theme of little importance under the Ancien Régime. Laurière's mysterious localities of Persanni and Prelley may easily have been mischievous transpositions of two towns near Pontoise, Persan and Pierrelay, recognizable to Laurière's friends as the sites of domestic exploits of some opponent to whom he attributed lubricious tendencies.[13]

Another and less hypothetical case derives from the traditional jokes of law clerks—*la basoche*. Laurière, and the entire tradition of *cuissage* after him, recalls the famous tale of the curé of Bourges told by Nicolas Boyer (1469–1532), a jurist born in Montpellier who was named to a chair in law at the University of Bourges before becoming *président à mortier* of the Parlement de Bordeaux. In his *Decisiones* (with commentary) we find: "I have seen at the court of Bourges before the Metropolitan [the archbishop of Bourges] a suit in appeal in which a rector or parish priest claimed to have by custom first carnal knowledge of the bride; this custom was annulled and he was sentenced to [pay] a fine."[14] This tale quite obviously has not the least chance of being true. Even without considering the absurdity of the situation (a parish priest requesting his archbishop's approval of a right to practice adultery and spiritual incest), the curé could only have claimed enjoyment of the right to *cuissage* if he held a secular seigniory, where a religious court would have no jurisdiction. If the author of the tale was suggesting the existence of an ecclesiastical droit du seigneur, he was moving into a more complex realm (to which we shall return).

How can we explain the presence of this narrative in a serious treatise? This work was in fact not written by Boyer: It followed a widespread custom of honoring a great judge or lawyer on his retirement or after his death by publishing a collection of his opinions, sentences, and briefs in volumes variously called *Actions, Arrêts notables,* and the like. The *Decisiones Burdegalenses* appeared in 1551, twenty years after the death of President Boyer. No compiler is mentioned, but there is a foreword by one Jean Alesmius. In 1576 the jurist Charles Dumoulin commented, well before the affair of the curé of Bourges created such a stir, "Many things in these *Decisions* have been inserted to increase their volume; [they] do not come from the opinions of Nicolas Boyer, already well advanced in years, but are the allegations of young people [allegationes juvenum]."[15] Rather than seeing it simply as a filler to add more pages, we should probably credit the incident to the sense of humor of young jurists having fun attributing salacious anecdotes to the grave memory of their old master.

Items 63 and 52: Boyer (or Pseudo-Boyer) adds that the lords of Gascony had the right to place a bare leg across the newlyweds' bed. This strange detail, perhaps borrowed from the ritual for marriage by procuration, had a great success, and in the eighteenth century it lent the *droit de cuissage* its name. René Choppin, a distinguished late sixteenth-century jurist and lawyer, relates that the canons of the cathedral chapter of Lyons "who were at the same time counts of Lyons had the patronal right to 'place the thigh' [jus coxae locandae] on the bed . . . of subjects, male and female, contracting marriage on the first day of the conjugal union; that obscene obligation was changed into the gift of a banquet on the wedding day."[16] Thus seventeen out of the seventy-two "facts" reported by Delpit (nearly one-fourth of all cases) were humbugs. It is not sure, moreover, that he himself was fooled by these fictions: During his long discussion of the forgery of Saint-Amans, he not only refutes in minute detail the highly misleading accusations amassed by Veuillot and his clan but also takes care to distance himself from the suspect text "without pronouncing on the real value of this document, whose authenticity matters little to us."[17] What Delpit considers important is to show Veuillot's blind excess; indeed, Veuillot, ignoring the original date of publication of Saint-Amans's work, sees it as evidence of a liberal plot against the Duras family, the beneficiaries of *cuissage* in the forgery and the ancestors of a prominent figure in the Restoration government. For Delpit, a scholar who posed as a peasant from the Dordogne, the essential thing was to win over public opinion in a political combat he held to be a just cause.

It is hard to draw conclusions from this little anthology of legends about *cuissage* in the early modern age: Authors and circumstances seem too scattered to be fitted into any all-inclusive causality. The worlds of Boece, Ghilini, and Saint-Amans do not make up a coherent universe. The droit du seigneur was one theme among many available to anyone interested, for a variety of purposes, in the citation, recall, or pursuit of mythic creation. Only two names on the list of inventors—Laurière and Choppin—were men in the sure line of transmission of royal jurists and magistrates, a connection shown more by their recall and comparison of facts than by their active intervention on the corpus. We shall meet them both again, for their importance seems to grow with the construction of the myth.

Mistranspositions

A second group of items (nos. 9, 10, 51, and 53 on Delpit's list) are based on a distorted reality: The faithful contested certain levies the Church imposed on them when they married. The opposing parties in a famous case resulting in a series of suits before the Parlement de Paris between 1393 and 1409 were the municipalities of Amiens and Abbeville against the bishop of Amiens, who asserted the validity of a tax levied for dispensation from respect of three days of prescribed chastity at the beginning of a marriage. This affair is of capital importance and will be discussed at length later; for the moment it is enough to note that none of the four cases makes any mention of disguising an ecclesiastical *droit de cuissage* as a dispensatory tax. That interpretation appeared only later, in the sixteenth century.[18]

A third group of items is easily distinguished because it uses authentic documents of the thirteenth to seventeenth centuries to put together forty-one mentions of the due, real or symbolic, a subject had to pay his lord at the marriage of his daughter. Most of these texts come from the publication of seigniorial documents from 1841 to 1857 by Mazure and Hatoulet, Bouthors, Delisle, and Beaurepaire. In his version Delpit amalgamates these cases skillfully, lending social credence and day-to-day concreteness to the great scandalous and legendary examples of ancien régime tradition. One might put under this same heading the Bollandists' unjustified interpretations of *bathinodium* examined above (items 41 and 42).[19] None of these texts mentions the *droit de cuissage*, but Delpit and his successors considered the dues in question to be payments replacing the *jus primae noctis,* a possibility explicitly stated in four or five texts. One of these forty-one innocent occurrences, dated 1507 and borrowed from Bouthors, is interesting because it introduces the word *cullage* (I have restored within brackets portions of the original text tendentiously omitted by Delpit): "The lord of Barlin had several handsome rights [privileges, and prerogatives over all men and tenants], among them a certain right of *cullage*, which is such that all women who hold fief from him, each and as many times as they marry or change husband [they or their said husbands] are held to pay for the said fiefs limited *reliefs* and *coteries* of one-sixth of their value. Of the which right of *cullage* the said lord of Barlin is held to give equal right to Madame de Humbercourt (item 3)."[20] This is a classic case of a tax on *formariage*. When a female subject married a man who did not belong to the lord, she deprived him of seigniorial rights over their offspring, who passed to the husband's lord or, if the husband was a freeman, were no longer dependent. We shall return to marital taxation in chapter 5—a question complicated by the various types of dependence and by paternal or maternal transmission of dependency. I might note here that one-sixth of a dependent's wealth corresponded roughly to the price of personal emancipation. When the religious communities held dominion over land, they could demand the same tax (item 2). The documents call this right *cullage* (items 2, 3, 19), *regards* (items 15, 26–29, 31), *droictures* (item 16), or *gerson* (item 13). In most cases the marriage of a female dependent involved a payment ranging from 18 deniers to 60 sous parisis. Comparative values are unimportant for the moment, because the documentation covers too broad a span of times and places for them to be comparable.

In other circumstances payment was only symbolic, or else monetary and symbolic forms were combined. Delisle gives a number of authentic examples. In 1400, when a subject of Étienne de Saint-Martin married in his fief of Saint-Martin (near Étrépagny in Normandy), he demanded a share of the wedding banquet and performance of an act equivalent to renewal of homage: "Item: when anyone marries in the said fief, he owes a cut of meat, two loaves of bread, and two jugs of wine, the same for the bride's fief, and it must be brought to the hostelry in the company of musicians playing fiddles."[21]

Elsewhere a new groom was subjected to a festive and sporting trial (the famous *droit de quaintaine*). In 1303 the lord of Branville, in the viscounty of Coutances, stated: "And my vavasors—that is, those who marry—are all obliged to joust on horses and strike a target with a lance with a full handle until each one has broken a lance or falls to the ground, and everyone who falls [will pay] a fine of 18 sous, and those who will not joust [will give] 18 *res* of oats, and these proceedings are called *quictaines.*"[22]

Delisle's chapter on marriage includes other attestations of the infinite variations on this late medieval ritual. Its point is obvious: As subjection became less and less a fiscal reality, the lord had to be content with a joking or humiliating ritual that made a public show of a fossilized form of a dependence by then long gone. These seigniorial practices certainly had some connection with the folk customs reflected in letters of remission that Dom Carpentier noted in the same age. Structurally speaking, the lord occupied the same place as the youth abbey or the unmarried village men *(varlets)*. Before the new family nucleus closed, the community being left behind (the bachelors or the former suzerain) marked this departure as negotiated by social control in the form of a personal act. Obviously, all intermediate stages existed between rigorous extraction of a high tax on marriage and purely formal seigniorial folklore. That genuine taxation could occur on occasion is richly exemplified by a famous suit brought before the Parlement de Paris in 1601, to which we shall return in chapter 7.

Five Troublesome Proofs

Once the seventeen legendary sources, the four cases of ecclesiastical taxes, and the forty-two mentions of seigniorial levies have been set aside, only eight items remain in the dossier. We can eliminate two items that Delpit never should have put on his list. Item 14, borrowed from Delisle, does not concern marriage. It is a donation made by Harculf de Soligné in favor of the local monastic community. The monks renounce all services from their subjects except the *cens* and probably the *corvée (servicia)*, "which [the abbot] himself judged unenforceable because of the honor of our order [pro honestate nostri ordinis]." This sort of monastic renunciation, although not systematic, can be found here and there in cartularies; it seems very forced to see it as a renunciation of a right to *cuissage.*[23] Item 61 is no more relevant: It regards a trial ritual set up by a lord in the Limousin who, once every seven years, had his peasants elect a *roi de la tirevesse* (a break-wind king) who was put to all sorts of difficult and humorous tests. This early seventeenth-century text, though fascinating to anthropologists, belongs at the limit under the heading of the "abusive rights" of late feudalism. There is such doubt connected with the "proof" in item 8 concerning the right to *braconnage* that it too should be eliminated. As we have seen in chapter 2, both Julien Brodeau and Dom Carpentier made much of the documents backing this allegation, but no documents are to be found.

When these three items are eliminated, five proofs remain. Given their importance I shall give their texts at length. The authenticity of these documents, still preserved in the Archives Nationales and the Archives Départementales of the Somme, the Pyrénées Atlantiques, and the Manche, is beyond question.

In 1419 the lord of La Rivière-Bourdet, in Normandy, declared: "In the said place I also have the right to take from my men and others, when they marry in my land, 10 sous tournois and a loin of pork from the whole spine up to the ear, and the tail generously included in that loin, with a gallon of whatever drink there is to be at the meals, or I can and I must, if it please me, go to lie with the bride in the case that either her husband or someone sent by him not pay to me or my representative one of the things declared above."[24]

On 28 September 1507 the lord of Rambures in Picardy proclaimed:

> When any of the subjects, male or female, of the said locality of Drucat marry (and the celebration and wedding take place at the said place of Drucat), the husband cannot lie the first night with his wedded lady without the acceptance, permission, and authority of the said lord; or else the said lord will have lain with the said wedded lady; in order to obtain dispensation of which the said husband is held to present a platter of meat (of the sort eaten at the said wedding), with two *los* of beverage (of the sort drunk at the said wedding) and the said right is called right of *cullage* (and the said lord and his predecessors have enjoyed the said right of *cullage* from time immemorial, so there is no memory to the contrary).[25]

The first of two seigniorial declarations drawn up in Béarn in 1538 and written in the local dialect states:

> In order to satisfy the command made to the nobles and to those who hold lands nobly in the territory of Béarn by you, Illustrious Reverend Father in God, Monsignor Jacques de Foix, bishop of Lescar, chancellor of Foix and of Béarn, first and great almoner and lieutenant general of the most high and all-powerful Henri, by the grace of God king of Navarre, sovereign lord of Béarn, the commissioner expressly deputized by the said lord to receive the homages and censuses [dénombrements] of the nobles in the said land of Béarn, the noble Augier, lord of the noble house, the domain, and the country house [gentilhommerie] of the locality of Bizanos and its dependencies, gives his present census in which he makes declaration and specification of the goods and things by him held and possessed in the present territory of Béarn, as lord above-

mentioned, for which reason he is held to make homage and oath of loyalty to the said lord of Béarn. First, he says that he holds and possesses and is immediate lord and possessor of the said locality of Bizanos.... Furthermore, as in times past and as everyone knows, in the said place and in the said seigniory dependents were subjected to, and the lords of that place, predecessors to the writer of [this] census, had the right, authority, and preeminence, every time that a wedding was held in the said locality of Bizanos, to sleep at their pleasure with brides on the first night of the said wedding; but, among his predecessors and the said subjects, that subjection was converted into another tribute: He, both in his own right and by his said predecessors, has the right to have, to take, and to conserve what the above-mentioned subjects are held to and have the usage and custom to give and to carry to his house, every time that there is a wedding, to wit, a hen or capon and a shoulder of mutton and two loaves of bread or a flat bread [fouasse] and two bowls of drink [bibaraou]. Petition is made to you, my said lord lieutenant and commissioner, to maintain him in his said rights, nobility, and possession: the said writer of this census offers to do homage and swear fidelity and to furnish to the said lord sovereign, in case of war, what he shall be commanded according to the cartularies and archives of the said lord, and in all [other] points as is expected of a good vassal and subject.

Augier de Bizanos[26]

One of Augier de Bizanos's successors, Jacques de Vignau, lord of Bizanos, repeated the same declaration in a *dénombrement* dated 12 October 1674:

Item: in times past the said subjects were in such subjection that the predecessors of the said census-writer had the right, whenever and as many times as they took a wife in marriage, to lie with the bride the night closest to the wedding. This duty has been converted, however, by his said predecessors into another, to wit, that the subjects are held and obliged, every time that a wedding is held in the said place, to bring him a hen, a capon, a shoulder of mutton, two loaves of bread or a cake, and three bowls of a sort of porridge popularly called *bibaraou.*

The second occurrence in Béarn makes more stringent demands:

In order to satisfy the order and command made to the nobles and to those who nobly hold possessions in the present territory and seigniory of Béarn ... Noble Jean, lord of Louvie-Soubiron, of Listo, of La Sauvetat, and of Buziet ... gives his census, in which are declared and specified the goods and the things held and possessed by him in the present territory and supreme seigniory of Béarn ... in reason of which he must and is held to do homage and swear fidelity to the lord of Béarn. And first I, noble Jean de Louvie ... recognize that I am the man, subject, and liege vassal of the lord king as sovereign of Béarn.... Furthermore, that when the people of these houses [the nine houses of Aas, now

Eaux-Bonnes] marry, before being united with their bride, they are held to present her, the first night, to the same lord of Louvie in order that he do his pleasure with her, or else to give him their value or tribute. Furthermore, for each child they may engender they are held to pay a certain sum of money. And if it should happen that the firstborn is a male child, he is free because he could have been engendered by the works of the said lord of Louvie on the said first night and of his said pleasure. The above things being seen and weighed. . .I petition you that it please you to leave them in the state and the liberty in which they have been to the present, are at present, and should be; and you will do good and do justice as is proper of a good lord toward his subject.

Jean de Louvie[27]

The Veuillot clan and later erudition found these texts highly embarrassing. Their authenticity is beyond question. Admittedly, none of these sources presents the *droit de cuissage* without also mentioning its indemnification by money or gifts. Still the origin of that substitution cannot be eluded. The geographical dispersion of the sources (Béarn, Normandy, Picardy) makes it impossible to see these events as specific or marginal aberrations. On the other hand, how could such a right have left so few traces?

The nature of the source may help to clarify the mystery. All are *aveux et dénombrements.* In the theoretical feudal system (an abstraction rarely realized), an *aveu* or an *aveu et dénombrement* was a text in which a vassal enumerated everything he held under the authority of his suzerain; it included complete mention of all revenues, quitrents *(cens)* responsibilities, and miscellaneous rights attached to his lands. The document declares the present state of a situation in relation to a superior to whom the lord owed services, but also in relation to inferiors who were sources of revenue. In a rigorous system (scarcely ever realized except at a high level of territorial organization, notably in the crown domains and the great principalities), a *dénombrement* had to be verified and registered by a chancery or a chamber of accounts to be valid. The customal of Vaudémont in Lorraine clearly describes the validation process for these documents (the bracketed portions are explanatory additions):

> The vassal's *dénombrement,* verified and received by the Chambre des Comptes, [acts as proof in favor of the vassal who drew it up in an eventual legal contention with his suzerain, who had it verified and by that token accepted it], and against the vassal toward all [the elements of the text, because they come from his pen, can be used against the writer of the *dénombrement* if he should go beyond the limits he himself has fixed]; but it can have no consequence or profit for the said vassal against other persons not heard or consenting.[28]

Louis Servin made the same point when he argued a case regarding seigniorial rights (to which we will return) before the Parlement de Paris in 1601: How could a subject submit to a rule he had no knowledge of, given that verification involved only the suzerain-vassal relation?

The *dénombrement* was a document that expired if it was not renewed periodically. The courts usually required a document drawn up within the last thirty years. Actual practice seems another matter: Far from the chanceries and the centers of power few censuses were drawn up. For example, we have a clear idea of the situation in Auvergne in the seventeenth century, thanks to the archives of the Grands Jours:[29] The lords themselves seldom thought to draw up an *aveu* and even less to renew it in due time. Often they did not even know this was necessary. Minor lords might draw up a *dénombrement* without having it verified or keep documents of no value. They were quick to argue bitterly when conflict arose, however, evoking the weight of tradition and hoping that in case of litigation an invalid *dénombrement* was better than no parchment at all. The archives of the Cour des Comptes also contain unverified and rejected *aveux:* The fact that a document was kept by no means implied registration or informal legitimation. The two *dénombrements* from Béarn end with a petition to the chancellor and the king of Navarre, overlord of Béarn, to register the document, but there is no trace of such registration, though late medieval chanceries and the courts had a tendency to keep everything. A *dénombrement* was part of a negotiation: A lord made protestations of loyalty, recognized his obligations, and stated his expected revenues; he hoped the chancery would accept the whole declaration, registering it without examining too closely what the lord was extracting from his subjects in items listed well below the services and dues he owed his overlord.

The special structure of this source explains the few cases of aberrant claims. In chapter 2 we have seen an extraordinary but authentic example of a similar document involving a right of *cognage* in Chauny where permission to cross a bridge was paid in pubic hairs. These fantasies were not limited to the sexual domain but applied to all the "bizarre rights" of the Ancien Régime. Their importance should not be exaggerated: The French national and departmental archives contain tens of thousands of *dénombrements,* and enormous numbers of documents were solemnly destroyed during the French Revolution. The aberrant documents are very few: Four for the *droit de cuissage,* twenty or so for some truly bizarre rights, perhaps a few dozen fairly odd claims. Scrutiny of the entire corpus—an unthinkable task—would probably turn up other cases, but my reading of inventories and an occasional sounding of the archives persuade me that they are extremely rare.[30] The typical *dénombrement* is a minutely detailed, sober summary of the state of taxes and revenues.

How are we to explain the exceptions, the four claims to the *droit de cuissage* in particular? We have already seen that when the relation of land domination or personal domination is viewed in terms of folk culture, there is a tendency to interpret the customs and signs of symbolic compromise in sexual terms. The mention of a deferred participation in the wedding feast clearly shows the cultural proximity in small domains where differences in wealth between the lord and the peasants might be slight. More precisely, the allusions to *bibaraou* in the Bizanos *dénombrement* and *breuvaigne* in Normandy correspond to the *chaudel* or *cochet* of peasant folklore. The dependent, under threat of gross and terrible consequences, had to give his "chick" *(béjaune)* to the lord. Moreover, as we shall see in chapter 5, it became increasingly difficult to justify or enforce *formariage* payments.

We can imagine that in a milieu of country squires both close to peasant culture and eager to set themselves off from the peasantry, a mixture of fierce ambition, ribaldry, boasting, fabrication, and mockery went into the preparation of *aveux et dénombrements*. The "P 300" series in the French National Archives, which contains an enormous number of these documents, reads like a scene in a village Café des Sports at seven in the evening: men converse gravely; once in a while someone boasts of his exploits, an off-color joke is told to enhance the teller's own reputation for sexual prowess, threats are exchanged, then everyone goes away peaceably and returns to work in the morning.

Still, we must guard against restricting our view of seigniorial exactions to this idyllic scenario. Participation in a common culture did not exclude cases of genuine social brigandage backed by violence. Seventeenth-century Auvergne will soon provide us with a convincing illustration of this. But rape did not need legitimation through *cuissage*.

Dénombrements in Picardy and Béarn shed light on the nature of this source. The situation in Picardy in the early sixteenth century seems to have been quite different from that of Béarn, but the effects were similar. In November 1505 a conflict broke out between the city government (the mayor's office and the *échevins* of the city council) of Amiens and the king's representative, one Saint-Delys, lieutenant general of the *bailliage*, over a question concerning royal jurisdiction over the city. The affair was brought before the Parlement de Paris. Sieur de La Grutuze, the governor of Picardy, offered his services as mediator. On 14 January 1507 the case was argued before King Louis XII in a session of the Grand Conseil. On 2

June 1507, despite the opposition of the Parlement, a royal edict dated 2 April 1507 was registered, ordering a general inquiry into the various rights in practice in the *bailliage* of Amiens. The various lords in the area hastened to draw up the "customs" mentioned in the title of Alexandre Bouthors's *Coutumes locales du bailliage d'Amiens* (1845), which was not a summary of customs but a collection of *aveux et dénombrements*.

The texts resulting from the royal order were to be examined by an assembly of the three estates called for 2 October 1507, but the royal edict had been circulated late in the summer, leaving only a month to prepare the statements. Saint-Delys refused to verify these declarations, however, and ordered a global, coherent compilation of general customs, a task completed 25 June 1508 and approved in 1513. The bundle of documents produced in September 1507—four hundred heterogeneous texts, never verified (a nearly impossible operation given their disparity)—was thrown into a chest in the audience hall of the *bailliage,* where they remained until the eighteenth century, when the Benedictine Dom Grenier exhumed them and had them moved to the archives. This was a century before Bouthors thought of publishing them. A reading of these so-called *coutumes* of 1507 gives a good idea of how exorbitant the writers' claims could be when they padded the list of their rights and multiplied their assurances of loyalty in the naive hope that their rights would be registered officially. Mentions of rights of *formariage,* quite numerous for a region where personal subjection no longer existed, reflect tactics of this sort. The myth of *cuissage,* which appears in one case out of four hundred, is simply an isolated case of raising the stakes in a cacophonic pursuit of individual interests.

THE CASE OF BÉARN

The texts produced by the lords of Bizanos and Louvie-Soubiron were written in response to a vast inquiry launched in 1534 by Jacques de Foix, bishop of Lescar and chancellor of the county of Béarn for Henri II d'Albret. In 1517 Henri II (1503–55) had succeeded his mother, Catherine de Foix, queen of Navarre (a kingdom reduced to Basse-Navarre by the annexation of southern Navarre to the crown of Aragon and Castile in 1512). The young king, who spent his adolescence and youth at the court of Francis I and married Francis's sister Marguerite d'Angoulême in 1527, set out to modernize his principality on the model of the kingdom of France. Modernization meant gaining tighter control over the nobility of Béarn and restricting local liberties. In 1519 Alain d'Albret, Henri II's grandfather (who administered the viscounty for him), created a sovereign council that absorbed a good share of the prerogatives of the États de Béarn, a venerable institution founded in the late fourteenth century. In 1551 the king of Navarre ordered a new compilation of the *fors* (customs) of Béarn, a move that also cut into the power of the États. The call for *dénombrements* in 1534 (which was connected with the creation of the Chambre des Comptes in 1520 and its further organization in 1535) should be understood in the context of these moves to gain better control over a highly independent nobility and to subject it to state control. Above all, the sovereign of Béarn, not a wealthy man, was seeking a way to improve his own revenues. He succeeded. Between 1531 and 1551 (thus after the *dénombrements*) the viscount's revenues doubled (from 11,676 écus to 21,468 écus), simply by the reinstatement of revenues that had been forgotten or usurped.[31] Understandably, he considered the detail of relations between the lords under him and their own subjects less important than specification of the revenues due the sovereign from the lords.

A strong threat accompanied the letter patent of 8 October 1534: It informed the commissioners charged with organizing the inquiry that territories not under direct seigniory, as proven by witnesses or documents, were to be returned to direct county control. Customs of dependence varied enormously and had shifted since the end of the Middle Ages, so they were not easy to prove. The *dénombrement*, a technique in use nearly everywhere in France since the thirteenth century, does not seem to have been current practice in Béarn. Jean de Louvie-Soubiron says as much himself at the end of his *dénombrement* of 1538: "Considering that presenting a *dénombrement* is a new and unusual thing in the present land and seigniory of Béarn, in the case of some omission having been made in the present *dénombrement*, the said deponent promises to amplify, correct, amend, and put it in proper form within the space of one year and one day, as accorded by you."[32] The nobility thus reacted by attempting to grant itself the greatest possible privileges. Still, the texts from Bizanos and Louvie-Soubiron stand out as odd among the dozens of *dénombrements* preserved in the departmental archives at Pau.

The seigniory of Bizanos, one of the twelve baronies of Béarn, was immediately outside Pau. The inventory of his goods taken after the death of Baron Augier de Bizanos, who submitted the 1538 *dénombrement*, shows his estate to have been quite modest, however: a manor house and 3 other houses, some 40 hectares of land (half of it fallow), a mill, 2 teams of oxen, 2 horses, 14 pigs, 35 geese, 17 capons, 12 hens, a rooster, and little more. Like many Béarnais nobles, Augier de Bizanos lived like a wealthy peasant. The inventory of household goods lists a few tools, coffers, and some barrels of wine, but no luxury objects. He married twice, which probably helped his finances somewhat, but he seems to have benefited more from his revenues from the *dime* of Pau, one-half of which he held (Pau was at the time a small town) and from *créances* (promissory notes) in which he had invested the *douaire* of his first wife, who died in 1544. Not many years later the barony passed to Mathieu du Pac, a man close to Henri II d'Albret, a doctor of laws, president of the sovereign council, future chancellor of Navarre, and a member of the commission that worked for the new compilation of the *Fors* in 1551.[33] Baron Augier—a man half peasant, half merchant, and the last of a dying lineage—is a good illustration of a pauperized lord who creates or maintains a festive rituality in his contacts with his tenant farmers partly as a game, partly to show his superiority to them. The text of his declaration lays claim to no more than a share of the wedding banquet, a demand barely distinguishable from those of the youth abbeys.

Some of the persuasiveness of the Béarn case comes from reinforcement by the text from Louvie-Soubiron, a strangely violent document. We know more about the circumstances in Louvie-Soubiron, thanks to a series of suits continuing into the mid-nineteenth century, but also thanks to the special status of the village.[34] It is a story worth telling, as it combines the strongest expression of a claim to *cuissage* and the best-documented context. Moreover, historians of *cuissage*—including scholarly circles in Béarn—have never considered this context. Even Paul Raymond, a great archivist, let his antifeudal convictions keep him from exploring the circumstances of this text.

The villages of Louvie-Soubiron and Aas, whose strong rivalry is reflected in the 1538 *dénombrement* of Jean de Louvie-Soubiron, lie in the high valley of the Gave Ossau, a river system that carves a path north from the Pyrenees from the crest (the Somport and Pourtalet passes and the Pic du Midi d'Ossau) to the Béarn piedmont south of Pau. Some twenty-five village communities lie along forty kilometers or so, squeezed in between the mountains and the limestone plateaus. From extremely early times they formed a strong unit, largely because they all raised sheep and cattle and practiced transhumance. The Val d'Ossau, a densely populated strip opening up to the south into vast high pastures, has little arable land aside from a few meager terraces. Immense herds of livestock were led to high pasture in summer and down to the plains in winter. The sheep might be taken far into Aquitaine but the cattle, the valley's chief wealth, were taken to the Pont-Long, a vast heath near Pau that the mountain people claimed to own. They showed astonishing obstinacy in claiming ownership of a moor so far from their valley: An agreement between Pau and Ossau concerning the Pont-Long is documented as early as 1278, but their ownership, claimed in a petition to Jeanne d'Artois in 1319, was recognized only in a suit settled in 1829. Through the ages the people of the Val d'Ossau vigilantly defended their *lande* near Pau and their pasturage, if need be descending from the upper valley in armed bands or seizing the animals that strayed over the borders in accordance with a right of *carnal* (seizure of livestock) that the courts of Béarn reaffirmed at regular intervals. As late as the 1960s the city of Pau continued to avoid setting building projects on that great stretch of uncultivated land.[35]

Throughout that long period the summer pastures and the trails to the winter pasture lands remained collective property, in part controlled by a valley organization whose seat or capital was at Bielle, not far from Louvie-Soubiron (where laboriously collected archives are kept in the church of Saint-Vivien de Bielle). These remarkable cartularies from the Val d'Ossau were edited by Pierre Tucoo-Chala, a scholar who possesses vast knowledge of Béarn. Other pasture lands belonged to the various communities and were subject to precise rules.[36]

The Val d'Ossau was brought into the viscounty of Béarn in the eleventh century, at the same time as the viscounty of Oloron, but it retained a high degree of autonomy, recognized by the *For d'Ossau* of 1221. The Universitat of the Ossau villages did not need to consult the viscount to conclude treaties on *lies et passeries* (governing pasturage and transhumance) with the Aragonese valleys on the southern slopes of the Pyrenees. A small mountain republic calling to mind a Swiss canton, the valley created its own political identity. Each community chose *jurats* who served one-year terms; the Universitat delegated one of these to settle questions internal to the valley and to negotiate—amiably or through the courts—matters that arose with the viscounty or the communities and lords of the piedmont and the plains. The valley's almost total autonomy was further enhanced by the nearly complete absence of church institutions (there was only an extremely modest hospital in Gabas in the upper valley).

What were relations like between Aas and Louvie-Soubiron during the Middle Ages? The two communities lay only a few kilometers apart on either side of the Cauceigt, a small west-running stream that joins the Gave d'Ossau. Aas, oriented toward the north, got less sun, and its meager fields and meadows petered out at a lower altitude. Both communities were small: In the census ordered by Gaston Phébus in 1389 Louvie-

Soubiron had 9 *feux allumant* and Aas, 16. Estimating the number of inhabitants on the basis of this information is not an easy task, as the term *feu allumant* designated the head of the house and master of the *oustau* (household), which might include several younger siblings. There were also inhabitants of a village whose humble status excluded them from the *oustau* structure. Still, comparison with neighboring communities (Bielle, the capital of the valley, had 82 *feux allumant*, and the larger community of Laruns had 114) emphasizes the smallness of our two villages, which perhaps had populations of 80 and 150 people, respectively. Unlike the lower Ossau valley and Laruns, Aas and Louvie-Soubiron had population figures that remained quite steady: A *dénombrement* of 1546 notes 11 *feux* (hearths) at Louvie and 15 at Aas. In the little "republic" of the Ossau, relations between the two villages do not seem to have posed any special problem. Between 1338 and 1492 sixteen documents mention that *jurats* from the two communities were present or voted by proxy when decisions were taken by the Universitat.

How could the inhabitants of nine households in Aas be claimed to be under servitude in 1538? Clearly, there was no hierarchical relation between the two communities, which were equal partners in the life of Val d'Ossau, where feudal relations were unknown because the near total absence of arable land provided no base for feudalism. The villagers' entire wealth was in livestock, and their collective use and protection of pasture lands circumvented any feudal confiscation. Their dependence on the viscounty was not fiscal: The counts of Foix dispensed the passage of animals in the valley from all payment of tolls, and the viscounts preferred to take part in the pastoral exploitation of the valley by sending their own herds there. The viscount's suzerainty was limited to the castle of Castet in the lower valley (the valley's inhabitants later obtained its gradual dismantling) and a *service d'ost* of 150 men-at-arms who served under precise and limited conditions. The viscounty relied above all on the valley's economic strength, for example in contracts for *gazaille* permitting the people of the plains and the piedmont to send herds to high pasture in the Ossau in exchange for rights to a proportion of the livestock.

There was a strong internal hierarchy, however, created by a type of lordship peculiar to Val d'Ossau. A strict mode of succession held in the valley (and in what has been called "Pyrenees law"), according full rights of succession to the eldest child, male or female, to the detriment of younger siblings. The system gave the *oustaux*, or households, a remarkable stability. Younger sons emigrated or became shepherds, eventually building up a sizable herd and, in the best of cases, marrying an heiress.

Thus every community had a strong internal hierarchy, both patriarchal and social, of *casalers naturaus* (house owners), *casalers ceysous* (homeowners who had acquired their house and who paid a *cens*), *boyoyers* (subject to *cens*), and *nouveaux poublants* (newcomers to the valley). Certain wealthy and influential heads of house gradually obtained title to a lordship connected with possession of a noble house or *domenjadure*. In the age of Gaston Phébus seven of the communities had a noble house: Sainte-Colome and Louvie-Juzon in Bas-Ossau; Béon, Louvie-Soubiron, Béost, Assouste, and Espalungue in Haut-Ossau. These seigniories were extremely limited, however, having no right of justice; their status as seigniories does not appear to have implied any suzerainty. Serfdom seems never to have existed in the Val d'Ossau.

Aas may have suffered from the presence of the two seigniories of Louvie-Soubiron and Béost in the Cauceigt valley. In the fifteenth century the Universitat marked out the pasture lands, assigning portions to the various communities: The pasturage of Ger, for example, belonged to Aas, and in 1440 it was distinguished from the pastures of Anouillas, which belonged to the Universitat. The two communities with a lord may have enlarged their shares of pasturage to the detriment of Aas. In 1853–55, when the Haut-Ossau divided up the common pasturage, then known as the Montagnes Générales, the three communities on the Cauceigt had joint use of the pasturage of Art; unlike Aas, however, Béost and Louvie-Soubiron had other pasture lands they could exploit. When Henri Cavaillès was studying transhumance in the Pyrenees in 1928, only four communes—Castet, Laruns, Béost, and Louvie-Soubiron—had enough summer pasturage to continue to receive herds from outside the valley. The two communities near Aas were thus in a stronger position regarding pasturage than the valley as a whole.[37]

As Aas grew poorer and was increasingly threatened by its neighbors' ambition, it withdrew, de facto, from the Ossau federation. This is confirmed by its inability to remain a commune: In the sixteenth century it was attached to the new town of Eaux-Bonnes, which thrived on its exploitation of thermal waters.

Still, there is a large step between a conjectural decline of Aas and the state of servitude implied in the 1538 *dénombrement*. It is made more plausible by the withdrawal of the lords of Louvie-Soubiron from the economic milieu of the Val d'Ossau. In 1518 the lord of Louvie-Soubiron (probably François, the father of the Jean who signed the 1538 *dénombrement*) hired workers from Spain to construct a forge in the Catalan style so he could manufacture iron from ore mined in the nearby Ouzon Valley and sell it in Morlaas, Oloron, Tarbes, and Lourdes. The absence of subsequent documentation suggests that neither the mine nor the forge remained in operation for long. This attempt to launch the Val d'Ossau into the modern world had perhaps been inspired by the viscounty, since in 1547 the king sponsored the installation of another forge to treat silver-bearing lead at Gère-Bélesten, not far from Louvie-Soubiron (a venture soon recognized as unprofitable by the Chambre des Comptes of Béarn). After his father had failed as an industrialist, Jean de Louvie-Soubiron turned to another type of "modernity" by attempting to reconstruct his domain on the model of late feudalism and taxing his unhappy neighbors in Aas. The fiction of serfdom and *cuissage* may have been a foundation narrative aimed at obliterating centuries of Val d'Ossau political culture.[38]

Who was supposed to be fooled by this bawdy tale? Probably not the inhabitants of Aas, who continued to pursue their ancestral pastoral practices until the twentieth century; probably not the viscount's men, who cared little about the management of a domain that brought in no revenues (nor did the village of Aas). More probably Jean de Louvie-Soubiron was attempting to patch together a feudal fiction in view of negotiating the sale of the seigniory, selling seigniorial rights, or constituting a dowry. Beginning in the sixteenth century Béarnais nobles with little land and little ready cash pursued something resembling real estate and matrimonial speculation. The end of the story corroborates this version: Aas continued to be subjected to repeated but vain fiscal pressures.

But to return to the *dénombrement* of 1538: The document shows every sign of a combination of haste, anxiety concerning the viscounty's investigation, and eagerness to profit from an opportunity for feudal "promotion." On 1 September 1534, a month before the arrival of the letter patent requiring the *dénombrement*, Jean de Louvie-Soubiron drew up a written statement of mutual fidelity that he should have made when he took possession of the domain at the death of his father, François. He excuses his tardiness with some embarrassment, stating that he had not had time. It is in fact that oath, with its few indications of seigniorial rights, that was registered with the Sovereign Council in Béarn on 30 October 1538, not the *dénombrement* dated 27 January 1538. The latter had indeed been received by the commission of the Chambre des Comptes, but the *procureur*, one Deufour, noted reservations regarding it, though without giving particulars. Jean de Louvie had thus made exaggerated claims in the hope of negotiating a compromise during the grace period of a year and a day before the document had to be registered or rejected. The negotiations obviously failed, and the compromise was to accept the text of the oath as the charter to the seigniory.

The text of the *dénombrement*, which abounds in various rights of justice, control over pasture lands, and more, gives no figures for *cens* or dues—a sign either of haste or of lack of legal training. The passage on the *droit de cuissage*, unlike the document from Bizanos, offers no details concerning symbolic marriage dues. The situation seems to have differed in the two localities: In Bizanos, at the gates of Pau, the text stresses "folklore," and a detailed description of terms implies that the lord both participated in the wedding festivities and dominated them, though no money was paid. The sexual threat is on the order of a mendacious provocation.

In Louvie the half-frightening, half-facetious Bizanos ritual seems to give way to brutal exclusion. The paragraph preceding the mention of *cuissage* justifies this harsh treatment by stating, "They are called and named in the popular tongue and from earliest antiquity the Bragaris of Louvie." The term *Bragari* appears nowhere else; it probably has some connection with the root of the Béarnais verb *braga* (to act proudly, to boast) and its derivatives, *bragardise* (impudent boastfulness) and *bragar* (a person who creates confusion).[39] The expression "Bragaris de Louvie" has a dual thrust: It annexes Aas by denying the village a specific identity, and it marginalizes its population. It recalls the fabrication of a race of *cagots* in medieval Béarn (analyzed by Alain Guerreau and Yves Guy), allegedly the descendants of lepers, who were subjected to rigorous segregation in certain trades and quarters of the town and had separate places in church.[40] The lord of Louvie-Soubiron might have attempted to play an individual game of putting social pressure on his neighbors, as the Béarnais lords of the plain and the piedmont had been doing for centuries.

The mountain valleys of Béarn, which, as we have seen, had no feudal structures, did not have any great acquaintance with *cagots*. We would have to ascertain (but how?) that the pastoral society of the Val d'Ossau had no caste model of the sort. Henri Cavaillès states that a group of men who specialized in castrating cattle lived in the village of Bilhères, just down the valley from Louvie-Soubiron. These men were called *crestadous*, a word that irresistibly recalls *chrestiaas*, an earlier term for *cagots*.[41] Moreover, the lord of Louvie-Soubiron also owned land in Buzy, near Oloron, where there are several attestations of the presence of *cagots* from the fourteenth century on.[42]

One might object that the figures are disproportionate and that the segregation of the *cagots* is out of all measure with Jean de Louvie-

Soubiron's claim to have a right to sexual promiscuity. The history of slavery has accustomed us to mixtures of proclaimed revulsion and actual attraction. The archives attest to the collective rape of *cagot* women by a troop of soldiers in the sixteenth century.[43] Be that as it may, the 1538 attempt to turn the village of Aas into a *cagot* colony failed, and any attempt to give ideological coherence to social fantasies practiced by one man in one *oustau* of the Val d'Ossau seems an exercise in futility.

The later history of Louvie throws some light on what happened to both the 1538 document and the inhabitants of Aas. The seigniory, which passed to the Incamps family, figures in a *dénombrement* dated 2 November 1674 and registered on 24 November 1676. The only documents to back up lordship were the 1534 oath and a lost *dénombrement* of 1612. There are traces of another *dénombrement* made on 24 March 1702 and registered on 12 July 1708, probably when the seigniory passed into the hands of the family of the marquis d'Argosse.

The most interesting episode, however, is a suit brought before the Parlement de Navarre, decided on 15 April 1756, between the *jurats* of Louvie and the marquis d'Argosse. In 1667 the lord of Louvie sold his rights to the village community in exchange for an annuity of 600 livres. Since that date the inhabitants of Aas had obstinately refused to pay anything. This is perhaps proof that those rough mountain people considered themselves free and exempt from all taxation from time immemorial. If so, the ferocious text of 1538 could be read as invective against obstinate recalcitrants.[44]

The *jurats* turned against the lord, claiming they could no longer pay; they demanded that he have his rights verified or guarantee the revenues himself, lowering rents. They state that the 1538 *dénombrement* is the only available document founding their obligations in principle, but add that it fails to state the amounts or confirm the legitimacy of those dues. In ordinary times and for a routine *dénombrement*, the lords omitted all mention of the bizarre 1538 document, taking it out of the seigniorial archives only when they wanted to enhance a sale price. The Parlement decided in favor of the *jurats*, obliging the inhabitants of Aas to pay what had become a communal tax. State taxation was instituted not long after.

If we wanted to generalize on the basis of this contextual explanation of the 1538 document, we would need to examine the tactics used and the sexual content of the arguments in the small number of documents claiming the existence of a *droit de cuissage* in France beginning in the mid-thirteenth century. Analysis of the situation in the Val d'Ossau proves that these were bawdy provocations or strong threats rather than rights or traditions. Ritual menace seems to have played a large part in the construction of power in the Ancien Régime. In a recent book on the representations of power in biblical glosses of the central Middle Ages, Philippe Buc shows that in medieval political discourse the management of the *potestas* implied exhibition of its more terrifying side, notably as the monarch's anger *(ira)*. Buc follows Otto Brunner to cite an astonishing text of Jean de Viktring (1336): When the dukes of Carinthia came to power, they had an "incendiary, said to be juridically named for that purpose, who set fires in order to elicit a respectful terror toward the prince [pro reverentia principis]."[45]

The sexuality of power is clear from a gloss of Pierre le Mangeur (late twelfth century) quoted by Philippe Buc. In a passage in his *Historia scolastica* Pierre comments on the status of woman after the fall (Genesis 3.16): "You will be under the power of the male. Under the violent power, to such a point that he will even inflict wounds on you by deflowering you. For now, after the Fall, the female, who was before submissive to the male out of love, is subject by condition and out of fear."[46] Male power meant social power and vice versa. André le Chapelain's *De amore* (early twelfth century) offers a crude example of this principle. In the first part of this work he presents various ways to court a woman according to her social condition. The short chapter on "love of peasants" gives the following advice:

> In case you think that our earlier discussion on the love of commoners is applicable to farmers, I briefly append for you a note about the love of peasants. I maintain that farmers can scarcely ever be found serving in Love's court. They are impelled to acts of love in the natural way like a horse or a mule, just as nature's pressure directs them. So for a farmer regular toil and the continuing uninterrupted consolations of ploughshare and hoe are enough. But sometimes, however rarely, it happens that farmers are roused in a way transcending their nature by the prick of love. But it is not appropriate to instruct them in love's teaching, in case we find, through their concentrating on behaviour naturally alien to them, that men's estates which are normally harvested by their toil turn out unfruitful for us through negligence of the cultivator. But if the love even of peasant women chances to entice you, remember to praise them lavishly, and should you find a suitable spot you should not delay in taking what you seek, gaining it by rough embraces.[47]

Should this text be seen as justifying the rape of peasant women? Probably not. The third and final part of André le Chapelain's treatise condemns all the tactics and aims of the first two books, and thus his advice should not be taken literally. It seems quite probable that the fragment given here ought to be read as a description of copulation within an erotic typology where amorous courtship and social divisions between partners serve as a metaphorical screen. And it is precisely the metaphorical power of sexual possession that makes it a crude sign of threatened domination.

If after examination of this dossier little doubt remains and it seems sure the *droit de cuissage* never existed, the myth nonetheless existed and from an early date—at least since 1419, the year of the *dénombrement* of the lord of La Rivière-Bourdet. That the myth was repeated in 1507 and 1538 in places remote from one another and before it had spread among jurists attests to its erratic presence as early as the late Middle Ages. There is more, however: The fifth and last of the troublesome proofs in the dossier takes the representation of *cuissage* back to the thirteenth century. In 1247 a poem in French inserted into a fragment of the cartulary of the Abbey of Mont-Saint-Michel mentions the existence of a *droit de cuissage* indemnified by a money payment in a secular seigniory: "Roger Adé has told me what shame the villein escaped. If the villein marries his daughter outside the seigniory, the lord has the *cullage* of her: He gets 4 sous for the marriage. Sire, I tell you by my faith, once upon a time the serf took his daughter by the hand and delivered her over to his lord for him to do his will with her unless he gave him an annuity [une rente], goods, or an inheritance to [have his] consent to the marriage."[48]

This text cannot be taken as evidence of a real right or even a real belief: This quite strange piece of the cartulary (in verse and in the vernacular) is clearly a satirical fiction. The text deserves close analysis. I will propose one below, along with a reconstitution of the history of the myth and of its operation. For the moment it is enough to note that the monks were raising the specter of lay barbarity by accusing lay lords of practicing a *droit de cuissage*. The thread connecting the tradition of *cuissage* from the thirteenth century to prerevolutionary protest in the eighteenth century: Unregulated power—denounced or claimed, imagined or represented—engenders threats to the individual and to what he or she holds most dear. Thus the individual must draw the consequences, negotiate local rules (payments or subjection), or take refuge in the Church or the state. But if we are to grasp the nature of this late medieval negotiation that persisted until 1789, we must analyze the terms defining the limits of the individual sphere—that is, personal subjection and Christian consensual marriage. That definition of terms will then enable us to return to the construction of statements regarding *cuissage* from the twelfth century to 1789.

CHAPTER FIVE

The Body and the Land

I n 1789 the *cahier de doléances* of the commune of Sénargent, now in the department of the Doubs, demanded the abolition of a scandalous right: "Every leap-year, each household pays 15 sols for a right that is called *de cuisse;* it would be indecent to explain it further. It seems that it must, like the others, undergo the fate of being abolished."[1] The four neighboring communes copied this paragraph word for word. Another allusion can be found in one of the manuscript pamphlets drawn up on the eve of the Estates-General and conserved in the Doubs departmental archives: "It is truly a shame that the Bourguignons let the rights of *marquette* and *cuissage* be extinguished along with so many other institutions useful in the feudal regime; you would probably not pass up the opportunity to make entries of them and seek to reinstate some of these ancient turpitudes in our future constitution."[2]

Franche-Comté presents a special case in the France of the Ancien Régime because the peasants' personal servitude lasted longer there than elsewhere. By a curious reversal, if we recall the monastic origin of the earliest denunciation of the *droit de cuissage,* serfdom lasted the longest in Church lands, which were densely implanted in Franche-Comté. The aristocrats and the bourgeois cooperated fully, however, to defend it. In 1780 and again in 1788, following a royal edict in 1779 abolishing servitude, the Parlement de Besançon drew up a remonstrance attempting to give a more modern cast to seigniorial rights. A century before the comte de Foras raised the question, these documents present *mainmorte* (a verbal crystallization of the servile condition and a term to which we shall return) as deriving from a right of property. Subtly twisting the physiocrats' vocabulary, the remonstrance transferred all the old feudal terms to the property ethic. The Parlement was not trying to revive feudalism; rather it was attempting to combat depopulation and encourage colonists from outside the region. Far from being a form of slavery, *mainmorte* established conventions of exchange; it was a contract founded on the freedom of the contracting parties and on the need for community bonds. The *droit de suite* (right to pursue a fleeing dependent) was further security for the proprietor's rights.[3] In the *cahier de doléances* of Maisières in Haute-Saône, one Monsieur Brun, a bourgeois, rose to the defense of servitude: "Everything belongs to me; as long as I have a shadow of a right, I will consent to no sale contract that does not involve my direct *mainmorte*. Who would dare resist me? I am fairly powerful in Parlement, where I have brothers, nephews, cousins."[4]

This personification of the proprietor from the mouth of a Monsieur Brun, too cynically typical to be true, casts doubt on the sources of this last "real" mention of the *droit de cuissage* (incidentally, mentioned only rarely in the *cahiers de doléances*) before the French Revolution. The *cahiers*, documents often copied from one commune to another and even from one *bailliage* to another and imbued with the style of the philosophes, are insufficient proof of the reality of the right or even of widespread belief in it.[5] When *marquette* is mentioned in the *cahiers*, it reflects juridical culture and shows acquaintance with the sort of text that unfailingly offered up the fable of King Evenus. The very term *droit de cuissage*, present in the Sénargent *cahier*, was of recent (eighteenth-century) and literary origin. One might wonder whether these few allusions to the droit du seigneur did not simply come from the immense success of Beaumarchais's *Marriage of Figaro*, a play that showed a lord's abusive sexuality as a striking emblem for his social power.

Voltaire had prepared the way for Beaumarchais's dramatization of seigniorial abuses in Franche-Comté: In association with the lawyer Charles Christin, he constructed one of the *causes célèbres* that shook the foundations of the Ancien Régime. Between 1770 and 1777—thus before the royal abolition of servitude—Voltaire and Christin published pamphlets and instituted several suits against the canons of Saint-Claude, the successors of the monks of a large abbey with 12,000 dependents.[6] Despite their virulent attacks the Parlement de Besançon ruled on 18 August 1775 that servitude would be maintained.

Although occurrences of the *droit de cuissage* were extremely rare, a fragile thread connects them through the long period perceived as "feudal," tying together the very first and the very last direct mentions of indemnification of *cuissage*. Both the "Chanson des vilains de Verson" of

1247 and the *cahiers de doléances* of 1789 pertain to rural servitude, whether servitude is denounced in the name of enlightened ecclesiastical or bourgeois values or brandished like a big knife by laughable ogres in Béarn and Picardy. In five centuries the themes of denunciation or provocation scarcely changed, even when the actors in the incidents and the structures involved differed enormously. The *droit de cuissage* always epitomized servitude.

The connection between the *droit de cuissage* and rural servitude is not as circumstantial as the polemical presence of Voltaire, as a predecessor of Beaumarchais in exploiting the myth for dramatic purposes, might make it seem. *Formariage,* or strict regulation of subjects' marriages—along with *mainmorte* and tallage (both direct taxes on the dependent's person) one of the three essential characteristics of dependence—seems constantly linked, then and later, to mentions of *cuissage,* usually through the ambiguous term *cullage.* Throughout the "feudal" period the right of *cullage* was presented as the origin, perversion, or emblem of servitude: It justified attributing an almost innate or psychological continuity to seigniorial domination. The substitution of the bourgeois proprietor for the feudal lord perpetuated this strong theme of man's exploitation of his fellow man and, at worst, the powerful man's domination and sexual oppression of the woman. As we have seen, the French version of sexual harassment is heir to that historical tradition. The unreliable evidence of the *cahiers de doléances* and the pamphlets of 1789 needs to be linked to the ideological construct of feudalism within jurists' circles beginning in the sixteenth century and with the rise of royal and state power from the late thirteenth century. We shall return to this point in chapter 7; for the moment, we need to grasp why rural dependency was depicted as tyrannical and the lord as an ogre, how that image could have persisted for centuries in a virtual state, and why it was expressed so infrequently and in such widely scattered places. The cultural bias that operated so effectively in 1789 did not exist between 1247 and 1538. The aim of this chapter is to establish in what social context the *droit de cuissage* was asserted and to define the perception of dependence that constructed that possibility. The difficulty of the task lies in the extreme rarity of instances when that possibility was realized. It is easy to account for the presence—or absence—of a frequent phenomenon, but it is extremely difficult to generalize about rare and scattered events or to discern their context. This means that rather than trying to trace the continuing force of an image in the history of medieval dependency, we must piece together the fragments of a possible discourse.

Memories of Servitude

We might begin by positing that the only conceivable form personal dependency could take was an individual and psychological relation based in the extreme possessiveness of the master of the land, the lord lay or ecclesiastical, noble or bourgeois. The very vocabulary of dependency crystallized this psycho-individualistic reduction of the social bond: Beginning in the central Middle Ages, when the word *servus* tended to disappear, the most current term for designating a dependent was a "body man" *(homo de corpore)*. Variants were simply "man" (as in "the man of. . .") or "own man" *(proprius)*. The possibility of the "own body" of an individual being split up among several lords made him a eucharistic being whose social sacrifice was played out on the somberly lit stage of sexuality. The powerful plot of this drama involved the emancipation of the individual in Western society in the name of this "own body" ceaselessly alienated, ceaselessly claimed. We need to comprehend the conditions of production of this ideological narrative of emancipation, posing the fundamental questions of poverty and wages, and of the inalienable subject and the community.

In short, the fragmentary but persistent narrative of tyrannical oppression and *cullage* turned rural dependency into a poorly disguised slavery. But what was the full geographical extent of that representation in the Middle Ages? It is tempting to explain discontinuous occurrences by the extreme variety of actual conditions of dependency. Robert Fossier has proposed a map of serfdom: even though it is drawn on a fairly large scale, it is a motley affair.[7] If we look more closely we can see variations almost from village to village. Thus in the same Pyrenees that furnished the few cases of claims to *cuissage* we have already examined, we find that in Bigorre during the fifteenth century the dependent—known as *questau*—had the official status of serf as in the twelfth century, while in Salies-de-Béarn, not far from there, dependency had completely disappeared, the nobility exercised no right of justice and was defined uniquely by the possession of many noble lands (the locality had 18 *domenjadures* and 231 inhabitants), and little but fiscal privilege distinguished the noble from the peasant.[8] Notions of dependency and property operated within an infinitely varied whole; each instance has to be seen in a different context. The juridical, the economic, and the political intermingle: Although it is relatively easy to discern the political implications of shifts in dependent status in moments of dramatic change—on the extension of royal jurisdiction, for instance—it is much more difficult to grasp phases and zones of prosperity that could empty certain categories of dependency of meaning without immediately affecting their juridical definition. This explains why historians of the Middle Ages, even when their studies are grounded in solid fieldwork, often produce broadly contradictory generalizations about serfdom and personal dependency. Even if we could make a highly detailed map of dependency, however, we would still be unable to show any overlap between the real intensity of seigniorial exploitation and the presence of denunciations of claims to *cullage.*

Moreover, when we speak of serfdom, we slip into an attitude that may not necessarily be justified and that reflects one of the major debates in medieval studies today: Did medieval serfdom derive from classical and Carolingian slavery? This debate, which I shall do no more than touch on briefly, is central to our investigation because the hypothesis of continuity supposes a real remembrance of slavery and a symbolic marking of the slave-serfs. The pressure of continued exclusion thus might have provided the basis of a representation shared by masters and slaves.

The thesis of continuity is undoubtedly a product of the liberal history of the nineteenth century, which saw humanity as progressing constantly from ancient slavery, through the intermediate stage of serfdom, to culminate in a peasantry of small-scale farmer-landowners. The question was revitalized, however, and given a strong scholarly foundation by the Belgian historian Léo Verriest, though during his long career his work was subjected (from 1920 to 1940) to the equally scholarly objections of Marc Bloch.[9]

For Verriest, starting in the eleventh century first serfs and then personal dependents *(homines)* formed a specific group of servile ancestry, noted and remembered in rural communities as a stigma *(macule)* and an indelible trace of the dishonor of the Carolingian slave, heir to the Roman system of slavery. Verriest saw the juridical specificity of servile status in numerous documents that carefully noted the dues and rights of various categories of individuals. One of these, a charter of emancipation given in 1250 (thus at a late date) by the Abbey of Saint-Germain-des-Prés to its dependents in Villeneuve-Saint-Georges, Valenton, and Crosnes clearly defines two groups of individuals according to criteria unrelated to socioeconomic considerations. A first group did not figure in censuses and was dispensed from paying *mainmorte, formariage,* and the *taille à miséricorde*—taxes connected with the status of the land being farmed *(ratione dominii)* that Marc Bloch considered specific to serfdom. A second group of thirty-three men and women benefited from the same exoneration but on the basis of their person *(quantum ad personas eorum).*[10] Among peasants who owed the same labor and paid the same taxes, we can pick out and name the ones who bore the stigma of servitude. From Carolingian times to the thirteenth century, Verriest argues, a strong opposition persisted—more juridical and symbolic than socioeconomic—in relatively unvarying proportions between a population of free peasants and a minority of personal dependents, slaves or serfs.

For Marc Bloch, to the contrary, the disappearance of the Carolingian domains and the public power of the counts beginning in the tenth century led to widespread dependency gradually structured into degrees as castellan lordship and then banal lordship developed. The mechanism of seigniorial domination made the idea of personal liberty completely outdated. There were simply degrees of dependency. Beginning in the twelfth century emancipations deepened gaps in status. The serf was not marked by any remembrance of exclusion, but he did support the triple and specific burden of tallage *(la taille)*, *mainmorte*, and *formariage*. This basic notion, asserted from the beginning of his career in a series of articles and minor works, underlies Bloch's full elaboration of the social history of feudalism in *La société féodale (Feudal Society*, 1939), a work that shocked the study of feudalism out of narrowly institutional studies focused on vassality.[11] The work of many contemporary scholars (Georges Duby, Robert Boutruche, Robert Fossier, Pierre Bonassie, Guy Bois, Pierre Toubert, Dominique Barthélemy, and others) derives from Bloch's approach.

Without going into detail regarding a complex controversy still very much ongoing, I might mention an original position of a third type. Dominique Barthélemy's recent study of the Vendômois radicalizes Marc Bloch's propositions, to the point of contradicting him on certain questions.[12] We must, of course, take into account the specific situation in the Vendômois, where serfdom disappeared around 1100 and the "new serfdom" failed to take root in the thirteenth century. Barthélemy disagrees with the view held by Bloch and most contemporary medievalists that a discontinuity existed as a partially slave society evolved toward a society of serfdom; for him, a long continuity privileged the relation of relative dependence over the notion of slavery. In the absence of a strong public institution capable of imposing structures of exclusion, slavery soon (by the third century) became diluted, turning into a loose dependency clearly discernible by the start of the second millennium. In this view, peasant dependency becomes a "variation on the seigniorial relation." Servile homage reproduced vassalic homage on a different scale, stressing the corporal aspect of dependency (limitations on marriage and succession, corporal punishment, constraints on physical mobility). Thus serfdom was no longer a separate status but a moving point in a dynamics of dependence. Voluntary servitude may be a sign of a desire for social promotion, as with men anxious to serve as *ministeriales* in posts of professional, artisanal, or administrative status directly serving the seigniory. Inversely, emancipation might signal a simple change of master. The most telling social distinction was not between the free and the nonfree, but between nobles and nonnobles. This bold absorption of juridical condition, based on an impressive amount of fieldwork, has much that is attractive and convincing. For our purposes it has both the drawback and the advantage of undermining the concrete basis for a slaveholding representation over the long term. We may have to give up the idea of continuity in slave and slaveholding "mentalities" and radically historicize the scheme of the seigniorial ogre, setting its origin in what Robert Fossier has called the "new serfdom" after the mid-thirteenth century.[13] After all, what we are pursuing—the words *cullage* and *formariage*, the first mention of the myth of *cuissage*—are no older than that.

The shorter time span is helpful because it concentrates on contemporary ideological instruments rather than hypothetical memories of real slavery. The rediscovery of Roman civil law in the twelfth century implied rediscovery of the juridical status of the slave and permitted a revival of an archaic way of categorizing dependents. Canon law, itself firmly anchored in Roman law, drew an absolute distinction between the *servus* (a term impossible to translate without arbitrarily deciding the question of the transposition of categories) and the *liber*. Thus a decretal in Raymond of Peñafort's codification of canon law, published in 1236 under the patronage of Gregory IX, stipulates that freemen had the right of asylum in churches but *servi* did not.[14] Until the early modern age the magistrates of the various parlements often referred to Roman law to describe or justify situations of dependence.

We need to look at two superimposed movements. In the first, a slow social evolution from slavery to serfdom and then to banal dependency produced a gradual emancipation (aided by waves of emancipation in the twelfth and thirteenth centuries); in the second, an efficacy inherent in the law often provided arguments for reappropriating dependents during the various cyclical "feudal reactions" and "new serfdoms" that occurred up to the end of the Ancien Régime. In the eleventh century, the epoch of genuine serfdom, remembrance of public law seems to have maintained certain forms of social classification: Servile condition, for instance, was transmitted uniquely through the mother. The term *ancilla,* much less ambiguous than *servus,* persisted. Late survivals of slavery reinforced the strong bond in Roman culture between sexuality and property, and made the female slave more slavish than the male: Although the demesnial slave had disappeared from rural life nearly everywhere during the tenth century, the image of the slave then became linked to the household. Once again, domestic concubinage marked the condition of the woman servant.

Thus the representation of slavery may have emerged during the thirteenth century, precisely when two inverse currents were meeting head-on—enfranchisement (though we should keep in mind Dominique Barthélemy's reservations regarding that concept) and a tighter control over the peasantry. The dramatic construction of that representation supposes a dialogue imbued with tension.

One important dimension of twelfth-century serfdom, the distinction between land dependence and personal dependence, aggravated both the real situation and the image of servitude. In the ninth century and perhaps earlier peasants of all conditions (freemen, coloni, slaves) slowly became fused in what Robert Fossier calls a "slippage of agrarian burdens from the man to the holding."[15] This primacy of control over land tenure continued to be one of the major characteristics of feudalism (in the broad sense) until 1789. Beginning in the twelfth century, however, when the more complex and more effective framework of banal seigniory and of seigniorial, princely, and royal justice permitted it, control over land tenures was supplemented by taxation of men.

At that point one can distinguish within a fairly homogeneous condition marked by hereditary obligations some people who were dependent in their body and others who were dependent in their holdings. Mastery over the lands that supported the men came to differ from mastery over the men who happened to cultivate those lands. Emancipations widened the gap between the two types of control, especially when a royal or county "bourgeoisie" developed. In Champagne in the early thirteenth century any freeman could declare himself a "bourgeois of the count" by paying a *droit de jurée* (oath fee) instituted in 1230.[16] Two ordonnances of Philip the Fair (in 1287 and 1295) set out the conditions of an appeal to royal sovereignty. Elsewhere communal autonomy suspended or eliminated land dependency. The *Coutume de Toulouse* drawn up in 1286 describes a process parallel to the one for creating royal or county bourgeois:

> Similarly, it is the practice and custom of Toulouse that if someone living outside Toulouse in some villa or castle or elsewhere should declare his disavowal in the place in which he lives or elsewhere by saying, "I wish to enter Toulouse and make myself a citizen of Toulouse," and if someone coming on his way—with the exception of the master of his

body [domino corporis] if such there is—has taken that man, or has "marked" him or stripped him of his goods, then the consul and the commune of Toulouse must demand such a man, take possession of him, and, if he is a prisoner, get him back with all his goods, as if he were a citizen of Toulouse.[17]

The parallel is not just structural; it refers to a specific instance of political interaction. The *Coutume*, which was authorized by Philip III, followed the ordonnance of Alphonse de Poitiers promulgated in Nîmes in 1283 discriminating between the aspirations to autonomy of the city of Toulouse and the claims of the county.

Of course, one ought not to follow liberal history's confusion of these waves of acquisition of "bourgeoisie" or "citizenship" with simple emancipation. In large part these measures served to transfer personal fiscality to stronger institutions. Nonetheless, the process gradually deprived seigniories of revenues, notably profits of justice. Domination based on land was becoming simple landownership. When that happened, domination over men, preserved by the requirement of free status for entry into the bourgeoisie or citizenship, became more clearly defined, and many charters of emancipation exclude "men of the body." A distinct aggravation of servile condition came with a change in perception.

Until the thirteenth century the Middle Ages was unaware of the Roman or the modern notion of property; mastery over things and men was understood by the notion of *saisine*, a concept based on practical management and ongoing use with no notion of either preeminence or subjection (that is, without being embodied in a subject-proprietor). A piece of property could fall under multiple and simultaneous *saisines* if discernibly different uses of it were present.[18] The rediscovery of Roman law and of property (the scholastics' *dominium*) gradually marginalized *saisine* by indexing mastery over things and people to the absolute model of divine domination over the world. The symbolic nexus of dependency had become narrower.

Tallies and Tales of Dependency

Two additional elements seem to me to enter into the construction of a common image of absolute servitude: The first was the religious implantation of an institution—voluntary servitude to the Church—at times real and at times symbolic, but always seen as liberation from the prison of secular life. The second was the monetarization of dependency. The circulation of money increased enormously in the twelfth century, which meant that dependency involved money transactions and was taxed.

This dual mechanism is evident in the constitution of the seigniory of the Templars at Douzens near Carcassonne. It will serve us as an example, without any claim to rigorous general application.[19]

The commandery of Douzens, known to us from a fine collection of documents, was founded around 1130 under the protection of the viscounts of Carcassonne and their principal vassals; it grew fairly rapidly in the twelfth century thanks to a series of donations, purchases, and exchanges, reflecting a contemporary model better known in connection with more illustrious foundations such as Cluny and Citeaux. Some 10 percent of the three hundred documents describing the progressive formation of the seigniory over a period of about sixty years concern the sale or donation of men and women as *donats* (voluntary serfs), dependent vassals, or personal dependents. It is difficult to distinguish among these categories because in all three cases the people involved become the *homines* or *feminae* of the commandery. An identical due (2 or 4 sous) called *usuaticum* or *hominium* marked the new dependency. The amount of this fee varied little, and we can categorize it somewhere between the personal *cens* and the *chevage* of northern France (which denoted the status of bondman or -woman and was so modest [usually 4 deniers] as to be clearly symbolic). Self-donation to the Temple at Douzens differed most obviously by its frequent use of the first person (in roughly one-half of the documents), but the formula of possession, here as in many other charters from commanderies and monasteries, is the same for the *donat* as for the "man of the body" given or sold: "Ad omnem voluntatem faciendam" (to do your will in everything).

Sale or donation of a "free" dependent can be inferred when there is precise mention of the *manses* (lands under feudal tenure) or *casali* making up the lot ceded to the institution. Léo Verriest's distinction reappears here: For example, one charter of 1147 mentions the donation-sale by Roger, comte de Carcassonne, in thanks (or in exchange) for liberation from a sizable pledge (3,000 sous ugoniens), where he gives a lot made up of one villa and two *casali* "with their men, their women, and their descendants." The people are not listed by name; it is the land that is the essential object of the transaction. Three men designated by name are joined to this lot, however, along with the *manse* "in which they seem to reside [ubi manere visi sunt]." The least transfer of land usually involved precise geographical description, but in this case an unspecified plot is attached as an accessory to the essential *saisine* exercised over the man.[20]

Human beings, whatever their condition, appear here as negotiable units capable of being expressed in monetary terms. In 1169, when Arnaud de Brasse sold a certain Dominique for the modest sum of 7 sous ugoniens, he specifies, "So that you will own him as your own goods and your alodium [pro vestro proprio et allodio possideatis]."[21] The donation-sale frequently mentions the man, his wife, and their descendants *(progenies)* in perpetuity, along with all goods, movable and immovable, acquired or future. Three-fourths of the acts of cession involve money payments corresponding to a sale, a liberation from a pledge, or a "charity" (modest sums serving as a counter-gift).

Ownership or partial *saisine* (one-third or three-fourths) of a male dependent by his holdings or by his body displays the fiscal aspect of this apparent reduction of people to property, and the painstaking calculations reflected in the documents attest to the growing role of the circulation of money in the rural economy of the twelfth century. The commandery of Douzens had monetary resources rare in the castellans' milieu, and by its ability to make middle-term investments it could transform unremunerative dependencies into cessions bearing a price, following up the transaction with a more rational exploitation of the land.

The case of Guillaume Paraire provides one example of such transactions. In 1165 Raimond Hugues d'Aiguesvives sold him for 120 sous melgueils, a round sum of money. Raimond states that he is ceding "one of my men [unum hominem meum] and all his posterity with all his goods both movable and immovable that he possesses and holds today and that he will acquire in the future, so that you and all the brothers of the Temple will possess and hold this man and his posterity with all that is said above and that you will have him in ownership to do your will in everything as your own alodium and with full right in perpetuity."[22]

Two months later (on 23 February 1166) the Temple gave Guillaume two *sétérées* of land under *tasque* and two vineyards, one in fief and the other under the regime of *la quarte*. The act mentions an *acapte* of 2 sous connected with this transaction and imposes an *usuaticum* of 4 sous melgueils.[23] Clearly, Guillaume was being set up as a land dependent of the Temple. What had his situation been before?

Guillaume was probably not poor, but before the 1165 sale his possessions must have been in such a state of confusion between personal and family holdings that their "owner" found it difficult to earn any profit from them. In 1158, seven years before the sale, a document mentions part ownership of the mills of Arrapesac in partnership with Pierre and Bernard Paraire.[24] A degree of confusion persisted after Guillaume entered into servitude: In 1188, twelve years after the sale, a document defines a landholding in relation to a *manse* of Guillaume and his brother.

Hugues d'Aiguesvives received a sizable cash payment in this transaction, Guillaume Paraire enlarged his farmland, and the Temple enhanced its stature as the principal lord of the locality. I do not mean to imply that these social operations were a game where everybody wins, as the lenifying conclusions of some brands of anthropological history would have us believe. The trend we are tracing on the basis of extremely sparse documentation was certainly connected with mechanisms for the constitution of banal seigniory, which often aggravated domination by putting it on a more rational basis.

Even in the south of France, where the "classic" forms of vassality were relatively undeveloped, the condition of servitude took the form of vassalage. This is clear from Paul Ourliac's study of servile homage in the Midi on the basis of charters of seigniories of the Temple in and around Toulouse.[25] Giving homage, designated by the term *ominium* (at Douzens the term also defines dues of servitude), *homagium,* or *hominatio,* involved joining hands, kneeling, at times swearing an oath and exchanging a kiss on the mouth *(osculum).* The charter transmitting the act repeated the formula of appropriation, "per omnem vestram voluntatem faciendam."

Thanks to their financial resources and their ability to plan for the middle and long term, ecclesiastical institutions had a privileged position in the process of monetarization and concentration of ownership of men and women. We can see the same dynamic at work in a totally different environment from Douzens at Battle Abbey in Sussex. The abbey's possessions extended out from an initial nucleus (the *leuga*), thanks to the purchase of direct dependents set up as *censitaires.*[26] This means that despite appearances of vassalage, the Church (or rather various ecclesiastical institutions) went beyond banal seigniory to a systematic appropriation of dependents that prefigures or parallels princely or state domination. Until 1789 the Church was the largest owner of people in France. Where first castellan seigniory and then banal seigniory faced contradictions between ownership of land and ownership of people, and struggled with emancipation movements and royal or princely power, the Church unified its domination over human beings by establishing a broader and more ambivalent ideological base than strict property. Church domination combined in a homogeneous vocabulary three distinct types of subjection: that of the serf or the bondman, who could be sold, exchanged, or donated; that of voluntary servitude (of the vassalic type, also found among lay lords); and that of dedition, or self-donation to the Church (as with the *donats* of seigniories to the Templars). At times only the enumeration of goods and holdings attached to the act of self-donation enables us to distinguish between one status and the other: A *donat*, for example, might bring with him a number of serfs.

It would of course be absurd to think that a homogeneous vocabulary confusing obedience to God and to his representatives with terrestrial subjection sufficed to create one standard model of dependency. The Church knew perfectly well how to distinguish metaphor from reality and how to make good use of its own language. In the twelfth century, for instance, when John of Salisbury addressed Pope Hadrian IV to denounce what John considered to be the pope's abject dependence on wealthy Roman houses, he used the ancient and venerable title of "slave of slaves [servus servorum]," bringing it violently and polemically up to date.[27] The meaning of words can shift, only lightly veiling reality.

In the seigniory of Douzens the long history of one self-donation clearly illustrates the ambiguities of voluntary subjection. In 1137 Arnaud de Gaure gave himself and all his possessions to the Temple "in order to become a brother in the community [per confratrem vestrum in ipsa militia]." He confirmed his dedition the following year. No mention is made of money: this seems to have been an act of spiritual subjection, like others to be found in the same cartulary and in the archives of many other ecclesiastical seigniories. In 1145, however, eight years after the first donation, Arnaud renewed his act, not confirming it but as if instituting it. He speaks of his ill health: "I, Arnaud, when I drew up that act, I found myself in sickness and I delivered over [or rendered] my body to the service of God forever, along with all that I possess." In a moment of pressing danger Arnaud remembered his vow, which had not been executed. When his illness passed, though, his fervor must have cooled, because in 1150 Arnaud had a new act drawn up reiterating the terms stated thirteen years earlier: "I give myself to you and I constitute myself your brother in the militia," and so forth. He must have married in the meantime because he also gives his two sons, requesting their upkeep *(victum et vestitum)*. A new fact appears: The last act is in exchange for freeing him from a sizable pledge (324 sous ugoliens and 96 sous melgueils). Nor does the matter end there: In 1167, thirty years after Arnaud's initial act, his eldest son, Raimond, confirmed the preceding act in exchange for 100 sous and the right to lifetime enjoyment of revenues from his holdings.[28] This little landholding chronicle confirms the complexity of the monetary and spiritual bonds involved in subjection. From one point of view this is a long negotiation regarding censitary and alodial lands and services. From another point of view it shows the spiritual domination of a community dedicated to salvation. A unifying religious vocabulary blurs clear contours in the picture of a landholding relation.

One final document from Douzens will help clarify the extent of this ideological and lexical unity in ecclesiastical subjection; it also brings up the question of marriage within the dependent relation. On 25 August 1167 Hugues Inard, his sister Garsen, and Garsen's husband gave one of their men, Pons Mirabel, to the Temple. The resulting act is of the ordinary type, using the habitual formula for transferral of ownership applied to all the goods and persons bound to Pons: "Ad omnem voluntatem vestrum deinde faciendam habeatis et teneatis et pro vestro jure plenario absque ulla reservatione nostra omni tempore possideatis." As with Guillaume Paraire, the Inards drew up a second document on the following day, attesting to an agreement with the prior of Saint-Jean: Pons Mirabel was to give 2 sous per year (in *usuaticum* and *servitium*, taxes on personal dependency) on the feast of the nativity of the Blessed Virgin Mary in September. This fee, symbolic in nature and a concrete sign of dependency, did not involve enrollment on the *cens*. What was Pons's real economic dependency? Apart from his spiritual subjection, where did he stand between this symbolic due and the total alienation of his possessions and those of his descendants?

The operation seems to have been of another order completely. The first contract setting up the donation was also an act of emancipation involving a strange condition: "We make this emancipation and liberation [solutionem et libertatem] of the previously cited men under the condition that Pierre, son of Pons Mirabel, wed Alazaïs, our aforementioned sister." We can surmise that Pons, a serf of Hugues Inard's family, had prospered to the point that his son was a good match for the youngest Inard daughter. Servitude made the union inherently difficult: Hugues Inard and his sister Garsen would have nephews and nieces who were their serfs through their father (in Douzens in the twelfth century offspring were serfs if only one parent was a serf) or through the status of their lands. By the same token Alazaïs's children would be her own serfs. Emancipation pure and simple, followed by a marriage, would recall too recent a stigma. The Temple served as a symbolic intermediary: the ambivalence inherent in subjection to the Temple—where dependency was simultaneously land-related, fiscal, and spiritual—permitted a redistribution of conditions.[29]

Marriage, the source of social mobility and its consequence, was the most visible aspect of the dependency system: When it forced people to think in concrete terms and make a precise accounting of their offspring, their inheritance, and the intricacies of their dependent status, it clarified the difficulties and dangers of that dependency. This example helps us better understand the genealogy of the myth of the *droit de cuissage* in the founding episode of Verson: In a period of strong social turbulence when categories were shifting, a monastery's recall of the abuse of persons (enveloped in a lenifying lexical homogeneity) clearly situates the myth within a triangular structure of dependence whose three corners—the sovereign (prince, city, or king), the Church, and the lords—surrounded the subject. This triangular figure produced three dependencies and three virtual conditions of subjection, whether variations in context produced an equilateral triangle or an irregular triangle where one power or another was stronger.

THE SOCIAL LOGIC OF *FORMARIAGE*

Competitive interplay among the various systems of personal domination crystallized, fixing the status of some dependents beginning in the twelfth century. As we have seen, the same period and the same dynamic produced emancipations and the expression *homme de corps,* a label for a relation of dependency that changed only quantitatively until the French Revolution. The relative rarity of dependency only accentuated its oddness and redoubled the number of interpretations given to its origin. The intensity of the representation of personal dependency was in inverse proportion to its quantitative reality. There is no reason to doubt solid studies establishing that after the pause of the "new serfdom" servitude regressed continually, except in certain regions (the Nivernais, Franche-Comté). The great crises of the fourteenth century were powerless to stop this movement: In 1313 20 percent of the population of Bigorre were *questaux,* in 1429 only 3 percent.[30] The socioeconomic marginality of servitude has caused recent historians of late medieval society to lose interest in the question (hence in the *droit de cuissage*), leaving it to the jurists. This trend had already begun in Marc Bloch's time, and it reached a peak in an important work, Guy Bois's *Crise du féodalisme,* which never even mentions the question of different kinds of subjection.[31] In my opinion, however, servitude, a social horizon sometimes near to hand but often remote, bathed conflicts between lords and peasants in a special light quite distinct from the more lively reflections of landholding alone.

Even before attempting to summarize the juridical characteristics structuring the bondman's condition, we must clarify what dependency meant over and above the various forms of feudalism and its "emergences" and "reactions." The probably universal ideal of the master of the land lay in joint dominion over the soil and the peasants in what I will call the "peasant nucleus," a small, tightly controlled agrarian-human unit. That ideal, of course, did not withstand the dynamics of production and accumulation. Better systems of control over both land and men were needed. What by inertia we call feudalism attempted to create such a system. Before we trace its complicated etiquette, I would like to illustrate the simple social logic involved by presenting one case of dependency that shows a desire to define the boundaries of exploitation with no explicit appeal to such juridical and social categories as *mainmorte, formariage, forfuyance,* and so forth.

The cartulary of the priory of Saint-Étienne-de-Vignory, a dependency of the Benedictine abbey (of the Cluniac reform) of Saint-Bénigne-de-Dijon contains a charter drawn up before a notary in 1377 for Jean d'Ambonville, lord of the village of the same name.[32] The charter puts order into a fairly complex situation among men and women "of the body" of both the priory and Jean d'Ambonville. Jean Leulier, a bondman of the prior's, was about to marry Jeannote Putte Beste, a bondwoman of Jean d'Ambonville's, while at the same time Leulier's daughter (also named Jeannote) by a first marriage with Ysabel, a bondwoman of the prior's (Ysabel does not reappear so we do not know whether her dependency was transmitted by her father, her mother, or both), was about to marry Nicolas Bourse Trousse, a bondman of Jean d'Ambonville's. *Formariage* is not mentioned in the document, but the very fact of having the charter drawn up by a notary and keeping it in a seigniorial cartulary shows that the event involved the matrimonial status of four dependents. From a demographic point of view, the situation of the two lords was unchanged by the two marriages: Possible offspring aside, each seigniory held one man and one woman both before and after. The division of goods, however, is noted with particular care: Jean Leulier gave Nicolas and Jeannote one-third of his possessions (excluding his share in Ysabel's estate). Jeannote Putte Beste brought Leulier her possessions (furniture alone). Thus Jean Leulier could put together a dowry by shifting to Jean d'Ambonville a portion of what he held under the prior. The most remarkable detail in this transaction, however, is that Jeannote Putte Beste and Leulier's daughter Jeannote exchanged their patrimonies, each bride leaving her "inheritance" in the seigniory of her birth (*heritage* here very probably refers to immovable goods and tenancies).

It looks as if movable goods and people could move from one place to another, while land had to keep its original seigniorial assignment. The history of the village of Ambonville is lost, so we cannot know how much in this episode is happenstance and how much the result of patient negotiations, perhaps spiced with threats of seizure. It seems probable that the peasants' family strategies regarding widows' rights *(douaire)* and succession played an important role. Still, in spite of the fragmentary nature of the documentation, this banal episode in Ambonville, which complicates the simple notions of "classic" feudal exchanges (noted by such terms as *commutatio* and *cambitio*, for example, in the charters of Saint-Corneille-de-Compiègne in the twelfth century),[33] hints at one major meaning of personal dependency: It fulfilled the impossible dream of the "peasant nucleus."

It is difficult to give an overall picture of the life of the bondman or bondwoman under the Ancien Régime, but certain constants do exist. As we have seen, three distinctive traits defined personal dependence: *la taille, mainmorte,* and *formariage.* I might add the lord's right to pursue a fleeing dependent, *forfuyance.* We can of course concede to Verriest's hypothesis that these characteristics might apply to peasants who were free in their person as far as taxes were concerned, given that mechanisms of dominion over land tended to increase fiscal pressures beyond the traditional juridical forms. All dominion over land strove for both real and personal subjection. Nonetheless, competition and peasant resistance limited overlaps between personal and land subjection.

The three taxes connected with personal dependency were universally perceived as marks of the servile condition and its juridical definition. To pick one example of this: In 1393 the Parlement de Paris, whose jurisdiction had already expanded to include a large part of France and whose adjudications influenced a good many other courts, ruled on an interesting case. In Flanders Jeanne La Niepce, the wife of Guillaume Bouilli, claimed to be a free woman and a *bourgeoise* of the count of Flanders ("dictum Cureboys desaoando ac se burgensem dicti patrui nostri advoando"). Her lord, Erard Cureboys esquire, sued her before the court of the *bailliage* of Lille, which decided in his favor. Guillaume Bouilli appealed to the royal *bailli* in Troyes. The *procureur* of the count of Flanders, who backed Guillaume and Jeanne, also entered a request, but Parlement upheld the Lille ruling in a decision dated 14 June 1393. The reasons it adduced defined Jeanne's condition as "woman entirely of the body, by reason of her servile condition, to the benefit of Cureboys . . . liable to high tallage and low and subject to the lord's will in matters of *formariage, mainmorte,* pursuit, and like conditions, as were the men and women of the body of the said Cureboys and his wife."[34] That eminent jurisdiction, deciding on an affair not from some remote archaic region but from an urban and dynamic Flanders, displayed no hesitation.

The only one of these rights that had any relation to the *droit de cuissage* was *formariage*, but it cannot be understood outside the overall system of personal dependence. The *taille* was a personal tax due to the lord, who freely stipulated its amount and frequency. Tallage gradually replaced the older *chevage*, which (paradoxically) became a sign of the relative emancipation of a bondman who had negotiated or bought his way out of subjection to the *taille* and *mainmorte*. Free subjects also paid a tallage, but only under specific and justified circumstances. In 1439 lords were forbidden to levy feudal tallage, by decree of Charles VII, who instituted the royal *taille*, a true national tax, instead. Bondmen, still subject to servile tallage, were exempt from the royal tax. Servile tallage, an arbitrary and particular tax, was a clear sign of strong domination, as shown by the contemporary expression, *taillable à merci* (taxable at will).

That is not the nub of the question, however: It even seems that in certain cases the tax burden on bondmen was lighter than state-imposed taxes. Jean Gallet's careful study of the small barony of Fénétrange in Lorraine shows that in 1752, when the seigniory, attached to the duchy of Lorraine, passed into the royal domain, the ducal "subsidy" was ten times what the seigniorial *taille* had been.[35] This is no argument in support of gentle seigniorial governance, a thesis dear to antirepublican historiography in the nineteenth century: As we shall see, the levies were simply carried out differently.

The extreme complexity of the fiscal system under the Ancien Régime meant that *mainmorte* and *formariage* had a stronger quota of symbolic investment than seigniorial taxes. Even though the arbitrary (a word of the age) nature of servile tallage made it the epitome of dependency, universal taxation leveled differences of condition within dependency and set up another opposition, no longer between free and dependent men and women but between those subjected to or exempt from taxation—that is, between nobles and clerics to one side and members of the third estate to the other. Although this polarity was strong in 1789, it needs to be qualified: We know, for example, that the monarchy succeeded in imposing high taxes on the Church, a move that in fact if not in law cut into the personal exemption of clerics.[36] On the other hand, the nobility's exemption became systematic only at the very end of the sixteenth century.[37] Perceived differences between orders or groups among the privileged were more telling than a representation of differences of social condition (which, however, were never completely obliterated). From the fifteenth century to the eighteenth, public opinion gradually came to oppose the third estate to the social orders exempt from taxation.

One special characteristic connected with the image of *cuissage* deserves mention: Only bondmen and bondwomen who lived independently, outside the parental house, were liable to servile tallage. In practical terms tallage entered the picture when they married. Thus the canons of the chapter of Saint-Pierre de Troyes had a special heading in their registers for "New Spouses of the Year."[38] This registration was unrelated to any tax on marriage or to *formariage,* but the coincidence may have reinforced an association between marriage and dependency.

Mainmorte was the most important mechanism in the system of personal dependency. Because it persisted to such a late date, it enables us to map servitude in 1789 by mentions in customary law and notarial acts. More than thirty fifteenth-century customals mention *mainmorte* in a vast zone stretching across French territories from northeast to southwest: Lorraine, Franche-Comté, Burgundy, the Nivernais, Berry, Auvergne, Bresse, Savoy, Dauphiné, and Béarn. In 1789 in Franche-Comté (the region of the Saint-Claude affair noted by Voltaire), nearly one-half the village population—400,000 out of 700,000 inhabitants—was subject to *mainmorte.*[39]

We shall return to the lexical origin of the term *mainmorte* and the myths it gave rise to. Its practical definition seems simple: A dependent could bequeath wealth only to direct heirs. Other restrictions pertained: The heir had to live within the "nucleus" of the family farm, understood as one unit of life and work. If there were no offspring, the holding passed to the lord. Infinite numbers of local variations applied to *mainmorte,* but its principle was unvaried: The dependent's capacity to bequeath wealth was subjected to very strict limitations. We can thus understand the symbolic importance of the "last will and testament," the ultimate and at times the only "liberty" of people who lived in want and were ruled by necessity.

The system of *mainmorte* had practical consequences that were just as important. Anne-Marie Patault's fine study of the bondmen and bondwomen of the chapter of Saint-Pierre de Troyes demonstrates the continuous and increasing pauperization of dependents from the fifteenth to the seventeenth century, largely because of the application of *mainmorte.*[40] Saint-Pierre was undoubtedly an extreme case of a lord creating multiple restrictions on the right of succession and seeing to it that principles were strictly applied. Moreover, the wars and the plagues of the fourteenth century decimated the rural population, offering increased opportunities for seigniorial succession. As a general rule, when the system was applied with that sort of rigor, it made any lasting accumulation of goods and lands impossible. Worse, far from being dissolved when feudal ties were relaxed in the late Middle Ages, *mainmorte* was defined even more rigorously in the fourteenth century precisely because in general dominion over land was becoming less personal and was no longer producing as much in dues.

It seems clear that by its rigor the ecclesiastical seigniory of Troyes was killing the goose that laid the golden eggs, in the long run impoverishing itself. Its land management policies stand in clear contrast to those of the Templars' commandery in Douzens or Battle Abbey in the twelfth century, where a sacrifice of immediate interests enhanced future return on investments. But this one case in Troyes is not enough to signal global change, since in most lands under *mainmorte* only a part of an estate was liable to taxation or confiscation. The Troyes case must be taken into account, however, as an example of the extreme limit of seigniorial power. We need to distinguish once again between the symbolic existence of *mainmorte* as the signature of a global, ongoing system always present on the horizon in the dependent's mind and its real economic existence in a world where dues bearing the same name were collected in very different situations. That diversity challenges the coherence of *mainmorte* as an object of historical investigation. Although it made possible slavelike exploitation in Troyes (where the peasant was simply an instrument, and biological reproduction was the only means for increasing the peasant population), elsewhere *mainmorte* operated to shift a fiscal levy from the point of production to the point of accumulation. Still elsewhere it was an inducement to stability, favoring direct transmission of land over sale or dispersion.

The third element in personal servitude, *formariage*, played an essential role in the construction of the fiction of *cuissage*. As we have seen, thirty-seven out of Delpit's seventy-two proofs of *cuissage* were connected with the collection of a marital tax that was explicitly linked to *formariage* in eight cases, more loosely a part of seigniorial domination in another twenty-nine. Well before the republican controversy introduced its approximations, certain authentic texts founded *formariage* in emancipation from an ancient right of *cuissage*, and the word *cullage*, with its ambiguous etymology, suggested sexual origins for the right of *formariage*. These mechanisms warrant a closer look.

The term *formariage* appears late, toward the end of the twelfth century, just when the breakup of the notion of dependency produced the term *homme de corps*, land-based dependency became dissociated from personal dependency, and human beings began to be seen as property. The dependent subject to *formariage* married "out"—outside the lord's lands and/or out of his or her condition. Marriage did not in itself modify personal status, but it could change the status of descendants, thus constituting what feudal law called an *abrègement de fief,* a reduction in the value of the domain. This loss was compensated by a money payment or by renunciation of succession rights or goods. Thus *formariage* designated a situation (marrying outside one's habitus), an interdiction, and payment of a due.

The threat to feudal wealth was not simply a pretext for fiscal exactions. In her study of Saint-Pierre de Troyes, Anne-Marie Patault sees *formariage* as the principal cause for a considerable decrease in the number of the seigniory's *hommes de corps:* During the fifteenth century the canons granted few emancipations (which occurred elsewhere out of financial need or complicated successions), and dependents' disavowals seem rare. *Formariage* depopulated the ecclesiastical seigniory. In the domain of Orvilliers no *formariage* appears on the tallage rolls for 1309; in 1395 it accounts for 10 percent of revenues; in 1489, for 58 percent of revenues.[41] At the end of the Middle Ages freedom was probably acquired less by solemn proclamation of mutation (emancipation by the lord, disavowal on the part of the dependent) than through a slow centrifugal trend. This makes the symbolic power of hindrances to marriage and the dues connected with it understandable: In the long time span and despite statistical evidence, marriage offered the mirage of social change. Cinderella and Suzanne are opposite faces of the same social fiction, whose force also relied on the bit of reality it contained.

The social origin of *formariage* seems fairly clear in an abstract feudal system never realized in its pure state. The question of practical application is less clear. Were such dues dissuasive? Were they aimed at protecting dominion over land or personal domination? The overall system linking *taille, formariage,* and *mainmorte* appears in its functional coherence only rarely. The ecclesiastical seigniories seem most likely to have maintained and improved the system as a whole: In the seigniory of Saint-Pierre de Troyes the burden of *formariage* was heavy. In 1407 one dependent who married a *bourgeoise* of the king had to pay one-third of the value of his holdings. Not long after the due disappears from the canons' account books, but to the profit of an extended and increased *mainmorte.*[42] The same proportion of one-third is repeated in the customal of Chaumont-en-Bassigny, where a distinction is drawn between a fine for an unauthorized marriage out of the domain and the indemnity due after authorization: "No fine [is] fixed by the custom of the *bailliage;* in certain localities by common observance the fine practiced is of 60 sols 1 denier tournoi." The indemnity was *le tiers de son vaillant* (one-third of the estimated patrimony).[43] In Bigorre in the fifteenth century a male *questal* owed the king of Navarre a fixed sum of 20 sous malgueils; a woman serf owed only 10 sous.[44] Around Verdun (one of the regions where strong control over dependents lasted the longest), the fee for *formariage* seems to have been high, and constraint approached pure violence: The canons of the church of Mary Magdalene and the cathedral and the religious of Saint-Mihiel and Saint-Vanne were known to throw marriageable women into prison (unless they paid a sizable bail) if they seemed about to "marry out." Infractions could result in the seizure of all goods, according to the terms of the Verdun customal drawn up in the sixteenth century. We should not believe blindly in these legal texts, however, because the measure could at times be more a threat to encourage negotiation than a genuine sanction. Alain Girardot cites the case of a female serf of the Hospitalers in Doncourt, near Verdun, who was *formariée* to a diocesan dependent and whose *moble et héritage* the Hospitalers seized. Her "goods and inheritance" were returned to her, however, in exchange for an annual payment of a hen in token of dependency.[45] Only very rarely is a fixed rate specified for *formariage.*[46]

Clearly *formariage* was a term with no more unity than *mainmorte:* When it refers to a fixed tax, we know it was one of the many penalties applied to dependents within the framework of seigniorial justice, but when it designates a levy equivalent to a sizable portion of the dependent's wealth, it was a step in emancipation or change of dependency circumstantially connected to the dependent's marriage.

This social and "feudal" dimension of *formariage* is not sufficient reason for founding the myth of *cuissage* on it. The fiscal aspect of *formariage* and its clearly functional nature, in a world that never ceased debating and reformulating modes of taxation in continual evolution, do not provide the shadows propitious to the primordial mysteries of seigniorial concupiscence. The most one can say is that personal dependency was so marginal and affected such a small minority of the population at the end of the Ancien Régime that it became a sign of underdevelopment and consigned the lords of regions where it was still practiced to a barbarity accounting, a posteriori, for the ethical aberration of *cuissage.* We shall soon see an example of this in the matter of the lord of Montvallat in the seventeenth century. First, however, we need to examine other functions of *formariage* that seem to have produced clearer results on the level of representations.

In a society of orders and classes personal dependency, an occasion for strange differences without any strong relation to empirical reality, produced the fantasy of caste.

FORMARIAGE AS A CRITERION OF CLASSIFICATION

We cannot be sure whether the social agents involved had any clear awareness of the ways in which *formariage* functioned. In Chaumont in the seventeenth century the notion of *formariage* seems to have been so obscure that an assembly was called and witnesses interrogated in an inquiry *par tourbe*.[47] Some juridical texts attempted to define it: One example is the classification of dependents in the *Coutumier bourguignon*, compiled and glossed in the late fourteenth century, one of the most explicit categorizations of the customary law of the Middle Ages.

This document refers to the dependent population as a whole as *mainmortable*. "Of the *mainmortable* persons, some are of simple *mainmorte*, others are serfs of *formariage*, others are servile serfs."[48]

The first of these cases, simple *mainmorte*, applied only to land dependency; it was limited to one or more landholdings and had no consequence either for the dependent person or for holdings subject to another dependency. Subjects could disavow their dependency by abandoning the holding; they were free except for attachment to the land: "For when a person is emancipated, the goods outside the control of the lord whom he has disavowed are freed." From the lord's point of view, this was like a right of eminent domain and a trace of the feudal relation. One phrase of this paragraph of the *Coutumier* is perplexing though: "And if he has nothing under him, he loses nothing, as long as he has other goods under another lord." What, then, was this dependency, which was attached neither to the person (the subject is free) nor to a holding (there is none in this last instance), which received no sanction, and which was nonetheless called *simple mainmorte?* Was this category an empty slot to permit further differentiation of the system, or is it a vague record of an ancient dependency that might be resurrected in case of litigation? Perhaps this fossil relation resulted from a series of partial emancipations that failed to eliminate the category. Whatever the reason, *formariage* did not apply to that category of dependency: No matter what the subject's marital status might be or what he or she might or might not inherit, the land remained under dependency. Aside from the contradiction involved in putting this category of freemen with dependent holdings under the heading of *mainmorte*, we can see that a slippage had taken place: Because of emancipations and repurchases of rights (in a region where ducal power was strong), the lords lost much of their power of dominion over men. This first and certainly largest category of *mainmortables* joined the mass of free peasants.

The second category (*personnes serves de corps et de poursuite*, "serfs 'of the body' over whom the lord had rights of pursuit") is harder to grasp. These were persons who fell under personal dependency, signaled by the term *corps*. The right of pursuit indicates that they could not remove themselves from that domination even to transfer to another dependency: "And should he appear before a lord under whom he advows himself, if the lord he left should pursue him, in all circumstances, even if he had just cause for his disavowal, by law he will forthwith lose all his holdings, wherever located." Right of pursuit is not to be confused with obligatory residence. Pursuit came under penal law, but it implied no direct physical coercion. The situation it reflected was the inverse of that of the first category: Because persons had mobility, they could cease having a landholding relation with the seigniory. Control over goods derived from personal domination: "His serfs cannot acquire or sell without permission."

The two first categories seems clearly contrasted, but it is harder to see how the second type was distinguished from the third, that of serfs *de formariage*. Pierre Petot, an expert in servile status in the Middle Ages, defines the right of pursuit (central to this distinction) as the "right to demand of an exiled *homme de corps* payment of his dues and, on that occasion, to collect *mainmorte* or a *formariage* fine." The *homme de corps*, a bondman with no attachment to the land, had a fiscal existence only when his person produced some change in wealth, which means when he was sold or purchased (possibilities mentioned only in connection with this category), when he inherited possessions, or when he married. Succession is quite understandably not mentioned because all four categories are defined as *mainmortable*. But why create a separate category for serfs "of *formariage*" when marriage or disavowal had the same effect? And how are we to imagine constraint to have been applied for *formariage* without pursuit? We would have to suppose either that this highly detailed text displays an obsessional attachment to an outdated categorization or else that *formariage* had become a tax on marriage guaranteed by social pressure alone.

A document from Bordeaux edited and translated by Robert Boutruche offers a possible example of *formariage* with no other form of dependency.[49] It was drafted in 1426 by Guillaume "Debrauyce," notary public of the duchy of Guyenne, for Bernard de Lamothe, lord of Roquetaillade, to emancipate Aymar de La Palanque et de Pompignac and his descendants. Like his ancestors before him, Aymar was the *questal* of his lord *à taille et à merci* "by reason and because of their bodies and of all the things and wealth they have." The document states the reason for the emancipation: "moved by compassion and wishing to reward the same Aymar . . . in contemplation of God our lord and out of charity." But Aymar abandons everything that had belonged to his father, Pierre de La Palanque. Robert Boutruche comments, "This means he puts [his wealth] at [the lord's] disposition. But the very terms of the charter prove that [his possessions] were returned to him immediately, without losing their servile character, however."[50] A codicil in fact states that *questal* status remains attached to all that Aymar or his lineage might acquire by inheritance or purchase within the jurisdiction of the lord as well as "to the goods and things that belonged to Pierre de La Palanque." This complicated ritual, which may conceal a repurchase, shows, on the one hand, that the rule stating that all wealth was confiscated when a dependent rose out of his condition was not rigorously enforced but was negotiable and, on the other hand, that the logic of social categories was carried out to the full. One could not move from the condition of an *homme de corps* to one of an *homme de bien* without fulfilling one's destiny, if only for a few minutes. There is more, however, and the next paragraph gives the former *questal* a new type of vassality: "Aymar has promised . . . to be good, loyal, and faithful toward Messire Bernard [and] his heirs . . . [and] to guard their secrets, their goods and things, and their honor." He also promised them that "if he should wish to withdraw [from this agreement] to marry or to install himself otherwise, he will marry and install himself within the seigniory and power of lord messire Bernard de Lamothe and not elsewhere without the will and permission of the said lord."[51] The notary carefully recorded that any transgression would be submitted for adjudication to the *sénéschal* of Guyenne, the *prévôt*, and the *official*. Although the landholding relation had become purely contractual and fiscal, the lord attempted to maintain a sort of personal dependency disguised as vassality, limited to marriage and residence, and based on honor.

To return to the *Coutumier bourguignon:* The fourth category of mainmortable persons takes us back to the stable and solid framework of classic feudalism. The customal states: "Servile serfs are those who are serfs of their person and their head and who owe 4 deniers each to the lord in payment of their person." Here the word *chef*, repeated by the word *teste*, the mention of a *chevage* (head tax) of 4 deniers, and the enumeration of constraints (goods must be available to the lord, the lord may sell or exchange serfs, the serf cannot disavow himself) all refer to the "ideal" condition of the serf of the golden age of feudalism. In exchange the lord promised survival: "When the serf has nothing to eat, the lord is held to provide him sustenance."

Article 340 on the following page of the customal brings down this entire edifice: "By custom no one is a serf of the body in Burgundy who, when it pleases him, cannot disavow his lord and advow another lord in freedom or in servitude as it pleases him; and for that reason such persons are called serfs."[52] There is a reason for the flagrant contradiction between articles 338 and 340: One case presents a theoretical system and a juridical classification, the other gives its particular application in Burgundy. The task of compiling customary norms consists precisely in combining universal principles and local practices. Thus article 339 begins by stating that usages vary: "In various places in Burgundy *mainmorte* takes various conditions." That article goes on, however, to attribute diversity to different types of origins rather than to geographical localities. Hence forms of partial servitude, *formariage* among them, appear as attenuations of an earlier condition.

We might well wonder what purpose was served by the juridical self-legitimation of this customal. It is absurd to think that a dependent subject to *formariage*, if such existed in Burgundy, ever had an opportunity to admire the coherence and generosity of this juridical text. Who provided an audience for customary law in its new Roman dress? Perhaps there was none, given that compiling customs was also an autonomous exercise practiced by professional jurists intent on producing impeccably reasoned arguments and classifications. The glossator of the *Coutume de Toulouse* at the end of the thirteenth century took particular pains over the impossible task of making feudal divisions of servitude coincide with a classification of types of agricultural status in the *Code* and the *Digest*.[53] It is not impossible that one of the principal target audiences for the new romanizing versions was royal and princely justice. When customary law was adorned with some universalizing coherence, it could be a respectable complement to royal law. When seigniorial violence excepted itself from common evidence, it had to mimic the style of the civil law, a source it shared with royal law.

The effects of such classifications merit investigation. The words used and the archaic ambivalence of expressions combining a Roman vocabulary and vernacular terms were apt to raise difficulties or lead to error. To return for a moment to the third category of the *Coutumier bourguignon*, serfs of *formariage*, we read: "Whenever a man marries in another jurisdiction and takes a wife in the place, if he takes her to lie the first night under his lord, he loses nothing, for he acquires the woman for the lord and brings her into his condition."[54] One wonders why Jules Delpit did not add this text to his dossier: The dependent avoids payment of a fine and confiscation of his property by leading his bride to *gésir soubs le seigneur!* The juridical reality, well attested elsewhere, is quite simple: In the logic of the declaratory value of gesture, specifying that the wedding night must be spent within or "under" *(dessous)* the lord's jurisdiction was equivalent to avowing dependency; it bore the same weight as a written engagement. By publicly displaying his wife's presence in the seigniory, the dependent enabled his lord to acquire a new dependent and any ensuing offspring. The counter example of the female dependent who marries outside her lord's territory confirms this reading of the expression: "But to the contrary if the woman, serf and of *formariage,* [marries] elsewhere than under her lord, whether she wants to lie under her lord or not, she is married outside and silently disavowed; for if she lies in the place she cannot acquire the man; and if she lies elsewhere the man acquires her because she is married outside and loses all she has."[55]

In real life the complex and outdated juridical categorizations sometimes found in seigniorial charters had little real effect. The immense majority of the peasant population drew up wills and married within the narrow limits of its social capacity but according to its own strategies.

Still, the society of the Ancien Régime cannot be reduced to a practice of exactions and constraints; the division of a local population into apparently arbitrary categories did not necessarily respond to strictly fiscal criteria. In a society defined since the Middle Ages by a constant tension between human equality and a hierarchy of conditions, differentiation seemed to function to produce social forms. We find an extremely late example of this in a tiny village community in Burgundy that claimed and applied a distinction between free and nonfree, apparently without pressure from the lord. This case deserves a closer look because it provides an exemplary illustration of unequal conditions under the Ancien Régime—the question underlying *formariage,* hence *cuissage.* It also offers a rare chance to examine what the people of the locality had to say about social divisions—interpreted, of course, by the scribes of the judiciary system.

As part of a vast study of the peasantry of Burgundy under the Ancien Régime, Pierre de Saint-Jacob published the text of a suit brought before the Grands Jours—thus brought to seigniorial justice—of Marsannay-en-Montagne (now in the department of La Côte-d'Or) in August 1703. The nub of this ordinary judiciary episode was a question of tithes *(dimes)* on vineyards. The question was an important one as the villagers, who had always agreed to a *dime* of one-twenty-fourth of the harvest, complained that *forains* (people not of the village community) did not pay the *dime* but instead paid a monetary fee proportional to the area of their vineyards. This conflict was typical of the later Ancien Régime: Peasants, acting in concert with burghers in the nearby towns and hamlets, took advantage of better fiscal conditions allowed them by relations with their patrons or protectors among the local lords and members of Parlement to infiltrate the land market, to the detriment of the villagers. The villagers claimed the *forains* were "able to make better conditions that the said inhabitants in favor of the vendors." The representatives of the village put forth a perfectly constructed argument. The document goes on, however, to draw a curious distinction: "All the said inhabitants assembled have stated to us that they were willing to receive the declarations that they are ready to make to us, that is, the free inhabitants on one side and the nonfree on another." At this point the court records divide the page into two columns, even though the tithing was strictly identical for the two groups. Somewhat later in the document the difference is explained:

> Furthermore the inhabitants have declared to us that they are of two sorts of inhabitants, some free, the others not free, according to how they are named in the above columns. [They] claim that there is no difference between them except that the free inhabitants have the use, uniquely among themselves, of a section of woods called the Freemen's Woods of the size of about 100 royal *arpents* and that the said nonfree inhabitants must pay a yearly *taille* of 10 sols per year to the lord who holds high justice in the said place, who is none other than the abbot of St. Benigne of Dijon. The above-named nonfree inhabitants have all declared they admitted to owing the said *taille*.

The difference between the two groups of villagers was only minimal. A tallage of 10 sols was not a great sum (equivalent to the royal tax on a cow). The freemen's right to the little woods would bring them only a bit of firewood. In all, the difference of status between two comparable households in the village would amount to no more than 5 percent of total yearly tallage. What is curious is that they themselves seem to insist on the distinction. They take the initiative to make the declaration; they insist on the listing in two columns. The *seigneur justicier*, the Abbey of Saint-Bénigne in Dijon, would never have had to put pressure on them to collect a seigniorial tallage that must have been meager, given the small numbers of the nonfree. Three nonfree men of the Chicheret family declare they have not paid the *taille* but will do so henceforth.

For no apparent reason the inhabitants of the village also tell the officers of the Grands Jours how social condition was transmitted, seemingly by their consent alone:

> The said free inhabitants have also declared that their children enjoy the same privilege of freedom along with their descendants—to wit, their sons, whether they marry the daughters of nonfree inhabitants of the said place or outsiders, and their daughters who marry outsider inhabitants. [In that case] the husband acquires the quality of free inhabitant during his marriage, but if his wife should happen to die and he remarries the daughter of a nonfree inhabitant or an outsider or if he remains a widower, he loses his privilege of freedom. It is nevertheless the custom that the children descended from the outsider father who has married the daughter of a free inhabitant keep their privilege forever, provided, however, that the daughters not marry a son of nonfree native inhabitants of the said Marsannay.[56]

The terms for this matrimonial transmission of social condition were fairly generous: Free status was the condition most easily extended. Behind its juridical simplicity this description shows how social division seems to have worked, something that probably should be linked to the capital question of the *forains* in the villagers' complaint about tithing on the vineyards. "Outsiders" were associated with or even substituted for the nonfree in defining the criteria for access to full "free" *(franc, franche)* status in the village. This means that nonfree status was a sort of transition stage permitting the integration of *forains* on the condition that they act as if they were resident villagers (and that they be subjected to the same taxes and fees as the native free villagers).

A document drawn up three years earlier throws further light on the question. In 1700 Jean Berthon, the parish priest of Marsannay, submitted a complaint to the royal *sergent* stating that the freemen of the village were giving him only a small share of the firewood from the freemen's woods, whereas the curé "should have his share, as being the principal free inhabitant in his quality of prior and parish priest." The freemen, he continues, "hold several assemblies to deliberate on the affairs of the said woods and on the division of its area without calling the said sieur Berthon to them." Division seems to have been made in a complicated manner: According to Berthon, the woods were divided unequally, and a sector left out was subject to obscure appropriations. He demanded the right to attend the meetings and keep "one of the keys to the coffer containing the titles to the said woods to which he will have access."[57] The wooded area was of an appreciable size (100 *arpents*) but it could not have provided large amounts of firewood. Its management, however, created remarkable forms of sociability—archives, assemblies, negotiation of unequal shares. Concerning its woods the small community of Marsannay created a four-class system: First came the *francs pléniers* (freemen with full rights), then came one "honorary" freeman (the curé may have thought himself the *premier franc* by virtue of his ecclesiastical dignity, but he was treated as a second-class freeman); then came the nonfree; finally the *forains*. (The last two categories were open to conditional promotion.) Although the regional socioeconomic context privileged the dynamics of networks of power and money as means of social promotion, in the village system marriage was the only recognized means of mobility—which perhaps explains why the parish priest came after the village-born freemen. Should we place the story of Marsannay in the dossier of the great controversy between Marc Bloch and Léo Verriest on the long-term persistence of social condition? Probably not. There is no reason to suppose that the dual division of the village was particularly ancient. It seems more probable that the nonfree group had been formed out of a *forain* population before the land market had been opened to burghers. The anecdote teaches us, however, that new social configurations can easily be translated into the old language of seigniorial domination.

Although the example of Marsannay shows how widespread the passion for social fragmentation was under the Ancien Régime, it must not distract us from the fact that those who owned the land dictated the terms of divisions into social categories. Beyond any seigniorial nostalgia for the mythic times of the "peasant nucleus," what mattered to the masters of the land (first nobles, then bourgeois) was to position themselves as the initiators of complex and strongly differentiated hierarchies. We have seen in chapter 4 how the lord of Louvie-Soubiron, a modest seigniory, fabricated a caste of sub-peasants on the scale of his own village and the neighboring village. The same fascination for caste in a society that was not based on it underlay the segregation of Jews and *cagots;* the idea of a primordial legitimacy for domination evolved in a society where, beginning in the late Middle Ages, the idea of nobility was founded in no identifiable function.[58] The rare and marginal diffusion of the myth of *cuissage,* which constructed a violent origin for seigniorial oppression, was part of the categorizing mentality that placed the master as the origin of the law.

FORMARIAGE AND THE RACE FOR SOVEREIGNTY

In the fourteenth century the strict notion of property formed by both the civil law inherited from Rome and canon law began to spread. One has the impression that beginning in the early fourteenth century there was a race for inalienable rights of ownership that granted the most titles to the strongest, along with the surest guarantees of legitimacy. As Brian Tierney has noted,[59] around 1200 the two meanings of the word *dominium* ("ownership of things" and "powers of high justice") were clearly distinct, but two centuries later that distinction was blurred. This was by no means a conceptual regression. Accumulated meanings aimed at constructing zones of absolute power over things and people. This phenomenon has been studied from the viewpoint of royal sovereignty,[60] but no one has sufficiently stressed that aspirations to absolute power could be found on all levels of society. It is precisely in rights of succession that the race for absolute power can best be seen. Jacques Krynen has shown the important role played by royal succession in 1315 and 1328, when the Capetians had no more male heirs in the direct line and had to define a doctrine of succession. He points out that another essential moment began when the Treaty of Troyes in 1420 excluded the dauphin Charles from succeeding his father Charles VI. On that occasion the Nîmes jurist Jean de Terrevermeille coined the adage, "le mort saisit le vif" (the dead [king] vests the living), a phrase that implies a substitution of persons in royal succession with no intermediary and no recourse.[61] The old notion of *saisine* was put to the service of Roman concepts making the *de cujus* and his heir one and the same person. Royal doctrine attempted to show that kingship did not derive from the common law regarding succession (it is inalienable, it excludes women, it is not open to being tested) and to translate that exception in terms of general law. We find the same conceptual duality applied to bondmen. A document of the chapter of Saint-Pierre de Troyes published by Anne-Marie Patault states explicitly: "And as by custom it is popularly said that the dead vests the living among the free, the dead man vests his lord among serfs."[62] Archaisms found a place in this modernization: The lord retained a bonus from feudalism because, unlike current norms regarding succession (notably after the application of the principle of *saisine*), the transmission of the patrimony of a bondman did not imply an unlimited obligation to pay his debts. Because serfs remained outside norms regarding succession (in both the royal and the common law) that were increasingly marked by the notion of inalienable property (an idea that later achieved wide currency), they were even more transformed into property. Once again we can see the tendency of feudal domination to strive for mastery over both men and land. Eventually it undermined the economic coherence of the system.

A late example (thus valuable for our purposes, as it is contemporary with the dramatized versions of the *droit de cuissage*) gives a clear idea of how *formariage* functioned in these sovereign micro-units. I borrow this example from a recent study by Jean Gallet that is particularly interesting for its systematic and exhaustive exploitation of the archives of Fénétrange, a minuscule seigniory in Lorraine situated on the Sarre between Nancy and Strasbourg.[63]

In 1761 Odile Huller had to pay a sum equivalent to nearly one-tenth of her possessions and expected legacies in order to marry outside the barony. When she did so, she ceased to be a dependent. This form of emancipation had become rare in the eighteenth century, though not unheard of. The case is interesting, however, because it demonstrates the relatively important part this sort of payment played in the seigniorial economy. The barony was formed of a fortified castle, Fénétrange, and eighteen villages spaced fairly compactly in the territory but situated in a region of interpenetrating seigniories. Despite a strong tendency to village endogamy, tallage and dovetailed jurisdictions made marrying outside the seigniory—that is, *formariage*—inevitable. The barony, an alodial land of the empire, recognized no superior power until the eighteenth century. By the late Middle Ages it had been divided as a result of successions and sales, with one portion remaining undivided. In 1664 seven barons shared lordship. Despite a slow trickle of purchased enfranchisements, nearly all the village population was under personal servitude. When the barony was attached to the duchy of Lorraine in 1752, every dependent was a member of one dependent category or another and knew which of the three remaining barons (all by maternal transmission) was his or her own lord. In 1752 these dependents were no longer under *mainmorte* but were still subject to *formariage* and *forfuyance* (under pain of confiscation), paid tallage *(schafft),* and owed *corvées* and various minor dues (providing roasting chickens, paying tallage on livestock, paying occasional special tallage). Servitude brought the barony some 20 percent of its revenues, as compared to 41 percent from direct exploitation of the demesne, 23 percent from consumption taxes, and 16 percent from tithes. *Formariage* brought in an extremely small proportion of total revenues (0.56 percent) but was the key to maintaining demographic strength.

These figures clearly show that a radical transformation had taken place in feudal exploitation. The barony was a major proprietor but also a local example of a statelike micropower (40 percent of its income came from its own revenues and 40 percent from fiscal receipts exempt from royal and imperial taxes). Servitude, although not a negligible item in this budget, was not central to baronial finances; rather, it reflected the anachronistic sovereignty of baronial power. It linked the general condition of the political subject and the condition of the personal dependent. The overall situation of the individual subject hardly changed when the barony disappeared: The "subsidy" paid to the duchy of Lorraine was ten times the *taille* due under servitude, but it also replaced other and much higher payments that had accompanied tallage.

In its most derisory and archaic forms, dependency was a way to keep up an appearance of political sovereignty. A customal in Vaudémont, also in Lorraine, offers an example of a control likening the status of royal subject to that of a seigniorial subject. The small county of Vaudémont was independent in the early seventeenth century but had as its sovereign the duke of Lorraine. He ordered the compilation of customs, charging the *bailli* with collecting texts and usages and submitting them to the count's Estates, a task completed in 1605, although restive nobles caused delays in the final compilation. The "reformed customs" of 1605 offers a remarkable normative and rational description of a microstate. Article 27 limited the arbitrary nature of tallage by restricting the right to set amounts to nobles with powers of high justice *(hauts justiciers):* "The said *hauts justiciers* may not at will put supplementary charges of tallage on landholdings on outside goods, but [only] such that the proprietors are not crushed, and it would be good to stipulate the amount that the said tallage should be for each *jour* of land, both empty and built upon; it being found in several ancient documents that the said tallage was fixed at 2 blancs per *jour* empty or built upon."[64] The nobles demanded "surcease and opposition" at this point because they wanted to eliminate the distinction between tallage on land and on persons (*taille réelle* and *taille personnelle*) as given in article 26 of the draft. Above all they objected to the connection between powers of high justice and collection and control of tallage. A new article 26 was more to their liking: "In several and various seigniories of the said county, both in the domain of his Excellency and in the villages of the lords prelates and vassals, tallage is at will; and in others it is limited; and by this means the said tallages will remain as formerly." This dispute clarifies what was at stake in the reforms. More than ever, the chief characteristic of sovereignty was justice, a source of both profits and power, particularly since the end of the Middle Ages, when state power came to be measured by its ability to institute a new penal law, which had been largely abandoned to local custom in medieval law. Seigniorial rights and the notion of dependency constituted the raw material (sometimes lowly or inert) of this capital form of political sovereignty. When late dependency is read in this political key, the critical representation of the lord is translated in terms of tyranny, and at the height of his personal enjoyment of the common wealth the tyrant might seize the goods that the female subject (and her male kin) held most sacred, her virginity.

The astonishing persistence of bizarre rights—what the Enlightenment referred to as "feudal abuses"—was in large part due to such political interests. It was not limited, as has too often been said, to a "feudal reaction," nor was it a purely discursive phenomenon that arose when Enlightenment thinkers or the monarchy militantly amplified exceptional but existing customs. To bring this survey of possible contexts of the *droit de cuissage* to a close, we need to examine another considerable rift in ancien régime societies where dependency played a very different role.

INTERACTIONS: *FORMARIAGE* AND THE WAR BETWEEN THE SEXES

Until around 1100 dependency was transmitted on the model of slavery in the ancient world, and a child's social condition was determined by the mother. As the Roman adage said, the child "followed the womb [sequi ventrem]." The slave was by nature a thing, and since marriage between slaves had no juridical reality, the child could only be the product of his mother. This was in direct contrast with the free citizen defined by his patrilineal ancestry; moreover, as we have seen, the father and the son constituted one person at the moment of succession.

Within the framework of serfdom, the first mentions of dues or exchanges for a *formariage* (before the fact) concern women. Georges Duby notes an early instance in a serf of the Abbey of Cluny in the mid-eleventh century who married a female free dependent of Saint-Vincent de Mâcon and paid *pro ea* (for her)—that is, he compensated Cluny for its loss of their offspring—giving the abbey two of his own slaves *(mancipia)*, following a logic of evening up the demographic score.[65]

The predominance of this principle of compensation probably explains why most mentions of *formariage* concern only the woman and future mother. The customs of the female abbey of La Sainte-Trinité de Caen in regard to its English manors set rules only for the daughters of servile dependents: "The freeman will give his daughter by requesting permission [cum licentia] but will not buy her; the nonfree will buy her."[66] The male dependent "cannot marry his daughter outside the domain [extra villam] without authorization [sine licencia] or if he fails to deliver the *guare* [a due found elsewhere under the name of *gerson*]."[67]

When dependency broke up in the late eleventh century, the rules for transmission of social condition and for succession tended to become unified, confusing statutory distinctions. In real life the bondman became too similar to the freeman dependent in his land for parallel systems for the transmission of condition to be maintained—which had obvious consequences for inheritance. The patrilineal principle spread everywhere during the twelfth century. The best proof of the abandonment of maternal transmission of condition may be the attempts of castellan lords to impose the rule of the "worst condition," attributing servile status to the offspring if either parent, irrespective of gender, was a serf. In an infinitely varied mosaic of conditions, mention of this rule can still be found in the seventeenth century in the ecclesiastical lands of the chapter of Sainte-Croix de Verdun, in the Nivernais, and in the Bourbonnais. Here and there the rule of maternal transmission persisted, reinforced by the rediscovery of Roman law. The rule of maternal transmission may have mitigated the rule of worst condition: Some fifteenth-century documents state that "the womb emancipates." Maternal transmission was also maintained or reestablished (among other places) in the official customal of Troyes drafted in 1509,[68] in a customal of Bar (1506), and in one of Chaumont-en-Bassigny (1509). The last of these states, "Between the Aube and the Marne rivers, the offspring follows the womb and the condition of the same."[69] This customal adds a qualification: "The offspring follows the womb except if one of the two spouses is noble."

This marginal resistance to a patrilineal standardization of succession systems throws light on one of the fundamental aspects of *formariage*, analyzed in masterly fashion by Eleanor Searle in an article on merchet in England (as we have seen, merchet was among the "proofs" of the existence of the *droit de cuissage*).[70] The specifics of the English setting preclude any literal application of Searle's conclusions to France. Personal dependence was less widespread in Britain than in France, but also the efforts of the English kings to spread the common law stifled seigniorial claims much earlier than in France. Nonetheless, the practice of *cullage* and merchet was similar enough in the two lands to permit a parallel. Both were a tax, fixed or proportional to wealth, on dependents' marriages, and both first appeared in the thirteenth century; further, in both cases the precise etymology of the term remains a mystery.

For Eleanor Searle merchet was essentially aimed at controlling anticipated transmission of wealth by dowering daughters. Some aspects of vassality came into the picture as well: The lord retained the right to choose the vassal who would come into a tenure by marriage. In general, however, the lord took advantage of a tension within peasant societies torn between a tenacious habit of dowering daughters in advance of inheritance and an increasing adherence to the model of male primogeniture in imitation of the upper classes. Paradoxically, the lord's paid authorization made the peasant freer to dispose of his patrimony in his own way: If the property was free, the new customary practices strictly limited the peasant's capacity to bequeath it. In short, the dependent bought (and at times paid dearly for) the ability to give his marriageable daughters a relative advantage. This was not a bipolar but a tripolar relation, involving the lord, the peasant, and his heirs (on occasion backed up by local norms). Moreover, in practical terms *formariage* affected land dependency much more than personal dependency, despite the jurists' efforts to standardize procedures. This explains the fluidity we can observe in the definitions of dependent categories.

This interpretation of *formariage* and merchet thus offers another possible explanation for the very occasional emergence of the myth of *cuissage:* At the time it may have expressed a village community's hostility toward women's right to receive a portion of their father's wealth. The nubile young woman was pictured as a creature intent on capturing wealth, caught in her own trap and become a victim. In this view the lord, objectively the ally of fathers and daughters, undergoes a rhetorical reversal to take on the role of persecutor of young women's virtue, and the young women are seen as more surely protected by the legal autonomy of custom than by the incestuous solicitude of natural fathers or seigniorial father figures.

Thus this rapid survey shows that the contextual conditions for producing the myth of *cuissage* were many and heterogeneous, as were actual conditions of dependency. Servitude in the Middle Ages could not have engendered either the reality or the myth of *cuissage*. The relation of personal dependence was not widespread enough to create continuity or accumulate representations; it did not underlie collective social trauma, whatever may have been thought by the liberal historians of yesteryear or jurists of today specializing in the history of serfdom. Nonetheless, the archaic vocabulary and practices of dependency produced virtual representations that in particular circumstances incorporated into timeless images of oppression the more precisely contextual figures of the barbarian, the master, the tyrant, and the father. The picture of those contextual possibilities would be incomplete if it did not include the singular connotations of religious transgression of the ecclesiastical *droit de cuissage*.

CHAPTER SIX

The Ecclesiastical *Droit de Cuissage*

T here is something surprising in the very idea of an ecclesiastical *droit de cuissage*. Early in its history Christianity accorded a special value to marriage and to the necessity for free consent on the part of both spouses. The principle of equality before God pushed the Church to recognize the validity of marriage in all social conditions: In the third century Pope Calixtus I declared unions between slaves valid. Pope Julius I reaffirmed the doctrine in the fourth century in a decretal that was incorporated into Gratian's *Decretum* (twelfth century), the compilation of canon law that rapidly became the sturdiest pillar of Church law. The laity, obviously, was largely unaware of these measures. Ecclesiastical institutions also came to terms with the landholding interests of the great proprietors, however: In 813 the Council of Chalon decreed that the master must not withhold consent to marriage if the couple were serfs belonging to different masters. This canon also went into the *Decretum*. Pope Alexander III (1159–81) energetically resolved the contradiction by decreeing the absolute validity of marriages between dependents, irrespective of the form of their dependency.[1] This legislation was later entered into the collection of decretals published by order of Pope Gregory IX in 1236, the second pillar of canon law. In spite of all these efforts the ecclesiastical *droit de cuissage* figures largely in Delpit's dossier, where it reflects three centuries of tradition.

The affair of the curé of Bourges related by Nicolas Boyer (or more probably by a facetious disciple) by no means constitutes proof of the existence of the *droit de cuissage,* but it does point to some areas of tension. The tendency to link sexual and seigniorial tyranny with the Church was not limited to the Gallican and anticlerical nineteenth century. It already had a long history in the mid-sixteenth century, when the image of a priest of limited intelligence and lusty appetites playing the potentate in his parish was a fitting pendant among the secular clergy to the picture of the coarse and lustful monk. Its development had no need of the bitter satires of the Lutheran Reformation. Against all likelihood and despite the extreme rarity of "proofs," for centuries clerics were seen as crafty practitioners of the droit du seigneur. A first reason probably lies in a long critical and satirical tradition of portrayal of medieval clergy.

Lustful Priests

The origins of medieval anticlericalism coincide with the rise of the Catholic Church's new and specific power after the turn of the millennium, when the Gregorian reforms aimed toward Church control of all spiritual power, until then broadly dispersed. European societies put up a strong cultural and social resistance to this move, in a political and religious antagonism that came to a head in the investiture controversy, engendering a violent and at times scurrilous pamphlet literature that fills much of the three thick volumes *De lite* in the *Monumenta germaniae historica*. Virulent attacks on the clergy were not limited to imperial milieus but also animated a rich folklore aimed at the Roman Church that found a welcome in England and Spain and spread throughout Europe.[2] This pamphlet literature, mostly written by clerics, expressed the resentment of churches or ecclesiastical classes who thought themselves oppressed by the papacy or a corrupt high clergy. One twelfth-century canon named Garcia wrote a stinging parodic hagiography vaunting the efficacious virtues of St. Rufin (gold) and St. Albin (silver).[3] Even St. Bernard, a man close to the papacy and hostile to any challenge to the Church, writes ferocious passages on Rome in his treatise *On Consideration*.[4] The image of pontifical Rome elaborated when the Curia transformed the Roman Church into a veritable proto-state made it appear a locus of ambition, corruption, concupiscence, and hypocrisy. The various heresies or "evangelistic" dissidences of the twelfth century further accentuated criticism of the Church. Beginning in the thirteenth century Roman anticlericalism gradually became more "democratic," passing from religious and political circles to lay culture and shifting its focus to include not only the Curia and the high clergy but also simple parish priests and the mendicant orders.

The sexual tone of this dark image of the Church was one result of the moral renewal commanded by the popes of the Gregorian reform. An increased insistence on priestly chastity and celibacy (a tenet from then to

our own day often seen as strangely at odds with human nature) exposed
many offenders to general opprobrium, but the vanity of the effort also
elicited mocking skepticism. In the late twelfth century even the irre-
proachable St. Bernard was an indirect victim of a bawdy literature that
took revenge on the more determined champions of moral rigor by attributing the liveliest and most hypocritical sexuality to them. Walter
Map, himself a cleric, includes this anecdote in his *De nugis curialium*
(Courtier's Trifles):

> Two white abbots [Cistercians] were conversing about Bernard in the
> presence of Gilbert Foliot, bishop of London, and commending him on
> the strength of his miracles. After relating one of them, one of the ab-
> bots said: "Though these stories of Bernard are true, I did myself see that
> on occasion the grace of miracles failed him. There was a man living on
> the borders of Burgundy who asked him to come and heal his son. We
> went, and found the boy dead. Dom Bernard ordered his body to be car-
> ried into a private room, turned everyone out, threw himself upon the
> boy, prayed, and got up again: but the boy did not get up; he lay there
> dead." "Then he was the most unlucky of monks," said I; "I have heard
> before now of a monk throwing himself upon a boy, but always, when
> the monk got up, the boy promptly got up too." The abbot went very
> red, and a lot of people left the room to have a good laugh.[5]

What is more, the development of schools and then universities in fast
growing cities produced a sizable mass of "clerics" who had received minor orders but were not fully integrated into the Church and who sometimes led a merry life, enjoying the exemptions and privileges of a clerical
status that set them apart from their fellow-citizens. From the twelfth
century to the 1330s the literature of the fabliaux happily portrayed clerics' sexual exploits, focusing either on wandering goliards, clever and cynical opportunists who, with the naive or knowing complicity of wives and
daughters, took advantage of the burghers' simplicity (as in Jean Bodel's
fabliau of Gombert)[6] or, more often, on parish priests, bumbling or clever,
tormented by sexual urges.

The curé of the fabliaux is characteristically a creature who continually
demands sexual favors because he lacks a sexual outlet. His constant presence in the small world of the village community makes his search more
obsessive than the advances of various errant figures always ready to profit
from a sexual opportunity or to snatch a maidenhood. Priests' adventures
were abetted by their legitimate access to private homes, where they were
welcomed by pious burghers or peasants. They might not only show the
traditional cleverness of the "sly dogs" and vagrants but also possess a skillful professional understanding of human credulity. In one fabliau by Jean

Bodel the wife of a villein in Bailluel is waiting for her lover, the parish priest, when her husband returns home unexpectedly.[7] The wife immediately feigns fright and sets to wailing, exclaiming how sick he looks, and puts him to bed, all the while talking of the illness devouring him. The priest arrives, enters into the game, and with rites and prayers proclaims the unhappy man dead. The husband, persuaded that he is in fact dead and in hell or purgatory, is then obliged to watch his wife frolic with the priest. In *Le prestre qui abevete* (The voyeur priest) by Garin,[8] a concupiscent parish priest arrives at the door of a man whose wife he covets. Bending down, he peeks through the keyhole and sees the couple dining. He sets up a clamor, shouting through the door to denounce the fornication he claims he is observing. The peasant shouts back that they are simply eating. The priest insists, proposing to the husband that they change places. The priest goes into the house and makes love with the wife, all the while loudly proclaiming, for the benefit of the peasant, that he is having dinner: The door must be enchanted! On occasion it is a wily priest who is deceived. In *Le prestre taint* (The dyed priest) by Gautier Le Leu,[9] a priest lusts after the virtuous wife of a dyer. When the worthy woman refuses him and pushes him away, he enlists the services of a woman who serves him as sacristan and is an expert go-between. She too fails, receiving a good tongue-lashing from the dyer's wife. When the go-between complains to the priest, he goes mad with rage and desire and rings the church bells, calling the congregation together to decree the excommunication of the dyer and his wife. After vigorous negotiation he withdraws the sanction for the price of a mass, but the husband demands explanations from his wife and, once informed, plots revenge. The wife must pretend to be willing to give in to the priest if she is paid 10 livres and must set up a rendez-vous. When her priestly would-be lover arrives, the false adulteress must persuade him to take a bath, at which point the supposedly cuckolded husband will appear. Everything takes place as the couple had planned, and the wife, thinking ahead, gets the priest to jump into a vat filled with a brazilwood dye next to the basin containing bath water. When the husband arrives he tells his workers to extract the priest, naked and tinted mahogany brown, saying the figure is for a crucifix he has been preparing. The newly dyed crucifix is placed against the wall in the common room, and as the two eat their meal, they remark that the sculptor has exaggerated the dimensions of the divine subject's member and suggest rectifying such an unseemly attribute. The terrified priest, naked and dark brown, flees in shame. We can note in passing that this literature of a rare licentiousness took an obvious pleasure in profanation. A vast anthology could be made of such joyous tales about lubricious parish priests.[10]

Extensive reading of the fabliaux, and after them the fourteenth-century farces and nouvelles that picked up where the fabliaux left off, shows that this satirical and often indecent literature makes no mention of the theme of *droit de cuissage*, lay or ecclesiastical, before the mid-fifteenth century. The topic could obviously have provided amusing variations (abusive claims, ruses to escape enforcement of the right, and so forth), as in eighteenth-century plays and nineteenth-century novels—which, incidentally, did not enjoy the startling license of the medieval jongleurs.

How can we explain this absence? The simplest explanation would be to state that mentions are lacking because the *droit de cuissage* did not exist. The very few mentions noted previously (the "Chanson des vilains de Verson" [1247], the *dénombrement* from La Rivière-Bourdet [1419], the three *aveux* from Amiens [1507] and Louvie-Soubiron [1538]) were confined to private documents and thus were insufficient to circulate the myth. Nonetheless, the geographical distribution of those five independent occurrences suggests that they might have arisen from the same virtual notion. Thus we might think the theme failed to appear because it was irrelevant: The literature of the fabliaux and the nouvelles emerged in the free towns, which had little familiarity with the rural world of personal dependency. Villeins figure in them only as stock characters who give a social cast to human dull-wittedness. The satiric fables present a homogeneous universe where the lecherous priest is an ordinary figure who is moved by the same lust and greed as the other characters but enjoys specific advantages (access to homes, use of canonical sanctions, a professional manipulation of credulity) and suffers specific handicaps (imposed chastity, at times lack of common sense). The means for sexual conquest—physical force, corruption, and deceit—are homogeneous as well, distributed among all characters without any real social or cultural distinction. The literature of the fabliaux privileges the individual by showing desire's power of invention as stronger than principles or institutions. In other words, the fabliaux lack a representation of power—the dramatic sense of difference that guaranteed reception of the myth of *cuissage*. The time-honored medieval tradition of anticlericalism is thus a false lead.

More accurately, the old anticlerical tradition found no outlet or efficacy until the eighteenth century, when the combat between Gallicans and freethinkers took it out of its literary framework and reapplied it to a global vision of the Church. But in the sixteenth century the story of the curé of Bourges, although close to the thematic material of the fabliaux, did not make anyone laugh. He frightened people or aroused their indignation, with none of the joyous complicity depicted by the jongleurs of the twelfth and thirteenth centuries.

A rupture and a change of pace had taken place in the apprehension of the lecherous priest. Why? Are we to think that the traumatic experience of the Wars of Religion removed the parish priest from his familiar, comfortable setting to depict him as a terrifying personage and an agent of external History? Need we evoke the efforts of the Counter-Reformation and the Council of Trent to place a cope on medieval Christianity, definitively distancing the priest from his parish milieu? Both are possible, but other symptoms, noted in recent studies on the "flamboyant Christianity" of the latter half of the fifteenth century or in Denis Crouzet's fine book on the Wars of Religion, indicate that a fundamental shift had occurred earlier, when Catholicism stiffened even before the Protestant Reformation.[11]

Our curé of Bourges, confined within the world of the jurists, would be an extremely weak and isolated sign of a changed representation of the lubricious priest if we did not have a source of capital importance unknown to the laborious participants in the nineteenth-century controversy. In 1462 the anonymous author of the *Cent nouvelles nouvelles* (One Hundred New Tales) invented the literary motif of ecclesiastical *cuissage,* perhaps providing Pseudo-Boyer with his source. This work imitated a genre deeply rooted in the Middle Ages from the time of Boccaccio's *Decameron.* It was also, as Pierre Jourda has said, "the first modern collection of tales in our literature."[12]

The hundred tales that make up this work are related by thirty-six narrators. The most illustrious among them, "Monseigneur," is none other than Philip the Good, duke of Burgundy, the most powerful sovereign of his day, who commissioned the book and received it in 1462. The other alleged (or perhaps actual) narrators are often high personages in the ducal court: Philippe Pot, councilor and chamberlain to the duke; Philippe de Laon, the duke's squire; Michault de Chauzy; Monsieur de Fiennes; and the marquis de Rothelin. A well-known writer, Antoine de La Salle, is joined to this small company of tale-tellers. According to Pierre Champion, the work's most recent editor, the anonymous author was Philippe Pot.[13] The book was published in 1486 in the very early days of printing.

The thirty-second nouvelle, related by Monsieur de Villiers, tells of the installation of the Cordeliers (Observant Franciscans) in Catalonia in the town of Ostelleric (Hostalrich, not far from Gerona). Chased out of

Spain, the Franciscans are welcomed, first by the local lord and then by his son, who gives them a fine church and honors them with his generosity. They soon prosper, preach everywhere, and are accepted as confessors by the entire population. Women are particularly touched by their ministry. The tale relates:

> Now, however, you will hear the evil deception and horrid betrayal which these falsely pious hypocrites perpetrated on the very men and women who did them so much good from day to day. The Franciscans made each and every woman in the city understand that she was obliged to pay a tithe to God on all their goods. "You are bound to render us a tithe on the number of times that your husbands have carnal knowledge of you just as you tithe to the Lord, to your parish, and to your curate for any chattel or any property whatsoever. We do not exact proportional payment on anything else for, as you know, we carry no money at all. And if we do not seek any financial gain, it is because we have no interest at all in the temporal and transitory goods of this world. We seek and petition only for spiritual goods. The tithe you owe us and for which we ask you, is not of temporal goods. It is because of the divine, spiritual, holy sacrament which you have received by marrying. No one else but us is entitled to collect this tithe, for we are the Friars of the Observance." The poor simple women, who thought that these good brothers were more angels than earthly men, did not refuse to pay the tithe. There was not one of them, from the loftiest to the lowliest, who didn't pay when her turn came. Even the lord's lady was not exempted. Thus, all the women of the city [were prey to] these valiant monks.[14]

One could not ask for more in a founding text for ecclesiastical *cuissage*. The Cordeliers in this fable take their "tithe" in kind—that is, in sexual installments—as the "spiritual" equivalent of monetary taxes due lords, lay or ecclesiastical. The sexual due demanded here refers to no longstanding usage but is the invention of these Observant Franciscans. The notion bears repeating: Lay *cuissage* has no place here; this universe, quite different from the realm of the fabliaux, represents all levels of society, lords, magistrates, squires, merchants, and peasants. The tale by no means neutralizes the question of power. The lustful lords never invoke seigniorial rights: In the twenty-fourth tale, told by Monsieur de Fiennes, a count tormented by desire for one of his female subjects tries first seduction, then brute force, but his attempted rape is foiled when the woman cleverly succeeds in immobilizing her aggressor by getting him tangled up removing his leggings while she escapes.[15]

The tale about the Franciscans offers an extreme example of the tendency, noted above in connection with Walter Map, of attributing the most extravagant sexual demands to the most ascetic churchmen. Franciscan Observance had grown up gradually during the fourteenth and fifteenth centuries as a counter-movement to the "conventual" current in the Franciscan Order; in imitation of the "spirituals" of the late thirteenth century, the Observance preached absolute fidelity to the testament of Francis of Assisi and radical rejection of property in any form, real or disguised. The Cordeliers preached a stringently ascetic version of Christianity: In 1462, the Observance, for some twenty years an independent institution, underwent a phase of rapid development and gained prominence for its sharp criticism of secular power and its insistent intervention in the life of the faithful. St. Bernardino of Siena, the most illustrious early fifteenth-century Observant, preached sexual abstinence on the wedding night, a precept closely connected, as we shall soon see, to the construction of the myth of ecclesiastical *cuissage*.[16]

The manipulation of female credulity, already present in the fabliaux, is highly refined in the tale about the Cordeliers. There is no longer a question of simple use of the power of liturgy (as when the villein of Bailluel was led to think he was dead) or enchantment (as with the magical door and its optical illusion); instead, the tale uses the theological concept of the sacrament filled with grace and distributed in superabundance—the same concept that justified the practice of selling indulgences beginning in the thirteenth century. There is another radical change here: The targets of the Cordeliers' lubricity are no longer simple-minded peasant men and some concupiscent peasant women but all females from the lord's wife to the least of his female subjects.

The tone of this nouvelle is important as well: Where the fabliaux made a show of fantasy (particularly in their preliminaries), the nouvelle plays the game of reality and chronicle. In this tale the Cordeliers' acts are set within a precise geographical and chronological framework; the order's arrival is explained historically, and the Catalan town opens its gates to the friars when they have been chased out of Spain because of their exactions. Still, the action takes place far from where it is narrated and received, in a relative "elsewhere" propitious, as we have seen in chapter 1, to the wildest sexual fantasies. It would be pointless to ask whether any listener or reader believed in the accuracy of a fable that was, if not true, at least clever. It is more important to note a shift in tone: The fable of the Cordeliers collecting their tithe is narrated with muted hatred rather than in the joking register of the fabliaux.

The rest of the nouvelle tells how the deplorable custom, which could last only as long as the tithe-paying women kept a conspiratorial silence, came to an end. One day a newly married couple pass before the Franciscans' church on their way home from supping with relatives. The young woman insists on stopping at the church for a moment, and when her astonished husband cannot understand what devotions could be so pressing, the young woman speaks of a tithe she owes Brother Eustachius. The husband conceals his fury in order to find out more, only to learn that each of the friars has been collecting the "tithes" of fourteen or sixteen women. He invites Brother Eustachius to dinner the next day, threatens to strangle him to make him confess, then goes off to report the facts to the lord of the city. The lord calls a general assembly of the townspeople, where he feigns concern about whether the women have paid their debts to their protectors, the Cordeliers. All the women, without exception, assure him they have paid their tithes, at times in advance. Only a few old women remain silent. The lord has them interrogated. They protest their willingness to tithe but state the confessors had rejected their offerings and, against their will, changed their tithe into "textiles, sheets, cushions, bench-coverings, pillows, and other such items." When the women have been heard, the men remain to deliberate alone.

> It was finally resolved that the husbands would go set fire to the convent, and would burn the monks and their church. They removed the *Corpus Domini* from the building, along with some other relics, and sent them to the parish. Without further inquiry, they set fire to the monastery in several places and didn't leave until the fire had consumed everything, monks, convent, church, dormitory, and all the buildings, of which there were many. Thus the poor friars paid very dearly for the unaccustomed tithe which they had levied. God himself, who could do nothing to remedy the situation, had his house burned.[17]

We must take seriously the tragic conclusion of this nouvelle. It announces an epoch soon to come when many houses of God were burned in the name of fidelity to him. We have moved beyond the joyous revelry of the ducal court in Burgundy to another world where assemblies decide on radical acts of arson in the name of God, "qui n'en povoit mais." The only elements of divine sacrality that are spared in the terrible punishment meted out to the Cordeliers are the Corpus Domini (the monstrance and the consecrated hosts) and some relics, just as in the great Catholic uprisings in the Wars of Religion of the following century, with their many political-religious processions linked, precisely, with the feast of Corpus Domini or patron saints' feast days featuring monstrances and relics.[18]

Burgundian literary fiction returns us to the episode of Montauban. I have suggested above that the legend of the town's founding by peasants in revolt against a monastic *cuissage* demanded by the monks of nearby

Montauriol could be connected with the burning of the cathedral of Saint-Martin (the former monastery of Saint-Théodard) in 1562 by the Protestants. The chronologies correspond fairly closely, if we allow for an anti-institutional obsession with purification in late fifteenth-century Catholicism. Protestants who burned churches were not a new human species springing up in the steps of Luther or Calvin; they followed one or more generations of fanatical Catholics. In both Montauban and Dijon the sexual motif seems appropriate to the context: Denis Crouzet has studied innumerable texts relating, even glorifying, a monstrous series of sexual misdeeds inflicted by Protestants on priests or vice versa.

Twenty years after this nouvelle the bawdy Gallic motifs of the fabliaux underwent another mutation. In 1484 two Dominicans, Heinrich Krämer (Henricus Institoris) and Jakob Sprenger (Jacobus Sprengerus) wrote their summa, *Malleus maleficarum,* the first text to present proofs of the existence of sorcery. The witch-hunting frenzy that ensued is a familiar story. This precise, well-documented text, informed by a solid Thomism, was written with irrefutable rigor and gravity.[19] Among the many practical examples of sorcery the authors cite, one occurrence might have fit well into the world of the fabliaux. One day a peasant finds that his genitals have disappeared. He is upset. He immediately accuses a neighbor woman suspected of sorcery, and after many threats and entreaties she leads him to a tree bearing a large nest that contains many penises of varying form and size. The witch invites the man to climb up to find his own. Seized with delusions of grandeur, the peasant picks a member much bigger than his own and gets ready to appropriate it when the witch dissuades him by saying that the model he chose could not possibly be his own and must belong to a priest.[20] This episode has the malicious wit of a fabliau, but the requisite fantasy has disappeared. The tone of the narration and the way events are perceived have changed completely: The event is cited as a proof; there is nothing to laugh about. Once again, a motif takes on meaning only from context.

The nouvelle about the Cordeliers in Catalonia provides a foundation for the fable of ecclesiastical *cuissage,* but it lacks specific mention of the wedding night. Although the sexual tithe extracted by the Franciscans was founded in a moral theology of the sacrament of marriage, the specific circumstance of a wedding night is only a point of departure. Another of the *Cent nouvelles nouvelles* from Burgundy, the fifty-second, narrated by Monsieur de La Roche, does focus on the wedding night. The tale is constructed on an old model: A noble father on his deathbed gives his son three final pieces of advice. They seem ridiculous, but the son's later adventures prove them apt. This is a classical scheme for a magical tale. The father's first piece of advice to the son is to stop his visits to a house if the master should serve him dark bread instead of white. The point soon is made clear: The son frequents the house of a neighbor who has a charming wife. He is unaware of his friend's mounting jealousy until one evening his neighbor serves him dark bread rather than the usual white. The son immediately understands, leaves the house never to return, and hangs a crust of the dark bread in his own house to remind him of his father's sage advice. The second warning was not to let his horse run in a valley. A serious accident corroborates the value of the father's second bit of wise counsel, and the son memorializes it too by hanging the skin of the dead horse in the great hall. The third piece of advice was not to marry a foreign woman. As it happens, the son soon leaves for a distant land, where he serves a noble lord who rewards him with the hand of his daughter in marriage. On the wedding eve, he is told that the custom of the land is not to lie with one's wife on the wedding night. The young man acquiesces, "since that is the custom." By chance, however, his room is next to the one where his wife is to sleep. He makes a little hole in the dividing wall to "see his wife's face," but he sees more: "It was easy for him to see his wife climb into bed. A short time afterwards, he also saw the household's chaplain climb into bed next to the bride to keep her company, so that she would not be afraid. Perhaps he wanted to try to take payment of future tithes, as did the Franciscans discussed previously." At that point the son understands the meaning of his father's third piece of advice. The next day he surreptitiously takes the chaplain's breeches from the room next door, then he pretends not to want to sleep with his wife until he can show his parents-in-law his own house. They make the voyage, and his wife's parents admire the house but wonder at the crust of dark bread, the horse skin, and the chaplain's breeches hanging in the great hall. The son relates the lessons he has learned and delivers their daughter back into their hands.[21] Ecclesiastical *cuissage* seems more firmly constructed here because the author explicitly connects this episode with the tale about the Catalonian Cordeliers.

How, though, was this serious, aggressive motif of the odious sexuality of churchmen prepared? How was the transition made from a smiling gauloiserie to this grating, violent fantasy? The tradition of *cuissage* itself may perhaps provide the missing link. If we want to trace the operations of this late medieval and early sixteenth-century transformation, we must turn to one of the few cases in which "proofs" of *cuissage* come from authentically medieval materials.

The tradition of ancien régime *cuissage* soon included another famous case of ecclesiastical *cuissage* founded on authentic records of an early fifteenth-century suit where the bishop of Amiens was the losing party. Boyer (or the Pseudo-Boyer of 1551) speaks first of the abusive lords of the Auvergne, then of the Amiens affair, to provide a context for the libidinous exaggerations of the curé of Bourges. This suit, which involved a bishop who dared demand monetary compensation for renouncing his claim to the infamous right, became a well-known precedent, unfailingly cited in juridical tradition of the seventeenth and eighteenth centuries.

THE DISPUTE BETWEEN AMIENS AND ITS BISHOP, 1336–1409

We need to follow all the stages of this shadowy affair, if we are to understand how the terrible accusation could have arisen and what *cuissage* signified within the Christian concept of marriage in the Middle Ages. Moreover, examination of this dossier in some detail will dispense us from looking at analogous affairs (the abbot of Rebais, the cantor of Saint-Vincent de Mâcon, the chapter of Nevers) that show few notable variants and lack the richness of the Amiens dossier.[22]

An ordonnance of the Valois king Philip VI published 10 July 1336 and reiterated by Charles VI signaled a serious conflict, brought before the Parlement de Paris, between the municipality of Amiens and its bishop:

> Philip by the grace of God king of the Franks gives his greetings to the bailiff of Amiens or to his lieutenant. The mayor and the magistrates of the city of Amiens have communicated a serious complaint to us; they have complained, in effect, in your presence, of the fact that the *official* [episcopal judge], acting for the bishop of the said city, as well as other people of the same bishop, have convoked and cited Jean d'Argeuve and several others of our bourgeois of the said city, for the reason that they allegedly had carnal knowledge of other women than their own wives, constraining them to pay a fine for that reason or even dragging them before our dear and faithful men who sit in our Parlement in Paris. They said that these facts would bring a great harm to ourself, to the said plaintiffs, and to all the said inhabitants of the said city. Furthermore, in following the oral injunction addressed to you by our aforesaid people, you attempted, by the seizure of his temporal wealth, to oblige the bishop in person to renounce his claims, however, under the pretext of certain royal letters transmitted to you by the bishop. According to hearsay [those letters] stipulated, among other things, that his temporal [possessions] could only be seized by our express command. You completely ceased proceedings, thus prompting, as they claim, great harm and peril for the said plaintiffs and all the inhabitants of the said city. To conclude, after a hearing of the parties before our above-mentioned

people, it was ordained that the said bishop would be constrained to renounce his claims, or else you would without delay oblige him to do so
by seizing his temporal possessions. And this despite the letters on this
point that may be given to you or shown to you by the bishop himself or
by his people and despite the other letters obtained of us and even those
that he may obtain from us. Given in Paris in our Parlement on 10 July
1336 and sealed again with our own seal by ourself, Charles, by the grace
of God king of the Franks, on 3 July 1406, twenty-sixth year of our
reign.[23]

On the surface the conflict seems simple: The bishop arrogated to himself the right to pursue adulterers in his diocese. The question was not
new, but its ambiguity lay in whether such pursuit should be qualified as
penal or penitential. The early Church considered adultery a much more
serious sin than simple fornication (sexual relations between unmarried
persons): In the second century, Athenagoras recommended expulsion
from the Christian community for it. Various early councils reiterated a
similar sanction, but it had no validity in civil law. Imperial Christian law
(the codes of Theodosius and Justinian) included criminal repression of
adultery, but since imperial jurisprudence was inherited from classical
Roman law, adultery was essentially female. With the development of the
Celtic and Anglo-Saxon penitentials (sixth through tenth centuries), the
principle of penitence proportional to the offense arose—a more supple
notion permitting response to a great variety of cases. Adultery was punishable by a period of penitence varying from three to ten years, some of it
"hard penance" (bread and water).[24] The very logic of setting a price on sin
introduced the notion that sin might be "redeemed" or "commuted" by
means of a compensatory payment (not to be confused with a fine, for
Church doctrine precluded substituting ecclesiastical discipline for the
justice of the secular courts unless a cleric was charged with the offense).

This division of responsibilities—one of Christianity's most original
characteristics[25]—worked smoothly as long as the civil authorities did
their part in repression, despite a clear tendency to shut their eyes to male
adultery and leave the punishment of female adulterers to the families.
The civil authorities clearly understood the need for legislation to confine
the Church's pressures: As Jean-Marie Carbasse has shown, the towns of
the Midi, which began to draw up statutes and customals in the twelfth
century, always included penalties for adultery.[26] Such provisions generally took the form of making the lovers run nude through the town, along
with other humiliations. The punishment seems cruel, but it replaced
older measures inherited from barbarian or imperial law stipulating confiscation of wealth or exile. By the late Middle Ages the guilty parties

could choose between running the gantlet or paying a fine, usually of 60 sous, whatever the monetary system and the real worth of the sou, which clearly shows the sentence was increasingly benign and symbolic. There is obviously nothing necessary about that evolution: Elsewhere, in the cities of central Italy for instance, where the pontifical power was not counterbalanced by a strong secular sovereignty, the city statutes of the fourteenth century tightened the laws and introduced penalties for female adulterers up to then abandoned to private vengeance.[27] Things were different in the cities of northern France, where few such dispositions existed. It was as if local communities accepted the principle of repressing adultery by penitential sanctions but also in practice confused these with civil penalties. In the thirteenth century synodal statutes from western France and from Paris provided a full range of punishments for sexual offenses to accompany civil penalties: someone who raped a virgin had to marry her or dower her for a suitable marriage.[28] One concrete proof of evident recourse to the Church in sexual offenses comes from an anonymous fabliau (undoubtedly written in a city of northern France in the twelfth century), *De la damoisele qui sonjoit* (The damsel's dream).[29] A virgin is raped in her sleep. She awakens:

> Stop, she cries, you are caught!
> Before the bishop of Paris
> You will have to be judged.

The increased importance of marriage during the central Middle Ages made the Church even more intent on moving into this legislative void. The Church defined marriage as a sacrament in the twelfth century, bringing the total number of sacraments up to seven, though debate continued for some time concerning the dogmatic basis for its promotion.[30] This made adultery blasphemy as well as a crime and a sin. Churchmen were often tempted to move from the penitential to the penal sphere in a period of lively rivalry between civil and clerical powers.

Even before the Amiens affair took a more violent and more mysterious turn fifty years later, we can sense an echo of an older, more general recrimination in the townspeople's complaint. Beyond the black images of the Church, Christianity proposed and imposed a universal dogma of marriage, and it tended everywhere to practice a unified control over questions seemingly closest to the individual and the most subject to familial, local, and regional discipline. Celibates claimed a right to regulate matrimonial conduct: That was the fundamental abuse transcribed in a myth that was all the more intent on explaining this tyranny by hidden interest because clerical control was accompanied by a variety of exactions. The basic triangle of money, marriage, and power we saw in the secular realm in chapter 5 is particularly clear here. The fact that many seigniories held by clergy, secular or regular, imposed a *formariage* tax added to a general perception of ecclesiastical interference.

The burghers of Amiens, constituted as a free municipality in a royal domain, felt the Church had overstepped its bounds and found its encroachment intolerable. Their local sovereignty was at stake. The monarchic state seemed to hesitate, given that Philip VI annulled the royal letters that protected the bishop's temporal holdings, but the ordonnance was unambiguous. Thus an alliance arose (not for the last time) between civil society and the state against the Church.

The contention dividing the municipal government of Amiens and its bishop must have continued and grown more complicated, because an ordonnance of Charles VI dated 5 March 1388 repeats the terms of Philip VI's ordonnance with nearly the same wording.[31] Charles VI also reconfirmed Philip's ordonnance again in 1406, affixing his seal. The public nature of these ordonnances helped spread knowledge of the Amiens affair. Moreover, Eusèbe de Laurière, whose *Glossaire du droit français* (1704) did much to publicize the corpus of "proofs" of *cuissage*, was the general editor of the *Ordonnances royales de la troisième race* (publication completed in 1729).[32]

Between the promulgation of the 1388 ordonnance and its confirmation in 1406, a new lawsuit set the city and the episcopal power at loggerheads and introduced other objects of litigation:

> Appeal has been made on the part of the bishop of Amiens before our court of Parlement regarding a decision of our bailiff of Amiens in favor of the mayor and the magistrates in the name of the community of the said city of Amiens [and in the names] of Jean called Wicart and André Coutelier, inhabitants of the said city, and against our dear bishop of Amiens; a decision taken in the form of a withdrawal of opposition to marriage [récréance, mainlevée] concerning the object of the contention in a sure cause of novelty and possession [nouveauté et saisine] brought before the said bailiff; the which *mainlevée* the said mayor, magistrates, and inhabitants affirmed was their right because everyone among the said inhabitants, provided he be capable of and free to contract marriage and plight troth [épousailles], might on the day of the said troth-plighting and the solemnization of marriage receive the nuptial benediction, lunch, dine and—also on the same day—consummate the marriage [cubare] and do and accomplish the other solemnities on that day of the said troth-plighting including those necessary and opportune concerning the marriage contract, and do so without being held

or obliged to wait for the second or the third day except that, if it so pleased the said inhabitants or certain among them to do so, they must freely request permission and written authorization, addressed to their parish priests by the said bishop and his officers, and this without the least monetary payment. By this decision the said lieutenant had pronounced that, without prejudging the facts, the said parties could decide among themselves concerning the *mainlevée* to be accorded the mayor, the magistrates, and the inhabitants during the principal suit, between the parties in a suit of *nouveauté et saisine*—paying a sufficient caution, however—and without prejudice to the said principal suit; all this sentencing the said bishop to [pay] the expenses. Having thus heard the above-mentioned parties in our said court in this suit on appeal, after having engaged this procedure on the question of the right or wrong of this appeal, and after having considered and diligently examined it, it has been said by a decree of our court that the lieutenant had judged well and [rightly] rendered sentence, and that the said bishop had appealed wrongly. The appellant will pay a fine and be sentenced to pay the expenses of this suit in appeal, according to the taxation of these expenses reserved to our said court. Pronounced 17 January 1393.[33]

Although this affair remains somewhat obscure because the Parlement de Paris pronounced on the procedures followed, not on the basic question, and because no record of the decision in the principal suit can be found in the registers of the Parlement preserved in the National Archives (the bishop, defeated in the appeal, may have given up what seemed a hopeless cause), its terms are easily understood and are confirmed by other documents. On 19 March 1409, for instance, the Parlement de Paris rendered a quite comparable decision, this time on a quarrel between the bishop of Amiens and the city of Abbeville that began in a suit instituted by the burghers of Abbeville, deposed in March 1401. Thanks to his Chartist friends, Louis Veuillot published the text of this document in the first edition of *Le droit du seigneur*.[34] One final document of uncertain date copied in the eighteenth century by the Benedictine Dom Grenier from materials in the communal archives of Amiens should be placed with these sure, dated pieces. This document mentions a bishop named "Jean," but there were three prelates by that name in Amiens between 1325 and 1388. It is nonetheless worth reading because it clears up the mystery of the three nights of conjugal chastity mentioned in 1393 and again in 1401 and 1409. The chapter of Amiens registered a complaint against the bishop:

> And because for sixty years and more and all through a long period when no human memory has brought contrary mention a custom and a usage has reigned, unique to the praiseworthy city and diocese of

Amiens, preserved expressly and without change in the same city and diocese, including the following: The bed of the newly married couple must be blessed the third night after the engagement of marriage, accomplished by the words of present [vows] and by the handing over of the bride, and this usage has been preserved from all antiquity in the said city and diocese of Amiens, in known and public fashion. Now, despite the above-mentioned custom and usage and against prescribed custom, the lord Jean, in order to give permission to bless on the first night the above-mentioned beds of the newlyweds, demanded and obtained and [still] demands and obtains money from various persons of the city and the diocese of Amiens. Thus he has had 4 livres of Jean de Montdidier and from all the others whom poverty does not exonerate.[35]

Dom Grenier also published a grievance of the people of Amiens:

Item: to give permission to bless the beds of the newly married on the first night; the which beds must not be blessed, according to the ancient custom of the city of Amiens, before the third night. The said bishop or his people take for each day, as the case may be, 20, 30, 40 livres or more, according to the wealth of the persons, and if sometimes it should happen that they act without permission, he makes them pay a large fine according to his pleasure.[36]

The bishop demanded payment of a special tax for dispensation from an ecclesiastical prescription requiring chastity for three days before consummating a marriage. This requirement, although not widespread, was by no means an acquisitive or pious innovation of the bishop of Amiens: As we shall see, it is attested in the early Church councils, and two canons repeating the injunction of initial chastity (one of them included in Gratian's *Decretum*) had broad geographical distribution. Still, although an incitement to chastity returned to prominence in the thirteenth century, it had too little influence on dogmatics and pastoral literature not to seem somehow odd and suspect in the sixteenth century. The last two texts quoted show that this requirement took a particular turn in Amiens, where the conflict involved three parties, the chapter, the faithful townspeople, and the bishop. The chapter and the citizens base their arguments on tradition and custom, although it is hard to tell if that tradition applied to the principle of chastity or only to the blessing of the conjugal bed on the third day of the wedding festivities. There is nothing absurd in the hypothesis that the tradition referred to chastity, because scholars of folklore have found traces of three days of sexual abstinence in imitation of the biblical Tobias in rural France of the nineteenth century. In any event, the townspeople of Amiens felt that customary freedom of initiative precluded any episcopal interference or attempt to impose as law a custom they might or might not choose to observe. Whether or not the three days were spent in chastity, respect of the ritual three days tended to be commuted into a money payment; refusal to pay might seem to the bishop's men like a refusal to respect the prescribed chastity, leading them to withhold benediction of the bed and to impose a fine. Understandably, even before the jurists circulated their malevolent insinuations, the bishop's attitude could appear fundamentally opposed to the goal of piety it claimed to foster. Quite probably recent rivalries in the city lay behind a cultural and religious antagonism. Some of the residents of Amiens were still the bishop's dependents and paid a symbolic *cens*, the *répit de Saint-Firmin*.

It is hard to see why the canons should have posed as champions of the Amiens citizens' freedom of initiative. Conflicts between a cathedral chapter and its bishop happened often in the Middle Ages, but does this case reflect solidarity with the commune or perhaps a conflict of interests and jurisdiction opposing diocesan centralization and local networks of canons and parish priests? We would have to do a prosopographic analysis of the chapter in order to hazard a hypothesis.

Nor should we underestimate the role of the monarchy in this drama. Amiens and its surrounding territory were in the royal domain, and the commune was quick to appeal to the lieutenant of the *bailliage* or the Parlement de Paris for justice. Interests may have been more tangled than one might think: At the end of the Middle Ages the municipal government of Amiens included many king's men.[37] Moreover, one small detail hints at indirect monarchical action: The 1393 decree lists as plaintiffs—along with the mayor and the magistrates, men acting in the name of the community—two "inhabitants of the city" whose goods the bishop had probably confiscated when they refused to knuckle under. One of these is given as "Jean, called Wicart." As it happens, a document dated 9 April 1389 (four years before the suit) contains the homage to the king for all he possesses in and near Amiens of one Wicart, cup-bearer and secretary to the king.[38] The name Wicart seems new among Picard homages and *aveux*. He was probably a king's man who received possessions near Amiens, became a citizen of the city, and soon stood out for his resistance to the bishop.

Be that as it may, the isolation of the bishop of Amiens, who faced the combined forces of the commune, the chapter, and monarchical authority, shows him in the role of intruder often attributed to the Church in the Middle Ages in both the ethical and the fiscal domains. We will have to leave Picardy to examine that two-pronged intrusion.

Raphael or Tobias: The Struggle for Ethical Hegemony

As has been said time and again, by excluding pleasure Christianity spread everywhere an extremely constraining model of conjugal sexuality, a model downright "unnatural" in ordinary societies. From the second century on, marriage was justified only as a means for procreation and for the channeling of sexual impulses. Admittedly, the first and second scholasticism corrected this notion, but until the nineteenth century the prevailing doctrine viewed marriage as a necessity and a remedy excluding enjoyment. Denis de Rougemont's analysis of the individual in western Europe torn among marriage, love, and sexuality is as pertinent as ever.[39]

The Church used its institutional weight to control mores in the delicate equilibrium among the various social and cultural practices of marriage, and its constant vigilance increased throughout the Middle Ages as the network of parishes grew. Demographic statistics starting in the early Middle Ages show the effect of prohibitions regarding conjugal sexuality in certain liturgical seasons.[40] The clergy hammered at the principles of strict, uninterrupted monogamy and of equal censure for male and female adultery, neither of which was natural to many of the societies converted to Christianity, and they subjected parishioners to attentive inquiry in confession. This sort of symbolic violence, accompanied by a jurisdictional coercion to which we shall return, contributed significantly to the reticence and rejections that went into constructing an image of the despotic parish priest motivated by his resentment of celibacy.

Nonetheless, a simple opposition of clergy and faithful, doctrinal rigor and unbridled enjoyment, gives an incomplete picture of medieval reality. The events in Amiens, although particular, lead us in another direction. Somewhere short of the confusion and amalgamation that portrayed the bishop's claims as libidinous or rapacious attacks, the documents show a real rivalry for ethical legitimacy, with the contending parties claiming initiative by upping the stakes in matrimonial morality. What we see here is a different scheme of relations between the clergy and the faithful: The vigor of the antiepiscopal reaction has some analogy with the concept of the moral economy of the crowd so forcefully outlined by E. P. Thompson.[41] The multitude of the faithful saw their own ancient tradition, founded in a direct reading of Scripture, as authentic, contrasting it to the Church's purely institutional control, which lacked true legitimacy. During the fourteenth and fifteenth centuries such a representation rekindled tendencies once extremely active in the "evangelizing" heretical movements of the twelfth century.[42] Before the development of the myth of *cuissage* it was not the person of one bishop or another that was targeted, but a system: The prelate seemed just as much a prisoner of the system of dispensations and monetary commutation as the Church had been a prisoner of the feudal apparatus of the twelfth century. The importance of indulgences in building toward the Protestant Reformation is a familiar story. We might thus speak of an ethical archaeology of the myth of *cuissage* applied to the person of clerics when a sufficient satirical distance separated the antagonists of an evangelical rivalry.

An Old Testament text was the probable base for rival claims to Christian excellence in Amiens and elsewhere. In French rural cultures initial nuptial chastity was argued in the name of Tobias and in his memory. The Book of Tobias, a text not often glossed by the great medieval exegetes,[43] nonetheless gave the blessing of marriage—or at least the most frequent type of blessing—a scriptural framework. In the thirteenth century, the age of broad diffusion of the Church's pastoral teachings regarding matrimony, preachers made much of this text.[44] It thus presents a rare instance of an intermediate level of culture shared by the faithful and the clergy.

It presents a curious story, which explains its rather special career in western Europe. The Book of Tobias is not part of the Hebrew canon of the Bible but belongs among the marginal writings the Catholic Church calls "deuterocanonical" or second-rank canonical but that it still groups with the "normal" biblical texts. Fragments in Hebrew and Aramaic discovered recently at Khirbat Qumran suggest Jewish origin and use. Modern translations of the Old Testament are founded on two or three Greek versions of varying length, probably written down in the second century B.C., but the West also had a notably different version translated by St. Jerome from an Aramaic original that he had a rabbi translate into Hebrew. The detour seems complicated, but the Qumran specialists tell us that the original language of the Book of Tobias may have been Aramaic.[45] Since the Aramaic text is lost, we have no way of evaluating the contribution of the Christian translator, but we can suppose it was sizable, as we shall see. Let us briefly summarize this tale, which closely resembles the marvelous tales of the East.

The action takes place toward the eighth century B.C., during the Diaspora. Tobias the elder has had to leave his city and tribe of Naphtali in northern Galilee for captivity in Nineveh. In his youth in his native city he had acted justly: Alone among his tribe he had refused to worship the golden calf, had kept the memory of God and given alms, and had paid his tithes to the priests and the Levites. In Nineveh the loving care he lavished on the tombs of Jews persecuted by the pagan king got him sent even farther into exile with his wife and his son Tobias. At the king's death the elder Tobias returned to Nineveh, where he continued his pious inhumations. One day hot dung from a swallow's nest fell into his eyes, blinding him, but like a new Job (the parallel is found only in Jerome) he renders thanks to God but asks to be removed from this world. At the same time in far-off Media another Jew in exile, the young Sara, daughter of Raguel, lived unhappily, persecuted by her serving woman because the demon Asmodeus had killed seven fiancés in succession on their wedding day, before the consummation of the marriage. Sara, devastated by these events and by the reproaches addressed to her, fasts and prays for three days and three nights (another detail found only in the Vulgate). Her prayer to God was later inserted in the chapter on marriage of the Dominican encyclopedist Vincent de Beauvais in his *Education of Young Nobles,* a work written around 1246 and dedicated to Queen Marguerite of Provence, the wife of St. Louis. (One of the king's hagiographers reports that the royal couple practiced abstinence on their wedding night).[46] Vincent de Beauvais cites the passage in the Book of Tobias as justification (it is perhaps the only biblical instance) for refusing sexual pleasure within the conjugal union. In her prayer Sara states, "Thou knowest, O Lord, that I have never coveted a husband, and have kept my soul clean from all lust. . . . But a husband I consented to take, with thy fear, not with my lust."[47]

The prayers of both these unhappy people are heard, and God sends the angel Raphael to their aid. The elder Tobias, thinking himself near death, calls his son to his bedside and delivers a veritable testamentary discourse: He enjoins his son to honor his parents by caring for his mother and burying his father with dignity, to give alms, to abstain from all fornication and remain faithful to his future wife, and to give every person his due. Finally, he asks Tobias to leave for Rages in Media to recover a large sum of money he had left on deposit there on his travels in more prosperous days.

This discourse, in total conformity with Old Testament tradition, evoked a strongly sympathetic reaction in the central Middle Ages. The father justifies the need to give alms with a phrase more reminiscent of Western ideas of Purgatory than Jewish notions of what comes after death: "For alms deliver from all sin, and from death, and will not suffer the soul to go into darkness." Tobias's fourth piece of advice coincides with the moral principles of merchants as they developed in the thirteenth century: "If any man hath done any work for thee, immediately pay him his hire, and let not the wages of thy hired servant stay with thee at all. See thou never do to another what thou wouldst hate to have done to thee by another."[48] Tobias's last piece of advice to his son, a true bequest, mentions (in Jerome's Latin version) a chirograph—that is, a contract drawn up and then torn in two, each one of the contracting parties keeping one piece. Use of a chirograph, certainly an extremely ancient practice, spread rapidly in urban circles during the twelfth and thirteenth centuries.[49] Tobias's moral and religious teaching also corresponded to the Church's principal prescriptions for the laity. Secular culture may have appropriated this tale thanks to this rare concordance.

Young Tobias assents fully to his father's recommendations and prepares to leave. His father asks him to find a traveling companion, to be paid on their return. Leaving the house Tobias meets the angel Raphael in the form of a handsome young man, and his new acquaintance immediately accepts Tobias's invitation and introduces himself to Tobias as Azarias, the son of Ananias. Despite the tears of Tobias's mother the two set off right away accompanied by a dog. When they reach the Tigris River, Tobias washes his feet and is nearly bitten by an enormous fish. Raphael tells him to seize the fish by a gill and remove his heart, liver, and gall. In answer to Tobias's questions he explains that the smell of the heart grilling on coals will chase away the demons who prevent unions between men and women, and that the gall can be used as a salve to cure his father's blindness. Tobias then asks where they will stop next, and Raphael/Azarias answers that they must reach Raguel's house, where Tobias will marry Raguel's daughter Sara. At this point Jerome skips a passage in which Azarias explains to Tobias that Raguel cannot refuse his daughter's hand because Tobias is Raguel's closest kinsman. Eight centuries before the papacy of the Gregorian reform instituted strict rules governing consanguineous unions, the Vulgate eliminated culture-specific details about marriage from this Jewish tale.

Tobias expresses some fear: He has heard of the demon's terrible massacre of Sara's suitors. Raphael promises to show him how to deal with the demon. Here Jerome adds a detail essential to later rituals of abstention from conjugal sex. Raphael prefaces the specific prescription by an explanation (later quoted in Vincent de Beauvais's educational manual): "For they who in such manner receive matrimony, as to shut out God from themselves, and from their mind, and to give themselves to their lust, as the horse and the mule, which have no understanding, over them the devil hath power."[50] Next comes the prescription itself (not found in the Greek texts):

But thou when thou shalt take her, go into the chamber, and for three days keep thyself continent from her, and give thyself to nothing else but to prayers with her. And on that night lay the liver of the fish on the fire, and the devil shall be driven away. But the second night thou shalt be admitted into the society of the holy Patriarchs. And the third night thou shalt obtain a blessing that sound children may be born of you. And when the third night is past, thou shalt take the virgin with the fear of the Lord, moved rather for love of children than for lust, that in the seed of Abraham thou mayst obtain a blessing in children.[51]

Everything happens just as Raphael has said it would: The marriage takes place, the demon Asmodeus is chased away and put in chains in the deserts of Egypt. Raguel gives Tobias half his goods and promises that Tobias will be his heir. Raphael fetches the money deposited with the elder Tobias's friend Gabel, and the young couple and the angel return to Nineveh without further difficulty. As Sara is leaving her parents, they give her some last-minute advice, "admonishing her to honor her father and mother in law, to love her husband, to take care of the family, to govern the house, and to behave herself irreprehensibly."[52] These words in the Vulgate—in the Greek text Sara's parents recommend her to Tobias's care—also worked in support of pastoral marital policy in the thirteenth century. The text is cited by the Dominican Guillaume Peyraut in his brief treatise *De eruditione principum* (On the Education of Princes) and by Jacobus de Voragine in a very simple, practical model sermon obviously addressed to a common lay public.[53]

On his return to Nineveh Tobias cures his father's blindness with the fish gall. Raphael reveals that he is an angel. The aged Tobias celebrates the glory of God in a long canticle and goes on to live in happiness to the age of 102. Tobias and Sara have many children, and he eventually leaves exile in Nineveh and dies peacefully at age 99.

This text was popular in the thirteenth century because it corresponded to the mindset of the central Middle Ages, first of all by its very nature. This brief pious tale obviously manifests contextual transformations in the Jewish religion within the Judaic world of the second century B.C. In this relatively peaceful world of Hellenic domination before the Hasmonean revolt of the Maccabees in 167 B.C. and the great eschatological and political upheavals of Roman conquest, the Book of Tobias, perhaps a product of Pharisaic tendencies in Judaism, shows it possible to achieve a happiness founded on justice and devotion within the family. Its insistence that service to God, a social ethic, and family values are compatible made sense in the thirteenth century, a time of reconciliation between the Church and secular preoccupations.

This harmony was only partially fortuitous: As we have seen, Jerome's rewriting of the Book of Tobias, facilitated by the uncertain status of the text and the absence of a Hebraic version, tended to de-judaize the text, permitting christianization by editing out mentions of endogamic norms and Jewish rituality and adding ascetic admonitions. The edited text filled a void: The New Testament gives little advice on marriage. Christ shows the way to celibacy, but he also affirms the indissolubility of marriage and states that contamination by adultery nullifies a union—all of which is expressed in formulas difficult to interpret that required an entire apparatus of doctrinal glosses before they could be given juridical interpretation in canon law. St. Paul's teachings were just as ambiguous, oscillating between a high-minded resignation to marriage as a sorry necessity and a proclamation of its high "sacramental" value as a symbol for the union of Christ and his Church. The Fathers of the Church and the various synods and councils went no further than prescribing a certain asceticism. Thus we need to view the Church's reception of the Book of Tobias in the central Middle Ages in relation to the sacramentalization of marriage and the elaboration of a religious morality for lay consumption. The text also gave the faithful a basis for aspirations to ethical autonomy, however: Jerome's rewriting of the Book of Tobias seems to suggest that the personal asceticism of the spouses has as much to do with sanctifying their marriage as the angel's advice, rites, and protection. The relation between Raphael and Tobias is more like a salutary collaboration than a hierarchical subjection. Despite his status as an archangel, in the central Middle Ages Raphael figured as a good shepherd or guardian angel watching over the individual. The tale's ambivalence permitted opposite conclusions.

TOBIAS'S NIGHTS

The Book of Tobias also had the advantage of confirming an ancient and obscure ascetic tradition. Although consistent exegesis of this text does not exist, the Church of the late Roman Empire and the early Middle Ages seems to have taken inspiration from Raphael's guidance of Tobias to counsel conjugal abstinence during the first days of marriage. The principle of initial chastity (totally absent in primitive Christianity) first appears not in the decisions of the councils or central synods but in a brief normative treatise, the *Statuta ecclesiae antiqua*, a collection written in southern Gaul during the second half of the fifth century, probably by a priest, Gennade of Marseilles. The 101st and penultimate canon in his collection reads: "The husband and the wife, when they are to be blessed by the priest, are presented to the priest in the church by the relatives or the paranymphs, and when they have received the blessing they remain in virginity that night out of respect for that benediction."[54]

The canon *Sponsus et sponsa* had a remarkable career. It appears in two important collections, the *Hispana* (seventh century) and the *False Decretals* (ninth century, wrongly attributed to Isidore of Seville), where it is given a fallacious antiquity and said to have originated in the Fourth Council of Carthage (398). It was repeated later in the *Decretals* of Burchard of Worms (tenth century), the *Decretals* and the *Panormia* of Ivo of Chartres (Yves de Chartres, eleventh century) and in Gratian's *Decretum* (c. 1140), the pillar of canon law and its prime authority until 1917.[55] The recommendation of initial chastity was thus broadly known in Christendom. The injunction was repeated in an entire series of Anglo-Saxon, Carolingian, and post-Carolingian penitentials of the early Middle Ages.[56]

The canon is somewhat difficult to comprehend in its first version because for the most part the *Statuta* addresses discipline of the clergy, borrowing some materials from Gennade's *De ecclesiasticis dogmatibus* but even more from the *Apostolic Constitutions,* a disciplinary work compiled in Syria in the early fifth century. Canon 101 seems quite isolated in that collection. Charles Munier may be of help in grasping the context of an innovation with an important bearing on our topic. Around 480 Christianity in southern France, firmly implanted and strongly supported by the monks of Saint-Victor de Marseille and Lérins (which explains the Eastern influence and the use of the *Apostolic Constitutions*), had been cut off from Rome for some time; the Visigothic invasions brought the threat of Arianism. This means that Gennade was urging a moral reform of the clergy just as the elites were facing a need to come to terms with Visigothic power. Gennade accords spiritual primacy to the priest and to the community of the *presbyterium* over the monarchy's episcopacy. Hence we need to relate his advice to the laity to an insistence on the sacrality of the Eucharist and an attempt to separate that sacrament and the wedding ritual from the life of the flesh. Some time before, the Metropolite bishop Caesarius of Arles (d. 542) had told newlyweds not to come to church for thirty days to avoid desecrating the temple. Be that as it may, Gennade's admonition strongly marked Visigothic liturgy; much use was made of it, it spread rapidly, and it influenced much of French liturgy in the Midi at the beginning of the second millennium.

Reference to Tobias and his son had less effect in a world that was still using the *Vetus latina,* the Latin version of the Bible before Jerome's.

Moreover, the canon speaks of only one night of chastity—the most important one in the biblical tale, however, since it determines the defeat of the demon Asmodeus.

A three-day gap between the blessing of the couple and consummation of the marriage appears a half-century after Gennade, however, and in his same circles: Cyprian of Toulon states in his *Life* of his master, Caesarius of Arles, that the latter "also decreed, in normative fashion, that the blessing would be given the spouses in the church three days before their carnal union in consideration of the respect due the benediction."[57] It would be tempting to see the influence of the Book of Tobias, as diffused through the Vulgate, in this extension of the period of chastity, but a closer look at the wording shows that it stresses moving the blessing back in time in relation to the secular festivities. This is not an ethical effort asked of the couple, but a liturgical precaution commanding clerics to separate the blessing and preserve its sacrality. The injunction should be understood in relation to precepts forbidding newlyweds access to the church during the thirty or forty days following consummation of their marriage. Once again the story from the Book of Tobias was to be an instrument of compromise, combining aspirations to sanctity with separation from profane pleasures, and the active participation of the faithful with the purity of a sacramental act.

This compromise was founded in an interpretation of the text; it was made explicit only much later, during the Carolingian age. Around 775 the *Vita Haimhrammi*, written by Aribo, bishop of Freising, mentions the nights of Tobias.[58] An influential prelate, Jonas of Orléans (d. 843), wrote a brief treatise of pastoral instruction for the laity, *De institutione laicali*, in which he urges the greatest possible gravity on the wedding day, condemns joyous banquets, and admonishes the couple to follow the recommendations of the angel Raphael, citing the fragment on the three nights of chastity found only in the Vulgate (Tobias 6.16). Jonas explicitly states that the biblical text gives more solid legitimacy to conjugal chastity than an ecclesiastical canon: "There are men who wish to grant only little weight to the advice of the priest when they receive their spouse chastely; it seems much more necessary to give great weight to the warning of the angel."[59]

This use of the biblical narrative soon led to the drafting of a new canon. It seems to combine Gennade's canon (the *Statuta* was widely diffused in the Frankish Church) and new readings of the Bible favored in Alcuin's circle. In 847 Benedictus Levita's collection offered an early version of the new canon. The writer presents himself as a monk in the diocese of Mainz, but contemporary scholarship has established that the collection is a forgery from western France.[60] In a chapter on legitimate marriage this collection states, "And for two or three days they [must] say their prayers and preserve their chastity so that a good progeny may be engendered and they may please the Lord in their acts. In that manner they will indeed please the Lord and will engender sons who will not be impure but legitimate and worthy of inheriting."[61] A few years later (in 858) Hérard, archbishop of Tours, included the canon, with slight variations, in a collection of capitularies: "So that the husband and the wife can be blessed by the priest amid prayers and offerings, it is important that the young woman be married and given according to the laws, that she be guarded by the paranymphs and received publicly and solemnly; that they abstain for two or three days and be taught to keep chastity between them, and that they unite at determined moments in order to engender offspring who are not degenerate but worthy heirs in the eyes of both God and the world."[62] This rule is obviously based on the biblical source: The final phrase is a close paraphrase of Jerome's translation ("the third night, you will obtain the blessing that will make you procreate healthy offspring"). The canon *Ut sponsus et sponsa*, found only in the *Decretals* of Burchard of Worms and the *Decretals* of Ivo of Chartres, is not included in Gratian's *Decretum* (probably because it had no ancient precedent), and it had little influence outside the area of the Frankish Church. This may explain the absence of the nights of Tobias (and consequently of the myth of ecclesiastical *cuissage*) outside France and its bordering regions.

Another normative text on the three nights of chastity, in the *Penitential* of Pseudo-Egbert (tenth century), warrants mention because it introduces an important variant clearly showing how an ethical compromise was reached between the Church and the faithful: "The holy books teach us what every man must do when he has led his wife to his house for the first time: for three days and three nights they must preserve their chastity; then on the third day they attend mass and must both receive the Eucharist. Afterward they must keep their union before God and before the world."[63] Henceforth, attending mass and taking communion were recommended at the end of the preparatory period of chastity: The old interest in separating liturgical sacrality from carnal consummation of marriage seems to have disappeared in favor of an increased ceremonialization of marriage in rituals connected with celebration of the Eucharist—an early hint of promoting the blessing of marriage to the rank of a sacrament.

The marriage liturgy was probably the most effective means for spreading the story of Tobias and making the rule of one or more nights of absti-nence part of lay mores. Reference to Tobias is found in the earliest occur-rences of blessing the bridal chamber (missals of Durham in the tenth century, Normandy in the eleventh century, Lyre in the twelfth century), and the custom was widespread until the sixteenth century. In the eleventh century, when the complex rite preceding the wedding mass was elaborated, the story of Tobias was constantly and universally used. It ap-pears in the words spoken at the beginning of the ceremony to give away the bride (Visigothic liturgy of the eleventh century; rituals of Vich, Por-querolles, and Carcassonne in the twelfth century; widespread diffusion afterward), in the concluding prayer, during the mass itself (antiphons of the introit, the offertory, and communion), and after the mass at the mo-ment of the final liturgical handing over of the bride to her husband. Even the gesture of the priest joining the couple's hands was an explicit refer-ence to the angel Raphael: "And taking the right hand of his daughter, he gave it into the right hand of Tobias" (Tobias 7.15). Repeated allusions to the story of Tobias and Sara are at times accompanied by a recommenda-tion to practice initial chastity: The Gallic canon *Sponsus et sponsa* is picked up in the early Middle Ages in the Fulda sacramentary (which, de-spite its geographical origin, derives from Visigothic liturgy, where refer-ence to the story of Tobias was frequent) and in the *Liber ordinum* of Selos. In these two cases the rule is justified "pro sancta communione" ("because of the holy communion" of the nuptial mass). The Vich sacra-mentary (eleventh century) preaches the three nights of chastity for the same reason. The canon *Ut sponsus*—as we have seen, specifically linked to Tobias—figures in the Cahors missal (second quarter of the twelfth cen-tury).[64] At the end of the mass, one missal from the papal court under Nicholas IV (1288–92) enjoins the couple to "abstain from one another today, tomorrow, and the day after tomorrow, as the angel Raphael com-manded Tobias."[65]

Although not consistently present, this tradition persisted until the early modern age: The same advice is given in the final admonition when the bride is consigned to her husband in a Lyons pontifical of the fifteenth century. In the sixteenth century ten or more diocesan rituals urged one night of chastity; in the early seventeenth century Cardinal Santori in-cluded in the marriage ritual the admonition "Abstain from one another today, tomorrow, and the day after tomorrow. Go in peace, and may the angel of the Lord accompany you."

The Church, although not insisting on observance of this prescription, seemed to be keeping it in reserve and bringing it back from time to time.

Thus at a time close to that of the Amiens affair, the Synod of Nantes in 1350 renewed the recommendation.[66] The Amiens contention should probably be understood as the effect of secular appropriation of a text known through nuptial benedictions and sermons. Lay appropriation took place well below the heights of doctrine because, as we have seen, the Book of Tobias was not a text on the holiest level of the Church's scriptural references, partly because of its deuterocanonical status and partly because its simplicity did not inspire the complex exegesis that was the Church's specialty. The text was seldom glossed: One brief exegesis in a sermon of St. Ambrose refers only to the money Tobias had deposited with a friend, which Ambrose sees as a generous interest-free loan and contrasts to the usury rampant among his fellow-citizens in Milan, which he roundly condemns. For obvious reasons, this sermon presenting the generosity of a pious Jew as an example for money-grubbing Christians was hardly ever cited in later tradition. In the early eighth century the Venerable Bede composed an allegorical explanation of the Book of Tobias to represent the conversion of Israel to the true religion, a version repeated in the eleventh and twelfth centuries in the *Glossa ordinaria* that became the most prominent interpretation of the biblical episode.

During the twelfth and thirteenth centuries this text nonetheless reached beyond liturgy and preaching to pass into lay culture. Around 1180 Matthieu de Vendôme composed a lengthy poem in Latin paraphrasing the Book of Tobias in elegiac pentameters, and because his text was used to teach metrics in the schools it circulated widely.[67] Guillaume le Clerc wrote another poetic paraphrase (in French this time) in the early twelfth century. The Book of Tobias was also translated in secular and heterodox circles by the Waldenses (or Vaudois), probably at the end of the thirteenth century. A late Waldensian manuscript (fifteenth century) in a very small format—which means it was designed for itinerant preaching by the "Bearded Ones"—follows the Latin syntax exactly, showing a scrupulous respect for the letter of the Vulgate. The Book of Tobias was not chosen by chance: This manuscript contains only a few translations (Job, Maccabees) obviously selected for their relevance for a pious and persecuted laity. Other literal translations exist in Provençal and in French but are more difficult to assign to a specific group.[68] In all these adaptations and paraphrases, it was the story itself that was important, not the allegorical meaning the Venerable Bede attributed to it.

The laity would have had no trouble understanding the tale of Tobias and Sara as it was transposed in these familiar bits of Church discourse on pastoral care or in the liturgy of marriage. Not only was the Book of Tobias in harmony with familial culture in the thirteenth century, but also certain aspects of the text could easily be acclimatized into what we vaguely call "popular culture." The demon's curse threatening the young husband, if not with death at least with impotence, and the magical practice of burning animal entrails to obtain smoke are often encountered in folk literature. The Book of Tobias, unburdened by exegesis, affirmed the compatibility of ancestral practices with personal piety. Whether the practice of chastity resulted from an implicit negotiation or was a complement (more homogeneous than might be thought) to magical practices, the result was that Tobias's nights of chastity entered into lay culture. The survival of the rite in much later times bears witness to this: Arnold van Gennep gathered occurrences of it in Bresse, Brittany, Franche-Comté, Gascony, the Loire Valley, Normandy, Picardy, Poitou, the Vendée, and Savoy, as noted in many nineteenth-century investigations of folk practices. In some cases the bride returned to her parents' house after the ceremony, in others she was entrusted to the care of four people, in still others she slept with her women friends. Or the groom's man slept, fully clothed, between the fully dressed couple. The prescription might also be mixed somewhat ambiguously with traditional tricks played on the newlyweds to hinder their new intimacy. Tobias's name appears in almost all these folk instances.[69]

One of the tales in the *Cent nouvelles nouvelles* (1462) makes clear the optional, discretional nature of the nights of chastity; it also links the motif indirectly to ecclesiastical *cuissage*. In the forty-fourth tale, told by Monsieur de La Roche, a young girl rejects the ardent suit of her parish priest, fearing the dishonor of a premarital pregnancy. Still, she is touched by the holy man's desire and promises he can make love to her once she is married. The priest immediately sets about finding a husband for her and goes to see her parents, then the parents of a young man of the neighborhood. They reach an agreement, thanks to a loan from the priest to the father of the groom, who is too poor to pay the wedding expenses or provide the bride's *douaire*. The engaged couple goes to confession, but when the priest raises his voice to remind the girl of her promise, the husband-to-be overhears him. The night of their marriage the young man plays a trick on the priest (the details of which are unimportant for our purposes), and by a complicated succession of events the priest is persuaded to renounce his claim. The first phase of these adventures is the most pertinent: On the wedding night the young man keeps his distance from his bride in the conjugal bed, saying not a word and not touching her. The next morning when the women crowd into the nuptial chamber to ask the bride how her wedding night went, she tells them the truth. "The women were all totally flabbergasted, and each one of them thought more about it than the next one. Nonetheless, they all agreed that he had avoided her out of piety, and spoke no more of this matter for the time being." In the representational system of these Burgundian women, pious chastity thus seemed unusual but possible and acceptable. The groom's feigned indifference continues for the following nights, and the women conclude: "Perhaps he is not whole. He should be tested, for his conduct has not varied, and has lasted as long as the [third] night." Hence the pious young man had a grace period of three nights and no more to prove he was not impotent—precisely the length of Tobias's enforced chastity.[70]

The religious individualism manifested in this secular appropriation of the Book of Tobias may possibly have combined with what are generically called archaic "popular beliefs." In chapter 1, I expressed some diffidence about the ethnographic interpretations of the *droit de cuissage* that relate it to a sacred horror of virginity. I would have to admit, however, that an obsession of the sort was not unknown in the Middle Ages. We find it projected onto a far-off world in a passage in the relation of an imaginary voyage around the world by John Mandeville written in the mid-fourteenth century. The setting is a remote island at the ends of the earth:

> There is another fair and good isle, full of people, where the custom is that when a woman is newly married, she shall not sleep the first night with her husband, but with another young man, who shall have ado with her that night and take her maidenhead, taking in the morning a certain sum of money for his trouble. In each town there are certain young men set apart to do that service, which are called *gadlibiriens,* which is to say "fools of despair." They say, and affirm as a truth, that is a very dangerous thing to take the maidenhead of a virgin; for, so they say, whoever does puts himself in peril of death. And if the husband of the woman find her still virgin on the next night following (perchance because the man who should have had her maidenhead was drunk, or for any other reason did not perform properly to her), then shall he have an action at law against the young man before the justices of the land—as serious as if the young man had intended to kill him. But after the first night, when those women are so defiled, they are kept so strictly that they shall not speak to or even come into the company of those men. I asked them what the cause and reason was for such a custom there. They told me that in ancient times some men had died in that land in deflowering maidens, for the latter had snakes within them, which stung the husbands on their penises inside the women's bodies; and thus many men were slain, and so they follow that custom there to make other men test out the route before they themselves set out on that adventure.[71]

This alleged custom did not spring from the burgeoning imagination of John Mandeville: As early as the mid-twelfth century, Vincent de Beauvais speaks of it in his *Speculum historiale* (1:88).

It seems clear that in the central Middle Ages an implicit negotiation between cultures and a game of both upping the stakes and making concessions caused the Book of Tobias to serve as what might be called a "collective utterance"—that is, a representation situated where otherwise incompatible spheres of thought and discourse touch.[72] This precarious equilibrium could not last, however, as the Amiens affair shows. The forces momentarily stabilized in that equilibrium were not inert: The Church triumphant pursued its appropriation of lay mores and customs, notably in matrimonial matters. It took over from civil authorities jurisdiction over matrimonial alliances, stripped the laity of its authority over ethics, and—perhaps the most sensitive point—gave monetary values to its symbolic domination. By the end of the Middle Ages the great ruptures that would lead to the Protestant Reformation were already looming. The horizon of reception for both Protestant criticism and the myth of an ecclesiastical *droit de cuissage* grew out of the cleavage that opened up between individual piety and the institution of the Church, between ethical freedom and the taxation of prescriptions and permissions, and between initiative and control. It is the slow widening of that crevasse that we must explore next.

THE PRIEST AS THE SPOUSES' LORD

The Church's constant progress in establishing norms for matrimony made it impossible for the thirteenth-century compromise between the Church and the faithful to last. I shall touch on the question only briefly: It has already been mentioned in connection with criminality involving sex, and historians have treated it in depth. Still, a few essential characteristics of ecclesiastical jurisdiction bear repeating.

Besides the fundamental question of prohibiting close consanguinity in marriage (on which the Church and lay society differed from the eleventh century on), the major point of friction was the doctrine of consent. This doctrine insisted, beginning in the twelfth century, that because marriage was sacramental, it must be a free and individual act involving consent. Roman doctrine was based on consent as well, but in a very different sense, as Jean Gaudemet has shown. Roman law contrasted juridical decision and the fact of cohabitation: The concrete and personal aspect of decision was not relevant. Conversely, Peter Lombard (in his

Sententiae) and Pope Alexander III went so far as to state that paternal consent was not necessary to legal marriage. Marriage became effective and real both by virtue of the act of consummation and by the words of consent, but decision and its public expression gradually came to be what actually effected the act of matrimony. Even without portraying the diverse societies of the Middle Ages as a world where the individual was repressed by the clan, it is easy to see that the theoretical emancipation of young people was hard to reconcile with the social uses of alliance.

A literal application of consent was also a hindrance to efficient management of the subjects of a seigniory, because the various taxes levied when dependents married were founded on the rule that a subject could not marry without the authorization of his or her lord. Despite the canon promulgated by the Council of Chalon (813), pontifical tradition, reiterated by Innocent II and Eugene III, required that serfs be able to marry freely. Obviously, the ecclesiastical lords were not shy about demanding payment of taxes of *formariage* or recognition of this authorization, and recourse to Church law was of little help to a dependent. Still, doctrinal affirmation of the liberty of the faithful in matrimonial matters helped to challenge subjection. The various parlements and the king's officers infiltrated the closed world of seigniorial relations in the name of sacramental freedom. A decree of the Parlement de Toulouse of 24 January 1549 justified abolishing a seigniorial tax on hearths: "It was said and ordained that inasmuch as the said [lady] de Binet demanded to take *fouage* by right over the inhabitants and workers and during their marriage only so much as one-half basket of wheat and other rights that she insists upon, abusing and scorning the liberty of the sacrament of marriage, the syndic and the inhabitants were absolved and relieved [of such payments] and without expenses." The sacramental argument may not have been put forth in good faith here: The decree refers to an exaction on households, not on marriages. In any event, on 1 May 1558 the Toulouse magistrates had the wit to argue the same sacramental liberty when the abbot of Sorrèze made analogous claims.[73]

The primacy of consent, which had to be established during the wedding ceremony, introduced a good dose of juristic thinking into developing Christian liturgy in the beginning of the second millennium. Before the priest could bless the couple, he had to ascertain that no impediment to their union existed and that both were freely disposed to wed. The Church even tended to adopt certain aspects of Roman law, thus contravening some of the extremely varied, local, and complicated customary norms of the various matrimonial regimes in Europe. For instance, an adage collected in the ninth century by Benedictus Levita that appears in the *False Decretals* (thus giving it the authority of antiquity) states, "No marriage without dowry," and later ritual books state that the priest must verify that the bride was "legally dowered [legaliter dotata]." The Church had no means for imposing uniformity on practices, but its formal support probably contributed to the slow but irresistible spread of dowries as time went on. The nobility developed the habit of conducting the formalities regarding the dowry and the *douaire* along with the nuptial benediction before the mass in the porch or the atrium of the church. It is this custom that explains the expressions, "to go to the door of the church" or "to go to the monastery" that designate the contractual operation preceding the celebration of the marriage and the wedding festivities (we have seen a licentious version of these proceedings in the Montauban affair).

In the central Middle Ages the parish priest even functioned as something like a notary, particularly in regions where the Roman notarial tradition and the Germanic custom of *échevins* were not firmly implanted. The compilers of a customal in Poitou must have seen this encroachment as a threat. In 1417 (hence contemporary with the Amiens affair) they state:

> Although in past times priests and some religious were accustomed to be notaries and pass contracts under the seal of the secular courts, the which contracts frequently touched on cases judged and sentences handed down by the same secular courts, this is manifestly against their professions. It has been and is commanded that henceforth priests and religious will not be notaries and will not exercise the office of notaries of secular courts under pain of fines to be determined, taken from their temporal holdings. And if they passed any letters, no faith is to be accorded them.[74]

The marriage ritual developed in France beginning in the twelfth century, arising from both southern (Visigothic) and Anglo-Norman liturgy, clearly reflects this jurisdictional struggle. Before that date there are scattered traces of liturgy connected with the church building, but the marriage ceremonies usually took place, by long tradition, in the house of the bride's parents with the priest coming to bless the nuptial chamber. The refinement of the theology of the sacrament of marriage during the twelfth century put marital ritual on a more and more solid foundation. In 1215 the Fourth Lateran Council imposed formal engagement and the publication of bans. Until the Council of Trent (in the canon *Tametsi*, 1563) it was strongly recommended but still not obligatory for marrying couples to go to church, although in France it was customary to do so. The ceremony was a symbolic manifestation dispossessing the parents and the family of the bride. The priest took the place in the ritual that had formerly been the father's; he "delivered the bride" to her husband and joined their hands. He declared himself the effector of the act of marriage: He alone was capable of "making the marriage [perficere matrimonium]" and of pronouncing "I marry you [ego conjungo vos]" and "I give you to one another [vos affido]."

As marriage ceremonies grew longer and more charged with sacrality, their institutional solidity allowed them to appropriate certain elements from secular culture. Thus the wedding gifts, the groom's gifts, and the bride's counter-gifts all received priestly blessing. The thirteen coins that husbands gave their brides passed through the hand of the priest. The clearest encroachment of secular customs into ecclesiastical culture came with the blessing of the nuptial bed, at times accompanied by the benediction of the bread and wine for the nuptial mass. That ritual, which corresponds to both the liturgy of communion (and the blessing did in fact sometimes take place in church) and to ancient secular usages (it was once the only ceremony of marriage) may have absorbed or concealed the popular customs discussed in chapter 2 involving the *chaudel* or the various beverages served and drunk on the wedding night. In that case the priest who shared the *vipae* (bits of bread steeped in wine) with the couple took the structural place of the youth abbey or the lord. In 1565 the Council of Milan forbade benediction of the couple's bread and the wine inside the church: The decree uses the term *bibaria vini*, an expression that recalls the *bibaraou* demanded by the lord of Bizanos in compensation for his droit du seigneur. The proximity of secular cultures is just as clear in a negative sense: A recommendation in a ritual book from Meaux in 1617 permits the blessing of the nuptial chamber but states that "the parish priest will take care that as he carries out this [blessing] no one indulges in loud laughter and other improprieties that would stain the sanctity of these holy ceremonies."[75] The post-Tridentine Church looked with a more and more jaundiced eye at such blessings and festivities, but they persisted to the nineteenth century: Arnold van Gennep states that at the end of the century this custom could be observed only in Picardy.[76] Amiens remained loyal to its medieval choices.

A subsidiary question raised by the Amiens affair—pecuniary exploitation of ritual or symbolic domination in matrimonial matters—connects all these processes of mutual and rival appropriations. A letter of remission from Normandy, written in 1386, takes us from a sphere of shared festivities to one of competition for the master's rights and their monied compensation. This particular case resulted in the death of a man: "The parish priest wanted to bless the bed of the said newlyweds [but] the said *varlets* . . . stated that the bed would not be blessed and prevented the said curé from doing so unless they had from the said couple 2 gold florins for the pillows."[77]

The priest's exactions, like those of the village youths, stand half-way between a symbolic gift and true taxation. They seem to have come into being gradually and in ways that vary from place to place. For example, the symbolic thirteen coins end up in the hands of the married couple in a ritual from Thérouanne but are shared (unequally: 10 deniers for the priest and 3 for the couple) in Amiens; in Lisieux and Agen the priest keeps the entire sum.[78] Habitual (but bitterly contested) exactions for liturgical services seem to have multiplied in connection with marriage: The cartulary of Saint-Étienne-de-Vignory contains a charter dated 1336 that would have excited the imagination of the partisans of ecclesiastical *cuissage* because it is the bride who pays: "Item: the day after the wedding, when the bride returns to the monastery, the said chaplain takes back all the bread and all the wine and all the candles offered for the mass . . . and the offering in money."[79] The faithful complained about these small exactions that grew more numerous as ritual became more complex; even though they knew that little of the money remained in the parish priest's purse, they felt that the burdensome exactions of the *dîme* ought to cover liturgical services.

In Amiens exactions for dispensation from Tobias's nights of chastity were paid to the bishop. That posed the infinitely more serious question (but it probably mingled with the question of liturgical taxation) of money payments for graces and penances. We all know what happened to the question in Luther's time. The accusation of simony had kindled resentment in the twelfth-century communities of "evangelistic" faithful, and since that date both the development of indulgences and the growing needs of the Church (but also the greed of some prelates) had spread the image of the institution of Christ's poor rotted by money. After the Reformation parlementary and royal milieus (the circles where the myth of ecclesiastical *cuissage* thrived) incessantly lashed out at the decadence of the clergy (even though they contributed to it). After 1560 the monarchical state never relaxed its pressure on the Church, initially in an attempt to wipe out the public debt aggravated by the Wars of Religion, and with the Church's "free gift [don gratuit]" to the monarchy in 1636, its contributions ceased to be justified in the name of Christian causes, becoming an important part of monarchical fiscal policy.[80]

As the Middle Ages drew to a close, the Church's avidity on all levels and its tight control over mores had opened a crevasse between the faithful and their clergy. The fables of the *droit de cuissage* slipped into that gap. The chronology is clear: In the thirteenth century in France a clerical culture that had reached an accommodation with secular society enjoyed a precarious equilibrium with communities by then well christianized. Satire of the clergy was culturally marginal and expressed joyously and with a sense of play. This cultural rivalry lost its serenity from the fourteenth century to the mid-fifteenth: The Church heightened its demands and tightened its institutional structure, while the faithful increasingly accepted individual responsibility for the ethical and religious teachings of Christianity. Raphael, Tobias's angel guide, might figure as an image of individual conscience and an early version of the guardian angel, just as easily as he serves as a prototype for the clergy as dispenser of the sacraments.

Criticism of the institution of the Church took a more serious turn in the time of prophets and seers. Then, during the fifteenth century, after the collapse of the Great Schism, the separation between the faithful and the institutional Church was further accentuated. At that point hostility toward the Church took the form of a bitter guerrilla warfare. We have seen one aspect of that conflict in the hatred that fills one of the nouvelles in the *Cent nouvelles nouvelles,* the founding text for ecclesiastical *cuissage.* It is but one example; there were thousands of representations of the fall of the church of Babylon that prepared the bloody vengeance of the Wars of Religion. When the priest-Raphael collected money for chastity, he became Asmodeus.

CHAPTER SEVEN

The Politics of *Cuissage:* The Social Uses of Persiflage

D|uring the Middle Ages the two versions of the myth of *cuissage,* ecclesiastical and lay, developed out of an ethical refusal to equate liberty (or grace) with money. Those who promoted this form of commutation were accused of brutal concupiscence, the height of tyranny and alienation, which made them unworthy of distributing that liberty. Conversely, free choice in matrimony was the most sensitive and most highly charged point of impact in personal liberty (or in the free assumption of broadly shared customs). Thus the third apex in the basic triangle of social relations—power, money, and sexuality—stressed freedom of choice in salvation and life more than sexuality in itself. Hence the chronology of the two scenarios is fairly easy to explain: A widespread monetarization of the seigniorial bond, detectable as early as the twelfth century, preceded the conversion into monetary terms of religious graces and dispensations that became systematic after the late thirteenth century. That historical structure may explain why a representation was possible, but it does not tell us how it was put into operation, which requires agents. Strong representations do not circulate in the "air of the times"; they follow earthly paths winding among a variety of cultures. This chapter will thus attempt to use case studies (geographically dispersed but with some common characteristics) to reconstruct strategies, virtual in the contexts described in the previous chapters, that led to a deliberate, politically motivated elaboration of the myth of *cuissage.*

From the late sixteenth century on it is easy to see who is diffusing the myth: The frequency of mentions of *cuissage* in the writings of jurists and members of the various parlements points to a collusion (which should surprise no one) between the king's men and parlementary circles, equally interested in reducing the symbolic prestige of the seigniorial class and the Church. The extreme rarity of medieval sources regarding *cuissage* means we cannot trace any continuity in the elaboration and diffusion of the myth; what is more, the two versions, lay and ecclesiastical, had different outcomes. The fact that the first occurrence of *cuissage* in 1247 emerges in a monastic milieu might induce us to think that the Church, in this domain as in many others, prepared the way for the monarchical state by operating as a source of a detached and serene governance freeing the population from local tyrannies and maintaining a distinction among the three points of the power-money-freedom triangle. Sustaining that hypothesis requires examination of the precise context and the events of 1247, to be followed by analysis of two other well-documented sets of events where we can observe the processes involved in the social setting of *cuissage* some centuries later.

THE VILLEINS OF VERSON (1247)

As we have seen, the inaugural text introduces the complete scenario of secular *cuissage:* A feudal due of 3 sous on marriages, called *cullage,* replaces a tyrannical demand either that the future bride be brought to the lord for sexual abuse or, later, that an enormous fee be paid in the form of an annuity, movable goods, or a "heritage" in exchange for the lord's consent to marriage.

This text is a poem in French consisting of 235 assonantal lines, signed by one Estout de Goz, otherwise unknown ("Cest conte fist Estout de Goz," line 234). The work, which enumerates at length the dues and *corvées* owed by the peasants of the village of Verson, was found inserted into a fragment of the cartulary of the Abbey of Mont-Saint-Michel compiled under Abbot Richard III Tustin (1237–64), preserved in the departmental archives of La Manche.[1] The poem appears before a detailed listing in Latin of the revenues of the abbey in the villages of Verson and Bretteville, both near Caen. Although the two documents differ greatly in both language and genre, there is little doubt that they are closely connected: They contain comparable data and are recognizably written by the same hand. Moreover, the census listing begins on the verso of the second folio of the poem (fol. 24v) and continues through folio 34. The first lines of the poem clarify the relation between the two texts:

To God and by the mediation of St. Michael
Who is the messenger to the king of heaven

I complain of all the villeins of Verson
And of Osbert, that wicked felon:
He is trying to disinherit St. Michael.

The poet is referring to a specific situation: In the 1240s Viscount Osbert, lord of Fontenay-le-Pesnel and kin to the ducal family of Normandy, incited the abbey's tenants to free themselves of excessive payments by forwarding a complaint to the treasurer of Normandy. The fiefs of Verson and Bretteville lay fairly far from the abbey but close to the ducal court, and their particular structure made their management delicate. A painstaking study by Commander Navel showed that despite their limited area the twin fiefs were divided among twenty vavasors in 1172.[2] Two vavasories were held by powerful lords, Guillaume de Tancarville, grand chamberlain of Normandy, and Jourdain Tesson, baron of Cinglais. Eight other vavasors held baronial rank. We can probably conclude that these tenancies were established before the fief was donated to the abbey and that they fell under an ancient ducal fiscal system on the Carolingian model connected, since the tenth century, with fief-bearing offices.

The abbey made repeated attempts to break this noble stranglehold.[3] In 1233, fourteen years before the compilation of the census that concerns us, the abbot bought all the possessions in Verson and Bretteville of Guillaume de Brée, one of the vavasors. By 1247 the monastery also had control of six of the seven mills that the vavasors had received in perpetual fief from the duke. Overall, the 1247 census document lists the vavasors as possessing 862 acres of land (as opposed to 1,021 acres in the 1172 census) out of a total of 2,400 acres (or 1,620 hectares) for the whole domain.

Viscount Osbert was thus working to win homages to combat the monastery's slow but effective efforts to gain control—a frequent occurrence in the difficult relations between monastic and lay seigniories. The poem by Estout de Goz (whose mysterious name doubtless conceals a scribe in the abbey's chancery) is evidently aimed at pointing out the dangers of a harsher secular seigniory more intent on profit. Before analyzing the specific terms of this bit of monastic propaganda, we must look at its practical aims and note the function of the vernacular text in relation to the Latin census.

The task is not simple: The three editors of this poem have viewed it as little more than a transposition of the census into verse. If this were the case, the allusion to *cuissage* would refer to actual past events in the domain under the dukes of Normandy. But could the monks have conceivably accepted to take over a fiscal privilege originating in an ignominy? We can only answer this question by looking more closely at the parallels between the dues mentioned in the two texts.

Lines 6–15 of the poem describe *corvées:* "They have to bring stone every day it is needed, without complaint or commentary. And at the bake-ovens and the mills (they are more slavelike [culverts] than dogs)— at the bake-ovens and the mills they owe service every day. When there are houses to be built, they must serve the masons with stone and mortar." In the census, article 23 on the extraction of stone reads: "All the said men [the villeins] must bring the stone to the manor buildings when there is need for it, and each wagon must receive 1 sou manceau per day, the month of August excepted." The census document seems less stringent, given that it stipulates remuneration and excepts the harvest season. On the other hand, article 29 states: "The said *bordiers* [bordars] of Verson and Bretteville are to furnish the masons with rusticated stone, make mortar, and furnish [such materials] for the manor, the bake-ovens, and all the buildings attached to the said manor." This harsh *corvée* concerns the *bordiers*, however, a category of sharecropping tenants installed on lands recently put to culture, whose conditions were more stringent than those of the villeins.

Lines 16–26 of the poem refer to the conflict, but in highly ambiguous terms: "The *vilain plénier* does all that, despite Osbert Pesnel, who brings bad innovations. The *vilains* make him their viscount, for which they will die in miserable shame. They make him their advocate to disinherit their lord. Did they not do the same in the time of Ogier, of Robert le chevalier, and in the days of the other priors? They did it always." Thus the poem seems to describe obligations specific to the seigniory of Verson and contested through Osbert's influence—unless the poet presents a general situation of peasant tenancy the viscount could not free them from. The difficulty of the text requires further investigation.

The poem goes on to enumerate the peasants' obligations in chronological order, following the agrarian calendar. On St. John's Day, 24 June, their first obligation is to cut the meadow grass of the demesne (lines 27–36). The cut hay has to be gathered into bunches and taken to the manor barn. Article 26 of the census speaks of the same obligation, specifying that each *plein vilainage* (full tenancy) owed one-half acre of hay cutting (roughly 3,000 square meters) and that the service could be fulfilled by a worker paid by the tenant. The poet may be opposing an unlimited *corvée* to a clearly specified and relatively modest task, a likely possibility because there were few *vilainages pléniers* in Verson.

Lines 37–42 of the poem refer to cleaning out the drainage ditches. Article 19 of the census document attributes the task to the bordars ("with the villeins") but the task does not appear on the list of villeins' tasks. The poem stresses the difficulty of the task: "Everyone goes, spade on shoulder, to clean out the mud, hard and soft."

The month of August (lines 43–54 of the poem) brought the harvest *corvée*. Here again, article 17 of the census document limits the work to one-half acre per *vilainage plein*.

Next, still during the harvest season, the poem speaks of payment of the *champart*, an exaction proportional to crops harvested (lines 55–89) and levied "if their lands are *champartables*" (line 55). The passage evokes the harshness of the checkers and their insistence on getting the lord's share of the harvest into the barn before the peasants' share, should a storm threaten. Are we to imagine the text would add this cynical note if it were a true description of monastic exploitation? Moreover, tenancies under *vilainage* in Verson do not seem to have been liable to the *champart*, a levy reserved to *coutures à ferme muable* (terrains under adjustable contracts) carved out of newly cleared lands in the domain. It is possible the monks were contrasting the villein's traditional service to new methods of exploitation promoted by secular lords.

On the Nativity of the Virgin, 8 September, the villein owed *porcage* (lines 90–98), a tax on his pigs amounting to 1 denier (the census document specifies "tournois") per pig for up to seven animals. If the villein owned seven to ten pigs he gave the lord the handsomest animal. Article 18 of the census confirms the amount of this due but adds an exemption: Nothing was owed for pigs born after St. John the Baptist's Day. The census also specifies that *porcage* was due in the tenancies and the lands under *champart (terra campartaria)*, thus confirming their particular status. The *cens* was due on St. Denis's Day, 9 October (lines 99–102).

The villein also had to pay the *pourport (porprestures)*, an annual payment for permission to fence in the fields (lines 103–17). There does not seem to be a corresponding exaction in the census document. Was this an agronomic novelty introduced by the monks? Or was it a version of *surprestures* mentioned in articles 13 and 14? Should we see it as an innovation of lay entrepreneurs that broke with the monastery's management of the domain? The next exaction does not appear in the census document either: When land passed into new hands, the monastery took one-thirteenth of the sale price (lines 115–18). The *sèche-moute*, a tax on grain milled outside the domain (lines 119–30), is not mentioned in the census document, nor are restrictions on purchases and sales among dependents (lines 131–34).

A *corvée* of plowing appears in both texts. The peasant is obliged to plow and sow one acre of the demesne (poem, lines 135–39; census, article 19), though the census document requires such labor only if the villein owns a plow, on his own or together with a *franc*, a freeman. On St. Andrew's Day (30 November), the villein paid *oublies*, but where the poem specifies that these could be paid in *baconnel* (surely pork products) the census does not define them but states they were paid by only a minority of the villeins (article 9). At Christmas the peasant offered the lord hens (*gélines*; poem, lines 145–48; census, article 36).

Next came *brésages*, a complement to the *cens* paid in grain: 2 *sestiers* of barley and 3 *quartiers* of wheat (lines 149–58). This due in the poem corresponds to articles 9 and 10 of the census document, which calls for only 1 *quartier* of wheat but accompanied by 1 denier manceau. I should note that the census, which painstakingly notes the calendar dates for exactions, shows the *brésage* due on St. Andrew's Day rather than Christmas.

The passage concerning the right of *cullage* discussed in chapter 4 is part of this calendar of obligations: lines 159–74 of the poem stipulate a payment of 3 sous. The equivalent passage in article 25 of the census calls it *licentia maritandi:* "It should be noted that whoever holds a full villeinage, when he marries his daughter outside the land of Saint-Michel, is held to pay 18 deniers; and he who has less will pay in proportion to what he has." The question of the nonmatching amounts for the *cullage* and the *licentia* cannot be resolved because the census document speaks interchangeably of sous manceaux and sous tournois, and one of the former was worth two of the latter. Thus if the 18 deniers mentioned in the census document are deniers manceaux, they are equivalent to the 3 sous of the poem, on the condition that it refers to deniers tournois. This seems probable: In Normandy coinage struck in Tours was more common than Le Mans coinage during the thirteenth century, and a text addressed to the laity would be more likely to have conformed to the customs of the times than a census document in part copied from earlier texts. The *porcage* tax is identical in the two texts, but the census puts it at 1 sou tournois, the poem simply at 1 sou. Similarly, the firewood *corvée* is remunerated at 2 deniers in the poem and 1 denier manceau in the census document. Finally, a census from Verson in the fifteenth century—more than two centuries later—stipulates a payment of 3 sous tournois for permission to marry.[4] We might hypothesize that the poet, who obviously had the census before his eyes and who could not have invented a lay *cullage* of known amount, deliberately plays on the ambiguity between types of coinage—a confirmation of the polemical intent of this poem about the peasantry.

Moutonnage was collected at Pâques Fleuries (Palm Sunday; poem, lines 175–80; census, article 21). Only the census gives a specific figure: the third lamb or a sum of 6 deniers manceaux if no lambs were born. At Easter came the *corvée* of plowing (lines 181–85). The census document notes this in combination with the autumn *corvée,* since both refer to planting wheat, winter and spring. Once again the poem increases the labor burden by adding the plowing of an acre of barley to that of the acre of wheat.

The next point in the inventory concerns what is called *boscage* in the census document (article 22): Every man who owns a horse (a restriction not mentioned in the poem), whatever his mode of tenure, must fetch firewood for the demesne once a year. The poem (lines 186–92) mentions 2 deniers paid for the day's work; the census gives 1 denier manceau per cart.

The following lines in the poem (193–200) regard wagon service, and article 25 of the census gives the historical background of this obligation. Formerly each one-half tenancy owed one wagon-trip to the barn at Danjean every Saturday except in the month of August. A payment of 1 *quartier* of wheat per year could be substituted for this *corvée.* I might note that for once the vernacular poem is less demanding: *Charriage* is due for a full rather than a half veilleinage, and payment frees the peasant from an annual *corvée* rather than a weekly one.

To end the list, the last exaction noted (lines 201–29) concerns *banalités* (payments for use of the lord's mill and bake-oven); the poem stresses the rudeness of the servants who work there. The text concludes with a passage on the sad fate of the villeins of Verson (lines 230–35): "Sire, hear this statement: I know of no species more slavelike [culverte] than the villeins of Verson; this we know with certitude. Estout de Goz has made this tale."

The poetic text stands up under analysis. Its contents are a transposition—at times an accurate translation—of the census document in Latin. Here and there it exaggerates burdens and omits restrictions; above all it accumulates the worst cases. We get the impression that its portrait of the villein of Verson is a negative synthesis of the varieties of status in the domain. The census document presents several strata: The first paragraphs note the dues of villeins, strictly speaking, taken from earlier census documents. The second part (articles 15–26) constitute a customal. Next it adds a list of exactions from bordars, then from vavasors, and finally from tenants on land under *fermes muables*. The novelty of the census lies in these last paragraphs: A reduction in the number of vavasories required serious revisions; the status of the tenants under *fermes* and of the bordars seems new and connected with land-clearing. Conditions for these new categories are a good deal harsher than for villeins. Villeins' holdings represent 672 acres out of the 2,400 acres of the seigniory as a whole (as opposed to 859 acres for the vavasories, 450 for the *fermes muables*, and 350 for the demesne). Thus villeinage was a minority and relatively privileged condition. The *cens* was light; total dues amounted to from 2 to 5 sous tournois per acre, whereas the rent for the farms held as fiefs was as high as 15–20 sous tournois. These categories were not inflexible, however: A villein could hold lands *à ferme* as well as his villeinage. The nub of the controversy seems clear: New developments in status were a degradation, and Osbert's proposals risked tipping the peasants into a new condition obeying the harsh laws of the land market.

We need to understand, however, who was the target audience for this text. An eyewitness to the events, the poet Estout, addresses St. Michael to denounce Osbert's attempts, and in the process draws a terrible group portrait, without sympathy, of the villein of Verson. He poses as a close witness on the village level ("Roger Adé has told me") aware of the practical details of exactions and sensitive to a thousand little acts of fraud and expressions of disdain. The writer poses as a well-off peasant who feels detached from the other dependents and scorns his companions still mired in obligations. His subtle mix of attested norms and deformations or omissions aims at verisimilitude. If this text, composed to be spoken or recited (which is probably why vernacular metrical verse was chosen as its medium), is indeed addressed to the comfortably prosperous villein, the monks were counting on a complicity induced by privileges and profits to guarantee acceptance of their persiflage both of peasants incapable of negotiating better terms and of brutal and deceptive lay lords. Where the census document cites a specific law, moderated by exceptions and opportunities for paid dispensation, the fictive picture of the average villein—in the domain in question or contemplating a new subjection—presents overall obligations that unfold implacably according to the rhythms of the calendar.

How are we to understand the allusion to the origins of secular *cullage?* I should point out that in Verson *cullage* (or *licentia maritandi*) was the only personal, not land-based, tax. As we have seen, all exactions are linked to one mode of tenure or occupancy, hence it seems clear that here dependency was landed and not personal—to the extent that the distinction has any meaning. This particular tax is the only obligation susceptible of direct disqualification on ethical grounds, which is just what made it so important in a polemical situation. The poem's descriptions of *banalités* hinted at abuse or fraud, but the lord could not be attacked in his person. The monastery's scribes could easily have imagined a libidinous origin for *cullage,* following a time-honored tradition of the concupiscence of tyrants. One local circumstance may have suggested this theme much more directly.

The two villages of Verson and Bretteville were part of the *douaire* of Gonnor, the second wife of Duke Richard I of Normandy, who gave Bretteville to the Abbey of Mont-Saint-Michel around 1015. His son Richard II completed the donation around 1024 by adding Verson. Curiously, a legend concerning Gonnor seems to nudge our domain in the direction of a setting for a tale about *cuissage.*

Duke Richard's first wife was Emma, the daughter of Hugues le Grand, duke of the Franks and father of Hugh Capet. Some decades after the Treaty of Saint-Clair-sur-Epte, which had given the invading Northmen the province of Normandy in exchange for their conversion to Christianity and their promise to put an end to their pillage, that prestigious alliance crowned the new dukes' integration into the western Frankish kingdom. While married to Emma, however, Richard had a Danish concubine, Gonnor. At Emma's death he legitimized the relation by marrying Gonnor. A legend transmitted by the chronicler Guillaume de Jumièges (eleventh century), the poet Wace (twelfth century), and later writers gave a different version of this second marriage, making Richard a brutal lord given to the sexual oppression of his dependents. Guillaume de Jumièges writes:

> Count Richard, having heard tell of the beauty of the wife of one of his foresters who lived not far from the castle of Arques in the domain named "Schecheville" hastened to go hunting in that direction, eager to test the truth of what he had learned by hearsay. Lodged in the forester's house and struck by the beauty of the woman's face, he ordered his host to bring his wife Sainfrien—for that was her name—to his bed. As [the forester] sadly informed his wife of this, she consoled him like a good wife, telling him that she would have her sister Gonnor, a virgin even more beautiful than she, take her place. This was done. The duke was told of the ruse and was delighted not to have sinned with another man's wife.[5]

There is probably some relation between the composition of the poem of 1247 and the fact that the donation of Verson resulted from (and seemingly compensated for) a story of sexual abuse. The menace of secular power recalled that origin and threatened to negate the benefits of monastic management. The legend must have had broad circulation around Verson: Wace, who was born in Jersey, spent the greater part of his life in Caen. His position as *clerc lisant* (reader) to three Henrys who were kings of England and dukes of Normandy made his *Roman de Rou* an authoritative source for Norman history.

This gives us a fairly firm schema for this first emergence of *cuissage*. A rivalry between lay and ecclesiastical lords engenders a polemical text that refers, by implication, to a legend about the origins of the sovereign family's power by presenting the image of a tyrant—an image, as we have seen, capable of being the source of inspiration for a tale.

Unfortunately, this vernacular text could not have had many readers since it was closed up in a cartulary of the monastery of Mont-Saint-Michel. At best we can imagine that the lord of La Rivière-Bourdet, also in Normandy, may have known of the tradition when he drew up his *dénombrement* in 1419.

The fact that this thirteenth-century occurrence is unique should not be seen as a limit on its possible influence. It is remarkable that *cullage* was given a legendary interpretation in the service of persiflage precisely when another term, *mainmorte*, was undergoing a similar transformation. There is nothing mysterious about the name of this seigniorial right so often associated, as we have seen, with the *cullage* paid for marriages. In the juridical Latin of the age *manus* designated power that holds or "seizes"; hence possessions under *mainmorte* were considered still held by the deceased, which for reasons of landed or personal dependency, were not automatically transmissible to the heirs. The expression contradicted the adage "le mort saisit le vif" (the dead invests the living), which functioned only among the free. Not only in the thirteenth century but in the precise year (1247) when the "Chanson des vilains de Verson" was written, a canon in Liège, Gilles d'Orval, invented a foundation legend crediting St. Albero, bishop of Liège (1123–28), with abolishing the barbarous custom of cutting a dependent's hand in sign of possession of his inheritance. According to Gilles, when Albero abolished this right, it was replaced with the right of *mainmorte* or the *droit du meilleur catel* (right to the best chattel). The fourteenth-century chronicler Jean d'Outremeuse, a clerk of the diocesan court in Liège, repeated the legend in his *Myreur des histoires*. In the following century an anonymous religious in Neuss am Rhein repeated the anecdote in his *Chronicum magnum belgicum* (1480). The career of the myth of *mainmorte* paralleled that of the myth of *cuissage:* Both were created in ecclesiastical circles, but by the seventeenth century the myth of *mainmorte* served a bourgeois and monarchist culture. Du Cange's *Glossarium* (1678), a work that played a major role in the diffusion of various terms related to *cuissage*, as we have seen, includes the tale and cites this chronicle. Another popularizer of *cuissage*, Eusèbe de Laurière, mentions the myth of the origin of *mainmorte* in his *Glossaire du droit français* (1699). The two myths remain solidly implanted in perception of the Middle Ages in our own day: The popular historian André Castelot has recently rekindled this dubious flame.[6]

These legends were forged at approximately the same time as the juridical notions that fueled them. Admittedly, exactions for marriages and succession have an extremely long history; the precise formulations of *cullage*, *mainmorte*, and merchet go back no further than the early thirteenth century, however, and the establishment of the principle that seigniorial rights could be commuted into money payments. The contention played out in 1247 in Verson and Liège involved rival claims to the legitimacy of these commutations. In the late sixteenth century, when the state took on the task of creating a monopoly on taxation, justice, and the problem of fiscal exemptions, juridical-monarchical culture picked up where that rivalry left off. This means that we need to take seriously this notion of persiflage and identify its historical function: It was aimed at undermining an adversarial power without confronting it directly through criticism or denunciation. Indirection was necessary because the contending factions relied on analogous fiscal exactions for the social basis of their power. The *licentia maritandi* of the monks bore the same price as the *cullage* of the lay lords; its legitimation had to be shifted without challenging the right itself.

It might seem surprising that ethical persiflage is not found elsewhere in the ecclesiastical seigniories of the Middle Ages. The extreme fragility of this sort of documentation may have something to do with this. The "Chanson des vilains de Verson" was preserved by pure chance. We might also conjecture that the rumor of ecclesiastical *cuissage* in the fifteenth century made ecclesiastical institutions more prudent. The particularly oppressive and backward nature of clerical and monastic seigniories in areas where personal dependency persisted may enter the picture as well.

This scarcity of documentation obliges us to move on to the juridical and monarchic persiflage of the late sixteenth century.

THE SUIT OF THE LADY OF SOMLOIRE (1600)

Until the sixteenth century the motif of *cuissage* existed only in documents related to social practice—first in the Verson polemic and then in *dénom-*

brements in Normandy, Picardy, and Béarn. At that point the story of per-siflage becomes complicated, because it mixes with several autonomous traditions. In chapter 1 we noted the importance of merchet, which began its literary existence with Hector Boece's *History of Scotland* (1526), apparently because he thought it necessary to have a primitive and barbaric king on whom to found a national and Christian history. We have traced a second tradition, the ecclesiastical *droit de cuissage,* from the *Decisiones* of Boyer or Pseudo-Boyer (1551), connecting the extravagant episode of the curé of Bourges with the Amiens affair and mentioning in passing the dread mores of certain lords in the Auvergne (who figure here to signify barbarity more than secular custom). We have also noted a third genealogy in travel narratives, many of them accounts of voyages to the Americas, which Montaigne used to such good effect.

All elements for a criticism of the mores of the French nobility come together in the *Recueil d'arrests notables* (1556) of the jurist Jean Papon (1505–90). Papon comments on a decree of the Parlement de Paris in 1401 regarding a contention between the citizens of Amiens and their bishop—a decree he probably confuses with the 1409 decree we know well—but the clerical aspect of the question interested him very little, and he moves on to a commentary that (for the first time) condemns certain practices in the name of humanity and natural law:

> It is execrable that in some places of this kingdom, and even in Auvergne, we can find the custom observed and tolerated that the lord of the place had the right to lie the first night with the bride. This is not far from what Diodorus Siculus wrote in the sixth book of his history, that in some places in Sicily a girl marrying for the first time was prostituted to several unmarried young men and remained with the one who knew her last. These are barbaric and brutal acts, unworthy not only of Christians but of men.[7]

It was not long before François Ragueau, *lieutenant de bailliage* at Mehun in Berry, then regent doctor of the University of Bourges, effected a political synthesis of tradition. In a much reprinted work, *Indice des droits royaux et seigneuriaux* (1580), completed a century later by Eusèbe de Laurière, Ragueau combined under the heading "marquette" materials from Boece (via Buchanan) and an allusion to the customs of the lords of Auvergne (citing Papon). His most salient point comes in a short comment in Latin (the language of juridical science) inserted among quotations in French from Buchanan and Papon: "These rapes and adulteries were banished long ago by the decisions of the Parlement of France."[8] The unfortunate Amiens affair (which Ragueau does not mention) is probably what inspired this glorification of the civilizing wisdom of the

Parlement. From then on the fate of the myth was sealed: *Cuissage* exemplified the all-out struggle of the central power and its Parlement against archaic and repugnant nobilities lurking in the Auvergne.

After 1580 one can follow an uninterrupted line of reiterations of this construct, but they brought little that was new. Moreover, we have already seen (in Piedmont, Montauban, Buch, and elsewhere) that juridical tradition was capable of incorporating local legend. I shall concentrate on two practical occurrences that display not only the reality of the new persiflage but also the assent of a certain seigniorial stratum to archaic representations of itself. These two affairs are not comparable: In the first, royal jurists treated a presumption of *cuissage* in 1600–1601 with a mixture of indignation and scorn; in the second (in 1665), the political aspects of persiflage are fully developed.

The first affair was an appeal heard by the Grand'Chambre of the Parlement de Paris on 6 March 1601 opposing Demoiselle Charlotte du Bois, widow of Joachim Barillon esquire, lord of Somloire (now in the department of Maine-et-Loire), to Gabriel Ragot, lord of La Faye and husband of Demoiselle Renée de Guynemoire, and Michel Breat, a sharecrop farmer of the same La Faye. The suit was filed to appeal a decision handed down by the lieutenant of the seneschal of Anjou, who ruled against the lady of Somloire on 4 March 1600. The question under litigation seems slim—only certain symbolic seigniorial rights—but it mobilized some remarkable personalities. Gourreau, the lady's lawyer, has left little trace in history, but the same cannot be said of the lawyer for the defense, René Choppin, or of the king's prosecutor, Louis Servin. Choppin, a lawyer and a jurisconsult, undeniably was called into this affair as an expert with a thorough knowledge of Anjou custom, a topic he treated in a lengthy volume.[9] His stature transcended this technical competence, however: He was known, along with Charles de Grassaille and Jean Bodin, as one of the theorists of nascent French absolutism, and he was part of a group in the late sixteenth century who constructed (or reconstructed) the image of the mystical marriage of the nation and its king, and drew a parallel between the royal domain and a bride's dowry.[10] Louis Servin started from a totally different ideological horizon but arrived at monarchism, just as Choppin had. In his own day Servin was considered a hidden Protestant. Be that as it may, he stood out consistently for a wholehearted attachment to the Gallican cause and for his fierce opposition to the Jesuits. In 1589, when he had just been named *avocat du roi* (public prosecutor) for the Parlement de Tours, he published *Revendications pour la liberté de l'église gallicane* (*Vindiciae secundum libertatem ecclesiae gallicanae*, 1590), a work that placed him among Henry IV's most effective partisans and won him the post of *avocat du roi* at the Parlement de Paris in 1594. It was thanks to his ardent petition, twenty-three years later, that the Parlement de Paris publicly burned (on 20 June 1613) a work that enjoyed the backing of the pope, the *Defensio catholicae fidei contra anglicanae sectae errores* of the great Jesuit Francisco Suarez. On 2 February 1615 Servin persuaded the Parlement to approve the first of the third estate's demands—the temporal power's strict autonomy from the Church—at a moment when the assembly of the third estate was too timid to put the question to a vote. For thirty years he was one of the most prominent of the *gens du roi*, the "king's men," in the Parlement. On 14 May 1610, the day Henry IV was assassinated, Servin accompanied Achille de Harlay, first president of Parlement, and Cardin Le Bret, another of the king's men, to the Louvre to prepare the *lit de justice* held the next day, thus to proclaim the immediate succession of the young Louis XIII.[11] Servin's discourse on that occasion is a major text in support of the principle of hereditary and instantaneous succession. All this may seem beyond the scope of the modest affair that concerns us here, but it provides a basis for the hypothesis that juridical and monarchical questions lay behind the treatment of *cuissage* under the Ancien Régime. I might add that Servin himself did not think this affair unimportant: A résumé of his final arguments is included in the many editions of his requisitories.[12]

Servin gave a clear summary of the question at law:

> The appellant claims for her children by reason of the seigniory of Souloire [now Somloire] a right over every wedding that is held in the said seigniory [and claims] that her sergeant must be invited eight days beforehand to go to the wedding festivities with two matched running dogs and a greyhound, and that the said sergeant must be seated at dinner facing the bride and be served like her. Moreover, the said sergeant must say the first song and the newlyweds must give the dogs and the greyhound to eat and drink.

We see here the chief characteristics of the rites of nuptial participation associated in *dénombrements* of the late Middle Ages with perception of the *droit de cullage* or with a recall of an earlier *droit de cuissage*. We can note a desire both to humiliate and to participate: The sergeant's dogs are given things to eat and drink by the couple, who by that gesture accept the rank of submissive animals. At the same time, however, the sergeant eats, sings, and is part of the wedding party. No *droit de cuissage* is mentioned, but it is clear that the sergeant occupies the symbolic place of the groom: Seated facing the bride, he is the first to offer a song, and he eats the same food as the bride.

The juridical basis for these demands lay in a series of *aveux et dénom-*

brements: "And for proof of this claimed right she says that it was given in these terms by *adveu* of the sieur Count of Maulévrier to whom the fief of Souloire owed loyalty and homage, and this in the years 1408, 1448, 1458, 1517, 1518, [and] 1546. [The lady] adds that by extracts dated from the years 1501, 1505, 1507, and 1511, 1514, 1531, [and] 1540 she has proof of the possession of this claimed *droict de nopces* made in the said years." We see here the painstaking care that lords of minuscule territories took to authenticate their rights, even though the *droit de noces* was undoubtedly only one small item in the *dénombrement*. The comte de Maulévrier probably had these *aveux* registered and verified, given that he agreed to provide extracts of them. The irregular series of dates is probably a sign of perpetual contestation: Seigniorial rights, ceaselessly attacked, continually threatened with obsolescence, seemed fragile indeed before the majestic judiciary machinery culminating in the Parlement de Paris. Royal justice was not indifferent to these local tyrannies and conducted inquiries. The appellant could no longer rely on old texts but had to exhibit witnesses: "Then she produced information in the form of an ordonnance affixed to the bottom of a petition of the lieutenant of the seneschal of Anjou in Angers, and by that information some witnesses report weddings having been held to which the sergeant of Souloir was invited."

The brief goes on to state that the resistance of some dependents had prompted the suit: "But one of these [witnesses] says that having been told to submit to this due when he married, he was prevented by the defendant, the husband of the Demoiselle de Guynemoire, who told him not to submit, promising to guarantee him for his refusal." This witness seems to be of two minds: He resists the custom, but he agrees to be a witness at the trial in Angers: "In the last instance the appellant says that by the argument of the defendant made in Angers 4 March 1600, the day of the sentence appealed here, he recognized that the late Sieur de Somloire sent his sergeant to some wedding gatherings held by the sharecroppers of the farm of Guynemoire." The social stakes grow clearer: Seigniorial rights were applied to the sharecroppers employed by the defendant, Gabriel Ragot, and his wife; feudal relations had fallen to the distaff side. The seigniory of Somloire had passed to the wife of a lord who had known how to ensure respect of ancient prerogatives; the heiress to the domain of Guynemoire had married a city-dweller who brought a spirit of revolt to this remote territory.

At this point a witness (perhaps Michel Breat, the sharecropper who testified in support of the demoiselle de Guynemoire) "added that this had been only for seventeen or eighteen years, during the minority of the said demoiselle de Guynemoire or before the time of the troubles that have come since and in the absence of the defendant and his wife, who did not make their residence in that place but in Angers, and by force and violence of the sergeant of Souloire over rustic persons who feared and dreaded him." These are remarkable details: They point the way to the monumental social rupture of the Wars of Religion (the *temps des troubles*). The dominating community of folklore has been transformed into pure exaction; it is also possible that the lady of Guynemoire's residence in Angers was a refuge against those "troubles." The *dénombrements* stop in 1546. Later in his requisitory Servin suggests that social change might have made the once joyous practices of the lord of Somloire more unacceptable. Let us suppose, Servin states, a change in condition where a female vassal of one of the lord's vassals marries a man from outside the community. "It would not be right [honneste] for the sergeant of the lord of Somloire to come into the house to trouble the festivities."

The defendant's counterattack, written by Servin, is no less interesting:

> Furthermore the defendant denies this right and maintains that it has not been proven by sufficient title nor by well-justified possession. And first for the proof resulting from the extracts from *aveux*, he remarks an article preceding the one of this alleged right that states that the sergeant of Souloire has a right over every public concubine who passes on the road to take 4 deniers from her or the sleeve from the right arm of her dress or for the said sergeant to do his will with the said concubine once, at the choice of the said sergeant.

We cannot know either the exact meaning of this second article or the reason for it, because the *dénombrement* for Somloire has unfortunately not been preserved and the lady, who had asked that it be maintained in the Angers suit, had not included the point in her appeal, probably because it was judged too scabrous. It is evident that the two successive articles share the seigniorial gauloiserie we have so often seen. Moreover, to repeat the point anachronistically in modern terms, seigniorial micropower was fundamentally "macho," with all the connotations implied in the term of boasts and lies (as we recall, the lord of Louvie-Soubiron was the putative father of all the eldest children of the village of Aas). In a shift to a lower level, the sergeant representing the lord holds an imaginary *droit de cuissage* over an eventual though improbable prostitute passing through Somloire, a derisory equivalent for the female subject: He can "faire sa volonté à ladite concubine," but his right can be bought off by the small sum of 4 deniers, an equivalent of *chevage*. Microseigniorial bragging spawned imitators.

The personality of the imagined victim of this *cuissage* by procuration raises some doubts. The text speaks of a *concubine publique,* an expression that could perfectly well designate a public prostitute. But it might also refer to a woman publicly and notoriously adulterous. If that were the case, the gesture of taking the right sleeve of her dress would mark her as a prostitute. As is known, one of the signs imposed on prostitutes in the late Middle Ages was to wear colored sleeves (the "green sleeves" of English tradition).[13] In such cases the article of the *dénombrement* would have a more ambitious meaning: The lord was allotting to himself some sort of right of justice over moral failings. The lord of Somloire clearly did not possess rights of justice on his lands, but as we have seen, the repression of sexual offenses long remained fluid, sometimes falling under strictly local customs. At other times it was considered a penitential matter and was handled by the parish priest or by religious justice, the diocesan courts *(officialités)* in particular. Thus there was a power gap waiting to be occupied. On an infinitely higher level than the seigniory of Somloire, state or city authorities at the start of the early modern age worked consistently to bring penal repression within their powers.[14]

The second article of the *dénombrement,* not subject to judiciary debate in the appeal, gave Servin an opportunity to qualify the nature of the seigniorial relations between the lords of Somloire and their vassals. Marital rights (the *droit de noces*) retained the full ambiguity of folk customs of domination; it gave off a whiff of the *droit de cuissage* without expressly stating it. In contrast, persecution of women of easy virtue enabled Servin to describe the lord's socioethical habitus: "And as this right would be tyrannical and bears the mark of cruel treatments by a lord over the subjects of a vassal dependent on him, and by that token should not take place, the defendant sustains that the subsequent [article in the *dénombrement*] making mention of the right to attend wedding festivities must not be executed either, no matter what the appellant might say: 'utile per inutile non vitiari' [a useful element is not vitiated by a useless element]."

That said, Servin moved on to the question of the tasks and *corvées* imposed by the seigniorial regime, invoking the capitularies of Charlemagne and Louis le Débonnaire. These were by no means innocent references: At the dawn of seigniorial times the Carolingian monarchy already appeared as the protector of subjects; the monarchs even drew up rules for the *corvées* assigned to domestic animals. The other source of law in the early modern period, Roman law, restricted owed labor to what was promised in a "legitimate pact" or in an oath sworn to the current patron of a freedman, by implication excluding all services based on tradition or justified by inherited condition. The only exceptions to these rules concerned artisanal or "liberal" occupations: "Among the Romans, the emancipated obliged themselves to servile [tasks] according to their condition—as with workers in wood and other materials, physicians, and players of farces, each in his profession. Nevertheless, these duties were easily lost, in several cases by the patrons or when they rented them out to an outside party."

Servin clearly tends to limit the services demanded of dependents to a contractual framework of the wage-earning sort. The few exceptions (also derived from Roman law) concern a close dependency linked to an urban business or the patrician home (recalling the urban servitude we have noted in the late Middle Ages). According to Servin, that kind of dependency soon turned into wage earning. He conceived of the relation of dependence in rural areas as a sequel to ancient slavery, slowly eroded by the progress of law and by state authority—a schema we also find among the liberal historians but also in Verriest and even in Marc Bloch.

The minute a contract or personal promise is required to legitimate the relation between the dependent and the lord, marital rights apply only "if the master had freed the woman either through marriage or in concubinage . . . or if, by the will of the master, the freedwoman married another and passed into that family by marriage . . . or if the freedman had given money to the master to emancipate her [pour le main mettre]." The lord could take part in the wedding festivities only on a personal basis, as a former husband or partner in concubinage or as a substitute for the father, aiding or authorizing the bride's departure to another family. Later in his requisitory Servin stresses the point that wedding custom in Somloire did not constitute a *paction* (pact, agreement), since the bride could refuse to go along with it: "She would not want a constraint that is not 'secundum bonas mores' [in conformity with right conduct]."

Once the condition of dependence is reduced to an individual and patriarchal relation, seigniorial custom became barbaric and archaic: "And if liberty must take place in any act, 'certe magna in matrimonio esse debet' [surely it must be great in marriage] to avoid constraining the subjects of a vassal to render to the lord of the fief extraordinary reconnaissances recalling the compulsion of pagan servitude."

At this point in his argument Servin mentions the Amiens affair, dating it as having occurred in 1401, an indication that his probable source was Papon's commentary (where Servin also found his reference to Diodorus Siculus): "And certainly such tyrannical laws or customs as some of those of Denys, tyrant of Sicily, others recounted by Aristotle in his *Economics,* and [the custom] of Scotland, an example of which is reported in the time of King Malcolm, must be governed by the right of reason, either being tempered by mutation into another law or by total abolition of what is contrary to liberty." Through his references (by then familiar in juridical culture) and with the aid of his crypto-Calvinism, Servin amalgamated folk customs of domination, ecclesiastical taxes, and the mythical forms of barbaric *cuissage.*

At the end of his requisitory Servin moderates his tone somewhat. After suggesting an analogy between marital rights (the *droit de noces*) and sexual abuse in three successive shifts (from the article regarding women of easy virtue to marital rights, from the Somloire case to the Amiens affair, from the latter to *cuissage* in ancient Scotland), Servin condemns the intrinsic indecency of the rite itself. At best, the *droit de noces* arose from festivities no longer appropriate "in these times, when men need to be brought back to the exacting law of ancient frugality." Dependents "cannot be constrained to the sort of repast that the wisest do not hold in our times."

Servin ends with a discussion of forms of proof of enjoyment of marital rights. The ethical indignity of the form of servitude demanded excluded the right from falling within the area of privileges whose tacit enjoyment for thirty years assured them permanence under Anjou custom. We can see at work here two sorts of temporal logic: The seigniory hopes that time will be favorable to it and bring consolidation of its privileges; royal law, which infiltrated the new customals, imposed the renewal of oaths every thirty years, making time work against seigniorial rights. The state opposed a falsely immemorial tradition by insisting on law as continual creation and demanding that present relations be contractual. For Servin the *aveu* and the *dénombrement* were only caricatures of law: Vassals had no way of knowing what fate such written documents held in store for them; they "can say that when the Lords of Somloire, their liege lords, rendered their *aveux* to the lord count of Maulévrier, they put in them whatever they wanted to."

All we have of René Choppin's arguments for the defense is a brief summary in the court's decision. It is enough, however, to establish the illustrious jurisconsult as a figurehead for the new legality: "Choppin, for the defense, denies a right that the appellant had no title to and that is not received by custom; he sustained that it was ridiculous, inept, and against honest public freedom, concluding [that the original suit was] well judged."

The lady of Somloire's appeal marks the final throes of local sovereignty. By reaffirming a culture of domination that had lost its piquancy and its bite in the troubles of the times, a minor lord sought desperately to demonstrate that lords were more than just proprietors subjected to the general laws of the kingdom. But here he (in this case, she) confronted the state-backed majesty of the Parlement and powerful adversaries who made it clear that in France under the monarchical state, the age of the contract and the citizen had arrived to replace the times of tradition and the subject.

Still, Parlement did not follow Louis Servin's vehement requisitory:

> The Court has considered the appeal and the matter under appeal inasmuch as the seneschal of Angers or his lieutenant has rejected the right of the feudal lord concerning the weddings of his subjects, the point of contention between the parties, and emending the judgment in this regard it has maintained and kept and now maintains and keeps the appellant in possession and enjoyment of the said right. We decree that as for the rest, the sentence is compelling, and there will be no cost for the appeal. Given in Parlement on 6 March 1601. Voisin.[15]

The decision handed down by the Parlement de Paris shows that its members, magistrates who often possessed noble or commoners' seigniories, had every intention of preserving the fragile network of relations of rural dependency against the ethical and juridical power of the monarchic state echoed in Servin's strong words. We have already seen how the members of the Parlement de Besançon acted as vigilant guardians of seigniorial rights until the eve of the French Revolution in 1789. That same spirit of resistance probably explains why officials and magistrates tirelessly pursued a denunciation of *cuissage*.

We can consider the Somloire *droit de noces* as a *droit de cuissage* largely because of Choppin's and Servin's juridical tactics, but the real situation was more complex. The parlementary debates of 1601 signal a turning point, difficult to date with precision, in the "juridicalization"—offensive and defensive—of seigniorial and communitarian custom. As we have seen, certain obligations close to "folk" customs—symbolic dues, joking or humiliating acts or payments linked to key moments in the calendar or to weddings—had been placed, since the end of the Middle Ages, within the catalogue of seigniorial rights, for the most part through the channel of *aveux et dénombrements*. A "seigniorial right" was not truly in the juridical sphere unless it was contested, preserved, or appealed before a third institution. Little by little, however, these apparently marginal customs were either tested in lawsuits or described critically in juridical texts as "bizarre," "ridiculous," or "indecent" rights.

As a consequence what we for lack of a better term call "folklore" took on a new social reality. Martine Grinberg and Nicole Pellegrin have recently brought a new perspective to this question.[16] "Folklore," a nineteenth-century construct, set up the idea that practices of symbolic exchange, proofs of prowess demanded by groups of young unmarried males, and compensations related to marriage revealed an ancient, primordial village culture; when lords took command of these forms of sociability at the end of the Middle Ages, they presumably took to themselves guardianship of community autonomy. Other scholars more sensitive to the "democratic" pull of popular culture see the dues that unmarried males demanded of newlyweds as a manifestation of popular reconquest of "feudal" seigniorial rights. Nicole Pellegrin's study of the *bachelleries* of western France enables us to get beyond both overly simple chronological schemes. The *bachelleries*, a late arrival on the scene (in the fifteenth century), seem to have been contemporary with *aveux et dénombrements* that begin to list symbolic seigniorial rights. As the marital dues exacted by the seigniories and the *bachelleries* appear in these texts (which describe a theoretical situation before or after conflicts), they seem to complement one another, showing a division of jurisdiction more than superimposed layers of custom. This division of conflictual jurisdiction passed into law during the sixteenth century at the moment of highest tension in the construction of "modern" jurisdictions among the state, the Church, the seigniories, and the parish and village communities. Confirmation of this point of view would require a study of French rural areas analogous to Angelo Torre's study of Piedmont.[17] Torre shows how parish and community networks traced during the Middle Ages long remained ill-defined and uncertain but grew more rigid in the sixteenth and seventeenth centuries as a result of incessant jurisdictional conflicts bearing on minute questions of ritual or symbolic competence. "Folklore," canon law, and liturgy furnish the vocabulary of a jurisdictional discourse expressing the new ambitions of distant sovereign bodies, ecclesiastical and civil, over local powers.

Despite Servin's and Choppin's defeat before the Parlement de Paris, *cuissage* structured the representation of bizarre seigniorial rights. Moreover, the image of local tyranny projected in that suit spread far beyond the narrow circle of royal jurists, disseminated by the new court culture.

CIVILITY AND RUSTICITY (1610–40)

In 1575, twenty-five years before the lady of Somloire's suit, René Choppin, the lawyer for the lady of Guynemoire, published a treatise, reprinted several times, titled *De privilegiis rusticorum* (*Sur les privilèges des rustiques* [On Peasant Privileges]).[18] In the late sixteenth century, a time of a veritable race for group privilege within the framework of the nascent absolute state, there was nothing surprising about his title.[19] Nonetheless, Choppin's specific interest in the peasant world marked a turning point, prefiguring the famous *Théâtre d'agriculture et mesnage des champs* of Olivier de Serres (1600). *La ville* began to take an interest in *les champs* on levels ranging from Henry IV's chicken in the pot on Sunday for every peasant to Honoré d'Urfé's chivalric pastoral romance, *L'Astrée*. This interest did not necessarily imply genuine or genuinely attentive observation, but rather marked an attempt to infiltrate local powers in their milieu.

Choppin's analysis was highly ambivalent, even in defining his topic: Were "rustics" everyone who lived in the countryside or only peasants? The "privileges" of the rural population are ambiguous as well: Choppin advocates protecting things specific to the country when they are profitable to the nation, but he makes excuses for the scant capacities of country folk, marked by a "rusticity" that had long been equated with simplicity and even stupidity in European culture. The "great division" that long continued to separate local cultures from the dominant cultures took two forms. First, the rural world was seen as a place of passive resistance to the "enlightenment" of the cities and the courts; second, country people were considered, with benevolent condescension, as innocent and simple victims ("natural" rusticity) to be rescued from the savage rusticity of local tyrants. Choppin himself, a man who loved his "half-peasant" *(semipaganus)* life in his domain at Cachan, expressed both a genuine interest in rural things and a condemnation of rustic brutality. His first mention of the fable of *cuissage* occurs in this treatise, but he also takes pains to gather precise information on agricultural methods. Above all, he understood that the specificity of country people's juridical situation lay in problems of succession, precisely where civil law was weak.

Choppin's attitudes of sympathy and disdain were more complementary than opposed. That complementarity is clear in his treatment of custom. Anne Zink catches the essence of the definition of juridical doctrine since the thirteenth century when she states, "A custom is not a usage or a habit but a law imposed locally."[20] This incontestable formula contradicts a common opinion forged during the sixteenth and seventeenth centuries—the very culture of the law courts and princely courts—that took the variety of custom as a sign of rustic naïveté and a mark of savagery. A considerable number of customals were republished and glossed in the sixteenth century in the spirit of the two forms of the "great division," respecting usages but also drastically reducing their particularities.[21] The royal jurists pretended to confuse the bizarre aspects of seigniorial usages with the singularities of custom: In their commentaries on custom or when they rewrote customs, they often backed up their emendation with an appeal to the universality of natural law or to Roman law. Civility of mores was closely connected to the civility of the law, as Choppin recalls when he notes that the etymology of *civil* law referred to the world of the cities.[22]

Guy Coquille (1523–1603), a jurist who was Choppin's contemporary, is a striking example of this same tendency. Like Choppin, Coquille contributed to spreading the fable of *cuissage*, in his case in a commentary on the customs of the Nivernais. His social figure adds nuances, however, to the portrait of the royal jurist. Guy Coquille might have become a king's man: He was approached twice with flattering offers of a high magistracy or a place in the royal Council, once by Michel de L'Hospital in 1560 and again by King Henry IV in 1590, but he preferred to continue to live "rustically" in his domain of Romenay while serving the house of the duc de Nivernais. In speaking of royal jurists, we must remember to include men who gravitated in the orbit of the princes and great lords whose interests were closely connected with those of the monarchy.

There is one revealing difference, however: Guy Coquille composed and glossed a customal of the Rethélois, a dependency of the duchy of Nivernais in the Ardennes, that he made up out of whole cloth, borrowing freely from the customals of Vitry-le-François and Paris.[23] The usual procedure for compiling a customal was to use the oldest usages as a base and, above all, to conduct an *enquête par tourbe* by calling meetings and interviewing witnesses. This text thus gives a good idea of what a jurist committed to centralization considered the ideal customal. Indeed, the synthetic customal (synthetic as one might speak of a "synthetic image") of the Rethélois preserves the forms of seigniorial land domination but connects them with the preeminent sovereignty of the king. Coquille makes this clear in his preface: "The lord justices do not hold these rights as truly patrimonial and alodial 'necque jure proprio, sed quasi procuratores constituti a rege in rem et utilitatem suam' [not by an inherent right but inasmuch as procurators established by the king over a possession and for its service]; and as among commoners the proprietor pays an annual due to his direct lord in recognition of his superiority, so the lords do service of their persons to the king."[24] Coquille's text is rationally arranged and sparely written; it prefigures the civility of thought and language that was to triumph during the 1630s.

It was perhaps thanks to this early sixteenth-century interest in alienated rusticity in need of sovereign, juridical, and royal protection that the native *droit de cuissage* (not some exotic form) became an element of a court culture that finds its perfect example in Esprit Fléchier in 1665. Allusions in the works of Papon, Ragueau, Servin, Choppin, and Coquille did not go unnoticed, but they remained within a sphere of demonstrative discourse.

One extremely interesting text illustrates this important shift: It is a tale told by Béroalde de Verville in his work *Le moyen de parvenir*, written around 1610. This curious narrative (the complete text appears in appendix 1, below) does not deal with a case of *cuissage*, strictly speaking, but rather presents an episode of sexual abuse by an imaginary lord. The narrator and protagonist is one Monsieur de La Roche, a name that recalls the narrator of several of the tales of the *Cent nouvelles nouvelles*, the work that first mentions ecclesiastical *cuissage*.[25] When the daughter of his miller brings some cherries to the lord, Monsieur de La Roche, a local tyrant, he obliges her to strip off her clothes, scatter the cherries on the floor of the hall while his guests and dependents enjoy the spectacle of her unadorned beauty, then pick them up again. The company applauds, and in jest the men vie with one another in a verbal auction to put a price on their amusement. When the scene has ended the lord forces each of the assembled men to pay the price he has bid and gives the money to the victimized girl.

This transitional text stands at the meeting point of three cultural systems. On the one hand, Béroalde's collection of satirical and bawdy tales is the "perfect, last expression of the French tale" of the sixteenth century.[26] We have seen, however, that sixteenth-century French tales neglect rural social stratification. On the other hand, by its learned allusions and its caustic humor this text participates in the libertine movement (in both the technical and the broader sense of the term) of the early seventeenth century that served as a foil for the construction of court culture. Finally, by depicting local tyranny and innocence perverted, the tale belongs to the new juridical and courtly civility. In his sure sketch of what Sandra Gilbert and Susan Grubar call the "eroticism of social inequality" (as we saw in connection with masters and servants in chapter 1), Béroalde prepares the way for the dramatic use of *cuissage* that developed a century later. His boldness went further: The extraordinary reversal ending the tale, when the lord's courtiers have to pay the innocent victim for their voyeurism, presents a dizzying picture of a sovereign power establishing a generalized money equivalent to a representation it offers.

The entry of the *droit de cuissage* into literature seems to have occurred throughout Europe. Shakespeare mentions it;[27] in 1617 Cervantes fit the American fables into his novel, *Persiles y Sigismunda;*[28] the plot of Fletcher and Massinger's comedy, *The Custom of the Country* (1619), turns around *cullage.*[29] What made the theme specifically French was probably the connection between a fantastic custom and the sociocultural reality of rustic life.

The medieval dimension of rustic seigniorial savagery began to emerge in a treatise in dialogue by Jean Chapelain, *De la lecture des vieux romans* (1646). Chapelain played a central role in furthering Richelieu's cultural policies, thus he is a good representative of the new cultural civility of the French monarchy.

Chapelain's dialogue, dedicated to the future Cardinal de Retz, presents Ménage, Sarasin, and Chapelain himself conversing. The *vieux romans* of its title are medieval romances, regarded by these men of letters with a mixture of disdain and curiosity. They analyze this courtly literature (before the fact, since the term was coined by Gaston Paris in the late nineteenth century),[30] foreshadowing Georges Duby's judgment some three and a half centuries later.[31] Chapelain states:

> The ecclesiastical estate was shut up inside hermitages and monasteries; valor reigned supreme and all pleasures and honors were reserved for it. It was the favored estate and the right hand of the monarchy, which (for the reasons I have given) nourished that virtue with all the means that those rough times and the disposition of the sensual minds of youth could furnish to its imagination. It was for that reason that the Round Table was invented. . . . The politics of those olden days made it a law that ladies' hearts would be the reward of courage, thus sharpening the loyalty that vassals owed their lords in the hope not only of glory but also of the pleasure procured by possession of [ladies'] beauty.[32]

Sarasin expresses surprise at courtly morality: "These gentlemen legislators wanted women to be faithful to their lovers when they could have done otherwise without being discovered, but they also permitted women to be unfaithful to their husbands provided no scandal ensued." Ménage, a man with a critical mind, demands proof; Chapelain gives literary sources (*Lancelot, Tristan, Merlin, Artus* [King Arthur], *Perceforêt*) and postulates a homogeneity of mores that makes him a precursor of the history of mentalities: "Everyone spoke about the same things and wrote at a time when minds were neither very inventive nor capable of acting counter to the mores and customs of their centuries."[33] This leads Chapelain to postulate the existence of the *droit de cuissage:*

Because what makes you think my supposition is suspect is what I tell you about the facility of the ladies of those days, founded on the persuasion that certain things could be done without dishonor, I think I can make it more believable for you by the custom kept in Scotland, long after Christianity had been received, of the kings having the first fruits of the weddings of their principal ladies and the great lords a similar tribute from the ladies of their vassals—a custom formerly practiced in Normandy, as it appears by the similar right that certain lords still claim on their subjects' marriage. Anyone who will consider that institution carefully will find it of the same nature as the one I suppose on the evidence of romances, except that it is even more heinous because it did not have the excuse of love and was pure brutality.[34]

Chapelain's reference to Scotland is by now an old story to us, but it would be interesting indeed to know what were his sources concerning Normandy. Did he perhaps know the "Chanson des vilains de Verson"? It is not impossible: Until the mid-nineteenth century, the fragment of the Mont-Saint-Michel cartulary containing the poem was owned by the Léchaudé d'Anisy family, who had connections in the Parlement and at court in the seventeenth century. In any event, Chapelain's text is probably the first interpretation of a marital right couched in terms of compensation for the *droit de cuissage*.

More important for the history of how the fable became integrated into court culture is the bias displayed by these erudite men of letters who had some acquaintance with medieval texts and displayed historical leanings. The most striking manifestation of this convergence of royal jurists, men of letters, and court culture occurs in a text by Esprit Fléchier, our third example of social persiflage.

THE LORD OF MONTVALLAT AND THE GRANDS JOURS OF AUVERGNE (1665)

On 25 September 1665 an extraordinary court convened in full solemnity in Clermont (later Clermont-Ferrand). It was made up largely of members of the Parlement de Paris (a *président*, sixteen *conseillers*, an *avocat général*, two *greffiers* [clerks], and a *maître des requêtes*), all dispatched by Louis XIV to hasten the course of justice and enforce respect in Auvergne of a royal order presumed flaunted. The court remained in Clermont until 30 January 1666. *Grands Jours* was a term that since the early thirteenth century had designated periodic and solemn seigniorial assizes to hear and judge cases on appeal passed on from lower courts. When the French provinces were attached to the royal domain, the Grands Jours were retained but with a changed focus. Beginning in the fifteenth century they provided the French monarchy with a means of control and repression swifter and less corrupt than ordinary justice. As Arlette Lebigre, a learned and precise historian of royal justice in general and the Grands Jours of Auvergne in particular, has noted,[35] the Clermont Jours, which were held three decades after the Grands Jours of Poitiers (1634), signaled that the monarchy was taking the kingdom firmly in hand four years after the start of the personal reign of Louis XIV and a few months after the fall of Fouquet (December 1664).

One of the chief aims of this extraordinary commission was the repression of feudal abuses. It was charged with enhancing the image of a paternal sovereign, a distant but potent protector of his humblest subjects. The magistrates of the Jours stated that they had no intention of competing with or superseding the ordinary local jurisdictions; they would only initiate first hearings in cases of abuses aimed at the weak: "among feeble and poor persons against the powerful, as with peasants against gentlemen and officiers of justice."[36] One denunciation addressed to Chancellor Séguier explains why this type of offense was so difficult to grasp: It ends, "and of all [matters] it is impossible to bring to suit about, for these are verbal complaints that the peasants, for fear of worse, would not dare make in writing."[37] In 1663 a royal official, the intendant of the *généralité* of Riom, informed Colbert that certain lords in the Auvergne who had the right to demand five *corvées* per year of their subjects "force them to do more than a hundred and are using them as slaves."[38]

After vague but repeated allusions, beginning in the mid-sixteenth century, to the enforcement of the *droit de cuissage* by the lords of Auvergne (in Boyer, Papon, and others), one might expect the painstaking and determined examination conducted by the commission of the Jours to tell in detail about such turpitudes. There is in fact mention of *cuissage,* but only indirectly, through a text that made the literary fortune of that judiciary operation, the *Mémoires de Fléchier sur les Grands Jours d'Auvergne en 1665.*[39] Esprit Fléchier (1632–1710), who later became a preacher whose fame rivaled Bossuet's, was elected to the Académie Française and eventually became bishop first of Lavaur and then of Nîmes. At the time he was tutor to the son of Monsieur de Caumartin, *maître des requêtes* and keeper of the royal seal in the commission of the Grands Jours and the only member of that group not connected with the Parlement de Paris. Even more than Denis Talon, the *avocat général,* Caumartin was a king's man. The king insisted, over the objections of the Parlement, that Caumartin serve as interim president of the Jours should the president, Novion, be taken sick.[40]

Fléchier, who attended many of the sessions and heard daily discussions of the cases presented, kept an extremely precise and admirably written journal of the Jours. He gives us a unique opportunity to compare a cultural representation with the real situation it portrayed, as reported in the judiciary sources preserved in the parlementary archives. Admittedly, that reality was filtered through both the complaints and their translation into juridical terms, making Fléchier's account only an imperfect reflection of true seigniorial relations. Still, it makes the process of reference possible.

Fléchier writes, "M. le comte de Montvallat is a man who holds a quite honorable rank in the province, at once for his quality, for the goods that he possesses, and for his very reputation of not being overly tyrannical in his lands."[41] The count does not in fact have the criminal stature of some extraordinary brigand lords who appear in the registers of the Jours, such as the aged marquis de Canillac and Gaspard d'Espinchal, who terrorized their subjects with direct and finely organized violence.

Following the logic of the portrait or the "character," as we can see from the opening sentence of his sketch, Fléchier explains the misfortunes of the count of Monvallat by his situation, in this case, an unhappy conjugal life:

> All that seems reproachable in public is the disorder of his domesticity, which comes more from his wife's ill humor than from his own unruly conduct. According to the most prevalent rumor, far from having committed the murders or done the violent acts alleged to have broken out in the land, he passed for [a man] so gentle and so tranquil that for a certainty his peasants had often threatened him and his wife often beat him, and he had been just as good a lord as a husband. Since the court of the Grands Jours is established to punish the acts of oppression gentlemen commit and not those they suffer within their houses, it was believed that this man was safe and his only crime was having altogether too much innocence.

Here Fléchier adopts just the tone of persiflage defined earlier in this chapter as one of the major modes for the narration of *cuissage*. The narrator sets himself at a distance from what he describes by using such terms as "reputation," "rumor," and "public." His amused irony finds it astonishing that a gentle, tranquil creature should be set in this savage world. The roughness of mores in the Auvergne, at the antipodes from the Parisian world the Grands Jours had transported to Clermont for a few months, turns Fléchier's juridical and worldly chronicle into a narration of a voyage to some distant New World people. Everything is topsy-turvy in these strange lands (a familiar convention in ancien régime culture): The peasant beats his lord, the wife mistreats her husband, the victim is brought before the law courts. The least guilty are thrown into prison because the true criminals have fled. In such strange lands justice—even justice exercised in the name of the king—barely conceals personal hatreds: "But he had as a neighbor and an enemy the king's prosecutor in Saint-Flour who stirred up a large number of witnesses in his lands and presented more than thirty counts of indictment against him, for which he was arrested. One major sign that he was not very guilty is that he had not fled and believed himself in safety in his own house." What follows is a little scene of burlesque domestic comedy:

> Madame his wife, who pursued her separation from him even though she had at least ten living children, came to Clermont in great alarm, either out of a feeling that nature inspires on such occasions or out of an external propriety interested in saving appearances. She first had them ask him, according to what I have learned quite coldly, whether he accepted to have her plead for him. He answered her equally coldly that he was sure of his innocence and had no need of her help. This disdain piqued her so strongly that for some time she resolved to join his accusers since he refused her as solicitor, and to furnish information against him since he did not want to be defended by her; and in truth, she who mistreated him while he was free pursued him relentlessly in prison.[42]

For Fléchier the real story lay in this conjugal intrigue. He lists the conjectures of the "public": "I have no idea what was the reason for their domestic discord: Some have attributed it to the ill humor of Madame; others to minor passions of Monsieur for some of the girls of the neighborhood. Still others attribute it to a more considerable cause that a woman assuredly should hold in horror, and if they speak the truth she may justly be pardoned her aversion." The inversion of roles (and genders, Fléchier suggests) characterizing this provincial gentleman appears only on the surface of a social role Montvallat struggled to attain; in his Auvergnat heart he was as savage as his province:

> Although this gentleman was of a most peaceful humor and was incapable of doing great violence, he nonetheless did small ones, and was a tyrant . . . without causing a stir. Because in his lands he had rights of justice over his subjects, he found ways to make use of it for his own injustices and to profit from their crimes. If someone should happen to be accused of a killing, he would promise him surety in justice on the condition that he sign an obligation for a certain sum; if another had attempted the honesty of one of his female subjects, he would offer to burn

the evidence in exchange for an obligation, and in this manner he sold impunity to all the guilty. Nothing was more useless to him than an honest man in his lands. He sent criminals to the notary rather than to the judge, and he knew no written law but contracts for obligations.[43]

Fléchier pinpoints the complicity underlying successful systems of corruption: "This skill in having everything bought by money was very useful for him and very convenient for the others, and it was entirely safe since he tyrannized them to prevent them from seeking recourse in justice. Moreover, because the sentences he imposed on them were pardons, they could not sue without betraying themselves and losing their own cause."

It is at this point that Fléchier introduces the episode of *cuissage:*

He was also accused of another sort of extortion that was no less amusing. There is a right fairly common in Auvergne called the *droit des noces*. In past times it was not called so nicely [honnêtement] but language is becoming purified even in the most barbarous places. This right originally gave power to the lord to attend all marriages among his subjects, to be in the bed of the bride, and to conduct the ceremonies performed by those who marry queens by procuration in the stead of the kings. That usage is no longer practiced today, either because it would be inappropriate for lords to be at all the weddings in their village and hoist their legs into the beds of so many good people who are getting married or because this custom was somewhat contrary to proper behavior [honnêteté] and exposed the gentlemen who possessed authority and did not always practice moderation to dangerous temptations when they found attractive subjects. This shameful ceremony has been changed into a pecuniary acknowledgment; by mutual accord the lords have demanded more solid rights and the subjects have been happy to give redemption for a law so dangerous to their honor. Monsieur de Monvallat believed that the old customs were the best when some beautiful village girl was about to marry, and he refused to give up his rights. As he was held redoubtable in this matter and people feared he might pursue his aims without ceremony, they found it appropriate to capitulate and make him as considerable a gift as they could. Whatever the case may be, he insisted on this tribute and it often cost half the bride's dowry.[44]

Thanks to Arlette Lebigre's analysis of the minutes of the inquiry (now housed in the French national archives),[45] we know a good deal about Monvallat's dossier. The minuscule seigniory of Montvallat was in a poor region where the Haute Auvergne, the Gévaudan, and the Rouergue meet. The seigniory brought little income to a lord burdened with ten children and perpetually short of cash. The dossier of the inquiry shows no trace of *cuissage* or any sale of judiciary impunity; the seigniory was so small that no large number of serious crimes punishable by law could have been committed there. Fléchier's imagination led him to construct an image of a tyrannical, sovereign microstate, whereas in reality Montvallat's exactions more resembled the brigandage of a proprietor admittedly abusing his powers of justice but not to the point of creating a complex system of corruption.

The real situation seems simpler: The hearings conducted from 13 October to 19 November 1665 bear on twenty-four articles, and the commission heard sixty witnesses. Most complaints concerned abusive *corvées* and the levying of unwarranted *cens*. Montvallat kept no *terrier* listing his transactions, and he set all exactions, both in labor or in money, at will. When Nau, one of the *conseilliers,* asked him if he was aware that in Auvergne custom seigniorial rights not recognized within the last thirty years were null and void, he responded that he was not. Without trying to cover up the facts, he stated that he asked for a *corvée* whenever he needed labor. When a *corvée* or a *cens* was refused him, he went with a servant to confiscate the furnishings and, above all, the livestock of the peasant. On other occasions he thrashed recalcitrants or threw them in prison. When the intimidated peasant agreed to the tax but did not have enough money to pay it, the lord lent him money at usurious rates. Monvallat used his powers of justice to impose fines for the most frivolous reasons: 460 livres for "being present at a quarrel"; 120 livres for "having separated people who were fighting"; 30–200 livres for "having gotten a girl pregnant"; 20 livres for "having refused to marry a girl"; 12 livres (even though the man had the authorization of the parish priest) for "having harvested on a feast day."

The court records present a picture far from the piquant image Fléchier offers, but far from the formalities of feudal domination as well. The exactions Montvallat imposed reflect the pure violence of a landowner making use of direct force (his weapons, the help of one or more strong-arm men). His possession of *basse justice* gave him a pretext for supplementary exactions; more important, it deprived his peasants of immediate and effective recourse to the law courts. A year before the Grands Jours opened, Pierre Albaret, a "poor inhabitant of the parish of Lespinasse," had in fact deposited a formal complaint against Montvallat with the intendant of the *généralité* of Riom, who had in turn ordered the *lieutenant général* of Saint-Flour to conduct an inquiry, but the matter had dragged on and Montvallat had not been pursued.[46]

Councilor Nau, who conducted the inquiry, was particularly severe with Montvallat. The requisitory of the *avocat général,* Denis Talon, demanded perpetual banishment and the confiscation of all his goods. The court was more lenient, however, and in a decision handed down 27 November 1665 it sentenced Montvallat to pay a fine of 8,000 livres to be used to give alms and make restitution of sums unjustly collected; his seigniorial rights were reduced and his rights of justice permanently abolished. The court thought the Montvallat case sufficiently exemplary to warrant publication, joining to it a general ruling on seigniories forbidding arbitrary fines and seizures of movable goods or livestock without a court decision. Moreover, a ruling dated 10 December imposed such stringent conditions for the exercise of seigniorial justice (offering proof of professional capacity, keeping minutes, and providing a prison that met certain standards) that it became materially impossible in a small seigniory. Thus a minor affair had considerable consequences in the French monarchy's long effort to recover judiciary sovereignty.

This still does not explain Fléchier's version of *cuissage*. It seems to be pure social fantasy, since nothing in the official dossier even comes close to it. It is unlikely that the minutes of the inquiry were censored or that the witnesses were timid, since in both the parlementary archives and in Fléchier's journal the accusation that brigand lords committed rape appears on several occasions and is reported in the crudest terms. We do find among Montvallat's arbitrary fines and taxes an exaction of 1 sol for every marriage celebrated in one of the parishes in his domains. This sum—equivalent to 1/240 of the fine Montvallat levied for harvesting on a feast day—is the lowest of his exactions and must be purely symbolic. It places the lord, for once, within the norm concerning feudal usages. Fléchier was not a court clerk, and on several occasions he confuses one dossier with another, but in this instance he seems to have taken a case, proclaimed as exemplary by the publication of the decision and the sentence, and used it as the basis for his own ideal type of the Auvergnat lord, making him figure as the height of tyranny in both judiciary corruption and sexual persecution.

This distortion on the part of an eyewitness would not be of any great interest if did not reflect a more global perception. Our dashing abbé, a guest in parlementary and noble salons, belonged to the household of an *homme du roi;* he speaks in the name of a court culture when he displays an ironic and condescending curiosity and depicts the strange mores of an archaic caste. The *cuissage* episode seems to him more amusing *(plaisant)* than worrisome or scandalous. The *droit de noces* formerly called by a less "honest" name (undoubtedly *cullage*) does not have a libidinous origin for Fléchier; in this sense it is comparable to the seigniorial rite at Somloire, also called *droit de noces*. It was one among many ridiculous and primitive practices in the most "backwoods" provinces. We are in the world of the burlesque or the mock-heroic, where country squire and peasant girls are put on the level of "ceremonies performed by those who marry queens by procuration in the stead of the kings." Sexual abuse arises only when "dangerous temptations" overcome gentlemen as unruly as the lord of Montvallat.

This combination of ancient agrarian comedy and brutal savagery persists throughout Fléchier's journal. One of the cases investigated by the Grands Jours concerned an accusation of sorcery brought by a young couple incapable of consummating their marriage. Fléchier reports the start of this union as if it were a chapter out of Honoré d'Urfé's *Astrée:* "In a parish near Clermont a young shepherd had fallen in love with a shepherdess, the prettiest and the most upright [honnête] in her village." Just as the Grands Jours were about to be dissolved, the court attended a charivari, but the gentlemen found its ritualized violence and its exactions incomprehensible. Only when an elderly gentleman delivered a learned archaeological explanation did the court withdraw its disapproval.[47]

Sixty-five years after the lady of Somloire's appeal we can read Fléchier's evocation as symptomatic of a new social persiflage where an ironic condescension before customs that are ridiculous but potentially dangerous for mores replaces the ethical and militant tones of Servin's day. In both cases, however, a group and a mode of life were denigrated by a use of comparisons and shifts of meaning based in a sociocultural complicity referred to a "natural" norm.

The judiciary dossier of the Grands Jours and Fléchier's narrative do not coincide because they fulfilled different tasks. The king's men, assisted somewhat reluctantly by the magistrates of the Parlement de Paris, were interested in reducing seigniorial privileges; court literature used irony to stifle the last vestiges of local culture.

Beginning in the late seventeenth century juridical culture underwent a clear decline. From then on allusions to the *droit de cuissage* in jurists' writings no longer add anything new. As if in compensation, indignation at seigniorial abuses spread everywhere, blossoming in the literature of the Enlightenment. Our road comes full circle early in the eighteenth century, when the theme of the *droit de cuissage*, by then firmly established, gave rise to the dramatic tradition discussed in chapter 1 and to a reiterated political indignation that continues to our own day even though the judicial dossier is empty.

T hus the *droit de cuissage* never existed in medieval France. Not one of the arguments, none of the events insinuated, alleged, or brandished, holds up under analysis: Every time we inquire into the precise context of a case that did not arise out of a forgery or a misinterpretation, we find a pure effect of discourse motivated by tactical insinuation, strategic denunciation, or boastful intimidation, with no sign that these unilateral statements had ever been challenged or prompted the least interaction in law or in fact. The discourse of denunciations or claims never addressed reality.

The reader who has followed us this far might well ask whether this negative result really required such a lengthy demonstration. It has been clear from the start that no matter what social restrictions were put on conduct and the management of wealth, and no matter how violent mores became, the *principle* of free choice of an unfettered matrimonial life was the most sacred area of individual liberty in medieval Europe. The Church, European society's principal normative center, very early removed all restrictions on the marriage of dependents, and it imposed consent as a sacramental value. No juridical form, no custom could attack that principle, constantly recalled in pastoral literature and sanctified in the twelfth century by the establishment of the sacrament of matrimony. No right contrary to that principle could be advanced. A right not expressed did not exist, however: Only the patient efforts of royal jurists, beginning in the sixteenth century, could suggest that a pseudo-law called "custom" existed beneath the law and that if custom were not controlled by the state, it would perpetuate the worst horrors. In reality custom constituted an authentic "law" in the sense of a system of norms subjected to institutional control. Even seigniorial "rights," which strictly speaking had no juridical status, had to be reviewed, verified, and registered, as we have seen. The four or five cases of bizarre *dénombrements* (out of a mass of several tens of thousands of documents) whose contexts we have tried to restore have no more meaning or juridical value than obscenities scribbled by hand in a *Code Dalloz*.

In my opinion the demonstration was of use because the belief persists. In March 1994, just as I was putting the finishing touches on this book, I encountered a work by Marie-Victoire Louis titled *Le droit de cuissage: France, 1860–1930.*[1] The subject of this book is clearly the sexual abuse of women workers by their employers in French industry and crafts manufacturing. Why not use the term *harcèlement sexuel,* now a part of the French penal code? Was this a deliberate return to an expression current in trade union circles at the end of the nineteenth century? Perhaps, but at that time the quarrel on *cuissage* described above was still fresh in memory. The book's title has the serious drawback of reinforcing a false belief.

There is worse, however: The author herself believes in it. It is enough to make one's head spin. At least Jules Delpit, writing in 1857, gave the impression of only partly believing in a fiction he held necessary to combat the alliance of throne and altar. Marie-Victoire Louis devotes three singular pages to summarizing the old fable, beginning with Alexandre Bouthors (whom she rebaptizes André). Léon de Labessade (who becomes de la Bessade) is presented as the summit of erudition and the author of "the most complete bibliography to this day. Still unexploited, it contains over one hundred references in several languages." As we have seen, Labessade, a polygraph journalist, simply and rather clumsily copied from Delpit. And how could anyone overlook Karl Schmidt, who had at least read and carefully examined the texts in Delpit's dossier? The Amiens affair in 1409 comes next (via Eusèbe de Laurière, copied in Labessade), to present the bishop of Amiens as the chief deflowerer of the diocese.

Louis's work enjoys the seal of approval of a foreword by Michelle Perrot, an eminent specialist in the worker movement who unfortunately confirms that "the lord has the right to the maidenhood of female servants."[2] Perrot bases this assertion on an unfortunate phrase that escaped Georges Duby's usually sharp eye: "The same class division that existed among men carried over to women. Thus 'ladies' [dames] and 'maidens' [pucelles] were sharply distinguished from peasant women [vilaines], whom the men of the court could treat as brutally as they pleased [que le 'courtois' était autorisé à traquer à sa guise pour en faire brutalement sa volonté]."[3] The ambiguity here resides in the skillful ordering of words to suggest the *droit de cuissage* ("était autorisé," "à sa guise") without actually mentioning it. The phrase—especially the word *traquer* (pursue, hunt down)—also suggests rape. I have read all Georges Duby's works, and I know that illustrious medievalist does not believe in the reality of the *droit de cuissage* (at least no book of his implies that he does). I may even have found the matrix for the statement in an article Duby wrote in 1964: "That was what aristocratic youth was like in the twelfth century: a pack of hounds that noble houses loosed to relieve the surplus of their expanding power, out to conquer glory, profit, and feminine prey."[4] Except that in this article the *proies féminines* Duby speaks of were not women of the masses but rather wives to be obtained by younger sons when noble houses concentrated their efforts on matrimonial alliances for their elder sons or their offspring destined to inherit. Duby's recent statement, quoted above, comes from a collective popularizing work in five volumes, *A History of Women in the West*. Medieval *cuissage* enters into the public's expectations; the editors and authors resisted the temptation to include a chapter on the topic, but at the price of one or two unfortunate phrases.

But let us be clear: I am not trying to deny that groups of young knights ever practiced rape. It is evident that rough mores, here as elsewhere, made rape fairly current. Jacques Rossiaud discusses the frequency of rape in medieval cities (which lay outside the feudal sphere) in a fine study of medieval prostitution.[5] Just as clearly, male-dominated societies were indulgent about rape: Even in modern France rape was only a *délit* (misdemeanor) tried before a judge until ten or twelve years ago. But it is going too far to move from a "male chauvinist" attitude that has nothing either medieval or feudal about it to the idea of a norm, let alone a juridical norm.

I might add that belief in the possible existence of the *droit de cuissage* supposes what I take to be a major failing in a historian: a scorn for the human beings he or she is observing. The notion of a *right* to *cuissage* seems to imply consent on the victim's part. To imagine that such consent might have been obtained in defiance of the victim's most dearly held values amounts to depicting the people of the Middle Ages as simpleminded, mired in their alienation. I am not moralizing, nor am I saying that monogamous association derives from a natural universal law that furnishes the ramparts of an unshakable faith. Anthropologists have demonstrated that there is great variety in human institutions of sexuality and cohabitation. But when we know that matrimonial autonomy constitutes an explicit and assumed value in a culture, it is important to recognize that history's agents are capable of evaluating the implications. The myth of the alienation of the oppressed lower classes had its hour of success in the

1950s; in our own day it has been succeeded by a brand of cultural relativism that ends up as a radical objectivation of human beings, remote in both space and time. The strange fortune of the *droit de cuissage* is in part due to that dubious "passion for being another,"[6] a pleasure by procuration that sometimes satisfies history and anthropology.

Conversely, historians who rejected the fable of *cuissage*, explicitly or implicitly, attempted to expunge the Middle Ages from it as if it were simply a prerevolutionary argument unconnected to authentic medieval history. As we have seen, however, the discursive reality of *cuissage* is old, going back at least to the year 1247. A few mentions, rare but sure, can be noted in the fourteenth and fifteenth centuries. This means that the historian cannot be content with testing the institutional reality of the *droit de cuissage* and stating that it never existed. The legends referring to the institution are themselves historical objects, for they engendered discourses and practices; they contributed to weaving social and political ties by eliciting or justifying quarrels and allegiances, and by polarizing the field of the memory. That structuring role of "beliefs" (in the broader sense) was what I attempted to show in a book about Pope Joan.[7] Here as there, I have tried to account for the historical functions of the active survival of legends beyond their formative moment and beyond the historical event of their creation.

It might seem useless to claim legitimacy for a history of schemas of historical representation, much developed in recent years. It is important, however, to recall the imperative need to privilege interaction between social history and the history of discourses. Realms of belief constantly rub up against worlds of events and practices. One entire trend in historiography today denies the possibility of attaining the reality of the past, reducing the historian's field to effects of language in a sort of systematic ecologism according to which all historical sources in the human world are polluted. Historiographical waters are often troubled, but the filter of criticism remains effective. The deconstruction of historical documents and concepts—which has had a long and fertile history in this century— has recently taken a relativist turn, leading to a greater and greater separation between empirical description of phenomena and contexts, on the one hand, and, on the other, an interpretation of the past taken as superimposed narrative strata with no bedrock. I have no intention of rehashing the challenge to the innocence of historical discourse; I am only trying to find the narrow way that leads to a global history accounting both for events and for their alienation in the documents that note them down. Two important books seem to me to point the way to this narrow path:

Arsenio Frugoni's *Arnaldo da Brescia* and Peter Linehan's *History and the Historians of Medieval Spain*.[8] These two works, written forty years apart, offer a painstaking problematization of the complex intermingling of events, their immediate narrations, and their later historical interpretation.

Once we admit the need to take the medieval reality of the legend of *cuissage* into account, we still have to comprehend why the legend had the frail and discontinuous existence that makes all explanation of belief in it or its use in discourse so difficult. How did denunciation of *cuissage* or its presentation as a threat come to be transmitted without any discernible tradition, seeming to materialize in documents with no readers? What was its status? How can we find any coherence in utterances produced in such different times and milieus?

I am tempted to use the handy notion of representation, in the sense of a configuration that constructs reality according to the interests of one or more groups.[9] It would not be hard to show how the *droit de cuissage* entered into several successful systems of representation: As we have seen, from 1864 to 1884 acceptance of the myth of *cuissage* or rejection of it as a fable was related to political attitudes, but also to strategies of social promotion in the field of learning. Similarly, between 1580 and 1640 we find a sociocultural motivation in denunciation of the *droit de cuissage* in the milieu of jurists close to the king's men. The Somloire affair shows that denunciation was an integral part of a relatively complex system of description of the social world. Even the enigmatic and isolated "Chanson des vilains de Verson" of 1247 suggests, by its virtual presentation of a wealthy peasant prospering under monastic protection, that it might be possible, if more sources were available, to reconstruct a fully articulated system of monastic representations.

It is still difficult, however, to connect these elements of systems of representation with one another, at least before the late sixteenth century. Beginning in the 1580s the substance of the successive social forms that are representations was transmitted with more continuity. Before that time the rare and scattered mentions of *cuissage* do not give an impression of cumulative knowledge available for reuse. I have offered a first response to this problem in chapter 1 by suggesting that the fear or threat of sexual abuse from dominant persons is a constant, simultaneously real and symbolic, in all cultures. After all, social tyranny can be exerted only over goods and persons. In the category of attacks on persons, the possibilities are limited, and they were all exhausted: imprisonment, mutilation and blows, assassination, kidnap or rape of the spouse, infanticide. The theme of the massacre of the innocents for the survival of the tyrant, reiterated from Herod to Ceaucescu by way of Louis XV, bears witness to that universality.[10]

The fact remains, however, that the more general form of rape or kidnap of the wife took the particular form of *cuissage* in medieval France. Mentions of "feudal" *cuissage* seldom crystallized outside of France, perhaps because there were stronger tensions between the central and peripheral powers in medieval France than in other regions of Europe. France has to be compared with the contrary cases of England, with its much earlier strong monarchy and free peasantry, and Germany, where the central powers were a good deal weaker. This means that even when local domination seems similar in these lands, social tyranny lacked the political and cultural channels available in France.

Finally, rare representations are incomprehensible only if they are viewed in relation to an exclusive model for the codification and communication of utterances (by imitation, selection, and appropriation). If we appeal to another logic for the production of discourses—induction—we might posit that on the basis of a specific historical situation, history's agents are capable of forming a variety of utterances, on different cultural levels, that they judge pertinent to that situation.[11] As we have seen, during the central Middle Ages the religious and social structures of Europe gave a new relevance to the individual. *Cuissage*, secular and ecclesiastical, was denounced in the name of a possessive and ethical individualism that developed just as much in the struggle for land as in religious devotion. Particular occurrences of this scheme cut across all the various layers of medieval societies.

I have tried to show elsewhere that an implicit collective utterance circulated in late medieval Europe: "I have a body that constitutes me as a singular subject, and I dispose of it as of a good alienable only to God." I based my chronology on the terrible Black Death of the mid-fourteenth century, an event that made human beings rare and precious.[12] I now think my chronology and my causality fell a bit short: Considerable importance should be attached to the emergence of the notion of the person in the twelfth and thirteenth centuries. Even beyond technical use of the notion of the moral or fictive person invented by canon law in the 1250s, the extraordinary development of trinitarian theology in the twelfth century gave meaning to Boethius's mysterious definition (which covered both the divine and the human person): "The person is the individuated substance of rational nature." Theological reflection gave its form to various tendencies that consolidated the individual's claims to ethical and juridical autonomy.[13] This by no means implies that a theory of the preeminent person was available in the thirteenth century. In a strongly stratified society the notion of the person could only be constructed differentially: The person was presented as a subject with rights, as opposed to subjects without rights or nonsubjects with rights. The immense question of noble, bourgeois, and ecclesiastical privileges had been raised. Extremely diverse social structures of dependency further complicated this race toward individual preeminence. This explains why the fable of *cuissage*, which provided a setting for themes of the body as one's own, of possession, and of social tyranny, had a certain relevance. The question of *cuissage* is only one chapter in a long, still incomplete history.

A Literary Setting of Seigniorial Sexual Abuse

From Béroalde de Verville, *Le moyen de parvenir* (The Way to Get Ahead, c. 1610).[1]

CEREMONY

The miller closest to his castle, having been the first to pick some very fine early cherries, sent them to him on that day. [At the castle] there were with Monsieur several gentlemen of the neighborhood (they were gentlemen of low lineage, you might say like the canons of Saint Mamboeuf in Angers as compared to those of Saint-Maurice; or those of Saint-Venant in comparison with those of Saint Martin de Tours[2]—I've been there and seen them!) He told his daughter to take them to Monsieur.

The girl, who was the age of a mature ox [i.e., fourteen or fifteen years old], desirable and fresh, came into the hall to make a curtsey to Monsieur, who was dining, and presented him with this fruit from her father. "Aha!" said La Roche, "here is something fine! . . . You there!" he said to his servants, "bring the four best sheets in the house and spread them out here." Note in passing that he was to be obeyed in everything he said, all the more so because he was the prefiguration of the Antichrist: the preachers said of him last Lent that he aimed his cannons on his tower just like a heretic, and he was such a good cannoneer, like Lord Santal, that he merrily shot the horse from under his friend who had just dined with him and got him while turning the corner; and to show off his skill, when the plowman turned his plow he shot right at the plow handle without hurting the plowman—and all that for laughs!

When the sheets were spread out, he ordered the beautiful young girl to disrobe. Poor Marciole began to weep. "Aha!" he exclaimed, "What a good girl you are! You would do better not to cry: a girl with a crying mouth has a laughing cunt. Hurry up and quit it, or I will summon all the devils. Hey, don't make me angry; do what I tell you." The poor girl takes off her dress and her stockings, undoes her hair, then, O! such modesty! she removed her chemise, and as naked as a fairy emerging from the water, she starts to scatter the cherries left and right, up and down on the sheets as Monsieur commanded her.

Her fine hair, scattered like dear little laces of love, floated over this fine masterpiece of Nature, polished, solid, and pleasingly fleshed, showing in her divers gestures a million admirable pretty little things; her two breasts, lovely round pleasure packets joined to the ivory of her chest, made their moundlike appearances, infinitely varied when seen from different angles. Lascivious eyes slid toward her fine round thighs, embellished by all that beauty communicates to those ramparts and comforts of the stamp of love; they ravished with greedy looks all the most perfect ideas that they could see. And no matter how many beauties were prettily displayed in this sweet spectacle, there was, however, only one little place that was most curiously sought with their eyes, so much did their gaze focus on the target every one of them wanted to hit, all of them totally absorbed by the precious corner that holds the register of amorous mysteries.

After the cherries were sown they had to be picked up again. Then it was that marvelous tricks appeared to try to hide above all the precious labyrinth of concupiscence; the poor little center of delight had a hard time finding gestures to make it disappear. That ultimate beauty, that fine stuff for engendering, that finely finished body was seen from so many and such delicious angles that it would be difficult to find eyes more satisfied that those of the spectators.

Looking at her one of them said, "There is nothing more beautiful in the world; I wouldn't want to have missed the contentment I have received for 100 écus." Another, recounting his fantasy occupied by delectation, set the price of his good fortune in this spectacle at more than 200 écus. A servant, just as flustered as the others, put his share of pleasure at 10 écus. And there were none among the masters who did not speak of 100 or 150 écus, some more, some less, according to how their tongues followed their eyes, in spirit licking the marble of this spectacle where speech hobbled behind a mind attaching its imagination to that beauty with a hundred thousand specious images. Each spectator tried to go the last speaker one better, raising the price of the delights that he imagined.

When all the cherries were back in the basket, the girl returned toward the windows to put her chemise back on. The men still stretched their gaze to peek into all its folds, hoping to have something more to see; thus they spied, little by little as she raised one leg, then the other, until she was back the way she started, completely coiffed and dressed. Her beautiful eyes—little cherubs—were humid from the waves of fire they had attracted and for the shame of showing their liquid in this adventure.

All this time Monsieur de La Roche had eyes in his head and his gaze fixed on the fine object, laughing heartily, but he nonetheless wanted to hear what those birds were chirping when, heedless of what they were saying, they were licking their chops. He observed them well and carefully remembered everything, especially the tax each had declared while recounting his pleasure. He even noticed a lackey who spoke of 1 écu ("Let yourself drop, there you are: all you have to do is bend down and take it!").

Marciole, fully dressed, was commanded by my said lord to sit at the end of the table, where he comforted her and encouraged her as best he could, giving her all that was most delicate. She was upset and weepy, ashamed at having shown all God had given her to show, and she regretted that so many people had seen her at once outside of church.

When La Roche saw this, he scolded the company and, rolling his eyes like the lions in the clock in Saint-Jean in Lyons, he started to swear his great evangelical oath (for the moment he was a Huguenot) and said: "By the certainty of God" (for that was how thieves of that religion swear), "Messieurs, do you think I wanted to play the buffoon for you? That I am your joker, your lackey, your purveyor of living flesh? By the double-worthy-great-triple horn of the most arrant cuckold here among you, you will each pay what you have said, or there will be no leg, head, member, guts, body, hair, or calf muscle left intact. Whore's belly! You will count it all out quickly unless you prefer to have your eyes blackened and your pricks [vits] cut off!" (If they had all been cut off, it would have been of service to the abbess of Montfleury, whose farm manager came to tell her, this last grape harvest, that the screw [vis] of her grape press was broken. On which, after long thought, she said, "On my faith as a woman, if I live [si je vis] I will made good provision of vis.")

The words of this Monsieur frightened the country squires, who paid what they had said, sent for it, or borrowed it from my said lord on good gages or good IOUs. Thus that terrified nobility spat into the basket some twelve hundred pretty little écus, bet and taken. ("I would much rather make my provisions in Paris: I could have a chemise full of flesh for 5 sous and a basketful of cherries for 4.") When the écus were all gathered into the basket, La Roche gave them to Marciole, who was biting her tongue with excitement and pleasure to know they were for her. And Monsieur said to her: "Take this, my dear, carry it to your father and tell him that you have earned them by showing your ass. There are many who have shown it and show it still who do not earn as much, and if they do, they run after even greater fortunes."

The *Droit de Cuissage* in Spain:
A Response to Carlos Barros

My investigation has for the most part been limited to the French domain. I have touched on merchet in England, on Piedmontese *cazzagio*, and on events in Flanders and Zeeland only to the extent that they played an important role in debate in France. These limits are inherent in the events and the method I have chosen: First, the myth of *cuissage* developed more completely in France than anywhere else; and second, the choice of a multicontextual analysis embracing events, their representation, and their later treatment in historiography does not permit serious treatment of too great a variety of regions. Nonetheless, what I propose here is a brief and perhaps imprudent excursion into the Iberian Peninsula, partly because Catalonia in the fifteenth century offers the only European instance of a troubling juridical text, partly because the Galician historian Carlos Barros has written an article on *cuissage* in Spain, the first explicit and resolute defense of the existence of the *droit de cuissage* by a competent medievalist for a very long time—since Delpit, if we neglect allusions with little genuine argument behind them by Robert Boutruche and others.[1]

Carlos Barros states that a radical distinction needs to be made between the sexual abuses of medieval lords and common manifestations of rape. The *derecho de pernada* was a "gesture of vassality" and an "admitted tradition" in feudal law. This means that the absence of documentary sources is not surprising, because this right belonged to a juridical realm of exclusively oral expression, whether it was taken as a usage under customary law or as one of a number of abuses contributing to a right to revolt. In an extremely interesting book Carlos Barros demonstrated the existence in fifteenth-century Galicia of a veritable though self-proclaimed right to revolt expressed within jurists' confraternities opposed to seigniory.[2]

Even this excellent scholar, however, for all his familiarity with Galician archives, has managed to find very few manifestations of this *droit de cuissage* opposed by a right to revolt. Only two or three affairs mention sexual abuses, and they appear to be simple individual offenses. Barros is thus forced to suppose that the "private nature of the practice of *cuissage* signals its degree of deterioration as customary law." But by that reasoning cannot any invisible phenomenon be constructed by showing that the logic of its production implies its appearance only in a degraded or fossilized state?

Barros finds little evidence for this right before the fifteenth century except for a few words in a *Fuero real* of Alfonso X forbidding "anyone from dishonoring the new groom or bride on the day of the wedding [alguu ome desonrrar nuoho casando ou nouha en dia de voda]." One really has to torture this phrase to make it refer to the *droit de cuissage:* No power relation is specified; the possible threat to honor concerns the man or the woman, not the bride alone, not the couple. This text needs to be viewed as one of a group of measures in *Las siete partidas* favoring marriage and procreation in a variety of ways, according to a royal policy of encouraging population growth. Peter Linehan has called attention to a measure authorizing priests to marry, in clear contradiction to formal and urgent church legislation.[3]

The Galician dossiers reduce the traces of a degraded state of the *droit de cuissage* to practically nothing. In 1385 the peasants of Aranga protested against seigniorial pressures from the monastery of Sobrado. Among their many grievances the report of the royal official mentions a complaint that the women have to do service twice yearly at a barn in Carballotorto, a *corvée* that does not seem to the peasants to be proper. The peasants' representative specifies that the service lasts two or three days and it is not generally known exactly what it consists of. Because the complaint is vague, it is taken to designate a practice of ritualized sexual abuse. One might object that the abuse in question has no connection with the wedding day; furthermore, it seems more likely that the nature of the work to be done suggested a gender-based division of labor. In the late fourteenth century an archaic, collective, and gender-based division of labor might easily have led to a protest that took the same ethical and accusative turn we have seen in French lands, especially those under ecclesiastical seigniory.

Another revolt in Galicia, in 1467, was prompted by abuses, one of which Barros presents as another degraded form of *cuissage*. The alcade of the castle of Allariz was accused of protecting friends and kin whom he permitted to kill male dependents and carry off married women. Here too we have acute forms—alleged or real—of seigniorial tyranny with no trace of any ritual or juridical aspect.

The last case that Barros cites concerns accusations against Rodrigo de Luna, archbishop of Santiago de Compostela, who was expelled from his ecclesiastical seigniory in 1458 and died in mysterious circumstances in 1460. In 1458 the archbishop received a royal command to gather an army for the war with Granada. The archdiocesan feudatories, in alliance with the neighboring towns and backed by a majority of the cathedral chapter, refused to obey the royal command and deposed the prelate, then attempted to impose their own candidate for the archiepiscopal throne of St. James. As part of a propaganda campaign directed at Henry IV of Castile and the pontifical court, they spread rumors about Rodrigo's bad conduct. In the abundant production of chroniclers and pamphleteers we find a statement by Diego de Valera that among the archbishop's many misdeeds he had ordered a bride kidnapped from the nuptial chamber and sequestered for an entire night. This is only one misdeed, however, and it lacks any hint of ritual or of an institutional exaction. What is more, Diego de Valera is alone among contemporary writers in citing this crime among the many accusations leveled at Rodrigo de Luna. Finally, the presentation of the height of infamy (here, a prelate's profanation of the sacrament of matrimony) was a familiar tactic in the Middle Ages for attacking a powerful ecclesiastic. We need only think of the floods of insults loosed first on the person and then on the memory of Gregory VII during the investiture controversy.

The dossier of *cuissage* on the Iberian Peninsula would be empty if late fifteenth-century Catalonia had not produced a famous and troubling text, the *Sentencia arbitral* rendered by King Ferdinand the Catholic in 1486 in Guadalupe. The decree was aimed at putting an end to a long series of antiseigniorial revolts; it permitted the suppression of or the substitution of compensation for "bad usages [malos usos]" that were crushing the *remenses* (Catalan peasants whose low status brought them close to harsh servitude).[4] Article 9 of this decree stated:

> We say by sentence, decree, and declaration that the said lords . . . cannot, on the night when the peasants have taken a wife, sleep with the spouse, nor can they, as a sign of seigniorial domination, on the night of the wedding when the bride is put to lie in the bed, pass over her, over the said spouse [ni tampoc pugan la primera nit que los pagès pren muller dormir ab ella, o en senyal de senyoria, la nit de las bodas, apres que la muller sera colgada en lo litt, passar sobre aquell, obre laita muller].[5]

The Catalan text is crystal clear; the royal document is authentic. This is thus the only document in Europe proving the existence of the *droit de cuissage.*

The situation is not really that simple, however.

First, if we analyze the document as a whole, we see that the six institutional (thus subject to satisfaction by a money payment) "bad usages" are grouped in article 1. They are roughly equivalent to tallage *(remença personal), mainmorte (intestia* and *xorquia),* and *formariage (cugucia* and *firma de espoli forzada).* The sixth, *arcia,* concerns fighting fires. Article 9, on the other hand, enumerates abuses deriving from previous abuses, not from earlier seigniorial rights, which are thus not open to being compensated by a money payment. The item immediately preceding this passage on weddings forbids lords to carry off peasants' wives against their will in order to use them, with or without pay, as wet nurses; the item that follows declares illegitimate any prohibition of the peasants' right to sell their agricultural produce. This means that the item in question is not a seigniorial right but, at worst, a repeated offense.

Second, an earlier document suggests that the 1486 decree had only a relative value. In 1462, after violent agitation on the part of the *remenses,* a first compromise text on seigniorial rights was drafted. It contains both the peasants' demands and the lords' commentaries. One of the articles in this text mentions nuptial abuse in terms quite close to those of the 1486 *Sentencia,*[6] but the lords add that they doubt that any lord ever demanded such a practice. The 1462 and 1486 documents are not direct legislation: Aimed at compromise, they combine the two discourses of the peasants and the lords. The fact that *cuissage* appears in either the discourse of demand or that of denunciation does not tell us anything about actual seigniorial practice. France, after all, had a tradition of denunciation going all the way back to the Verson episode. Both occurrences, unconfirmed by any other document, derive strictly from a context of social struggle through discourse.

Third, the disjunction between an actual act ("sleeping" with the bride) and a symbolic gesture (the lord straddling the bed with his body) evokes the alternative presented in *aveux et dénombrements* in fourteenth- and fifteenth-century France: lie with the lord or recognize his lordship with a real or symbolic payment. The disavowal or perplexity of the Catalan lords seems to indicate that the seigniorial gestures and acts having to do with weddings correspond—in Catalonia as in Béarn or Normandy—to an extreme and marginal crystallization of the offensive or defensive figure of the local tyrant. Despite the official nature of the document, the configuration suggested in Ferdinand's *Sentencia* is just like the one that we observed in detail in Béarn.

The *derecho de pernada* (a literal equivalent of the French *droit de jambage* and also a late term) is just as lacking in consistency as the French *cuissage*, even if recent tendencies in Spanish historiography, oriented toward reducing differences between the Iberian Peninsula and the rest of Europe, are intent on proving the feudal nature of medieval society by dressing it in the tattered glories of seigniorial domination.[7]

NOTES

INTRODUCTION

1. This definition appears in editions of the *Petit Robert* beginning in 1967; it was modified after 1977 to read: "the right of the lord to put his leg into the bride's bed on the first night of the wedding and, in some localities, to spend that first night with her" (1990 edition, 434). The lexicographer confuses the issue by reducing the notion to one particular version of it known as *jambage,* alleged by some authors beginning in the sixteenth century. Moreover, use of the phrase "in some localities" lends an appearance of greater reality.

2. See Marc Bloch, *La société féodale* (1939–40), 2 vols. (Paris: Albin Michel, 1970), 11–13; available in English as *Feudal Society,* trans. L. A. Manyon, 2 vols. (Chicago: University of Chicago Press, 1961), vol. 1, xvi–xviii.

3. Antoine Du Verdier, sieur de Vauprivaz, *Les diverses leçons* (1557), 2d ed. (Lyons: B. Honorat, 1580), 96; Jean-Baptiste Lacurne de Sainte-Palaye, *Dictionnaire historique de l'ancien langage françois, ou Glossaire de la langue françoise depuis son origine jusqu'au siècle de Louis XIV,* ed. L. Favre, 10 vols. (Paris: Champion), vol. 4 (1876), 434–35.

4. "Droits abusifs," in *Encyclopédie ou Dictionnaire raisonné des sciences, des arts et des métiers, par une société de gens de lettres. Mis en ordre et publié par M. Diderot de l'Académie royale des sciences et des belles lettres de Prusse, et quant à la partie mathématique par M. D'Alembert de l'Académie* (Paris), vol. 5 (1755), 142: "rights of *cullage, cuillage,* and *cuissage* in virtue of which certain lords claimed to have the first night of new brides." Boucher d'Argis had already written on the topic the previous year (but without using the new expression) in the article "Culage," in volume 4 of the *Encyclopédie* (Paris, 1754), 548, where he speaks of "the infamous custom that gave those lords the first night of brides."

5. Robert Boutruche, *Seigneurie et féodalité* (1959), 2d ed., rev. and enlarged (Paris: Aubier-Montaigne, 1968), vol. 1: *Le premier âge des liens d'homme à homme,* 128n.6. See also below, chapter 1.

6. Jean Gallet, *La seigneurie bretonne 1450–1680: L'exemple du Vannetais* (Paris: Publications de la Sorbonne, 1983), 241. Gallet provides the following gloss on the word *culléage* in his lexicon (p. 50): "The bride's first night, compensated by a gift." Nothing in the document cited (Archives Départementales du Morbihan, E 2704) authorizes this interpretation.

7. Carlos Barros, "Rito y violación: Derecho de pernada en la baja edad media," *Histo-*

ria social 16 (1993): 3–17. My thanks to the author for sending me an offprint of this article, which deals exclusively with Spain. For further discussion, see below, appendix 2.

8. George Orwell, *Nineteen Eighty-Four* (New York: Harcourt, Brace, 1949), 72–75. My thanks to Delphine Collomb for bringing this text to my attention.

CHAPTER 1: REMNANTS AND PERSISTENCES

1. *Le nouvel observateur,* 2–8 March 1989, 14–26.

2. Association Européenne contre les Violences Faites aux Femmes au Travail, *De l'abus de pouvoir sexuel: Le harcèlement sexuel au travail* (Paris: La Découverte, 1990), 5n.1.

3. *L'Espresso,* 10 May 1992, 128–34.

4. Marie-Victoire Louis, *Le droit de cuissage: France, 1860–1930* (Paris: L'Atelier, 1994).

5. Article 222-33, *Code pénal* (1992): "Le fait de harceler autrui en usant d'ordres, de menaces ou de contraintes, dans le but d'obtenir des faveurs de nature sexuelle, par une personne abusant de l'autorité que lui confèrent ses fonctions est puni d'un an d'emprisonnement et de 100 000 francs d'amende."

6. See Pascale Robert-Diard, *Le monde,* 23–24 June 1991, 9.

7. Catharine A. MacKinnon, *Sexual Harassment of Working Women: A Case of Sex Discrimination* (New Haven: Yale University Press, 1979). For bibliography complementing MacKinnon's, see *De l'abus de pouvoir sexuel.*

8. See "Sex Discrimination and Legal Equality," in *Congressional Quarterly's Guide to the U.S. Supreme Court,* ed. Elder Witt (Washington, D.C.: Congressional Quarterly, 1979), 631–39; Liliane Kerjan, *L'égalité aux États-Unis: Mythes et réalités* (Nancy: Presses Universitaires de Nancy, 1991), 93–95.

9. This text was published in a brochure written for Canadian students. For texts defining sexual harassment in the Western world, see the documents and appendices in *De l'abus de pouvoir sexuel.*

10. Margaret Atwood, *The Handmaid's Tale* (1985; Boston: Houghton Mifflin, 1986). My thanks to Colette Collomb-Boureau for bringing this text to my attention.

11. Johann Jakob Bachofen, *Das Mutterrecht* (Stuttgart, 1861), in *Gesammelte Werke,* ed. Karl Meuli, 10 vols. (Basel: B. Schwabe, 1943–67), vol. 2, para. 35.

12. Georges Bataille, *L'érotisme* (1957; Paris: U.G.E., 10/18, 1964), 120–28.

13. Kathryn Gravdal, *Ravishing Maidens: Writing Rape in Medieval French Literature and Law* (Philadelphia: University of Pennsylvania Press, 1990), 142.

14. On *cuissage* in the literary, theatrical, and cinematic tradition in our own times, see Frances Eleanor Palermo Litvack, *Le Droit du Seigneur in European and American Literature from the Seventeenth through the Twentieth Century* (Birmingham: Summa Publications, 1984).

15. François-René de Chateaubriand, *Analyse raisonnée de l'histoire de France,* in *Œuvres complètes,* 28 vols. (Paris: Ladvocat, 1825–31), vol. 5, 286.

16. Robert Boutruche, *Seigneurie et féodalité* (1959; Paris: Aubier-Montaigne, 1968), vol. 1: *Le premier âge des liens d'homme à homme,* 128n.6.

17. *The Letters of Lanfranc Archbishop of Canterbury,* ed. Helen Clover and Margaret Gibson (Oxford: Clarendon Press, 1979), 68–69.

18. See the translation of Giraud de Barri's text, with commentary, in Jeanne-Marie Boivin, *L'Irlande au Moyen Âge: Giraud de Barri et la Topographia Hibernica (1188)* (Paris: Champion/Slatkine, 1993).

19. Hector Boece, *Scotorum historiae ab illius gentis origine* (Paris, 1526), book 3, fol.

36r, quoted from *The History and Chronicles of Scotland Written in Latin by Hector Boece*, trans. John Bellenden, 2 vols. (Edinburgh: W. and C. Tait, 1821), 83.

20. Boece, *Scotorum historiae*, book 12, fol. 260, and elsewhere. In Bellenden's translation: "Amang mony werkis quhilkis he did, it wes not litill to be commendit, that he abrogat the wickit lawe maid be King Ewin the Thrid, and commandit half ane mark of money to be payit to the lord of the ground, in redemptoun of the womannis chastite and honour; callit, yit, The Merchetis of Wemen."

21. George Buchanan, *Rerum scoticarum historia* (Edinburgh, 1582), book 4, fol. 31v; book 7, fol. 62v. Published in English as *The History of Scotland* (London: Edw. Jones for Awnsham Churchil, 1690).

22. Sir John Skene, Lord Curriehill, *De verborum significatione: The exposition of the termes and difficill wordes, conteined in the foure buikes of Regiam Maiestatem*, in *The Laws and Actes of Parliament* (Edinburgh: Robert Waldegrave, 1597).

23. John Major, *Historia Majoris Britanniae, tam Angliae quam Scotiae, per Johannem Majorem . . . e veterum monumentis concinnata* (Edinburgh, 1521).

24. See Thomas Peter Ellis, *Welsh Tribal Law and Custom in the Middle Ages*, 2 vols. (Oxford: Clarendon Press, 1926; reprint, Aalen: Scientia Verlag, 1982), 396–98.

25. "De Sancta Margarita Scotiae Regina Edimburgi Civitate Regia," *Acta sanctorum, Iunii tomus II* (Antwerp, 1688), with commentary by the Bollandists, 320–40, especially 318–19.

26. "De Sancto Forannano," *Acta sanctorum, Aprilis tomus III* (Antwerp, 1675), with commentary by the Bollandists, 821–22: "Constituit praeterea quatenus ex his duabus partibus et potestatibus, quasi gens una et populus unus, sibi invicem familiae haerarenp, et sine exactione contraria et bathinodii quaestu Florinensis homo ex Walciodorensis, de Florinensi potestate mulierem sumendi faciet." "Bathinodium . . . intelligo quod nos leniori dialecto Bed-nood possemus dicere, quo significetur redimendi concubitus sive lecti necessitas: quae inter servos glebae (quales etiam in Belgio olim erant rustici et adhuc multi sunt in Frisia et Germania) et dominos eorum intercedebat."

27. See chapter 2, below, for an analysis of the controversy regarding the *droit de cuissage* among Dutch and Flemish scholars in the late seventeenth and early eighteenth centuries.

28. Marc Bloch, *Apologie pour l'histoire ou Métier d'historien*, 7th ed. (Paris: Armand Colin, 1974), 38, quoted from *The Historian's Craft*, trans. Peter Putnam (New York: Alfred A. Knopf, 1953), 31.

29. See Reinhardt Koselleck, *Kritik und Krise*, consulted in French as *Le règne de la critique*, trans. Hans Hildenbrand (Paris: Minuit, 1979); available in English as *Critique and Crisis: Enlightenment and the Pathogenesis of Modern Society* (Cambridge, Mass.: MIT Press, 1988).

30. *Les essais de Michel de Montaigne*, ed. Pierre Villey, revised by V.-L. Saulnier (Paris: Presses Universitaires de France, 1965), 112; quoted from *The Essays of Michel de Montaigne*, trans. and ed. Jacob Zeitlin, 3 vols. (New York: Alfred A. Knopf, 1934), vol. 1, 95.

31. Montaigne, *Essais*, 114; *Essays*, vol. 1, 97.

32. *Les neuf livres des Histoires d'Hérodote, prince et premier des historiographes grecs*, trans. Pierre Saliat (Paris: C. Micard, 1575), book 4, 168.

33. Francisco López de Gómara, *La istoria de las Indias y conquista de Mexico*, 2 vols. (Zaragosa: A. Millan, 1552). Other editions followed, and the work was rapidly translated into French, English, and Italian. The French translation by Martin Fumée was first published in 1569.

34. See Pierre Ragon, *Les amours indiennes, ou L'imaginaire du Conquistador,* preface by Serge Gruzinski (Paris: Armand Colin, 1992).

35. Montaigne, *Essais,* 109, 115, 117, 120; *Essays,* vol. 1, 92, 98, 104, 100.

36. See Margaret Mead, *Sex and Temperament in Three Primitive Societies* (New York: Morrow, 1935, 1968), essays written in 1928 and 1935, translated into French by Georges Chevassus under the title *Moeurs et sexualité en Océanie* (Paris: Plon, 1963). These texts present a veritable encyclopedia of all possible relationships among sexuality, affectivity, and social institutions. American anthropologists have recently challenged Mead's methods and results on some important points.

37. Quoted in Ragon, *Les amours indiennes,* 138. See chapter 6, below, for Vincent de Beauvais and Sir John Mandeville. For Westermarck, see Edward Westermarck, *The History of Human Marriage,* 2 vols. (New York: Macmillan, 1891), published in French as *Histoire du mariage,* trans. Arnold van Gennep (Paris: A. Picard, 1934–43), vol. 1: *La promiscuité primitive,* 217.

38. Sigmund Freud, "The Taboo of Virginity (Contributions to the Psychology of Love, III)" (1918 [1917]), in *The Complete Psychological Works of Sigmund Freud,* ed. James Strachey in collaboration with Anna Freud, 24 vols. (London: Hogarth Press, 1966, 1995), vol. 11, 191–208; consulted in French as "Du tabou de la virginité," in *La vie sexuelle* (Paris, 1964), taken from vol. 12 of the *Gesammelte Werke.*

39. See Alain Boureau, "L'imene et l'ulivo: La virginità femminile nel discorso della Chiesa nel XIII secolo," *Quaderni storici,* n.s. 75, 3 (1990): 791–813.

40. Pierre Augustin Caron de Beaumarchais, *Le mariage de Figaro,* 2 vols. (Paris: Larousse, 1934), act 1, scene 1, vol. 1, 47, quoted from *Phaedra and Figaro,* trans. Robert Lowell (for *Phaedra*) and Jacques Barzun (for *Figaro*) (New York: Farrar, Straus, 1961), 105, 211.

41. Beaumarchais, *Le mariage de Figaro,* final *vaudeville,* act 5, scene 19, vol. 2, 72; Barzun trans., 211.

42. Beaumarchais, *Le mariage de Figaro,* act 1, scene 1, vol. 1, 44; Barzun trans., 104.

43. See W. D. Howarth, "The Theme of the 'Droit du Seigneur' in the Eighteenth-century Theater," *French Studies* 15 (1961): 228–40.

44. Paris, Bibliothèque Nationale, MS 9295. This manuscript was discovered by W. D. Howarth.

45. This is roughly the thesis of Edward Shorter, *The Making of the Modern Family* (New York: Basic Books, 1975).

46. Peter Laslett, *Family Life and Illicit Love in Earlier Generations: Essays in Historical Sociology* (Cambridge: Cambridge University Press, 1977).

47. Jean-Louis Flandrin, "Vie de famille et amours illicites en Angleterre: A propos d'un livre de Peter Laslett," in *Le sexe et l'Occident: Évolution des attitudes et des comportements* (Paris: Éditions du Seuil, 1981, 1986), 305–6; quoted from "Family Life and Illicit Love in England: A Review of Peter Laslett's Book," in Flandrin, *Sex in the Western World: The Development of Attitudes and Behavior,* trans. Sue Collins (Philadelphia: Harwood Academic Publishers, 1991), 291–309, quotation on 293–94.

48. See Silvana Vecchio, "The Good Wife," in *A History of Women in the West,* ed. Georges Duby and Michelle Perrot, 5 vols. (Cambridge, Mass.: Belknap Press of Harvard University Press, 1992), vol. 2: *Silences of the Middle Ages,* ed. Christiane Klapisch-Zuber, 105–35. Originally published as *Storia delle donne in Occidente,* 5 vols. (Rome: Laterza, 1990); available in French as *Histoire des femmes en Occident,* 5 vols. (Paris: Plon, 1990).

49. Robert Jacob, *Les époux, le seigneur et la cité: Coutume et pratiques matrimoniales des bourgeois et paysans de France du Nord au moyen âge* (Brussels: Facultés Universitaires Saint-Louis, 1990).

50. Jacques Rossiaud, *La prostitution médiévale*, preface by Georges Duby (Paris: Flammarion, 1988); available in English as *Medieval Prostitution*, trans. Lydia G. Cochrane (Oxford: Blackwell, 1988); originally published as *La prostituzione nel medioevo* (Rome: Laterza, 1984). Also Leah L. Otis, *Prostitution in Medieval Society: The History of an Urban Institution in Languedoc* (Chicago: University of Chicago Press, 1985); Peter Schuster, *Das Frauenhaus: Städtische Bordelle in Deutschland (1350–1600)* (Paderborn: Ferdinand Schöningh, 1992).

51. Richard Trexler, "La prostitution florentine au XVe siècle: Patronages et clientèles," *Annales, ESC* 36 (1981): 983–1015.

52. Iris Origo, "'The Domestic Enemy': The Eastern Slaves in Tuscany in the 14th and 15th Centuries," *Speculum* 30, 3 (1955): 321–61.

53. Cissie C. Fairchilds, *Domestic Enemies: Servants and Their Masters in Old Regime France* (Baltimore: Johns Hopkins University Press, 1984), 164–81. Two excellent studies should be added to this fine work: Jean-Pierre Gutton, *Domestiques et serviteurs dans la France d'Ancien Régime* (Paris: Aubier-Montaigne, 1981); Sarah C. Maza, *Servants and Masters in Eighteenth-Century France: The Uses of Loyalty* (Princeton: Princeton University Press, 1983).

54. Peter Laslett, *The World We Have Lost* (London: Methuen, 1965; 3d ed., New York: Scribner, 1984); Edward Shorter, "Illegitimacy, Sexual Revolutions and Social Change in Modern Europe," *Journal of Interdisciplinary History* 2 (1971): 237–71.

55. Quoted in Fairchilds, *Domestic Enemies*, 169.

56. G. R. Quaife, "The Consenting Spinster in a Peasant Society: Aspects of Premarital Sex in 'Puritan' Somerset, 1645–1660," *Journal of Social History* 11 (1977–78): 228–44.

57. Documents on paternity searches have given rise to several studies. See Jacques Depauw, "Amour illégitime et société à Nantes au XVIIIe siècle," *Annales, ESC* 27 (1972): 1155–82. For a chronological comparison, see Alain Croix, *Nantes et le pays nantais au XVIe siècle: Étude démographique* (Paris: SEVPEN, 1974), 98; Pierre-François Alail, "Enfants illégitimes et enfants abandonnés à Clermont dans la seconde moitié du XVIIIe siècle," *Cahiers d'histoire* (1976): 307–33; Jacques Solé, "Passion charnelle et société urbaine d'Ancien Régime: Amour vénal, amour libre et amour fou à Grenoble au milieu du règne de Louis XIV," in *Villes de l'Europe méditerranéenne et de l'Europe occidentale du Moyen Âge au XIXe siècle*, actes du colloque de Nice, 27–28 March 1969 (Paris: Belles-Lettres, 1969), 211–32; Marie-Claude Phan, "Les déclarations de grossesse en France (XVIe–XVIIIe siècles): Essai institutionnel," *Revue d'histoire moderne et contemporaine* 22 (1975): 61–88; F. Galabert, "La recherche de paternité à Toulouse en 1792 et les volontaires nationaux," *Revue des Pyrénées* (1911): 353–92; Yves-Marie Bercé, "Aspects de la criminalité au XVIIe siècle," *Revue historique* 239 (1968): 33–42. I should note that in *Domestic Enemies* Fairchilds obtains singularly different results for Languedoc.

58. Quoted in Gutton, *Domestiques et serviteurs*, 207.

59. Joseph Nicholas Guyot, *Supplément au répertoire universel et raisonné de jurisprudence civile, criminelle, canonique et bénéficiale* (Paris, 1786), 8:68–69, quoted in Gutton, *Domestiques et serviteurs*, 146.

60. The article "Soubrette" is reproduced in Denis Diderot, *Œuvres complètes*, ed. Roger Lewinter, 15 vols. (Paris: Club Français du Livre, 1969–73), vol. 15, 380.

61. Edmond and Jules Goncourt, *Journal*, entry for 21 November 1871; quoted in Anne-Marie Martin-Fugier, *La place des bonnes: La domesticité féminine à Paris en 1900* (Paris: Grasset, 1985), 321.

62. See Pierre Tranouez, "La Maison Tellier ou le lupanar généralisé," *L'école des lettres* 84, 13 (1993): 53–67.

63. See Hubert Juin's preface to Edmond and Jules Goncourt, *Germinie Lacerteux* (Paris: U.G.E, 1979), 9–12.

64. Robert Mauzi, "Introduction," in Abbé Prévost, *Histoire d'une Grecque moderne* (Paris: U.G.E., 1965), xv.

65. Sandra M. Gilbert and Susan Grubar, *The Madwoman in the Attic: The Woman Writer and the Nineteenth-Century Literary Imagination* (New Haven: Yale University Press, 1979), 506.

66. Martin Heidegger, *Die Frage nach dem Ding* (1962), quoted from *What Is a Thing?* trans. W. B. Barton Jr., with an analysis by Eugene T. Gendlin (Chicago: H. Regnery, 1968), 2; consulted in French translation by Jean Reboul and Jacques Taminaux as *Qu'est-ce qu'une chose?* (Paris: Gallimard, 1971), 14. Heidegger notes that the book represents the text of a course given at the University of Freiburg im Breisgau during the winter semester of 1935–36 under the title "Basic Questions of Metaphysics." On Heidegger and his rectorate in 1933–34, see Hugo Ott, *Martin Heidegger: Unterwegs zur seinen Biographie* (1988), consulted in French translation by J.-M. Beloeil as *Martin Heidegger: Éléments pour une biographie* (Paris: Payot, 1990); available in English as *Martin Heidegger: A Political Life*, trans. Allan Blunden (Hammersmith: HarperCollins, 1993).

67. Heidegger, *What Is a Thing?* 2–4.

68. Pierre Vidal-Naquet, "Esclavage et gynécocratie dans la tradition, l'utopie," in *Le chasseur noir: Formes de pensée et formes de société dans le monde grec*, 2d ed. (Paris: Maspero, 1983), 267–88; available in English as "Slavery and the Rule of Women in Tradition, Myth, and Utopia," in *The Black Hunter: Forms of Thought and Forms of Society in the Greek World*, trans. Andrew Szegedy-Maszek (Baltimore: Johns Hopkins University Press, 1986), 205–23.

69. See Marcel Morabito, "Droit romain et réalités sociales de la sexualité servile," in *Droit, histoire et sexualité*, ed. Jacques Poumarède and Jean-Pierre Royer (Villeneuve d'Ascq: Publications de l'Espace Juridique; distribution Paris: Distique, 1987), 3–20.

70. Georges Dumézil, *Loki*, rev. ed. (Paris: Flammarion, 1986), 150 and note 33. My thanks to Jacques Merceron for having brought this text to my attention. It is regrettable that (as is so often the case in discussions of *cuissage*) Dumézil gives no references for his description of ancient mores.

CHAPTER 2: THE *DROIT DE CUISSAGE* IN THE CORRIDORS OF HISTORY (1789–1854)

1. *Le droit de jambage, ou Le droit des anciens seigneurs sur les nouvelles mariées*, "traduction libre de l'italien de Colombo Giulio" (Paris: Defer-Demaisonneuve; Nantes: Louis, 1790).

2. *Le vasselage, ou Droit des anciens seigneurs sur les nouvelles épousées*, "poème satirico-comique traduit de l'italien par C. Niort" (Paris, 1791).

3. *Le nouveau seigneur de village*, text by Auguste Creuzé de Lesser and Jean-François Roger (or perhaps Edmond-Guillaume-François Favières) (Paris: Barba, 1815).

4. Delacour [Alfred Lartigue] and Adolphe Jaime, *Les noces de Merluchet*, published in *Le magasin théâtral illustré* (1854).

5. Jacques Collin de Plancy, *Dictionnaire féodal, ou Recherches et anecdotes sur les droits féodaux*, 2 vols. (Paris: Brissot-Thivars, 1819; 2d ed., 1820), vol. 1, 162–79.

6. Collin de Plancy, *Dictionnaire féodal*, 2d ed., vol. 1, 169.

7. Eugène Allent (pseudonym of Jacques Collin de Plancy), *Abelina, nouvelle historique du XIIIe siècle, suivie des Aventures de M. Lebéjaune, et d'anecdotes et recherches sur le droit de cuissage* (Paris: Th. Grandin, 1823); Jacques Saint-Albin (pseudonym of Jacques Collin de Plancy), *Le droit du seigneur, ou La fondation de Nice dans le Haut-Monferrat, aventure du XIIIe siècle, traduit librement du Fodero de Jules Colomb, avec l'histoire de Monseigneur le Béjaune, et un grand nombre d'anecdotes sur le droit de cuissage et sur les variétés de ce privilège* (Paris: Th. Grandin, 1820).

8. On Migne's commercial ventures, see R. Howard Bloch, *God's Plagiarist: Being an Account of the Fabulous Industry and Irregular Commerce of the Abbé Migne* (Chicago: University of Chicago Press, 1994); published in French as *Le plagiaire de Dieu: La Fabuleuse industrie de l'abbé Migne*, trans. Pierre Antoine Fabre (Paris: Éditions du Seuil, 1995).

9. It is also mentioned in George P. R. James, *The Jacquerie, or The Lady and the Page* (London: A. and W. Galignani, 1842).

10. Jean Joseph Raepsaet, *Les droits du seigneur: Recherches sur l'origine et la nature des droits connus anciennement sous les noms de droits des premières nuits, de markette, d'afforage, marcheta, maritagium et bumede* (1817), reprinted posthumously in Raepsaet, *Œuvres complètes*, 6 vols. (Mons: Leroux, 1838–40), vol. 1, 199–229. An identical edition was published in Rouen (1877).

11. On Raepsaet, see the lengthy (and highly critical) entry by Victor Fris in *Biographie nationale de Belgique* (Brussels), vol. 18 (1905), cols. 562–76.

12. Raepsaet, *Les droits du seigneur*, 212.

13. Matthijs Smallegange, *Nieuwe Cronyk van Zeeland, eerste deel, vervattende de voor desen uitgegeven Cronyken van de Heeren Jacobus Eyndius, en Johan Reygersberg, veel vermeerdet outrent deses Landschaps Oudheden, en Herkomsten* (Middelburg: J. Meertens, 1695), 621.

14. Matheus Gargon, *Walchersche Arkadia*, 2 vols. (Leiden, 1715–17), vol. 2, 221.

15. Pieter van der Schelling, *Hollands Tiend-Regt, of Verhandeling van het Regt tot de Tiended, Toekomende aan de Graafelykheid, en de Heerelykheden van Holland, en Westvriesland*, 2 vols. (Rotterdam: P. Losel, 1727), vol. 1, 142–50.

16. Adriaan Pars, *Catti Aborigines Batavorum, dat is De Katten de voorouders der Batavieren, ofte De twee Katwijken, aan See en aan de Rijn* (1697), ed. Pieter van der Schelling (Leiden: J. A. Langerak, 1745).

17. Gerard van Loon, *Beschryving der Aloude Regeeringwyze van Holland*, 5 vols. in 3 (Leiden: P. Vander Eyk, 1744–50), vol. 1 (1745), 158–68.

18. Johann Voet, *Commentarius ad Pendectas*, 6 vols. (Halle: I. I. Beyerus and I. I. Curtius, 1776–80), vol. 1 (1776).

19. The heading for entries in Du Cange's *Glossarium*, rather than page numbers, will be given in the many references that follow. The typographical devices in the Henschel edition, reprinted many times and available in libraries, will enable the reader to trace the various layers of the text. A clearer idea of Dom Pierre Carpentier's colossal achievement can be had from his *Glossarium novum ad scriptores medii aevi, cum latinos tum gallicos, seu Supplementum ad auctiorem Glossarii Cangiani editionem*, 4 vols. (Paris, 1766).

20. Julien Brodeau, *Coustume de la Prévosté et Vicomté de Paris, commentée par feu Maistre Julien Brodeau*, 2d ed. (Paris, 1689), title 1, article 37, no. 11, p. 273.

21. See Jacques Le Goff and Jean-Claude Schmitt, eds., *Le charivari, Actes du Congrès de la Table Ronde de Paris, April 1977* (Paris: École des Hautes Études en Sciences Sociales, 1980).

22. Natalie Zemon Davis, *Fiction in the Archives: Pardon Tales and Their Tellers in Sixteenth-Century France* (Stanford: Stanford University Press, 1987), consulted in French as *Pour sauver sa vie: Les récits de pardon au XVIe siècle*, trans. C. Cler (Paris: Éditions du Seuil, 1988); Claude Gauvard, *"De grâce espécial": Crime, état et société en France à la fin du Moyen Âge*, 2 vols. (Paris: Publications de la Sorbonne, 1991). On the administrative aspects of letters of remission, see Michel François, "Note sur les lettres de rémission transcrites dans les registres du Trésor des Chartes," *Bibliothèque de l'École des Chartes* 103 (1942): 317–24.

23. These documents will be cited as transcribed in Roger Vaultier, *Le folklore pendant la guerre de Cent Ans d'après les lettres de rémission du Trésor des Chartes* (Paris: Guénégaud, 1965), 22–27. The extracts cited by Dom Carpentier are preceded and followed by an asterisk.

24. See Arnold van Gennep, *Manuel de folklore français contemporain* (Paris: A. Picard, 1943–46), vol. 1, part 2, 437–51.

25. Ibid., vol. 1, part 2, 560.

26. Ibid., vol. 1, part 2, 48.

27. Duvivier in *Revue des Ardennes* 4 (1825) and 8 (1829).

28. Jules Michelet, *Les origines du droit français cherchées dans les symboles et formules du droit universel*, in *Œuvres complètes*, ed. Paul Viallaneix (Paris: Flammarion, 1971–), vol. 3, 603–85.

29. Ibid., vol. 3, 760.

30. Frédéric Ozanam in *L'Univers*, 1 October 1837. The article is reprinted in the press dossier following the text of Michelet's *Origines du droit français* in *Œuvres complètes*.

31. Anatole de Barthélemy, "Le droit du seigneur," *Revue des questions historiques* 1 (1866): 95–123.

32. Charles de Robillard de Beaurepaire, "Charte portant abolition du droit de 'culagium' dans le fief de Pierrecourt," *Bibliothèque de l'École des Chartes*, 18th year, 4th ser., 3 (1857): 167–68.

33. Évelyne Sorlin, "La croyance au 'droit du seigneur' dans les coutumes du Moyen Âge" and "Le 'droit du seigneur' et les droits de la jeunesse dans le folklore français et piémontais," *Le monde alpin et rhodanien* 1–2 (1987): 69–82; 1–2 (1989): 7–22.

34. See Sorlin, "Le 'droit du seigneur.'"

35. For a painstaking modern edition of Cordara's text, see Giulio Cesare Cordara di Calamandrana, *Il Fodero, ossia il jus degli antichi signori sulle spose: Poema giocoso satirico in ottava rima sulla fondazione di Nizza della Paglia nell'Alto Monferrato*, ed. Alberto Migliardi (Alessandria: Società di Storia, Arte e Archeologia per la Provincia di Alessandria, 1934).

36. My thanks to Philippe Buc for suggesting this analogy.

37. See the notes to the modern edition of Ghilini's *Annals:* Girolamo Ghilini, *Annali di Alessandria*, ed. Giovanni Jachino (Alexandria: Amilcare Bossola, 1903–10), vol. 1, 204–5.

38. *Opere latine e italiane dell'abbate Giulio Cesare Cordara* (Venice, 1804), vol. 1, 66–67. See note 35, above, for the 1934 edition of *Il fodero*. For further information and bibliogra-

phy, see Magda Vigilante, "Cordara, Giulio Cesare," in *Dizionario biografico degli italiani* (Rome: Istituto della Enciclopedia Italiana, 1960–), vol. 28, 789–92.

39. See Carlrichard Brühl, *Fodrum, Gistum, Servitium Regis: Studien zu den wirtschaftlichen Grundlagen des Königstums im Frankenreich und in den fränkischen Nachfolgestaaten Deutschland, Frankreich und Italien vom 6. bis zur mitte des 14. Jahrhunderts,* 2 vols. (Cologne: Böhlau, 1968).

40. See, for example, Daniel Ligou, ed., *Histoire de Montauban* (Toulouse: Privat, 1984).

41. Charles Petit-Dutaillis, *Les communes françaises: Caractères et évolution des origines au XVIII⁰ siècle* (Paris: Albin Michel, 1947).

42. See Pierre Charpentier, "Les chartes urbaines dans la France centrale: Un movement seigneurial?" in *Les origines des libertés urbaines, Actes du XVI⁰ Congrès des Historiens Médiévistes de l'Enseignement Supérieur, Rouen, 7–8 June 1985* (Rouen: Publications de l'Université de Rouen, 1990), 261–80.

43. *Renaud de Montauban* is discussed in Jacques Le Goff, "Apogée de la forme urbaine médiévale: 1150–1330," in *Histoire de la France urbaine,* ed. Georges Duby, 5 vols. (Paris: Éditions du Seuil, 1980), vol. 2: *La ville médiévale, des Carolingiens à la Renaissance,* 395.

44. Henri Le Bret, *Histoire de la ville de Montauban* (Montauban: S. Dubois, 1668).

45. Antoine de Cathala-Coture, *Histoire politique, ecclésiastique et littéraire de Querci,* 3 vols. (Paris and Montauban: P. Th. Cazaméa, 1785).

46. Henri Le Bret, *Histoire de Montauban,* new ed., revised and annotated after the original documents by Abbé Marcellin and Gabriel Ruck (Montauban: Rethoré, 1841), 58–59.

47. "Lorsqu'elle fut assaillie par plusieurs fois et longtemps assiégée de chevaliers et grands seigneurs de France, l'an 1562" (Jean Fournier, *Chronique par Jan Fornier, de Montauban* [Montauban, 1564], 179).

48. Baron Chaudruc de Crazannes, "Observations sur le droit de monnayage des abbés de Montauriol," *Revue de numismatique* (1853): 140–46.

49. Léonce Cellier, "Le droit de congnage à Chauny," *Bibliothèque de l'École des Chartes* 85 (1924): 229–30.

CHAPTER 3: THE GREAT DISPUTE OF 1854–82

1. Stanley Mellon, *The Political Uses of History: A Study of Historians in the French Restoration* (Stanford: Stanford University Press, 1958).

2. See Rudolf von Thadden, *Restauration und napoleonisches Erbe; der Verwaltungszentralismus als politisches Problem in Frankreich (1814–1830)* (Wiesbaden: F. Steiner, 1972), consulted in French as *La centralisation contestée: L'administration napoléonienne, enjeu politique de la Restauration (1814–1830),* trans. Hélène Cusa and Patrick Charbonneau (Arles: Actes Sud, 1989), 27–42.

3. Augustin Thierry, *Lettres sur l'histoire de France* (Paris, 1827), 234, quoted in Marcel Gauchet, "Les *Lettres sur l'histoire de France* d'Augustin Thierry: L'alliance austère du patriotisme et de la science," in *Les lieux de mémoire,* ed. Pierre Nora, 3 vols. in 7 (Paris: Gallimard, 1984–92), vol. 2: *La Nation,* part 1, 250.

4. Ibid. Gauchet demonstrates this to stunning effect.

5. Edgar Quinet, *Histoire de mes idées: Autobiographie* (Paris, 1858), quoted from the edition by Simone Bernard-Griffiths (Paris: Flammarion, 1972), 154–55.

6. *Les Constitutions de la France depuis 1789*, ed. Jacques Godechot (Paris: Flammarion, 1979), 217.

7. See Robert-Henri Bautier, "Le *Recueil des monuments pour l'histoire du Tiers État* et l'utilisation des matériaux réunis par A. Thierry," *Annuaire-bulletin de la Société pour l'Histoire de France* (1944): 89–118.

8. See Von Thadden, *La centralisation contestée*, 85–87.

9. This interesting work is available in a facsimile edition: Léopold Delisle, *Études sur la condition de la classe agricole et l'état de l'agriculture en Normandie au Moyen Âge*, 2 vols. (New York: Lenox Hill Publishing, 1978).

10. "Rapport sur un ouvrage de M. Bouthors, greffier en chef de la cour impériale, intitulé *Coutumes locales du baillage d'Amiens* par M. Dupin," *Séances et travaux de l'Académie des Sciences Morales et Politiques*, 3rd ser., 8 (1854): 117–41.

11. There is no overall study of Dupin's highly edifying career. An interested reader might consult André-Marie-Jean-Jacques Dupin, *Mémoires*, 4 vols. (Paris: H. Plon, 1855–61).

12. Quoted in Guillaume de Bertier de Sauvigny, *La Restauration* (1955; new ed., Paris: Flammarion, 1963), 381; quoted here from Bertier de Sauvigny, *The Bourbon Restoration*, trans. Lynn M. Case (Philadelphia: University of Pennsylvania Press, 1967), 381.

13. Bertier de Sauvigny, *La Restauration*, 445; *The Bourbon Restoration*, 444.

14. Dupin, "Rapport sur un ouvrage de M. Bouthors," 121.

15. Ibid., 131.

16. The members of this commission were François Chamard, Adolphe Dureau de La Malle, Karl Benedict Hase, Alexis Paulin Paris, Louis Vitet, and Léon de Laborde.

17. Jules Berger de Xivrey, "Rapport fait à l'Académie des Inscriptions et Belles-Lettres au nom de la Commission des Antiquaires de France par M. Berger de Xivrey lu dans la séance annuelle du vendredi 18 août," *Séances annuelles de l'Académie des Inscriptions et Belles-Lettres* (1854): 24–25.

18. On Alloury, see Victor Gueneau, *Dictionnaire biographique des personnes nées en Nivernais ou revendiquées par le Nivernais* (Nevers: Mazeron Frères, 1899), 2–3.

19. Henri Martin, *Histoire de France*, 17 vols. (Paris: Furne, Jouvet, 1854–70), vol. 5, 568.

20. Louis-Firmin Laferrière, *Histoire du droit français*, 6 vols. (Paris: Joubert, Cotillon, 1846–58), vol. 5: *Coutumes de France dans les diverses provinces*, 454.

21. For a recent study on Veuillot, see Benoît Le Roux, *Louis Veuillot, un homme un combat* (Paris: Tequi, 1984).

22. By "journalism," I mean the modern journalism associated with mass-distribution publication. In France one of its earliest promoters was Émile de Girardin, the founder (in 1836) of *La Presse*. See also (of course) Honoré de Balzac, *Les illusions perdues*.

23. Quoted in Le Roux, *Louis Veuillot*, 26.

24. See R. Howard Bloch, *God's Plagiarist: Being an Account of the Fabulous Industry and Irregular Commerce of the Abbé Migne* (Chicago: University of Chicago Press, 1994), published in French as *Le plariaire de Dieu: La fabuleuse industrie de l'abbé Migne*, trans. Pierre Antoine Fabre (Paris: Éditions du Seuil, 1996).

25. Quoted in Le Roux, *Louis Veuillot*, 50.

26. Louis Veuillot, *Le droit du seigneur au Moyen Âge* (1854), in *Œuvres complètes*, 31 vols. (Paris: P. Lethielleux, 1924–), ser. 1: *Œuvres diverses*, vol. 6, 5. Subsequent references

will be to this edition rather than to the first edition, now rare. The text is identical in the passages quoted.

27. Ibid., vol. 6, 7 (publicity notice, 2d ed., 1871).

28. Ibid., vol. 6, 26.

29. Ibid., vol. 6, 13.

30. Ibid., vol. 6, 43.

31. Ibid., vol. 6, 49.

32. Ibid., vol. 6, 25.

33. Ibid., vol. 6, 51.

34. Ibid., vol. 6, 24.

35. See P. E. Bordeaux, *Le Comte Amédée de Foras* (Paris: 1933).

36. Amédée de Foras, *Le droit du seigneur au Moyen Âge* (Paris, 1884), 168–71.

37. Charles de Robillard de Beaurepaire, ed., "Charte portant abolition du droit de 'culagium' dans le fief de Pierrecourt," *Bibliothèque de l'École des Chartes,* 18th year, 4th ser., 3 (1857): 54–55.

38. Clearly the word *cullage* may have been overdetermined by its closeness to *cul* without that being a proof of a sexual origin to rights pertaining to marriage.

39. Foras, *Le droit du seigneur,* 35, 1, 122, 2.

40. For a fine critical edition, see Adolphe Mazure and Jules Hatoulet, *Les Fors anciens de Béarn,* ed. Paul Ourliac and Monique Gilles (Paris: Éditions du CNRS, 1990).

41. *Les Fors de Béarn: Législation inédite du XIe au XVe siècle avec traduction en regard, notes et introduction par MM. A. Mazure et J. Hatoulet* (Pau: E. Vignancour, and Paris, n.d. [1841]), 171n.A. The copy in the Bibliothèque Nationale, Paris, includes a copy of the subscription prospectus.

42. Marcel Barthe, *Le bon vieux temps en Béarn: Extrait d'un mémoire publié en 1845 dans l'intérêt de la commune de Louvie-Soubiron et Liste* (Pau: Véronèse, 1874).

43. Gustave Bascle de Lagrèze, *Le Trésor de Pau: Archives du château d'Henri IV* (Pau, 1851), 70, 156.

44. Gustave Bascle de Lagrèze, "Le droit du seigneur," *Le Droit,* 23 July 1854; republished as *Essai sur le droit du seigneur à l'occasion de la controverse entre M. Dupin aîné et M. Louis Veuillot* (Paris, 1855).

45. For his own account of his research, see Gustave Bascle de Lagrèze, *Histoire du droit dans les Pyrénées (Comté de Bigorre)* (Paris, 1867), 384–420.

46. Bascle published a fuller version of his communication to the academy in ibid.

47. Ibid., 131.

48. Victor Vallein, *Le Moyen Âge, ou, Aperçu de la condition des populations, principalement dans les XIe, XIIe, et XIIIe siècles* (Saintes: Z. Lacroix, 1855), 5–6. The *cuissage* question occupies only a modest place in this work (pp. 208–29).

49. Jules Delpit, *Le droit du seigneur: Réplique ou seconde réponse à M. Louis Veuillot* (Bordeaux, 1873).

50. *Notices et extraits de la Bibliothèque du Roi* 14 (1843): 296–458.

51. Jean de Gaufreteau, *Chronique bordelaise,* ed. Jules Delpit, 2 vols. (Bordeaux: G. Gounouilhou, 1876–78).

52. Karl Schmidt, *Jus Primae Noctis: Eine geschichtliche Untersuchung* (Freiburg im Breisgau and St. Louis: Herder, 1881).

53. Wilhelm Schmidt-Bleibtreu, *Jus Primae Noctis im Widerstreit der Meinungen: Eine historische Untersuchung über das Herrenrecht der ersten Nacht* (Bonn: Rörscheid, 1988).

CHAPTER 4: SEVENTY-TWO PROOFS

1. Jules Delpit, *Réponse d'un campagnard à un Parisien, ou Réfutation du livre de M. Veuillot sur "le droit du seigneur"* (Paris, 1857), 93–106. Henceforth, this work will be referred to by the initial *D.*, followed by the page numbers. Secondary documentary sources will be referred to by the abbreviations *De.* for Léopold Delisle, *Études sur la condition de la classe agricole et l'état de l'agriculture en Normandie au Moyen Âge* (1851); *B.* for Alexandre Bouthors, ed., *Les Coutumes locales du bailliage d'Amiens, rédigées en 1507*, 2 vols. (Amiens, 1845–53). Where Delpit tendentiously eliminates portions of the text, they have been restored in square brackets.

2. "Nec dissimile est quod haud longe a Lovanio in pago fit quondam, ubi suae sponsae struprum sponsus a loci praefecto redimit" (*D.*, 39–40, 59–63).

3. *D.*, 57–59.

4. *D.*, 107–14.

5. *D.*, 69–70.

6. *D.*, 67–69.

7. *D.*, 65.

8. *D.*, 92. Bellet's *Notes et observations sur Bordeaux* is unpublished. For Jean de Gaufreteau, see his *Chronique bordelaise*, ed. Jules Delpit, 2 vols. (Bordeaux: G. Gounouilhou, 1876–78), vol. 1, 27.

9. Gaufreteau, *Chronique bordelaise*, vol. 2, 46–47; vol. 1, 53; vol. 2, 75.

10. Ibid., vol. 1, 159.

11. Ibid., vol. 1, 237.

12. The basic study on the quarrel between Épernon and Sourdis is Christian Jouhaud, "Le duc et l'archevêque: Action politique, représentation et pouvoir au temps de Richelieu," *Annales, ESC* 41, 5 (1986): 1017–40. On Gaufreteau, see Albert Gaillard, "Jean de Gaufreteau et la *Chronique bordelaise*," *Revue historique de Bordeaux* (1914): 98–113, which rectifies errors in Delpit's presentation of both the work and the author. On Bernard d'Épernon as captal, see *Le prince ridicule, mazarinade inédite composée vers 1650 et accompagnée de quelques notes par Jules Delpit* (Bordeaux, 1873).

13. The case of the fictional Piedmontese villages of Persani and Prelley first appears in Eusèbe-Jacques de Laurière, *Glossaire du droit français* (1699), ed. François Ragueau, 2 vols. (Paris, 1704). Laurière was best known for his edition of the *Ordonnances des rois de France: Recueil d'édits et d'ordonnances royaux*, 2 vols. (Paris: Montalant, 1720). The fragile hypothesis of a cutting joke in the milieu of royal jurists is backed up by a passage in Saint-Simon's *Mémoires*. On the occasion of the retirement of Achille de Harlay from his presidency of the Parlement de Paris, the memorialist relates a savory anecdote reflecting the scornful attitude of great state servants toward the pretenses to nobility of some members of Parlement: "The two Doublet brothers, both of them councilors and the elder of whom had some merit, capacity, and esteem, had bought the lands of Persan and Croy, whose name they took. They went to the audience of the First President. He knew them perfectly well, but he kept asking them who they were. At their names, he bent into a low bow, then, rising again and looking at them as if surprised to recognize them: 'Masks,' he said to them, 'I know you' and turned his back on them." See Louis de Rouvroy, duc de Saint-Simon, *Mémoires*, ed. Yves Coirault, 8 vols. (Paris: Gallimard, 1983–88), vol. 2, 897 (under the year 1707, but the incident occurred much earlier). Saint-Simon repeats the anecdote in *Mémoires*, vol. 4, 34. Just as Harlay had feigned respect to humiliate these two men, Lau-

rière may have mockingly dressed the same *bourgeois gentilshommes* in the cast-off clothing of *cuissage* by changing Persan into Persani.

14. Nicolas de Boyer (Bohier), *Decisiones supremi senatus Burdegalensis* (Lyons, 1551; Geneva, 1690), decision 297, no. 17: "Et ego vidi in curia Bituricensi coram Metropolitano processum appellationis, in quo rector seu curatus parochialis praetendebat ex consuetudine primam habere carnalem sponsae cognitionem, quae consuetudo fuit annullata, et in emendam condemnatus" (*D.*, 80–85).

15. "Multa in dictis decisionibus ad augendum librum inserta sunt, quae non sunt e sententia Nicolai Boërii jam senio confecti, sed allegationes juvenum" (Charles Dumoulin, *Tractatus dividui et individui, cum nova et analytica declaratione, compilatore Gasparo Caballino* [Venice, 1576], part 3, no. 255, p. 400).

16. *D.*, 92–93, 71–74.

17. *D.*, 96.

18. *D.*, 36–37, 68–70.

19. *D.*, 64–65.

20. *D.*, 27; *B.*, 483.

21. *D.*, 51 (which does not quote this text); *De.*, 71; Paris, Archives Nationales (henceforth abbreviated A.N.), P 307, no. 206.

22. *D.*, 52; *De.*, 70–71; A.N., P 304, no. 16.

23. *D.*, 50; *De.*, 63.

24. *D.*, 52 (which does not quote this text); *De.*, 72; A.N., P 305, no. 38.

25. Item 1: *D.*, 26; *B.*, vol. 1, 481.

26. Item 69: *D.*, 115–18; Pau, Archives Départementales (henceforth abbreviated A.D.), Pyrénées-Atlantiques, B 834 (document dated 1538) and B 877 (document dated 1674).

27. Item 70: *D.*, 115–18; A.D., Pyrénées-Atlantiques, B 850.

28. Centre Lorrain d'Histoire du Droit, *La Coutume de Vaudémont* (Nancy: le Centre, 1970), 62–63.

29. For the Grands Jours, see chapter 7 below.

30. See, for example, the transcripts of *aveux et dénombrements* published in Jacques Monicat and Bernard de Fournoux, *Chartes du Bourbonnais (918–1522)* (Moulins, 1952; Paris: A. and J. Picard, 1953); and in André Barban, *Recueil d'hommages, aveux et dénombrements de fiefs relevant du comté de Forez du XIIIᵉ au XVᵉ siècle* (Saint-Etienne, 1885). For a listing of *dénombrements* in the Archives Nationales (series P, Chambre des Comptes), see Jean Favier, ed., *Les Archives Nationales: État des inventaires,* 4 vols. (Paris: Archives Nationales; distribution, La Documentation Française, especially vol. 1: *L'Ancien Régime,* by Anne-Lise Rey-Courtel (1985), 142–71.

31. Charles Dartigue-Peyrou, *La Vicomté de Béarn sous le règne d'Henri d'Albret (1517–1555)* (Paris: Belles Lettres, 1934), 250.

32. A.D., Pyrénées-Atlantiques, B 850.

33. Christian Desplat, *Le For de Béarn d'Henri II d'Albret (1551),* new ed. (Pau: Marrimpouey, 1986), 20.

34. See Marcel Barthe, *Le bon vieux temps en Béarn: Extrait d'un mémoire publié en 1845 dans l'intérêt de la commune de Louvie Soubiron et Liste* (Pau: Véronèse, 1874).

35. See Bernard Hourcade, *La vie rurale en Haut-Ossau (Pyrénées-Atlantiques)* (Pau: Société des Sciences, Lettres, et Arts, 1970).

36. Pierre Tucoo-Chala, *Cartulaires de la vallée d'Ossau* (Saragossa, 1970).

37. Henri Cavaillès, *La transhumance pyrénéenne et la circulation des troupeaux dans les plaines de Gascogne* (Paris: Armand Colin, 1931); Cavaillès, *La vie pastorale et agricole dans les Pyrénées des Gaves, de l'Adour et des Nestes: Étude de géographie humaine* (Paris: Armand Colin, 1931).

38. The case of Louvie-Soubiron is all the more interesting because it led nowhere: The domain soon changed hands, and its modest rights were eventually acquired by the community of Louvie-Soubiron.

39. Simon Palay, *Dictionnaire du béarnais et du gascon modernes,* 3d ed. (Paris, 1980), 159.

40. Alain Guerreau and Yves Guy, *Les cagots du Béarn: Recherches sur le développement inégal au sein du système féodal européen* (Paris: Minerve, 1988). See also Françoise Bériac, *Des lépreux aux cagots: Recherches sur les sociétés marginales en Aquitaine médiévale* (Bordeaux: Fédération Historique du Sud-Ouest, Institut d'Histoire, Université de Bordeaux III, 1990); Paola Antolini, *Au-delà de la rivière: Les cagots, histoire d'une exclusion,* trans. Gilles Demonet (Paris: Nathan, 1989).

41. Cavaillès, *La vie pastorale.*

42. H. Marcel Fay, *Histoire de la lèpre en France: Lépreux et cagots du Sud-Ouest* (Paris: Champion, 1910), 596.

43. Ibid., 613.

44. See Barthe, *Le bon vieux temps en Béarn,* 40–41.

45. Philippe Buc, *L'ambiguïté du livre: Prince, pouvoir, et peuple dans les commentaires de la Bible au Moyen Âge,* foreword by Jacques Le Goff (Paris: Beauchesne, 1994), 200. Buc refers to Otto Brunner, *Land und Herrschaft: Grundfragen der territorialen Verfassungsgeschichte Österreichs im Mittelalter,* 5th ed. (Vienna, 1985), 90–93; available in English as *Land and Lordship: Structures of Governance in Medieval Austria,* trans. and introd. Howard Kaminsky and James van Horn Melton (Philadelphia: University of Pennsylvania Press, 1992).

46. Buc, *L'ambiguïté du livre,* 200.

47. André le Chapelain, *De amore* I.11, in *Andreus Capellanus on Love,* ed. and trans. P. G. Walsh (London: Duckworth, 1982), 222. To set this work into context, see John W. Baldwin, *The Language of Sex: Five Voices from Northern France around 1200* (Chicago: University of Chicago Press, 1994). For an erotic reading of the social distinctions of André le Chapelain, see Betsy Bowden, "The Art of Courtly Copulation," *Medievalia et Humanistica* 9 (1979): 67–85; and, especially, Bruno Roy, "Un art d'aimer: Pour qui?" and "L'obscénité rendue courtoise," both available in Roy, *Une culture de l'équivoque* (Montreal: Presses de l'Université de Montréal, Paris: Champion-Slatkine, 1992), 47–74 and 75–88.

48. Estout de Goz, "La chanson des vilains de Verson," Saint-Lô, Archives Départementales de la Manche, Fonds du Mont-Saint-Michel. For further remarks on this text, see chapter 7 below, especially note 1.

CHAPTER 5: THE BODY AND THE LAND

1. Besançon, A.D., Doubs, B 7901–8, quoted in Robert Jouvenot, "Mainmortable ou pas, mainmortables quand même," *Mémoires de la Société pour l'Histoire du Droit et des Institutions des Anciens Pays Bourguignons, Comtois et Romands* 32 (1973–74): 272.

2. A.D., Doubs, L 2853, quoted in Jouvenot, "Mainmortable ou pas," 272.

3. See François Prost, *Les remontrances du Parlement de Franche-Comté au XVIIIᵉ siècle* (Lyons: Bosc Frères, M. and L. Riou, 1936), 171–73.

4. Quoted in Yves Tripier, "Le servage tardif et les survivances de la mainmorte en Franche-Comté dans le baillage d'Amont à la fin de l'Ancien Régime," *Mémoires de la Société pour l'Histoire du Droit et des Institutions des Anciens Pays Bourguignons, Comtois et Romands* 32 (1973–74): 319.

5. On the need for caution in consulting the *cahiers de doléances*, see Henri See, "La rédaction et la valeur historique des cahiers de paroisses pour les États Généraux de 1789," *Revue historique* 103 (1910): 292–306, an old article but still pertinent. Consultation of the *cahiers* is facilitated by Beatrice Fry Hyslop, *A Guide to the General Cahiers of 1789* (New York: Columbia University Press, 1936). An important corpus of *cahiers* can be found in J. M. Mavidal and E. Laurent, eds., *Archives parlementaires de 1787 à 1860* (Paris: Librairie Administrative de P. Dumont, 1862–1995), ser. 1, vols. 1–7 (1879). Volume 7 contains an index.

6. Charles Gabriel Frédéric Christin, *Dissertation sur l'établissement de l'Abbaye de S. Claude, ses chroniques, ses légendes, ses chartes, ses usurpations, et sur les droits des habitans de cette terre* (Neufchâtel, 1772); Christin, *Collection des mémoires présentées au Conseil du Roi par les habitans du Mont Jura et le Chapitre de Saint Claude, avec l'arrêt rendu par ce tribunal* (Neufchâtel, 1772).

7. Robert Fossier, *Histoire sociale de l'Occident médiéval* (Paris: Armand Colin, 1970), 162.

8. Pierre Tucoo-Chala, "La vie à Salies de Béarn au début du XVᵉ siècle," *Revue de Pau et du Béarn* 11 (1983).

9. Léo Verriest, *Le servage dans le comté de Hainaut: Les Sainteurs: Le meilleur catel* (Brussels: Hayez, 1910).

10. See Léo Verriest, *Institutions médiévales: Introduction au Corpus des records de coutumes et des lois des chefs-lieux de l'ancien comté de Hainaut* (Mons: Union des Imprimeries, 1946–), vol. 1, 194–98.

11. Marc Bloch, *Rois et serfs: Un chapitre d'histoire capétienne* (Paris: Champion, 1920).

12. Dominique Barthélemy, *La société dans le comté de Vendômois: De l'an mil au XIVᵉ siècle* (Paris: Fayard, 1993), 474–505.

13. Fossier, *Histoire sociale de l'Occident médiéval*, 315–17.

14. There are many works on canon law. See Antoine Bernard, *La sépulture en droit canonique du Décret de Gratien au Concile de Trente* (Paris: Domat-Montchristien, 1933).

15. Fossier, *Histoire sociale de l'Occident médiéval*, 63.

16. See Anne-Marie Patault, *Hommes et femmes de corps en Champagne méridionale à la fin du Moyen Âge*, Mémoires des *Annales de l'Est* 58 (Nancy: Presses Universitaires de Nancy, 1978).

17. Henri Gilles, *Les Coutumes de Toulouse (1286) et leur premier commentaire (1296)* (Toulouse: Picard, 1969), 148.

18. On *saisine*, see Paul Ourliac and Jean-Louis Gazzaniga, *Histoire du droit privé français depuis l'An mil au Code Civil* (Paris: Albin Michel, 1985), 205–29.

19. *Cartulaires des Templiers de Douzens*, ed. Pierre Gérard and Elisabeth Magnou, under the direction of Philippe Wolff (Paris: Bibliothèque Nationale, 1965), henceforth abbreviated as Douzens and followed by the call number of the document and the page.

20. Douzens, D4, 275–76.

21. Douzens, A71, 73.

22. Douzens, A31, 42–43.

23. Douzens, A19, 31. An *acapte* was the equivalent of a *droit de relief* (right of investiture for a fief). The *tasque* and the *quarte* designated fees paid in proportion to harvests.

24. Douzens, D7, 278–79.

25. Paul Ourliac, "L'hommage servile dans la région toulousaine," in *Mélanges Louis Halphen* (Paris: Presses Universitaires de France, 1951), 551–56.

26. See Eleanor Searle, ed. and trans., *The Chronicle of Battle Abbey (Chronicon Monasteri de bello)* (Oxford: Clarendon Press; New York: Oxford University Press, 1980).

27. John of Salisbury, *Metalogicon* 8.23, in *Patrologiae cursus completus, Series latina* (henceforth abbreviated as *P.L.*), ed. Jacques Paul Migne, vol. 199, cols. 813–14; available in English as John of Salisbury, *The Metalogicon*, trans., introd., and annotated by Daniel D. McGarry (Berkeley: University of California Press, 1955).

28. Douzens, A173, 155–56; A181, 160–61; A175, 157; A191, 167; A182, 161.

29. Douzens, A27, 39–40; A69, 72.

30. See Maurice Berthe, *Le Comté de Bigorre: Un milieu rural au bas Moyen Âge* (Paris: SEVPEN/École des Hautes Études en Sciences Sociales, 1976), 253.

31. Guy Bois, *Crise du féodalisme: Économie rurale et démographie en Normandie orientale du début du 14ᵉ siècle au milieu du 16ᵉ siècle* (Paris: Presses de la Fondation Nationale des Sciences Politiques, 1976); available in English as *The Crisis of Feudalism: Economy and Society in Eastern Normandy c. 1300–1550* (Cambridge: Cambridge University Press, 1984).

32. *Cartulaire du prieuré de Saint-Étienne de Vignory*, ed. Jules d'Arbaumont (Langres, 1882), 57–60.

33. *Cartulaire de l'abbaye de Saint-Corneille de Compiègne*, ed. Émile-Épiphanius Morel (Compiègne), vol. 1 (1904), 259, 260–61, 274–75, 281–82.

34. A.N., A X1A 40, fol. 351.

35. Jean Gallet, *Le bon plaisir du baron de Fénétrange* (Nancy: Presses Universitaires de Nancy, 1990).

36. See Claude Michaud, *L'Église et l'argent: Les receveurs généraux du clergé de France aux XVIᵉ et XVIIᵉ siècles* (Paris: Fayard, 1991).

37. See Davis Bitton, *The French Nobility in Crisis, 1560–1640* (Stanford: Stanford University Press, 1969), 14–23.

38. Patault, *Hommes et femmes de corps*, 132 and 132n.3.

39. Jacques-Jean Clère, "Servitude et liberté dans le baillage de Chaumont-en-Bassigny," *Mémoires de la Société pour l'Histoire du Droit et des Institutions des Anciens Pays Burguignons, Comtois et Romands* 32 (1973–74): 239.

40. Patault, *Hommes et femmes de corps*, n.38.

41. Ibid., 87.

42. Ibid., 258–59.

43. Clère, "Servitude et liberté," 253.

44. Berthe, *Le Comté de Bigorre*.

45. Alain Girardot, *Le droit et la terre: Le Verdunois à la fin du Moyen Âge*, 2 vols. (Nancy: Presses Universitaires de Nancy, 1992), vol. 1, 374 and 374n.3.

46. See Danielle Anex, *Le servage au pays de Vaud XIIIᵉ–XVIᵉ siècle* (Lausanne: Bibliothèque Historique Vaudoise, 1973). For a detailed study of the various forms of *formariage*, see Pierre Petot, "Licence de formariage et formariage des serfs dans les Coutumes françaises du Moyen Âge," *Annales d'histoire du droit* 2 (1949): 199–208; Jean-Auguste Brutails, *Étude sur la condition des populations rurales du Roussillon au Moyen Âge* (Paris: Imprimerie Nationale, 1891); M. Lebon, "Textes sur le formariage en Lorraine, des origines

au début du XIIIe siècle," *Annales de l'Est* (1951); Lebon, "Le formariage en Lorraine," law diss., Université de Nancy, 1952. The data and the analyses given by historians of institutions have to be treated with prudence, since they generally tend to ignore the contexts and rely excessively on the literal meaning of the charters. In general, historians of law follow Léo Verriest in emphasizing continuity between ancient slavery and medieval dependency.

47. Clère, "Servitude et liberté," 253.

48. Michel Petitjean, Marie-Louise Marchand, and Josette Metman, *Le Coutumier bourguignon glosé (fin du XIVᵉ siècle)* (Paris: Éditions du CNRS, 1982), 259–61.

49. Robert Boutruche, *La crise d'une société: Seigneurs et paysans du Bordelais pendant la guerre de Cent Ans* (Paris: Belles Lettres, 1947), 464–68.

50. Ibid., 259–60.

51. Ibid., 466.

52. Petitjean, Marchand, and Metman, *Le Coutumier bourguignon,* 261.

53. See Gilles, *Les Coutumes de Toulouse.*

54. Petitjean, Marchand, and Metman, *Le Coutumier bourguignon,* 259.

55. Ibid.

56. Pierre de Saint-Jacob, *Documents relatifs à la communauté villageoise en Bourgogne du milieu du XVIIᵉ siècle à la Révolution* (Paris: Belles Lettres, 1962), 133–35.

57. Ibid., 139–40.

58. See Jan Rogoziński, *Power, Caste, and Law: Social Conflict in Fourteenth-Century Montpellier* (Cambridge, Mass.: Medieval Academy of America, 1982).

59. See Brian Tierney, *Religion, Law and the Growth of Constitutional Thought, 1150–1650* (Cambridge: Cambridge University Press, 1982), 30–32.

60. See J. H. Burns, *Lordship, Kingship and Empire: The Idea of Monarchy, 1400–1525* (Oxford: Clarendon Press, 1992).

61. See Jacques Krynen, "'Le mort saisit le vif': Genèse médiévale du principe de l'instantanéité de la succession royale française," *Journal des savants* (July–December 1984): 187–221.

62. Patault, *Hommes et femmes de corps,* 264.

63. Gallet, *Le bon plaisir.*

64. *La Coutume de Vaudémont,* Centre Lorrain d'Histoire du Droit 22 (Nancy: le Centre, 1970), 86–87.

65. Georges Duby, *La société aux XIᵉ et XIIᵉ siècles dans la région mâconnaise* (Paris: Armand Colin, 1953), 125n.2.

66. Manoir de Minchinhampton, c. 1200; texts published in Marjorie Chibnall, ed., *Charters and Customals of the Abbey of Holy Trinity Caen* (London: Published for the British Academy by the Oxford University Press, 1982), 61, 75, 92.

67. Felsted Manor, c. 1223–24, in ibid., 92.

68. Patault, *Hommes et femmes de corps,* 55.

69. Clère, "Servitude et liberté," 240.

70. Eleanor Searle, "Seigneurial Control of Women's Marriage: The Antecedents and Functions of Merchet in England," *Past and Present* 82 (1979): 3–43.

CHAPTER 6: THE ECCLESIASTICAL *DROIT DE CUISSAGE*

1. The classic works on marriage in canon law are: Adhémar Esmein, *Le mariage en droit canonique* (1891), 2d ed. rev., ed. Robert Ginestal and Jean Dauvillier, 2 vols. (Paris:

Recueil Sirey, 1929–35), vol. 1, 323–24; Jean Dauvillier, *Le mariage dans le droit classique de l'Église depuis le Décret de Gratien (1140) jusqu'à la mort de Clément V (1314)* (Paris: Recueil Sirey, 1933), 180–90; Jean Gaudemet, *Le mariage en Occident: Les moeurs et le droit* (Paris: Éditions du Cerf, 1987), 99–100, 139–50.

2. See Josef Benzinger, *Invectiva in Romam: Romkritik im Mittelalter vom 9. bis zum 12. Jahrhundert* (Lübeck: Mattiesen, 1968).

3. Garsias, *Tractatus de Albino et Rufino*, ed., trans., and introd. Rodney M. Thompson as *Tractatus Garsiae, or The Translation of the Relics of SS. Gold and Silver,* Textus minores in usum academicum 46 (Leiden: Brill, 1973).

4. St. Bernard, *De Consideratione*, consulted in French as *De la considération*, in Pierre Dalloz's admirable translation (Paris: Éditions du Cerf, 1986); available in English in *Saint Bernard On Consideration*, trans. George Lewis (Oxford: Clarendon Press, 1908).

5. Gautier Map [Walter Map], *De nugis curialium*, available in French as *Contes de courtisans*, trans. Marylène Pérez (Lille, n.d.), part 1, chap. 24, 53; quoted here from Map, *Courtier's Trifles*, ed. and trans. M. R. James, rev. C.N.L. Brooke and R.A.B. Mynors (Oxford: Clarendon Press, 1983), 81.

6. Jean Bodel's fable of Gombert has been published, translated, and annotated by Luciano Rossi and Richard Straub in their anthology, *Fabliaux érotiques: Textes de jongleurs des XIIᵉ et XIIIᵉ siècles,* afterword by R. Howard Bloch (Paris: LGF, 1993), 119–35. I prefer this remarkable edition to the complete (and necessary) collections cited in note 10, below.

7. Ibid., 107–17.

8. Ibid., 155–63.

9. Ibid., 263–95.

10. For a corpus of fabliaux, see Anatole de Montaiglon and Gaston Raynaud, *Recueil général et complet des fabliaux des XIIIᵉ et XIVᵉ siècles,* 6 vols. (Paris: Librairie des Bibliophiles, 1872–90); Willem Noomen and Nico van den Boogaard, *Nouveau recueil complet des fabliaux,* 8 vols. (Assen: Van Gorcum, 1983–91). For a recent bibliography of studies and individual editions, see the bibliography in Rossi and Straub, *Fabliaux érotiques,* 61–70.

11. Denis Crouzet, *Les guerriers de Dieu: La violence au temps des troubles de religion (vers 1525–vers 1610),* 2 vols. (Seyssel: Champ Vallon, 1990).

12. Pierre Jourda, "Préface," in Jourda, ed., *Conteurs français du XVIᵉ siècle* (Paris: Gallimard/Bibliothèque de la Pléiade, 1956), xix; available in English as *The One Hundred New Tales (Les cent nouvelles nouvelles),* trans. Judith Bruskin Diner, Garland Library of Medieval Literature, ser. B, vol. 30 (New York: Garland, 1990). For a study of these texts, see Roger Dubuis, *Les cent nouvelles nouvelles et la tradition de la nouvelle en France au Moyen Âge* (Grenoble: Presses Universitaires de Grenoble, 1973).

13. Pierre Champion, *Les cent nouvelles nouvelles* (Paris: E. Droz, 1928). This is the edition Pierre Jourda uses to establish his text. The question of the work's attribution remains open and has given rise to a long series of studies in the last fifty years.

14. Jourda, *Les conteurs français,* 139–40; quoted from *One Hundred New Tales,* 133–34.

15. Jourda, *Conteurs français,* 99–102; *One Hundred New Tales,* 97–99.

16. Bernardino da Siena, *Le prediche volgari*, ed. Piero Bargellini (Milan: Rizzoli, 1936), no. 20, pp. 439–40.

17. Jourda, *Conteurs français,* 146; *One Hundred New Tales,* 138–39.

18. Crouzet, *Les guerriers de Dieu,* vol. 2, 297–369.

19. See Alain Boureau, "Le Sabbat et la question scolastique de la personne," in *Le Sab-*

bat des sorciers: Actes du colloque, École Normale Supérieure, Fontenay-Saint-Cloud, novembre 1992, ed. Nicole Jacques-Chaquin and Maxime Préaud (Grenoble: Jérôme Millon, 1993), 33–46.

20. Heinrich Krämer (Henricus Institoris) and Jakob Sprenger (Jacobus Sprengerus), *Malleus maleficarum*, consulted in French as Henry Institoris and Jacques Sprenger, *Le marteau des sorcières: Malleus maleficarum*, ed. and trans. Armand Danet (Paris, 1973; Grenoble: Jérôme Millon, 1990), 315.

21. Jourda, *Conteurs français*, 209–13; *One Hundred New Tales*, 203–6, quotation on 204.

22. Karl Schmidt, *Jus Primae Noctis: Eine geschichtliche Untersuchung* (Freiburg im Breisgau: Herder, 1881), 282, 243.

23. Paris, Bibliothèque Nationale (henceforth abbreviated as B.N.), Picardy collection, tome 158, Grenier, fol. 142. Karl Schmidt has published part of the Amiens dossier and analyzed it in his *Jus Primae Noctis*, 267–82.

24. See Allen J. Frantzen, *The Literature of Penance in Anglo-Saxon England* (New Brunswick: Rutgers University Press, 1983); Cyrille Vogel, *Les "Libri poenitentiales"* (Turnhout: Brepols, 1978).

25. See James A. Brundage, *Law, Sex and Christian Society in Medieval Europe* (Chicago: University of Chicago Press, 1987).

26. See Jean-Marie Carbasse, "*Currant nudi:* La répression de l'adultère dans le Midi médiéval (XIIᵉ–XVᵉ siècles)," in *Droit, histoire et sexualité*, ed. Jacques Poumarède and Jean-Pierre Royer (Lille: Publications de l'Espace Juridique; distribution, Paris: Distique, 1987), 83–102.

27. See Brundage, *Law, Sex and Christian Society*, 490–93.

28. See *Les statuts synodaux français du XIIIᵉ siècle*, 4 vols. (Paris: Bibliothèque Nationale, 1971–), vol. 1: *Les statuts de Paris et le synodal de l'Ouest (XIIIᵉ siècle)* (1971), trans. and ed. Odette Pontal, 203.

29. Rossi and Straub, *Fabliaux érotiques*, 84–85, lines 23–24.

30. See the very firm position taken by Peter Abelard, probably around 1135, in *Sententie magistri Petri Abelardi (Sententie Hermanni)*, critical edition by Sandro Buzzetti (Florence; La Nuova Italia, 1983), 135. Nearly two centuries later the great Franciscan theologian Pierre de Jean Olivi rejected the sacramental status of marriage: see David Burr, "Olivi on Marriage: The Conservative as Prophet," *Journal of Medieval and Renaissance Studies* 2 (1972): 183–204.

31. B.N., Picardy collection, tome 158, Grenier, fol. 143.

32. The Amiens affair is exemplary of the configuration examined in chapter 7 because it provides sources from the milieu of both the royal officials (for the ordonnances) and the jurists (for the decrees of the Parlement de Paris).

33. A.N., X 1a 40, fol. 128.

34. Louis Veuillot, *Le droit du seigneur au Moyen Âge* (Paris: L. Vivès, 1854). See chapter 3, above. Curiously, this authentic document disappears in the later editions of the work.

35. B.N., Picardy collection, tome 159, Grenier, fol. 28.

36. This second text is copied on the same page of Dom Grenier's manuscript as the text from the municipal archives of Amiens.

37. See Georges Duby, ed., *Histoire de la France urbaine*, 5 vols. (Paris: Éditions du Seuil, 1980), vol. 2: *La ville médiévale, des Carolingiens à la Renaissance*, 302–9.

38. A.N., P 17, no. 358.

39. Denis de Rougemont, *L'amour et l'Occident* (Paris: Plon, 1939); available in English as *Love in the Wester World,* trans. Montgomery Belgion (New York: Harcourt, Brace, 1940).

40. See Jean-Louis Flandrin, *Un temps pour embrasser: Aux origines de la morale sexuelle occidentale (VIᵉ–XIᵉ siècle)* (Paris: Éditions du Seuil, 1983).

41. E. P. Thompson, "The Moral Economy of the English Crowd in the Eighteenth Century," *Past and Present* 50 (1971): 76–136.

42. See Grado G. Merlo, *Tensioni religiose agli inizi del Duecento* (Torre Pellice, 1989).

43. Apart from a brief allusion in St. Ambrose, discussed below, the Book of Tobias received little commentary except from the Venerable Bede. In the early twelfth century the *glossa ordinaria* gave Bede's allegorical exegesis broad circulation.

44. See Silvana Vecchio, "The Good Wife," in *A History of Women in the West,* ed. Georges Duby and Michelle Perrot, 5 vols. (Cambridge, Mass.: Belknap Press of Harvard University Press, 1992), vol. 2: *Silences of the Middle Ages,* ed. Christiane Klapisch-Zuber, 105–35. This work was originally published as *Storia delle donne in Occidente,* 5 vols. (Rome: Laterza, 1990–92). Silvana Vecchio's essay appears in French as "Sarra, l'héritage du XIIIᵉ siècle," in *Histoire des femmes en Occident,* 5 vols. (Paris: Plon, 1992), vol. 2, 118–38.

45. See Paul Deselaer, *Das Buch Tobit: Studien zu seiner Entstehung, Komposition, Theologie* (Freiburg: Universitätsverlag, 1982).

46. Guillaume de Saint-Pathus, *Vie de Saint-Louis,* ed. H.-François Delaborde (Paris: A. Picard et fils, 1899), 129. See also Vincent de Beauvais, *De eruditione filiorum nobilium,* ed. Arpad Steiner (Cambridge, Mass.: Medieval Society of America, 1938), 197–206, for his advice to the laity.

47. Tobias 3.16 and 3.18, quoted from *The Holy Bible: With the Confraternity Text* (Chicago: Good Counsel Publishing, 1963).

48. Tobias 4.11, 4.15–16, quoted from ibid.

49. See Robert Jacob, *Les époux, le seigneur et la cité: Coutumes et pratiques matrimoniales des bourgeois et paysans de France du nord au Moyen Âge* (Brussels: Facultés Universitaires Saint-Louis, 1990), 77–81.

50. Tobias 6.17, quoted from *The Holy Bible: With the Confraternity Text.* See also Vincent de Beauvais, *De eruditione filiorum nobilium.*

51. Tobias 6.18–22, quoted from *The Holy Bible: With the Confraternity Text.*

52. Tobias 10.13, quoted from ibid.

53. Jacobus de Voragine, "Second Sermon for the Second Sunday after Trinity Sunday." The history of Tobias in thirteenth-century preaching remains to be written. A few examples can be found in the sermons to lepers edited by Nicole Bériou in *Voluntate Dei leprosus: Les lépreux entre conversion et exclusion aux XIIᵉ et XIIIᵉ siècles,* ed. Nicole Bériou and François Olivier Touati (Spoleto: Centro Italiano di Studi sull'Alto Medioevo, 1991), where the emphasis is on Tobias's suffering and miraculous cure: "Iob quidem et Thobias non propter peccatum sed propter maiorem gloriam puniti sunt infirmitate corporali, unde angelus ad Thobiam XII: Quia acceptus eras Deo necesse fuit ut temptatio probaret te" (Jacques de Vitry, "Sermon aux lépreux et autres malades" [after 1228], in *Voluntate Dei leprosus,* 107); "Sicut enim felle piscis sanati sunt oculi Thobiae, ita amaritudinibus corporalis infirmitatis sanatur oculi mentis" (Jacques de Vitry, "Sermon aux lépreux II," in ibid., 125). Guilbert de Tournai speaks of the four temptations mentioned in the Tobias 12 (ibid., 137).

54. "Sponsus et sponsa, cum benedicendi sunt a sacerdote, a parentibus suis vel a paranymphis offerantur. Qui cum benedictionem accepterint, eadem nocte, pro reverentia ipsius benedictionis, in virginitate maneant." This text is published in Charles Munier, *Statuta ecclesiae antiqua* (theology diss., Strasbourg, 1958; Paris: Presses Universitaires de France, 1960), 100.

55. The canon *Sponsus et sponsa* appears in the *False Decretals* (87–88), in the *Decretals* of Burchard of Worms (9.5), in the *Decretals* of Ivo of Chartres (8.6 and 8.143) and in his *Panormia* (6.20), in the *Decretum* of Gratian (D23, chap. 33, and C30 q, chap. 5). It appears as *Ut sponsus et sponsa* in the *Decretals* of Burchard of Worms (9.7) and in the *Decretals* of Ivo of Chartres (8.143).

56. These mentions are in the penitentials of Theodore (Anglo-Saxon, late seventh century), Pseudo-Egbert (Anglo-Saxon, eighth century), Halitgaire (Frankish kingdom, early ninth century), Regino of Prüm (Germania, early tenth century), Burchard of Worms (Germania, early eleventh century).

57. "Statuit etiam regulariter, ut nubentes ob reverentiam benedictionis ante tridum coniunctionis eorum eis benedictio in basilica dareteur" (*Vita s. Cesarii* I.59, ed. Bruno Krusch, in *Monumenta Germaniae historica, Scriptores rerum merovingiarum*, vol. 1, 481, lines 15–16). This text is mentioned in Korbinian Ritzer, *Formen, Riten und religiöses Brauchtum der Eheschliessung in den christlichen Kirchen des ersten Jahrtausends* (Münster: Westfalen Aschendorffsche Verlagsbuchlandlung, 1982), 206.

58. Arbeonis Episcopi Frisingensis, *Vitae sanctorum Haimhrammi*, ed. Bruno Krusch, in *Monumenta Germaniae historica, Scriptores rerum merovingicarum*, vol. 4 (1902), 515–17, and in *Scriptores rerum Germanicarum in usum scholarum* (1920), 88–90.

59. Jonas of Orléans, *De institutione laicali*, in *P.L.*, vol. 106, col. 171: "Si qui forte sunt qui in accipiendis caste uxoribus sacerdotalem parvipendere admonitationem, prorsus necesse est ut angelicum magnipendant agnitationem."

60. Benedictus Levita's collection was studied in detail by Emil Seckel in a long series of articles in *Neues Archiv für Alterer Deutsche Geschichtskunde* between 1900 and 1917. On Seckel's death J. Junker pursued the project in two long articles in the *Zeitschrift der Savigny-Stiftung für Rechtsgeschichte: Kanonistische Abteilung* 23 (1934): 269–377; 24 (1935): 1–112.

61. Benedictus Levita, "De Benedicti levitae collectione Capitularium scripsit F. H. Knust," in *Capitularia spuria: Canones ecclesiastici: Bullae pontificium*, ed. Georg Heinrich Pertz, *Monumenta Germaniae historica, Legum*, 5 vols., vol. 2 (1837), Pars altera, 17–158: "Et biduo vel triduo orationibus vacent et castitatem custodiant, ut bonae soboles generentur, et Domino suis in actibus placeant. Taliter enim et Domino placebunt, et filios non spurios, sed legitimos atque hereditabiles generabunt."

62. "Ut sponsus et sponsa cum precibus et oblationibus a sacerdote benedicantur et legibus sponsetur ac dotetur, et a paranymphis custodiatur et publice sollemniterque accipiatur. Biduo ad triduo abstineant et doceatur eis, ut castitatem inter se custodiant, certisque temporibus nubant, ut filios non spurios, sed hereditarios Deo ac seculo generent" (Hérard de Tours, *Capitula* 89, in *P.L.*, vol. 121, col. 770).

63. Quoted in Ritzer, *Formen, Riten und religiöses Brauchtum*, 251.

64. Jean-Baptiste Molin and Protais Mutembe, *Le rituel du mariage en France du XIIe au XVIe siècle*, foreword by Pierre-Marie Gy (Paris: Beauchesne, 1974), 248.

65. "Abstinete vos hodie, et cras, et aliud cras, sicut precipit angelus Raphael Tobie" (Vatican City, Vatican Library, MS Ottobon., quoted in Ritzer, *Formen, Riten, und religiöses Brauchtum*, 193).

66. Synod of Nantes, canon 3, in *Veterum scriptorum et monumentorum historicorum, dogmaticorum, moralum, amplissima collectio,* ed. Edmond Martène, 9 vols. (Paris, 1724-33), vol. 4, 439-40.

67. For Matthieu de Vendôme's poem, see *Mathei Vindocinensis opera,* ed. Franco Munari, 3 vols. (Rome: Edizioni di Storia e Letteratura, 1977-88), vol. 2 (1982). For a Provençal translation of Matthieu edited by Julius Wollenberg, see *Archiv für das Studium der neueren Sprachen und Literaturen* 32 (1862): 337-52.

68. For an edition of the Waldensian version of the Book of Tobias with commentary, see Maria Carla Marinoni, *La versione valdese del libro di Tobia* (Fasano: Schena, 1986).

69. Arnold van Gennep, *Manuel de folklore français contemporain* (Paris: A. Picard, 1943-46), vol. 1, part 2, 554-59.

70. Jourda, *Les conteurs français,* 91; *One Hundred New Tales,* 184.

71. Quoted from *The Travels of Sir John Mandeville,* trans. and introd. C.W.R.D. Moseley (Harmondsworth: Penguin Books, 1983), 175; consulted in French as Jean de Mandeville, *Voyage autour de la terre,* trans. with commentary Christiane Deluz (Paris: Belles Lettres, 1993), chap. 31, 214-15.

72. On the notion of the *énoncé collectif,* see Alain Boureau, "Propositions pour une histoire restreinte des mentalités," *Annales, ESC* 44 (1989): 1491-1504.

73. These decrees appear in Bernard de La Roche Flavin, *Arrests notables du Parlement de Tolose* (Toulouse: R. Colomiez, 1617), 338.

74. See *Coustumier de Poictou* 4.56, cited in Maurice Lacombe, *Essai sur la coutume poitevine du mariage au début du XVe siècle d'après le vieux "Coustumier de Poictou" (1417)* (Chateauroux: Mellottée, 1910), 70.

75. Molin and Mutembe, *Le rituel du mariage,* 269.

76. Van Gennep, *Manuel de folklore français,* vol. 1, part 2, 371-72; Pierre Saintyves, *Revue anthropologique* 44 (1934): 266-96. See also *Ephemerides theologicae lovanienses: Commentarii de re theologica et canonica* 12 (1935): 673.

77. A.N., JJ 97, fol. 138r, quoted in Roger Vaultier, *Le folklore pendant la guerre de Cent ans d'après les lettres de rémission du Trésor des Chartes* (Paris: Guénégaud, 1965), 22-27.

78. Molin and Mutembe, *Le rituel du mariage,* 285.

79. *Cartulaire du prieuré de Saint-Étienne de Vignory,* ed. Jules d'Arbaumont (Langres, 1882), 84-112.

80. See Claude Michaud, *L'Église et l'argent: Les receveurs généraux du clergé de France aux XVIe et XVIIe siècles* (Paris: Fayard, 1991).

CHAPTER 7: THE POLITICS OF *CUISSAGE*

1. Saint-Lô, A.D., Manche, Fonds du Mont-Saint-Michel. This text has been published three times: in the *Mémoires de la Société des Antiquaires de Normandie,* ser. in-4°, 2: 105ff.; in Léopold Delisle, *Étude sur la condition de la classe agricole et l'état de l'agriculture en Normandie au Moyen Âge* (Evreux, 1851), facsimile reprint, 2 vols. (New York: Lenox Hill Publishing, 1978), 668-90; in the volume of documents annexed to Victor Hunger, *Histoire de Verson* (Caen: E. Brunet, 1908). Delisle's edition, which appeared sixty years before Hunger's, is still the best.

2. H. Navel, "Les Vavassories du Mont-Saint-Michel à Bretteville-sur-Odon et Verson (Calvados)," *Mémoires de la Société des Antiquaires de Normandie* 45 (1937): 137-65, published separately with the same title (Caen: Bigot, 1938).

3. Robert Carabie, *La propriété foncière dans le très ancien droit normand: XIe-XIIe siècle,* 2 vols. (Caen: R. Bigot, 1943), vol. 1: *La propriété domaniale,* 25-146.

4. Cited in Carabie, *La propriété foncière*, vol. 1, 68.

5. Guillaume de Jumièges, *Gesta Normannorum ante Rollonem* . . . *ducem* VIII.26, in *Historiae Normannorum scriptores antiqui*, ed. André Duchesne (Paris: R. Fouet, 1619), 311. See also Wace, *Roman de Rou et des ducs de Normandie*, ed. Frédéric Pluquet, 2 vols. (Rouen: E. Frère, 1827), vol. 1, 293–94; Philippe Mouskes, *Chronique rimée*, ed. Frédéric de Reiffenberg, 3 vols. (Brussels: M. Hayez, 1836–45), vol. 2, 102, lines 14,869ff.; *Chronique de Normandie*, Recueil des Historiens de la Gaule et de France (Paris, 1767), vol. 11, 329.

6. See Jean Bart, "L'imaginaire de la coutume . . . ou les tentations de l'étymologie," *Mémoires de la Société pour l'Histoire du Droit et des Institutions des Anciens Pays Bourguignons, Comtois et Romands* 40 (1983): 315–24.

7. Johannes Paponius, *Recueil d'arrests notables des cours souveraines de France* (Lyons, 1556, 1568), 717. A slightly different version can be found in Johannes Paponius, *Corpus juris Francici, seu, absolutissima collectio arrestorum sive rerum in supremis Franciae tribunalibus et parlamentis judicatarum* (Grenoble, 1624), book 22, title 9, no. 18.

8. François Ragueau, *Indices des droits royaux et seigneuriaux, des plus notable dictions, termes et phrases de l'estat* (Paris, 1580; republished 1583, 1600).

9. René Choppin, *De legibus Andium municipalibus libri III* (Paris, 1600).

10. See Robert Descimon, "La métaphore du mariage politique du roi et de la république dans la France moderne, XVe–XVIIIe siècles," *Annales, ESC* 47 (1992): 1127–47. For earlier occurrences of this image, see Philippe Buc, *L'ambiguïté du livre: Prince, pouvoir, et peuple dans les commentaires de la Bible au Moyen Âge*, foreword by Jacques Le Goff (Paris: Beauchesne, 1994), chap. 6.

11. See Sarah Hanley, *The Lit de Justice of the Kings of France: Constitutional Ideology in Legend, Ritual, and Discourse* (Princeton: Princeton University Press, 1983), consulted in French as *Le Lit de justice des rois de France: L'idéologie constitutionnelle dans la légende, le rituel et le discours*, trans. André Charpentier (Paris: Aubier, 1991).

12. Louis Servin, *Actions notables et plaidoyez de Messire Lovys Servin* (Paris: E. Richer, 1640), 730–33. Many editions of this work were published from 1601 on.

13. See Jacques Rossiaud, *La prostitution médiévale*, preface by Georges Duby (Paris: Flammarion, 1988); available in English as *Medieval Prostitution*, trans. Lydia G. Cochrane (Oxford: Blackwell, 1988); originally published as *La prostituzione nel medioevo* (Rome: Laterza, 1984).

14. See Robert Muchembled, *Le temps des supplices: De l'obéissance sous les rois absolus, XVe–XVIIIe siècles* (Paris: Armand Colin, 1992).

15. This *arrêt* is published in Servin, *Actions notables*, 733.

16. See Martine Grinberg, "Dons, prélèvements, échanges: À propos de quelques redevances seigneuriales," *Annales, ESC* 43 (1988): 1413–32; Nicole Pellegrin, *Les bachelleries: Organisations et fêtes de la jeunesse dans le Centre-Ouest, XVe–XVIIIe siècles* (Poitiers: Société des Antiquaires de l'Ouest, 1982).

17. Angelo Torre, *Il consumo di devozioni: Religione e comunità nelle campagne dell'Ancien Régime* (Venice: Marsilio, 1995). My thanks to the author for making his book available to me in manuscript.

18. See J.-L. Halperin, "Le juriste de la ville et l'homme des champs: Le *De privilegiis rusticorum* de René Choppin," *Mémoires de la Société pour l'Histoire du Droit et des Institutions des Anciens Pays Bourguignons, Comtois et Romands* 44 (1987): 147–82.

19. Ibid., 148n.3.

20. Anne Zink, *L'héritier de la maison: Géographie coutumière du Sud-Ouest de la France*

sous l'Ancien Régime (Paris: Éditions de l'École des Hautes Études en Sciences Sociales, 1993), 21.

21. For an overall view of custom, see John Gilissen, "Typologie des sources du Moyen Âge occidental," in *La coutume, Typologie des sources du Moyen Âge occidental,* 41 (Turnhout: Brepols, 1982). Gilissen gives an abundant bibliography, which is brought up to date in more recent numbers of the series.

22. Halperin, "Le juriste de la ville," 182.

23. This unpublished customal is now available in Michel Petitjean, "Un ouvrage inédit de Guy Coquille: La rédaction et le commentaire de la Coutume de Rethélois," *Mémoires de la Société pour l'Histoire du Droit et des Institutions des Anciens Pays Bourguignons, Comtois et Romands* 44 (1987): 7–99.

24. Ibid., 20.

25. François Béroalde de Verville, *Le moyen de parvenir,* ed. with notes Ilana Zinguer (Nice: Université de Nice, Centre de la Méditerranée Moderne et Contemporaine, 1985), 13–18. My thanks to Sophie Houdard for introducing me to this text.

26. Lazare Sainéan, *Problèmes littéraires du XVIᵉ siècle* (Paris: E. de Boccard, 1927), 218.

27. "There shall not a maid be married, but she shall pay to me her maidenhead ere they have it" (William Shakespeare, *Henry VI Part II,* act 4, scene 7). What Jack Cade is in fact demanding here is a merchet on the marriage of girls without specifying the origin of that right. Still, this is an important literary instance of a feudal due.

28. See W. D. Howarth, "'Droit du seigneur', Fact or Fantasy?" *Journal of European Studies* 1 (1971): 291–312.

29. See W. D. Howarth, "Cervantes and Fletcher," *Modern Language Review* 66 (1961): 563–66.

30. R. H. Bloch, "'Mieux vaut jamais que tard'," *Représentations* (autumn 1992).

31. See Georges Duby, "The Courtly Model," in *A History of Women in the West,* ed. Georges Duby and Michelle Perrot, 5 vols. (Cambridge, Mass.: Belknap Press of Harvard University Press, 1992), vol. 2, 250–66, consulted in French as "Le modèle courtois," in *Histoire des femmes dans l'Occident,* 5 vols. (Paris: Plon, 1992), vol. 2, 261–76. This work was originally published as *Storia delle donne in Occidente,* 5 vols. (Rome: Laterza, 1990).

32. Jean Chapelain, *Opuscules critiques,* ed. Alfred C. Hunter (Paris: E. Droz, 1936), 230. My thanks to Christian Jouhaud for bringing this text to my attention.

33. Ibid., 231.

34. Ibid., 232.

35. Arlette Lebigre, *Les "Grands Jours d'Auvergne": Désordres et répression au XVIIᵉ siècle* (Paris: Hachette, 1976).

36. Ibid., 48–49.

37. Ibid., 24.

38. Ibid., 25.

39. *Mémoires de Fléchier sur les Grands Jours d'Auvergne,* presented and annotated by Yves-Marie Bercé (Paris: Mercure de France, 1984).

40. Lebigre, *Les "Grands Jours,"* 32–34.

41. *Mémoires de Fléchier,* 188.

42. Ibid., 189.

43. Ibid., 190.

44. Ibid., 190–91.

45. Lebigre, *Les "Grands Jours,"* 102–6; A.N., X2 B 1268.

46. Lebigre, *Les "Grands Jours,"* 74.

47. *Mémoires de Fléchier,* 107, 303–7.

Epilogue

1. Marie-Victoire Louis, *Le droit de cuissage: France, 1860–1930* (Paris: Atelier, 1994).

2. Michelle Perrot, "Introduction," in ibid., 3.

3. See Georges Duby, "The Courtly Model," in *A History of Women in the West,* ed. Georges Duby and Michelle Perrot, 5 vols. (Cambridge, Mass.: Belknap Press of Harvard University Press, 1992), vol. 2, 250–66, quotation p. 256; consulted in French as "Le modèle courtois," in *Histoire des femmes dans l'Occident,* 5 vols. (Paris: Plon, 1992), vol. 2, 261–76. This work was originally published as *Storia delle donne in Occidente,* 5 vols. (Rome: Laterza, 1990).

4. Georges Duby, "Les 'jeunes' dans la société aristocratique dans la France du Nord-Ouest au XIIᵉ siècle," *Annales, ESC* 19 (1964): 846.

5. Jacques Rossiaud, *La prostitution médiévale* (Paris: Flammarion, 1988), 26–40. This work, originally published as *La prostituzione nel medio evo* (Rome: Laterza, 1984), is available in English as *Medieval Prostitution,* trans. Lydia G. Cochrane (Oxford: Basil Blackwell, 1988), 27–38. See also A. Porteau-Bitker, "La justice laïque et le viol au Moyen Age" *Revue historique de droit français et étranger* 3 (1988): 499–504.

6. I am borrowing this fine expression from the title of Pierre Legendre, *La passion d'être un autre: Étude pour la danse* (Paris: Seuil, 1978).

7. Alain Boureau, *La Papesse Jeanne* (Paris: Flammarion, 1988, 1993).

8. Arsenio Frugoni, *Arnaldo da Brescia: Nelle fonti del secolo XII* (1954; Turin: Einaudi, 1989), available in French as *Arnaud de Brescia dans les sources du XIIᵉ siècle,* trans. Alain Boureau (Paris: Belles Lettres, 1993); Peter Linehan, *History and the Historians of Medieval Spain* (Oxford: Clarendon Press, 1993).

9. See Roger Chartier, "Le monde comme représentation," *Annales, ESC* 44 (1989): 1505–20.

10. See Arlette Farge and Jacques Revel, *Logiques de la foule: L'affaire des enlèvements d'enfants, Paris, 1750* (Paris: Hachette, 1988), available in English as *The Rules of Rebellion: Child Abduction in Paris in 1750,* trans. Claudia Miéville (Cambridge: Polity Press, Basil Blackwell, 1991).

11. See Deirdre Wilson and Dan Sperber, *Relevance: Communication and Cognition* (Cambridge, Mass.: Harvard University Press, 1986), consulted in French as *La pertinence: Communication et cognition,* trans. Abel Gerchenfeld and Dan Sperber (Paris: Minuit, 1989).

12. Alain Boureau, *Le simple corps du roi: L'impossible sacralité des souverains français, XVᵉ–XVIIIᵉ siècle* (Paris: Éditions de Paris, 1988).

13. See Alain Boureau, "Droit et théologie au XIIIᵉ siècle," *Annales, ESC,* 47 (1992): 1113–25.

Appendix 1: A Literary Setting of Seigniorial Sexual Abuse

1. François Béroalde de Verville, "Cérémonie," in *Le moyen de parvenir,* ed. and annotated Ilana Zinguer (Nice: Université de Nice, Centre de la Méditerranée Moderne et Contemporaine, 1985), 13–18. See also chapter 7, above.

2. Saint-Maurice is the name of a cathedral; Saint-Martin de Tours, a venerable and prestigious chapter of canons, included persons of high rank.

APPENDIX 2: THE *DROIT DE CUISSAGE* IN SPAIN

1. Carlos Barros, "Rito y violacion: Derecho de pernada en la baja edad media," *Historia social* 16 (1993): 3–17.

2. Carlos Barros, *Mentalidad justiciera de los Irmandiños, siglo XV,* originally written in Galician (1988), trans. Carlos Barros (Madrid: Siglo XXI España, 1990).

3. See Peter Linehan, *History and the Historians of Medieval Spain* (Oxford: Clarendon Press, 1993), 416–17.

4. See Paul Freedman, *The Origins of Peasant Servitude in Medieval Catalonia* (Cambridge: Cambridge University Press, 1991).

5. This text is available in Jaime Vicens Vives, *Historia de los remensas en el siglo XV* (Barcelona: Imprenta Clarasó, 1945), app. 2, 352.

6. Text in Catalan edited by Eduardo Hinojosa, *El régimen señorial y la cuestión agraria en Cataluña durante la edad media* (Madrid: V. Suárez, 1905), 318. See also Hinojosa, "Existió en Cataluña el jus primae noctis?" *Annales internationales d'histoire* 2 (1902): 204–6.

7. Linehan, *History and the Historians of Medieval Spain.*

GLOSSARY

From the year 1247 to the sixteenth century the *droit de cuissage* was called by a Latin name, *cullagium* or *culagium* (French *cullage*). This word does not necessarily derive from *cul* because the term *cullagium* was attached to a number of other taxes not connected with marriage, as the term *cullage des mariages* shows. Nonetheless, the more immediate etymology became dominant, restricting the use of the word in the early modern age. When authors wanted to avoid all hint of impropriety, they used the expression *droit de noces* or one of its equivalents. As late as 1665, as we have seen in chapter 7, Esprit Fléchier adopted that solution, adding that "in former times it was not called so nicely [autrefois, on ne l'appelait pas si honnêtement]." Beginning in the sixteenth century the fable of Evenus enabled jurists to speak of *cuissage* using such terms as *marquette* and *marchet* derived from the English merchet (see chapter 5). The greatest number of new designations arose in the eighteenth century, however. The synecdoche "droit du seigneur" seems to go back no further than an anonymous theatrical work produced in 1732 (rediscovered by W. D. Howarth) that Voltaire picked up and popularized in 1762. Voltaire played a central role in this lexical history: He not only popularized the *droit de cuissage* (a term coined by Boucher d'Argis in 1755) in his *Essai sur les moeurs* (1756) but also invented the term *droit de jambage* in *Défense de mon oncle* (1767). The success of the expression *droit de cuissage* can probably be attributed to the striking contrast between "right" and *cuissage,* the concreteness but presentability of the word *cuissage,* and the fact that such a "right" could be limited in scope to a symbolic gesture of domination analogous to the act of a high personage taking responsibility for the bride of an absent sovereign. Seventeenth-century erudition seems to have produced the learned Latin expression *jus primae noctis.*

Abbaye de jeunesse   Youth abbey. See also *Bachellerie.*
Abrègement de fief   Reduction in value of a fief
Acapte   Transfer tax; right of investiture. See also *reliefs.*
Accensement   Hereditary rental contract
Adveux   See *Aveu.*
Afforage   Tax on beer and wine
Alcade   Municipal official (Spain)
Alleu   Allod (alodial); freehold (without homage)
Amobyr, amachyr   Merchet

Ancilla   Female dependent (eleventh century)
Arcia   *Corvée* to help fight fires
Arpent   Land measure unit (roughly an acre)
Arrière-fief   Fief dependent from another fief
Aveu   Statement of holdings, revenues, rights. See also *Dénombrement.*
Avocat général   Barrister of Parlement de Paris; king's representative
Bachellerie   Association of unmarried village males
Baconnel   Dues paid in pork products
Baillettes   Charter (southwest France)
Bailli, bailliage   Local go-between for lord and tenants, high royal official; district of royal domain
Banalités   Payments to lord for using his oven, mill, etc.
Bannum   Coercive power (of king, later of feudal lord)
Basoche   Law clerks
Basse justice   Powers to judge minor cases. See also *Haute justice.*
Barthinodium   Various dues
Béjaune, beiaune   Lit., young falcon; inexperienced youth; "chick"
Bibaraou   A beverage; a sort of porridge
Bibaria vini   Wine offered in ritual circumstances
Bordier   Bordar (sharecropper on newly cleared land)
Boscage   Woodcutting duties
Bourgeois, bourgeoise   Burgher; special status of townspeople in royal towns
Boyoyers   Non–house owners (Pyrenees)
Braconnage (Lat. *braconagium*)   Poaching; allegedly a metaphor for a right of defloration
Braconner   To enforce *braconnage*
Bragaris, braga   Roughly, braggarts; to brag
Brésages   Quitrent payment in grain
Breuvaigne   A drink (Normandy)
Cagots   Alleged descendants of lepers forming a low-status caste in Béarn
Cahiers de doléance   Official registers of complaints from Estates General
Calenum   A drink. See *Chaudel.*
Cambito   Exchange
Captal   Person holding lordship of La Teste (Lat. *caput*, 'head'), near Bordeaux
Casalers ceysous   Homeowners who bought their land
Casalers naturaus   Homeowners
Catel   Chattel
Cazzagio   *Cullage* (Piedmont)
Cens   Quitrent
Censier   *Terrier*, survey, list of customs, holdings
Censitaire   Person who pays a quitrent or *cens*
Champart   Fee in proportion to crop
Charriage   Cartage
Chaudel   Drink, soup (Pyrenees)
Chef   Head
Chevage   Yearly payment from an enfranchised tenant; head tax or poll tax
Chevel   Feudal right of aid for son's knighthood, daughter's marriage, ransom from imprisonment

Chrestiaas   *Cagots*
Clerc lisant   Reader (official position)
Clie   Monopoly on fish trade
Cochet, cochetus   Young cock
Cognage   *Cullage*
Coillage   *Cullage*
Coin   A die, stamp (hence related to coinage)
Colonus, coloni   Freemen farming land for rent (late Roman Empire)
Commende (en)   In trust
Commutatio   Exchange
Concage   Right to tax of one-tenth the value of cargo discharged (Bordeaux)
Conseiller   Councilor (of Parlement de Paris)
Consulats   Form of municipal government by *consuls*
Corvéable à merci   Subject to *corvées* at the lord's will
Corvée   Dues paid in labor
Coterie   Land held by cottars
Coullase   *Cullage*
Coutumal   Customal; customary (collection of customs)
Coutume   Custom; customs; customal
Coutures   Tenancies
Créance   Letter of credit; promissory note; debt
Crestadous   Cattle castrators
Cubare   To consummate (marriage)
Cugucia   *Formariage*
Cuillage   *Cuissage*. See *Cuissage, droit de*.
Cuissage, droit de   *Droit du seigneur;* alleged right of lord to lie with brides on their wed-
      ding night
Cuisse   Thigh. See also *Cuissage, droit de*.
Cullage   *Cuissage;* marital tax. Also spelled *culache; culage; culagio; culagium; culéage; cul-
      lagium.* See *Cuissage, droit de*.
Culvert   From Lat. *collibertus*, 'freedman'; ex-freedman returned to servitude; particu-
      larly harsh form of servitude
Cul   Ass
De cujus   The person in question (Roman law)
Denier   A coin worth 1/240 livre; also a way of expressing proportion (e.g., *le sixieme de-
      nier,* 'one-sixth')
Dénombrement   Statement of holdings, rights, revenues
Derecho de pernada   *Droit de cuissage* (Spain). See *Cuissage, droit de*
Deschaussage, deschaussaille   Marital payment connected with removing shoes and stock-
      ings
Dime   Tithing (lay and ecclesiastical)
Domenjadure   A noble house (Béarn)
Dominium   Property ownership; powers of justice
Donat   Voluntary dependent (of a monastery)
Douaire   Spouse's rights to husband's estate
Droictures   Marriage tax
Droit   Right; law

Droit de cuissage, de cullage, de jambage, de jurée, de/des noces/nopces, de quintaine, de relief, de suite, du meilleur cattel   See *Cullage, droit de; Cullage droit de; etc.*

Échevin   Municipal officer

Emphytéose, emphyteotes   Emphyteusis, long lease; emphyteutas, lessors (Roman law)

Enquête par tourbe   Inquiry conducted by calling assemblies, hearing witnesses

Épousailles   Troth-plighting ceremony

Extra villam   Outside the domain

Feminae (pl.)   Female dependents

Ferme   Contract; *à ferme muable,* with adjustable contract

Feu/feux allumant   Head of household; hearth

Firma de espoli forzada   Formariage

Fodero   Marital tax

Fodrum   Feudal tax to provision troops

For, fors   Custom(s), customal

Forains   Outsiders

Formariage (Lat. *foris maritagium*)   Lord's marital tax for tenant who marries out of domain

Forfuyance   Lord's right of pursuit of fleeing dependent

Fouage   Hearth tax

Fouasse   Flat bread (foccaccia)

Fuero real   Royal law (Spain)

Fougage   Hearth tax

Franc, franche   Free status; freedman, -woman

Gazaille   Pasturage privileges

Gélines   Hens

Généralité   Royal administrive district

Gens du roi   King's men

Gentilhommerie   Noble country house

Gerson   Marital tax

Glèbe   Glebe, farm, land

Greffier   Court clerk

Guare   *Gerson*

Harcèlement sexuel   Sexual harassment

Haute justice   Highest form of judicial powers

Héritage   Estate; inheritance

Homagium   Homage

Hominatio   Homage

Homines   Men, male dependents

Hominium   Fee paid to become a dependent

Homme (femme) de corps (Lat. *homo de corpore*)   Serf; bondman; personal bondage; personal and hereditary subjects with special restrictions

Intendant   Royal official

Intestia   *Mainmorte*

Ira   Anger

Jambage, droit de   Right to put a leg on the wedding bed

Jour   Land measure

Jours   Circuits of the Parlement de Paris

Jurat   Village or municipal magistrate

Jurisprudence prud'homale   Decisions rendered by the Conseil des Prud'hommes, a conciliation board for industrial disputes (early nineteenth century)

Jus cunni (Lat. *cunnum*, 'cunt')   *Droit de cuissage*. See *Cuissage, droit de*

Jus primae noctis   Right to the first night

Lande   Heath, moor

Leuga   Initial nucleus of land held by an abbey

Liber   Freeman

Licentia maritandi   Cullage

Lieutenant général   Official of royal police

Lit de justice   Official session of king's justice at the Parlement de Paris

Los   Liquid measure (Arras, 2 pints; Paris, 4 pints)

Macule   Stigma

Mainlevée   Removal of interdict; withdrawal of opposition to marry; restoration of confiscated goods

Mainmorte   Lord's rights of succession over tenants (partial or whole, with or without restrictions about who inherits)

Maire   Officer of lord who keeps order, who polices; reeve; mayor

Maître des requêtes   Court official who receives suits and petitions and passes them on

Malos usos   Bad customs (Spain)

Mancipia   Slaves

Manse   Small feudal holding (one piece of land)

Marchet, marcheta, marchetis, markette, marquete, marquettee   Merchet

Manus (Lat. for 'hand')   Holding or seizing power

Maritagium   Marital tax

Mark   A silver coin; a horse

Mazarinade   Political pamphlet (after Jules Mazarin)

Merci, à   At will

Ministeriales   Feudal officials

Moutonnage   Tax on sheep

Mutage   Shift of tenant's obligations to lord's heirs

Mutuum   At interest; loan

Noblesse de robe   Persons ennobled through governmental service; judicial posts

Noces   Wedding; wedding festivities

Notae tironianae   Ancient Roman shorthand system

Nouveaux poublants   Newcomers (Béarn)

Nuptiaticum   Marital due

Official; officialité   Judge of diocesan court; that court

Ominium   Homage

Osculum   Kiss to seal oath

Ost   Military service; men in service

Oublies   Year-end payments

Oustau   Household

Paction   Contract

Pernada   Cuissage. See also *Derecho de Pernada*.

Plein, plénier (vilain)   Full (tenant)

Porcage   Tax paid on pigs

Potestas   Power
Pourport (also *porprestures*)   Annual fee to fence in land
Prélibation   Payment for wedding snack
Prévôt   Provost (king's representative in royal territory)
Presbyterium   Sacerdotal community in the early Christian Church
Progenies   Offspring
Proprius, proper proprius homo   Serf
Quaintaine   Sporting premarital competition
Quarte   Fee proportional to harvest
Quartier   Unit of grain measure
Questal, questau   Serf
Quictaine   *Quaintaine*
Rapchat, rachat   Payment for lord's consent to marriage
Ratione dominii   Relating to dominion over land or men
Récréance   Withdrawal of opposition
Regards   Marital tax
Reliefs   Investiture fee
Remença personal   Tallage
Remences   Near-slave serfs
Remontrance   Parlement's response to royal edict listing its drawbacks
Rente   Annuity; yearly income
Res   Measure of volume (oats)
Ricorsi   Returns (Vico)
Saisine   Enjoyment of rights on land without holding proprietary rights
Schafft   Tallage
Sèche-moute   Tax on grain not milled in lord's mill
Sénéchal   Seneschal (royal officer)
Sequi ventrem   Following the womb (of servile condition)
Sergent   Official of royal police
Servicia   *Corvée*
Servitium, pl. *servitia*   A dependent's obligation(s) to his lord (*corvée*, taxes, armed service)
Servus, servi   Dependent(s); in Latin, both serf and slave
Sestier   Unit of grain measure (150–300 liters)
Sétérée   Unit of land measurement (roughly, what 1 sestier of grain will sow)
Sine licentia   Without permission
Solutio et libertas   Emancipation and liberation
Soubrette   Ladies' maid
Squat   Squatting; occupying property illegally
Sufferte   Investiture fee
Suite, droit de   Pursuit, right of
Surprestures   Feudal tax on land
Taggage   Tagging, signing graffiti
Taille   Tallage; financial aid to lord, occasional or fixed; *taille à volonté* or *aborné; taille rélle; taille personnelle; taille à miséricorde*
Tasque   Fee proportional to harvest
Tempus, ad   For a limited time

Teste   Head
Terrier   Survey of tenements. See also *Censier.*
Usuaticum   Fee paid to become a dependent
Varlet   Young village male
Villa   Country estate, domain
Vilain   Peasant
Vilainage   Tenancy
Vin de cullage (Lat. *vinum maritagii*)   Wedding wine
Vipae   Ritual bits of bread imbibed with wine
Xorquia   *Mainmorte*

CHRONOLOGICAL BIBLIOGRAPHY OF WORKS
AND DOCUMENTS RELATING TO THE
DROIT DE CUISSAGE

This bibliography refers only to the *droit de cuissage* in the strict—that is, the feudal—sense. The only exceptions—Vincent de Beauvais (1257), John Mandeville (1356), López de Gómara (1552), Montaigne (1588)—are for figures who played a major role in the history of the feudal myth. The order of presentation permits a chronological reconstitution of the legend. At the same time it neutralizes the difference among primary sources, secondary analyses, and artistic elaborations precisely because, as I hope I have demonstrated, that deceptive distinction is an integral part of the myth. An individual author can be located by consulting the index.

1247   Estout de Goz. "La chanson des vilains de Verson." In a fragment of the cartulary of the Abbey of Mont-Saint-Michel, Saint-Lô, Archives Départementales de la Manche, Fonds du Mont-Saint-Michel. The text of the "Chanson" has been published three times: by Amédée Louis Léchaudé d'Anisy in *Mémoires de la Société des Antiquaires de Normandie*, série in-4°, 2:105ff.; by Léopold Delisle, in *Étude sur la condition de la classe agricole et l'état de l'agriculture en Normandie au Moyen Âge* (1851), facsimile reprint, 2 vols. (New York: Lenox Hill Publishing, 1978), 668–90; and by Victor Hunger, in *Histoire de Verson* (Caen: E. Brunet, 1908), supplementary volume of documents.

1257–58   Vincent de Beauvais. *Speculum historiale*. Part 1, chap. 88.

1356   John Mandeville. *Itinerarium (Travels)*. This text, originally written in Romance, had a number of translations, with variants, in the Middle Ages. See *Voyage autour de la terre*, trans. Christiane Deluz (Paris: Belles Lettres, 1993), chap. 31, pp. 214–15. For a modern English version, see *The Travels of Sir John Mandeville*, trans. with introd. C.W.R.D. Moseley (Harmondsworth: Penguin, 1983).

1419   Seigneur de La Rivière-Bourdet. *Aveu et dénombrement*. Paris, Archives Nationales, P 305, no. 38. Published, in part, in Delisle, *Étude sur la condition* (1851), p. 69.

1462 (probable date)   *Les cent nouvelles nouvelles*, 32d novella. See the edition by Pierre Jourda in *Conteurs français du XVIᵉ siècle* (Paris: Gallimard, 1956), pp. 139–46. Available in English as *The One Hundred New Tales*, trans. Judith Bruskin Diner (New York: Garland, 1990).

1482   Catalonian seigniorial declarations. Published in Eduardo Hinojosa, *El régimen señoral y la cuestión agraria en Cataluña durante la edad media* (Madrid: V. Suárez, 1905), p. 318.

1486　Ferdinand the Catholic (Ferdinand II of Castile). *Sentencia arbitral.* First published in *Constitutions y altres drets de Cathalunya, compilats en virtut de cap. de Cort XXIIII de las Corts per la S. C. Y Reyal Majestat del rey Don Philip nostre senyor, celaebrados en la vila de Montso any 1585* (Barcelona, 1588), vol. 1. Among modern editions, see Jaime Vicens Vives, *Historia de los remensas en el siglo XV* (Barcelona: Clarasó, 1945), app. 2, p. 352.

1507　"Aveu et dénombrement du seigneur de Rambures." In Alexandre Bouthors, ed., *Les coutumes locales du bailliage d'Amiens rédigées en 1507* (Amiens, 1845–53), vol. 1, p. 481.

1526　Hector Boece (Boethius). *Scotorum historiae ab illius gentis origine.* Paris, 1526. Book 3, fol. 36r. This work is available in English in a modern edition: *The Chronicles of Scotland,* edited in continuation of the work of the late Walter Seton by R. W. Chambers and Edith C. Batho, 2 vols. (Edinburgh: Blackwood, 1938–41).

1538　"Aveu et dénombrement du seigneur de Bizanos." Pau, Archives Départementales des Pyrénées-Atlantiques, B 834 (document dated 1538). Published in part in *Les Fors de Béarn,* ed. Adolphe Mazure and Jules Hatoulet (1841), p. 172.

1538　"Aveu et dénombrement du seigneur de Louvie-Soubiron." Archives Départementales des Pyrénées-Atlantiques, B 850. Published in part in Mazure and Hatoulet, *Les Fors de Béarn* (1841), p. 172.

1551　Nicolas Boyer (de Bohier). *Decisiones supremi senatus Burdegalensis.* Lyons, 1551; Geneva, 1690. Decision 297, no. 17.

1552　Francisco López de Gómara. *La istoria de las Indias y conquista de México.* Zaragosa: A. Millan, 1552. A modern Spanish edition was published in Madrid (1979), p. 74. For a contemporary French translation, see *Histoire géneralle des Indes Occidentales et terres neuves,* trans. Martin Fumée (Paris: M. Sonnius, 1569), p. 122a.

1556　Johannes Paponius (Jean Papon). *Recueil d'arrests notables des cours souveraines de France.* Lyons, 1556, 1568. p. 717. A somewhat different version appears in Paponius, *Corpus juris Francici, seu absolutissima collectio Arrestorum sive rerum in supremis Franciae tribunalibus et parlamentis judicatarum* (Grenoble, 1624), book 22, title 9, note 18.

1557　Antoine Du Verdier, sieur de Vauprivaz. *Les diverses leçons.* Lyons, 1580. p. 96.

1580　François Ragueau. *Indice des droits royaux et seigneuriaux, des plus notables dictions, termes et phrases de l'estat.* Paris, 1580; reprinted 1583, 1600.

1582　George Buchanan. *Rerum scoticarum historia.* Edinburgh, 1582. Book 4, fol. 31v; book 7, fol. 62v. This work was published in English as *The History of Scotland* (London: Edw. Jones for Awnsham Churchill, 1690).

1588　Michel de Montaigne. *Les essais.* Bordeaux, 1580; Paris, 1588, 1592. Book 1, essay 23. The text on *cuissage* among the Indians first appears in the second version, published in 1588. For a modern French edition, see *Les essais de Michel de Montaigne,* ed. Pierre Villey, rev. V.-L. Saulnier (Paris: Presses Universitaires de France, 1965), p. 112. Montaigne's *Essays* are available in several English translations.

1590–92　William Shakespeare. *Henry VI, Part Two.* Act 4, scene 7.

1597　Sir John Skene, Lord Curriehill. *De verborum significatione: The exposition of the termes and difficill wordes, conteined in the foure buikes of Regiam Majestatem.* In *The Laws and Actes of Parliament* (Edinburgh: Robert Waldegrave, 1597).

1598　Camillus Borrellus d'Oliveto (Camillo Borrello). *Consiliorum, sive contro-*

versiarum forensium centuria prima. Venice: J. Guerilium, 1598. *Consilium* 1, note 150, fol. 6v.

1600   René Choppin. *De legibus Andium municipalibus libri III*. Paris, 1600. Book 1, chap. 31, note 8, p. 269.

1601   Louis Servin. *Actions notables et plaidoyez de Messire Lovys Servin*. Paris: E. Richter, 1640. pp. 730–33. Many other editions were published.

1607   Simon d'Olive, sieur de Mesnil. *Œuvres*. Lyons, 1607. Book 2, chap. 1, p. 149. Toulouse, 1639. p. 155.

1610   Bonifacio Vannozzi. *Della suppellettile degli avvertimenti politici, morali e christiani*. Bologna: eredi di G. Rossi, 1609–13. Vol. 2 (1610), p. 253.

1617   Miguel de Cervantès. *Trabajos de Persiles y Sigismunda* (novel). See the modern edition by Rodolfo Scevill and Edolfo Bonilla (Madrid: B. Rodríguez, 1914), pp. 85–86. Available in English as *The Trials of Persiles and Sigismunda: A Northern Story*, trans. Celia Richmond Weller and Clark A. Colahan (Berkeley: University of California Press, 1989).

1617   Bernard de La Roche Flavin. *Arrests notables du Parlement de Tolose*. Toulouse: R. Colomiez, 1617. p. 378.

1619   John Fletcher and Philip Massinger. *The Custom of the Country* (comedy).

1621   Bernard Automne. *Commentaire sur les coutumes géneralles de la ville de Bourdeaus et pays Bourdelois*. Bordeaux, 1621. p. 477.

c. 1630   Jean de Gaufreteau. *Chronique bordelaise*. Jules Delpit, ed., 2 vols. Bordeaux: G. Gounouilhou, 1876–78. Vol. 2, pp. 46–47.

1637   Louis Charondas Le Caron. *Responses et décisions du droit français, confirmées par arrests des cours souveraines de ce Royaume et autres*. Paris, 1637. Book 7, response 79, p. 279.

1646   Jean Chapelain. "De la lecture des vieux romans." In Chapelain, *Opuscules critiques*, ed. Alfred C. Hunter (Paris: E. Droz, 1936), p. 230.

1650   Johannes Limnaeus. *Tomus quartus juris publici Imperii Romano-Germanici, additionum ad priores primus*. Strasbourg, 1650. Vol. 4, chap. 7, p. 603.

1658   Nicolas Henel. *Otium Wratislawiense, hic est variarum observationum ac commemorationum liber*. Jena, 1658. Chap. 47, p. 401.

1660   Antoine Despeisses. *Des droits seigneuriaux*. In Despeisses, *Œuvres* (Paris, 1660; other editions 1685, 1750), vol. 3, title 6.

1665   Esprit Fléchier. *Mémoires de Fléchier sur les Grands-Jours d'Auvergne*. This text was not published until the nineteenth century, when it was edited first by Benoît Gonod (Paris: Porque, 1844), then by Pierre-Adolphe Chéruel (Paris: Hachette, 1856). See the recent edition by Yves-Marie Bercé (Paris: Mercure de France, 1984).

1666   Girolamo Ghilini. *Annali di Alesssandria*. Milan: Gioseffo Morelli, 1666. See the edition by Giovanni Jachino (Alessandria: Società Poligrafico, 1903–10), vol. 1 (1903), pp. 204–5.

1668   Henri Le Bret. *Histoire de la ville de Montauban*. Montauban: S. Dubois, 1668. See also Le Bret, *Histoire de Montauban*, new ed., revised and annotated after the original documents by Abbé Marcellin and Gabriel Ruck (Montauban: Rethoré, 1841), pp. 58–59.

1674   "Aveu et dénombrement du seigneur de Bizanos." Archives Départementales des Pyrénées-Atlantiques, B 877, published in part in Mazure and Hatoulet, *Les Fors de Béarn* (1841), p. 172.

1675   "De Sancto Forannano." In *Acta sanctorum* (Antwerp, 1675), *Aprilis tomus III*, pp. 821–22 (for the Bollandists' annotations).

1678   Charles du Fresne, sieur Du Cange. Entries for "bathinodium," "braconagium," "marcheta" in *Glossarium ad scriptores mediae et infimae latinitatis*. 3 vols. Paris: L. Billaine, 1678; enlarged editions, 1733 and 1840–48.

1688   "De Sancta Margarita Scotiae Regina." In *Acta sanctorum* (Antwerp, 1688), *Iunii tomus II*, 1698 ed., pp. 320–40 (for the Bollandists' annotations).

1689   Julien Brodeau. *Coustume de la Prévosté et Vicomté de Paris, commentée par feu Maistre Julien Brodeau*. 2d ed. Paris, 1689. Title 1, *arrêt* 37, note 11, p. 273.

1695   Mattheus Smallegange. *Nieuwe Cronyk van Zeeland, eerste deel, vervattende de voor desen uitgegeven Cronyken van de Heeren Jacobus Eyndius, en Johan Reygersberg, veel vermeerdet outrent deses Landschaps Oudheden, en Herkomsten*. Middleburg: J. Meertens, 1695. p. 621.

1697   Pierre Bayle. Entry for "Sixte IV," in *Dictionnaire historique et critique*. 2 vols. Rotterdam: R. Leers, 1679.

1697   Adriaan Pars. *Catti Aborigines Batavorum, dat is De Katten de voorouders der Batavieren, ofte De twee Katwijken, aan See en aan de Rijn*. Leiden: J. du Vivié, 1697. The work was republished, ed. Pieter van der Schelling (Leiden: J. A. Langerak, 1745).

1699   Charles Dufresny. *La noce interrompue* (comedy). Paris: Pierre Ribou, 1699.

1699   Eusèbe de Laurière. *Glossaire du droit français*. Paris, 1699. Vol. 1, p. 307. The work was republished, ed. François Ragueau, 2 vols. (Paris, 1704).

1708   Barthélemy Auzanet. *Œuvres . . . contenant ses notes sur la coutume de Paris*. Paris, 1708. p. 5.

1715   Charles Johnson. *The Country Lasses, or, The Custom of the Manor* (play). London: J. Tonson, 1732.

1717   Matheus Gargon. *Walchersche Arkadia*. 2 vols. Leiden, 1715–17. Vol. 2, p. 221.

1717   Nicolaus Hieronymus Gundling. *Gundlingiana: Darinnen allerhand zur Jurisprudentz, Philosophie, Historie, Critic, Litteratur*. 9 vols. Halle: Renger, 1715–29. Vol. (1717), p. 503.

1720   Johann Georg Keyssler. *Antiquitates selectae septentrionales et celticae*. Hannover: Nicolas Foerster, 1720. p. 484.

1726   Ernst Joachim von Westphalen. *De consuetudine ex sacco et libro*. Leipzig, 1726. pp. 37–40.

1727   Pieter van der Schelling. *Hollands Tiend-Regt, of Verhandeling van het Reft tot de Tienden, toekomende aan de Graafelykheid, en he Heerelykheden van Holland, en Westvriesland*. 2 vols. Rotterdam: P. Losel, 1727. Vol. 1, pp. 142–50.

1732   Anonymous. *Le droit du seigneur* (play). Paris, Bibliothèque Nationale, MS. fr. 9295.

1733   Charles du Fresne, sieur Du Cange. Entry for "cullagium," in *Glossarium* (1678). Republished by the Benedictines of Saint-Maur (Paris, 1733).

1735   Louis de Boissy. *Le droit du seigneur ou Le mari retrouvé et la femme fidèle* (play). Paris, 1735.

1745   François de Boutaric. *Traité des droits seigneuriaux, et des matières féodales*. Toulouse, 1775. pp. 650–54.

1745   Gerard van Loon. *Beschryving der Aloude Regeeringwyze van Holland*. 5 vols. in 3. Leiden: P. Vander Eyk, 1744–50. Vol. 1 (1745), pp. 158–68.

1748   Christian Grupen. *De uxore theotisca (Von der deutschen Frau)*. Göttingen: J. W. Schmidt, 1748. Chap. 1.

1753   Johann Conrad Füssli. "Erörterung der Frage, ob der Meyer zu Mauer in der Grafschaft Greifensee das recht gehabt habe, mit seiner Hofjünger Bräuten die erste Nacht zu Bett zu gehen." *Hamburger Magazin* 12 (1753): 154–73.

1754, 1755   André Boucher d'Argis. Entries for "cuissage" and "droits abusifs" in *Encyclopédie ou Dictionnaire raisonné des sciences, des arts et des métiers, par une société de gens de lettres. Mis en ordre et publié par M. Diderot de l'Académie royale des sciences et des belles lettres de Prusse, et quant à la partie mathématique par M. D'Alembert de l'Académie*. Paris. Vol. 4 (1754), p. 548; vol. 5 (1755), p. 142.

1756   Voltaire. *Essai sur les mœurs et l'esprit des nations*. Ed. René Pomeau. Paris: Garnier, 1963. Vol. 1, chap. 52, p. 543.

1761   Heinrich Ernst Kestner. *Dissertatio juridica de jure connagii (Vom Recht der Jungferschafft)*. Jena: Heller, 1761.

1762   Germain-François Poullain de Saint-Foix. *Essais historiques sur Paris*. 3d ed. 4 vols. Paris, 1762–63. Vol. 2 (1762), p. 172.

1763   Voltaire. *Le droit du seigneur* (play). Geneva: Les Frères associés, 1763. First performed in 1762.

1763   P.J.B. Nougaret. *Le droit du seigneur* (play). Paris, 1763.

1764   Voltaire. Entries for "cuissage" and "taxes" in *Dictionnaire philosophique*. In Voltaire, *Œuvres complètes*, 52 vols. (Paris: Garnier), vol. 18 (1878), p. 299; vol. 20 (1879), pp. 488–89.

1765   François de Jaucourt. Entry for "marchet" in Diderot, *Encyclopédie*. Vol. 10 (1765), p. 89.

1765   Joseph Renauldon. *Traité historique et pratique des droits seigneuriaux*. Paris: Despilly, 1765. Book 5, chap. 10, p. 450.

1765–69   William Blackstone. *Commentaries on the Laws of England*. 4 vols. Oxford: Clarendon Press, 1765–69. Vol. 2 (1770), p. 83. Available in facsimile reprint, 4 vols. (Chicago: University of Chicago Press, 1979).

1766   David Hoüard. *Anciennes lois des Français, conservées dans les coutumes anglaises*. 2 vols. Rouen: Richard Lallemant, 1766. Vol. 1, p. 332.

1766   Dom Pierre Carpentier. Entries for "bannum," "calenum," "cochetum," "culagium," "nuptiaticum," "vinum maritagii" in *Glossarium novum ad scriptores medii aevi, cum latinos tum gallicos, seu Supplementum ad auctiorem Glossarii Cangiani editionem*. 4 vols. Paris, 1766. A supplement to the 1678 and 1733 editions of Du Cange, *Glossarium*.

1767   Voltaire. *La défense de mon oncle*. Ed. José-Michel Moureaux. Vol. 64 of Voltaire, *Œuvres complètes* (Oxford: Voltaire Foundation, 1984), p. 200.

1768   Sir John Macpherson. "Of the Marchetae Mulierum." In *Critical Dissertations on the Origin, Antiquities, Language, Government, Manners and Religion of the Ancient Caledonians, Their Posterity the Picts and the British and Irish Scots*. London: T. Becket and P. A. De Hondt; Dublin: B. Grierson, 1768.

1772   "Dissertation sur l'établissement de l'abbaye de Saint-Claude, ses chroniques, ses légendes, ses chartes, ses usurpations et sur les droits des habitants de cette terre." In *Collection des mémoires présentés au Conseil du Roi par les habitans du Mont-Jura, et le chapitre de Saint-Claude, avec l'arrêt rendu par ce tribunal in 1772* (Neufchâtel, 1772).

1776 Johann Voet. *Commentarius ad Pandectas.* 6 vols. Halle: I. I. Beyerus and I. I. Curtius, 1776–80. Vol. 1.

1776 Sir David Dalrymple, Lord Hailes. "Of the Law of Evenus and the Maercheta Mulierum." In *Annals of Scotland* (Edinburgh, 1776), vol. 1, app. 1.

1778 Willliam Kenrick. *The Lady of the Manor* (comic opera). London: E. and C. Dilly, 1778.

1780 Friedrich Christoph Jonathan Fischer. *Über die Probenächte der deutschen Bauermädchen.* Berlin: Decker, 1780. Published in French translation as *Les nuits d'épreuve des villageoises allemandes avant le mariage: Dissertation sur un usage singulier* (Paris: J. Gay, 1861; Brussels: Gay et Doucé, 1877).

1783 Desfontaines (François-Georges Fouques). *Le droit du seigneur* (comedy). Paris: R.-C. Ballard, 1783. Performed in Paris, 1772.

1784 Pierre Augustin Caron de Beaumarchais. *Le mariage de Figaro ou la folle journée.* Performed at the Comédie Française in 1781; text completed in 1784.

1785 Antoine de Cathala-Coture. *Histoire politique, ecclésiastique et littéraire du Quercy.* 3 vols. Paris and Montauban: P.-T. Cazaméa, 1785. Vol. 1. This work was published some time after Cathala-Coture's death in 1724.

c. 1785 Jean-Baptiste Lacurne de Sainte-Palaye. *Dictionnaire historique de l'ancien langage françois, ou Glossaire de la langue françoise depuis son origine jusqu'au siècle de Louis XIV.* 10 vols. Niort: L. Favre, 1875–82. Vol. 4 (1876), pp. 334–35.

1786 Wolfgang Amadeus Mozart. *Le nozze di Figaro.* Libretto by Lorenzo da Ponte after Beaumarchais (1784). The opera was first performed in Vienna.

1786 Giulio Cesare Cordara. *Il fodero o sia il jus sulle spose degli antichi signori, sulla fondazione di Nizza della Paglia, poema di Colombo Giulio.* Nizza della Paglia and Paris, 1786.

1789 *Cahier de doléances* of Sénargent (now in the department of Doubs). Besançon, Archives Départementales du Doubs, B 7901–8. Quoted in Robert Jouvenot, "Mainmortable ou pas, mainmortables quand même," *Mémoires de la Société pour l'Histoire du Droit et des Institutions des Anciens Pays Bourguignons, Comtois et Romands* 32 (1973–77): 272.

1790 Anonymous. *Le droit de jambage ou le droit des anciens seigneurs sur les nouvelles mariées.* Paris: Defer Demaisonneuve; Nantes: Louis, 1790. A translation of "Colombo Giulio" (Cordara), *Il fodero* (1786).

1791 Jacques Antoine Dulaure. *Histoire critique de la noblesse depuis le commencement de la monarchie jusqu'à nos jours.* Paris: Gullot, 1791.

1791 *Le vasselage ou Droit des anciens seigneurs sur les nouvelles épousées* (satirical-comic poem). Paris, 1791. A translation of Cordara, *Il fodero* (1786).

1791 Nicolas Restif de la Bretonne. "Sanclaudette soumise au droit de jambage-prélibation." In *L'année des dames nationales* (Paris, 1791), pp. 711–19.

1794 Thomas Astle. "On the Tenures, Customs, etc., of his Manor of Great Tey: A Letter Read in the Society of Antiquaries of London, May 22, 1794." *Archaeologia* 12 (1812): 25–37.

1795 August Friedrich Wilhelm Crome. *Die Staatsverwaltung von Toskana unter der Regierung seiner königlichen Majestät Leopold II.* 3 vols. Leipzig, 1795–97. Vol. 1 (1795), p. vi.

1796–98 Wilhelm Danz. *Handbuch des heutigen deutschen Privatrechts nach dem Systeme des Herrn Hofraths Runde.* 4 vols. Stuttgart: F. C. Löflond, 1796–98; Schweinfurt, 1801. Vol. 6, p. 45.

1811   Davide Winspeare. *Storia degli abusi feodali.* Naples, 1811. pp. 130–33. Available in a reprint of 2d ed. (Bologna: Forni, 1967).

1812   Jean Florimond de Saint-Amans. *Voyage agricole, botanique et pittoresque dans une partie des Landes de Lot-et-Garonne et de celles de la Gironde.* Vol. 18 (1812) of Conrad Malte-Brun, ed., *Annales des voyages, de la géographie et de l'histoire,* 24 vols. (Paris: F. Buisson, 1809–14).

1813   François Adrien Boieldieu. *Le nouveau seigneur de village* (comic opera). Libretto by Auguste Creuzé de Lesser and Jean-François Roger. Paris: Barba, 1815. Performed in Paris, 1813.

1817   Jean Joseph Raepsaet. *Les droits du seigneur: Recherches sur l'origine et la nature des droits connus anciennement sous les noms de droits des premières nuits, de markette, d'afforage, marcheta, maritagium et bumede.* Ghent, 1817. This text was republished posthumously in Raepsaet, *Œuvres complètes,* 6 vols. (Mons: Leroux, 1838–40), vol. 1, pp. 199–229. An identical edition was published in Rouen (1877).

1819   Jacques Collin de Plancy. *Dictionnaire féodal, ou Recherches et anecdotes sur les droits féodaux.* 2 vols. Paris: Foulon, 1819.

1820   Jacques Collin de Plancy. *Les regrets féodaux.*

1820   Jacques Saint-Albin (pseudonym of Jacques Collin de Plancy). *Le droit du seigneur, ou la fondation de Nice dans le haut Montferrat, aventure du XIIIᵉ siècle, traduit librement du Fodero de Jules Colomb, avec l'histoire de Monseigneur Le Béjaune, et un grand nombre d'anecdotes sur le droit de cuissage et sur les variétés de ce privilège.* Paris: Th. Grandin, 1820. A translation of Cordara, *Il fodero* (1786).

1821   Jacques Collin de Plancy. "Une chanson; les gémissements" (described as a "poème dialogué"). Paris, 1821.

1822   André Miot. *Histoire d'Hérodote* (described as a new translation). Paris: F. Didot père et fils, 1822. p. 217n.61.

1823   Eugène Allent (pseudonym of Jacques Collin de Plancy). *Abelina, nouvelle historique du XIIIᵉ siècle, suivie des Aventures de M. Le Béjaune, et d'anecdotes et recherches sur le droit de cuissage.* Paris: E. Grandin, 1823.

1823   Paul Louis Courier. *Gazette de village* (political pamphlet). Brussels: Demat, 1823. See also Courier, *Œuvres complètes* (Paris, 1956), p. 186.

1825   John Anderson. "Enquiry into the origin of the Mercheta Mulierum, a letter from Edinburgh 13ᵗʰ December 1825." *Transactions of the Society of Antiquaries of Scotland* 3 (1831): 56–73.

1826   Johann Philipp Gustav Ewers. *Das älteste Recht der Russen.* Dorpat: A. Sticinsky, 1826. pp. 71–75.

1827   Sir Walter Scott. *The Fair Maid of Perth.* London: 1827.

1828   Jakob Grimm, *Deutsche Rechts alterthümer.* Göttingen: Dieterich, 1828. See under 1887 for Jules Michelet's adaptation of this work in French.

1829   Ferdinand Langlé and Émile Morice. "Le droit de nopçage." In *L'historial du jongleur, chroniques et légendes françaises* (Paris: F. Didot, 1829).

1831   François-René de Chateaubriand. *Analyse raisonnée de l'histoire de France.* In *Œuvres complètes,* 28 vols. (Paris: Ladvocat, 1825–31), vol. 5.

1837   Jules Michelet. *Les origines du droit français cherchées dans les symboles et les formules du droit universel.* Paris, 1837. Republished in Michelet, *Œuvres complètes,* ed. Paul Viallaneix (Paris: Flammarion, 1971–), vol. 3, pp. 603–85.

1838   Johan Kaspar Bluntschli. *Staats- und Rechtsgeschichte der Stadt und Landschaft Zürich.* 2 vols. Zürich: Orell Füssli, 1838–39. Vol. 1 (1838), p. 190.

1839   *La Jacquerie.* Opera based on Langlé and Morice, "Le droit de nopçage" (1829).

1840   Gustave Brunet. *Notices et extraits de quelques ouvrages écrits en patois du Midi de la France.* Paris: Leleux, 1840. p. 172.

1841   *Les Fors de Béarn: Législation inédite du XIᵉ au XVᵉ siècle avec traduction en regard, notes et introduction par MM. A. Mazure et J. Hatoulet.* Pau: E. Vignancour, and Paris, n.d. [1841]. p. 171n.A.

1841   Republication of Le Bret, *Histoire de Montauban* (1668), with notes.

1841–48   Republication of Du Cange, *Glossarium* (1678). Ed. G.A.L. Henschel, incorporating the additions of the 1733 edition and Dom Carpentier's *Supplément* (1766). 7 vols. Paris: Firmin Didot, 1840–50.

1842   George P. R. James. *The Jacquerie, or The Lady and the Page.* (novel). London: A. and W. Galignani, 1842.

1843   Georg Friedrich Kolb. *Geschichte der Menschheit und der Kultur.* 2 vols. Pforzheim: D. Finck, 1843. Vol. 2, p. 72.

1844–45   Louis-Hector Chaudru de Raynal. *Histoire du Berry depuis les temps les plus anciens jusqu'en 1789.* 3 vols. Bourges: Vermeil, 1844–45. Vol. 2, pp. 203–10.

1845, 1853   Alexandre Bouthors. *Les Coutumes locales du bailliage d'Amiens, rédigées en 1507.* 2 vols. Amiens, 1845–53.

1846   Auguste Cassany-Mazet. *Annales de Villeneuve-sur-Lot et de son arrondissement.* Agen: P. Noubel, 1846.

1846   Antoine Masson. Review of Bouthors, *Coutumes locales* (1845). *L'Investigateur,* 2d ser., 6 (1846): 378–83.

1849–56   Eugène Sue. *La coquille du pèlerin ou Fergan le carrier* and *Li trépied de fer* (novels). Vols. 6 (1849) and 8 (1856) of *Les mystères du peuple,* 16 vols. (Paris: Administration de Librairie, 1849–57).

1850   Charles Fellens. *La féodalité ou les droits du seigneur: Événements mystérieux, lugubres, scandaleux, exactions, despotisme, libertinage de la noblesse et du clergé, suivis de la marche et de la décadence de la féodalité depuis le Moyen Âge jusqu'à nos jours* (novel). Paris, 1850. This work was translated into German (Weimar, 1851).

1851   Léopold Delisle. *Études sur la condition de la classe agricole et l'état de l'agriculture en Normandie au Moyen Âge.* Évreux, 1851.

1851   Gustave Bascle de Lagrèze. *Le Trésor de Pau: Archives du château d'Henri IV.* Pau, 1851. pp. 70 and 156.

1851   Karl Weinhold. *Die deutschen Frauen in dem Mittelalter.* Weimar: Voigt, 1851. pp. 194–95.

1853   Baron Jean-César Chaudruc de Crazannes. "Observations sur le droit de monnayage des abbés de Montauriol." *Revue de numismatique* (1853): 140–46.

1853   George R. Corner. *On the Custom of Borough English, as Existing in the County of Sussex.* London: 1853. pp. 8–10.

1854   Delacour (Alfred Lartigue) and Adolphe Jaime. *Les noces de Merluchet* (play). Published in *Le magasin théâtral illustré,* 1854.

1854   "Rapport sur un ouvrage de M. Bouthors, greffier en chef de la cour impériale, intitulé *Coutumes locales du baillage d'Amiens* par M. Dupin." *Séances et travaux de l'Académie des Sciences Morales et Politiques*, 3d ser., 8 (1854): 117–41.

1854   Jules Berger de Xivrey. "Rapport fait à l'Académie des Inscriptions et Belles-Lettres au nom de la Commission des Antiquaires de France par M. Berger de Xivrey lu dans la séance annuelle du vendredi 18 août." *Séances annuelles de l'Académie des Inscriptions et Belles-Lettres* (1854): 24–25.

1854   Louis Alloury. Article in *Journal des débats*, 2 May 1854.

1854   Louis Veuillot. *Le droit du seigneur au Moyen Âge*. Paris: L. Vivès, 1854. Enlarged ed. (Paris: V. Palmé, 1871). See also Veuillot, *Œuvres complètes*, 39 vols. (Paris: P. Lethielleux, 1924–), ser. 1: "Œuvres Diverses," vol. 6 (1925).

1854   Gustave Bascle de Lagrèze. "Le droit du seigneur." *Le droit*, 23 July 1854. Republished as *Essai sur le droit du seigneur à l'occasion de la controverse entre M. Dupin aîné et M. Louis Veuillot* (Paris, 1855).

1855   Victor Vallein. *Le Moyen Âge, ou, Aperçu de la condition des populations, principalement dans les XIe, XIIe, et XIIIe siècles*. Saintes: Z. Lacroix, 1855. pp. 208–29.

1855   Henri Martin. *Histoire de France*. 17 vols. Paris: Furne, 1854–70. Vol. 5 (1855), p. 568.

1856   Joseph Eugène Bonnemère. *Histoire des paysans depuis la fin du Moyen Âge jusqu'à nos jours, 1200–1850*. 2 vols. Paris: F. Chamerot, 1856. Vol. 1, p. 58.

1857   Jules Delpit. *Réponse d'un campagnard à un Parisien, ou Réfutation du livre de M. Veuillot sur "le droit du seigneur."* Paris, 1857.

1857   Charles de Robillard de Beaurepaire. "Charte portant abolition du droit de 'culagium' dans le fief de Pierrecourt." *Bibliothèque de l'École des Chartes*, 18th year, 4th ser., 3 (1857): 167–68.

1858   Louis-Firmin Lafferière. *Histoire du droit français*. 6 vols. Paris: Cotillon, 1852–58. Vol. 5: *Coutumes de France dans les diverses provinces*, p. 454.

1858   Eduard Osenbrüggen. *Deutsche Rechtsalterthümer aus der Schweiz*. Zürich: Meyer and Zeller, 1858. Chap. 12: "Das jus primae noctis."

1859   *Les droits du seigneur, ou Un drame à Jersey* (play). Adaptation for the stage of Sue, *La coquille du pèlerin, ou Fergan le carrier* (1849) and *Li trépied de fer* (1856).

1859   Charles Dickens. *A Tale of Two Cities* (novel). London: Chapman and Hall, 1859.

1859   Luigi Cibrario. *Della economia politica del medio evo: Libri III, che trattano della sua condizione politica, morale, economica*. Turin: Giuseppe Bocca, 1839. Fourth ed. available in French as *Économie politique du Moyen Âge*, trans. and ed. M. Barneaud, 2 vols. (Paris: Guillaumin, 1859), vol. 1, p. 38.

1860   John Retcliffe (pseudonym for Hermann Ottomar Freidrich). *Villafranca* (historical novel). Berlin, 1860. pp. 47–105.

1861   François Laurent. *Études sur l'histoire de l'humanité*. Brussels: Méline, Cans, 1861. Vol. 7: *La féodalité et l'Église*, p. 57.

1861   Jules Pinard. "Études sur les moeurs et les coutumes féodales du Béarn." *Revue des sociétes savantes des départements*, 2d ser., 5 (1861): 425–44, 625–42.

1861   Samuel Sugenheim. *Geschichte der Aufhebung der Leibengenschaft und Hörigkeit in Europa bis um die Mitte des neunzehnten Jahrhunderts*. St. Petersburg: Eggers and Co., 1861. pp. 103–4.

1861–76   Amalio Marichalar, marques de Montesa y Cayetano Manrique. *Historia de la legislacion y recitaciones del derecho civil de España.* 9 vols. Madrid, 1861–76. Vol. 6, pp. 66–70.

1863   Henry Stephen. *New Commentaries on the Laws of England.* London, 1863. Vol. 1, p. 216.

1864   Gabriel Legouvé. *Histoire morale des femmes.* 4th ed. Paris: G. Sandré, 1864. pp. 93–94.

1864   Felix Liebrecht. "Das *jus primae noctis.*" *Orient und Occident* 2 (1864): 541.

1865   Auguste Hanauer. *Les paysans de l'Alsace au Moyen Âge: Étude sur les cours colongères de l'Alsace.* Paris: Durand, and Strasbourg, 1865. p. 138.

1866   Anatole de Barthélemy. "Le droit du seigneur." *Revue des questions historiques* 1 (1866): 95–123.

1867   Gustave Bascle de Lagrèze. *Histoire du droit dans les Pyrénées (comté de Bigorre).* Paris: Imprimerie Impériale, 1867. pp. 384–420.

1869   Angelo de Gubernatis. *Storia comparata degli usi nuziali in Italia e presso gli altri popoli indo-europei.* Milan: E. Treves, 1869. p. 198.

1871   Otto Friedrich von Gierke. *Der Humor im deutschen Recht.* Berlin: Weidmann, 1871. p. 27.

1872   Antonio Pertile. *Storia del diritto italiano.* Padua: Fratelli Salmini, 1871–82. Vol. 3 (1872), p. 53.

1872   Adolph Bastian. *Die Rechtsverhältnisse bei verschiedenen Völkern der Erde.* Berlin: G. Reimer, 1872. p. 179.

1873   Jules Delpit. *Le droit du seigneur: Réplique ou seconde réponse à M. Louis Veuillot.* Bordeaux, 1873.

1873   Jacob Buchmann. *Die unfreie und die freie Kirche in ihren Beziehungen zur Sklaverei, zur Glaubens- und Gewissenstyrannei und zum Dämonismus.* Breslau: A. Gosohorsky, 1873. pp. 36–68.

1874   Paul Raymond. *Le droit du seigneur au pays de Béarn.* Paris, 1874.

1874   Marcel Barthe. *Le bon vieux temps en Béarn.* Pau: Véronèse, 1874.

1875   Friedrich von Hellwald. *Kulturgeschichte in ihrer natürlichen Entwicklung bis zur Gegenwart.* Augsburg: Lampart, 1875. pp. 451–94.

1877   Otto Henne am Rhyn. *Allgemeine Kulturgeschichte von der Urzeit bis auf die Gegenwart.* 7 vols. Leipzig: Wigand, 1877–97. Vol. 1, p. 245.

1877   Daniel Spitzer. *Das Herrenrecht* (epistolary novel). Vienna, 1877.

1878   Léon de Labessade. *Le droit du seigneur et La Rosière de Salency.* Paris: Rouveyre, 1878.

1878   Christian Meyer. "Zur Geschichte des teutschen Bauernstandes." *Preussische Jahrbücher* 42 (1878): 339–76.

1879   M. Kulischer. "Die communale Zeitehe und ihre Ueberreste." *Archiv für Anthropologie* 11 (1879): 215–29.

1881   Karl Schmidt. *Jus Primae Noctis: Eine geschichtliche Untersuchung.* Freiburg im Breisgau and St. Louis: Herder, 1881.

1883   Isadore Weil. "Bibliographie: *Jus Primae Noctis: Eine geschichtliche Untersuchung* von Dr. Karl Schmidt." *Revue des études juives* 7 (1883): 156–59.

1884   Amédée de Foras. *Le droit du seigneur au Moyen Âge: Étude critique et historique.* Paris, 1884.

1884   Karl Schmidt. "Der Streit über das *Jus Primae Noctis.*" *Zeitschrift für Ethnologie* 16 (1884).

1891   Edward Westermarck. *The History of Human Marriage*. 2 vols. New York: Macmillan, 1891. Published in French translation by Arnold van Gennep as *Histoire du mariage*, 2d ed., 6 vols. (Paris: Payot, 1934–45), vol. 1 (1934): *La promiscuité primitive*, p. 217.

1902   [[Alfred] Ernest Crawley. *The Mystic Rose: A Study of Primitive Marriage* (London and New York: Macmillan, 1902). Rev. and enlarged ed. published as *The Mystic Rose: A Study of Primitive Marriage in Its Bearing on Marriage*, ed. Theodore Besterman, 2 vols. (London: Methuen, 1927), vol. 2, p. 65.

1902   Eduardo Hinojosa. "Existió en Cataluña el jus primae noctis?" *Annales internationales d'histoire* 2 (1902): 204–6.

1905   Eduardo Hinojosa. *El régimen señoral y la cuestión agraria en Cataluña durante la edad media*. Madrid: V. Suárez, 1905.

1911   H. Gaultier de Saint-Amand. *Les droits du seigneur* (novel). Paris: Librairie du Temple, 1911.

1912   Hans Adolf Fehr. *Die Rechtsstellung der Frau und der Kinder in den Weistümern*. Jena: G. Fischer, 1912.

1918   Sigmund Freud. "The Taboo of Virginity (Contributions to the Psychology of Love, III)" (1918 [1917]). In *The Complete Psychological Works of Sigmund Freud*, ed. James Strachey in collaboration with Anna Freud, 24 vols. (London: Hogarth Press, 1966, 1995), vol. 11, pp. 191–208.

1918   *Jacquerie* (opera). Libretto by Alberto Donaudy, music by Gino Marinuzzi.

1919   Hermann Wolfgang Karl Sartorius, freiherr von Waltershausen. *Die Rauensteiner Hochzeit* (opera).

1921   "Pernada." Entry in *Enciclopedia universal illustrada Europeo-Americana*. Barcelona, 1921. Vol. 43, pp. 972–79.

1923   Aldous Huxley. *Antic Hay* (novel). New York: George H. Doran, 1923; London: Chatto and Windus, 1924; London: Panther, 1977. p. 193.

1925   Thomas Broadhurst. *The Right of the Seigneur* (play). Performed in New York, 1925.

1926   George Coulton. *The Medieval Village*. Cambridge: University Press, 1926. p. 466.

1949   George Orwell. *Nineteen Eighty-Four*. New York: Harcourt, Brace, 1949; Harmondsworth: Penguin, 1989. pp. 75–76.

1955   Leslie Stevens. *The Lovers* (play). Performed in New York, 1955.

1957   Georges Bataille. *L'érotisme*. Paris: Éditions de Minuit, 1957, 1964. pp. 120–28. Available in English as *Eroticism: Death and Sensuality*, trans. Mary Dalwood (San Francisco: City Lights, 1986).

1959   Robert Boutruche. *Seigneurie et féodalité*. 1959. 2d ed., rev. and enlarged (Paris: Aubier-Montaigne, 1968). Vol. 1: *Le premier âge des liens d'homme à homme*, p. 128n.6.

1961   W. D. Howarth. "The Theme of the 'Droit du Seigneur' in the Eighteenth-Century Theatre." *French Studies* 15 (1961): 228–40.

1961   W. D. Howarth. "Cervantes and Fletcher: A Theme with Variations." *Modern Language Review* 56 (1961): 563–66.

1965   *The War Lord* (film). Based on Stevens, *The Lovers* (1955).

1971   W. D. Howarth. "'Droit du seigneur,' Fact or Fantasy?" *Journal of European Studies* 1 (1971): 291–312.

1979   Eleanor Searle. "Seigneurial Control of Women's Marriage: The Antecedents and Functions of Merchet in England." *Past and Present* 82 (1979): 3–43.

1983   Jean Gallet. *La seigneurie bretonne: L'exemple du Vannetais, 1450–1680.* Paris: Publications de la Sorbonne, 1983. p. 241.

1984   Frances Eleanor Palermo Litvack. *Le Droit du Seigneur in European and American Literature from the Seventeenth through the Twentieth Century.* Birmingham: Summa Publications, 1984.

1987   Évelyne Sorlin. "La croyance au 'droit du seigneur' dans les coutumes du Moyen Âge." *Le monde alpin et rhodanien* 1–2 (1987): 69–82.

1988   Martine Grinberg. "Dons, prélèvements, échanges: A propos de quelques redevances seigneuriales." *Annales, ESC* 43 (1988): 1413–32.

1988   Wilhelm Schmidt-Bleibtreu. *Jus Primae Noctis im Widerstreit der Meinungen: Eine historische Untersuchung über das Herrenrecht der ersten Nacht.* Bonn: Röhrscheid, 1988.

1989   Évelyne Sorlin. "Le 'droit du seigneur' et les droits de la jeunesse dans le folklore français et piémontais." *Le monde alpin et rhodanien* 1–2 (1989): 7–22.

1990   Kathryn Gravdal. *Ravishing Maidens: Writing Rape in Medieval French Literature and Law.* Philadelphia: University of Pennsylvania Press, 1990.

1990   Évelyn Sorlin. "La démystification du droit du seigneur au sortir du Moyen Âge." *Bulletin de la Société du Mythologie Française* 158 (1990).

1993   Carlos Barros. "Rito y violación: Derecho de pernada en la baja edad media." *Historia social* 16 (1993): 3–17.

1994   Marie-Victoire Louis. *Le droit de cuissage: France, 1860–1930.* Paris: Atelier, 1994. pp. 15–18.

INDEX

Ney, Michel, duc d'Elchingen, prince de
La Moskova, 76
Niccolini, Paolo, 32
Nicholas IV, pope, 182
Niermayer, Jan Frederick, 49
Nivernais, 133, 137, 153, 214; duc de,
214
Normandy, 50, 59, 101, 103, 184, 189–90,
194, 197, 200, 201, 203, 217, 240
Nougaret, P.J.B., 30, 281
Novion, Nicolas Potier de, 218

Ogier, Viscount, 195
Olive, Simon d', sieur de Mesnil, 279
Olivi, Pierre de Jean, 261
Olivier, Gustave, 80
Oloron, 111, 114, 115
Origo, Iris, 32
Orwell, George, 5, 11, 287
Osbert Pesnel, lord of Fontenay-le-Pesnel,
194, 195, 199
Osenbrüggen, Eduard, 285
Ossau, Val d', 110–16
Oudinot, Nicolas-Charles, duc de Reggio,
71
Oudote (a bride), 53
Ourliac, Paul, 130
Ozanam, Frédéric, 58, 71

Pac, Mathieu du, 110
Papebroch, Daniel, 19–20, 47
Papon, Jean (Johannes Paponius), 203,
209, 215, 218, 278
Pardessus, Jean-Marie, 70
Paris: customal of, 214; Parlement de, 85,
100, 102, 106, 107–8, 135, 166–67, 170,
172, 203–6, 211, 212, 217, 218, 224
Paris, Alexis Paulin, 252
Paris, Gaston, 216
Pars, Adriaan, 47, 280
Patault, Anne-Marie, 137, 139, 149
Paul, St., 178
Pellegrin, Nicole, 212
Perceforêt, 216
Perrot, Michelle, 226
Persanni (Persan), 94, 98, 255
Pertile, Antonio, 286

Peter Lombard, 186–87
Petit-Dutaillis, Charles, 63
Petitot, Claude Bernard, 72
Petot, Pierre, 142
Peyraut, Guillaume, 177
Philip II (Philip Augustus), king of
France, 90
Philip III, king of France, 127
Philip IV (the Fair), king of France, 70, 126
Philip VI, king of France, 166, 169
Philip the Good, duke of Burgundy, 160
Picardy, 43, 52, 79, 103, 105, 107, 121,
172, 184, 189, 203
Piedmont, 42, 43, 60, 94, 98, 204, 212, 237
Pierre (tenant farmer), 84
Pierre le Mangeur, 117
Pierre Mirabel, 132
Pierre Paraire, 129
Pinard, Jules, 285
Pius IX, pope, 71, 81
Plato, 37–38
Poitiers, Grands Jours de, 218
Poitou, 184, 188
Pole, Marguerite de la, 96
Pons Mirabel, 132
Poret de Morvan, Jean-Baptiste, 76
Pot, Philippe, 160
Poujoulat, Jean, 73
Poullain de Saint-Foix, Germain-
François, 281
Pradt, Dominique-Georges-Frédéric de
Riom de Prolhiac de Fourt de, arch-
bishop of Malines, 76
Prelley (Pierrelay), 94, 98
Prévost, Abbé (Antoine-François
Prévost-d'Exiles), 36
Pseudo-Boyer. *See* Boyer
Pseudo-Egbert, 181
Putte Beste, Jeannote, 134

Quaife, G. R., 33–34
Quicherat, Louis-Marie, 90
Quinet, Edgar, 68–69

Rabelais, François, 4
Raepsaet, Jean Joseph, 44–49, 58, 81, 84,
86, 283